Today's MANNA

MIKE SMELLIE

WESTBOW
PRESS®
A DIVISION OF THOMAS NELSON
& ZONDERVAN

WestBow Press books may be ordered through booksellers or by contacting:

WestBow Press
A Division of Thomas Nelson & Zondervan
1663 Liberty Drive
Bloomington, IN 47403
www.westbowpress.com
1 (866) 928-1240

ISBN: 978-1-9736-0187-6 (sc)
ISBN: 978-1-9736-0189-0 (hc)
ISBN: 978-1-9736-0188-3 (e)

Library of Congress Control Number: 2017913944

Print information available on the last page.

WestBow Press rev. date: 10/18/2017

DEDICATION

To our wonderful daughters, Michelle-Anne, and Stephanie.

You are God's special gift to Mom and me. Your love,
humor and laughter have brightened our lives.

May you never neglect your spiritual growth and development.

INTRODUCTION AND ACKNOWLEDGMENTS

From a very young age I adopted the practice of using a devotional book along with the reading of Scripture for my daily times of meditation and prayer. The words of from these daily devotional books helped to provide structure to my devotions and challenged my mind for self-examination and prayer.

I never dreamed I would ever attempt to produce a devotional book. There are already so many of these books on the market. Furthermore, although I have been involved in ministry as a bible teacher for many years, I never considered myself sufficiently competent as an author for publication. However when my daughters left home to go off to college, and I realized that my direct influence on their lives had diminished, I felt a strong urge to continue to provide them with some biblical guidance. One of them suggested that I provide them with a daily devotional by email. I wanted to provide them with a devotional structured for systematic teaching on a topic, with daily passages to motivate them to reading of Scripture. I also hoped to provide them with an inspiration and challenge for each day. I wanted the devotionals to become daily manna to provide spiritual nourishment, strength and blessing for daily living. My wife Valerie became not only the main motivator and supporter for the project, but was also the daily reviewer of the product providing valuable critiques. Without her constant help and prodding, this project would never have progressed beyond the stage of being a good idea. I am indebted to her.

Initially the daily devotions were distributed to immediate family members. However, with Valerie's encouragement and promotion, many people were added to the distribution list. To meet the greater demand and more widespread scrutiny, my sister Jasmine Miller, began to assist with the daily reviews of the devotionals sent out by email. Her dedication and input were invaluable.

I also acknowledge the following people who, after becoming members of the email distribution family, began to urge me to produce the devotionals as a book. Although I resisted for a while, and delayed progressing to publishing, these friends never relented in their efforts. I am indebted to them for their encouragement and persistence: Mildred Hunt, Charmaine Tucker, Tamika Todd, Dorothy Trott. I am especially indebted to one of my mentors, Anthony (Tony) Williamson, who was a constant encourager and motivator on this project. Sadly, Tony recently passed away before the publication of the book.

Before submission to the publishers, my sister Valerie Kerr, graciously agreed to line edit the manuscript. I greatly appreciate her diligence and dedication to this tedious and monotonous assignment.

Mike Smellie
June 2017

ABOUT THE AUTHOR

Michael (Mike) Smellie is a Jamaican-born Chartered Accountant, who worked in Jamaica, USA and Bermuda where he lived for 28 years. He made a Christian commitment in his pre-teens, and began teaching a Sunday School class in his late teens. In 1980 he married Valerie, a Jamaican registered nurse, in London, England. They moved to Bermuda where he served as an elder of First Church of God under the pastorate of Bishop Vernon G. Lambe for twenty-five years, and became well known in the island as a bible teacher, preacher and Christian Education director. In 2008 he retired from his position as a Vice President of a company in the reinsurance industry, and along with Valerie, left Bermuda to enter full time studies at Dallas Theological Seminary, Dallas Texas. Mike graduated with a Masters of Theology in 2012 and returned to his native Jamaica, where he remains active in various church ministries. He and Valerie are the parents of two daughters, Michelle-Anne and Stephanie.

January 1

MANNA SERIES: GOD'S RECKONING AND OUR RECKONING
THE MINDSET FOR SUCCESS

Reading Passage: Phil. 3:7-16
Main Text: Phil. 3:13-14 Brothers, I do not consider myself yet to have taken hold of it. But one thing I do: Forgetting what is behind and straining toward what is ahead, I press on toward the goal to win the prize for which God has called me heavenward in Christ Jesus. (NIV)

Success begins with having the mentality for success. We can identify potential winners by their attitude even before they begin the race or start the project. It's the way they think about the goals they must achieve, the failures they have suffered, and their current status. This process is captured in the Greek verb *logizomai*, which means, to count, calculate, account for, to reckon, regard, or reason. In our current series, we will observe how God reckons or regards those who trust in Jesus, and how we in turn ought to reckon, consider or think about ourselves.

At the beginning of a new year we must be determined to develop a mentality for success so we may achieve the goals we set for the year and fulfill the purpose God ordained for our lives. Paul's statements in the text provide excellent guidelines that we can apply to various areas of our lives, such as business enterprises, personal development and spiritual growth. First, he set a goal that was noble and achievable but was beyond his current grasp, so it would take great effort to achieve. His goal was to know Christ and experience His power and suffering in order to become like Him. What goals will you set for yourself this year? Are they worth pursuing, possible to achieve, yet requiring great effort to accomplish?

Having fixed the goal, Paul set about programming his mind for success. He determined never to relax, thinking he had already achieved, or become complacent thinking he was fully qualified. Whenever we entertain any such thoughts we will reduce our efforts and immediately begin the slide into the path of mediocrity or non-achievement. Instead Paul focused his efforts in one direction, "one thing I do," to forget past failures that are irreversible, and to strain against every obstacle that could impede his progress.

Our enemy tries to keep us remembering the old races we failed to win, the business deals in which we lost money, the promises we broke, or the sins of our past. When our minds are occupied with our irreversible past we lose strength for the present, and are easily tripped up by the obstacles in our path. But when we learn from the past and treat the present as brand new opportunities, we maximize our energy in pressing through every difficulty and every challenge to pursue the irresistible future of achieving our goals.

Father, we thank You for the opportunity offered by a new year to begin again. Help us to reprogram our minds for the success You have prepared for those who make the effort to press through the challenges before us. We pray in the name of Jesus.

January 2

MANNA SERIES: GOD'S RECKONING AND OUR RECKONING
GOD'S UNIQUE ACCOUNTING SYSTEM

Reading Passage: Rom. 4:1-8
Main Text: Rom. 4:4-5 Now when a man works, his wages are not credited to him as a gift, but as an obligation. However, to the man who does not work but trusts God who justifies the wicked, his faith is credited as righteousness. (NIV)

As humans we have a natural sense of equity by which we seek to match reward with work effort. But we have difficulty understanding people being rewarded when they did no work, obtaining benefits without any qualifying status, or getting funds credited to their account without their making a deposit. Welcome to God's unique accounting system, which is the basis for the gift of salvation.

The only way a Holy Just God can offer anyone salvation is that the person must meet the divine standard of righteousness. If God lowered His standard for anyone He would no longer be holy and just. Because of an inherited sin nature, no human could ever be qualified to achieve God's standard of righteousness. Yet this fact has never dissuaded people from trying to prove to God, their neighbors, and themselves that they can do sufficient good works and religious activity to merit God's salvation.

How then can a man meet God's righteous standard and qualify for His salvation? Paul supplied convincing arguments in his letter to the Romans explaining that God has provided salvation for humanity only through Jesus' sacrifice on the cross, and the righteousness of Jesus can only be appropriated by faith. This method of obtaining righteousness as a gift, by trusting what has been provided by another, was demonstrated by Abraham. He believed God and was credited with righteousness (cf. Rom. 4:3). This basis by which God reckons (Gk. logizomai) even a wicked person as righteous is not whimsical, but recognizes that once a person trusts Jesus and His sacrifice, God substitutes the merits and status of Jesus for the demerits and evil status of that person. Concurrently, God begins the process of transforming the nature of the person to the status that Jesus established for him.

The result of God's unique accounting system, also known as grace, is that we no longer sweat for salvation, we just accept it; we no longer fear meeting God's standards, we just have faith in Jesus' finished work; we no longer judge the works of other people, we encourage their faith in Jesus. It is because of the Grace Accounting System that Jesus could accept humble, honest prostitutes, and reject proud self-righteous Pharisees, He could ignore the status of the high priest and justify a dying criminal who asked for forgiveness. The Message paraphrases Rom. 4:5,

> But if you see that the job is too big for you, that it's something only God can do, and you trust Him to do it—you could never do it for yourself, no matter how hard and long you worked—well, that trusting-Him-to-do-it is what gets you set right with God, by God. Sheer gift.

What a gift, what assurance, what relief!!

Father, we thank you for your great salvation and the good news of the gospel. Help us to be eager to share it with others, for Jesus' sake.

January 3

MANNA SERIES: GOD'S RECKONING AND OUR RECKONING
THE BLESSED ASSURANCE OF A GRAVESITE

Reading Passage: Rom. 6:1-14
Main Text: Rom. 6:11-12 In the same way, count yourselves dead to sin but alive to God in Christ Jesus. Therefore do not let sin reign in your mortal body so that you obey its evil desires. (NIV)

Someone is missing and presumed dead. The loved ones grieve with uncertainty, desiring closure. Will the missing person suddenly appear? Are they free to sell the assets, remarry, move on despite a conditional death certificate? Although extremely painful, there would be more acceptance and closure if only there was a body to be buried, and a gravesite that provides evidence of the burial.

When we trusted Christ for salvation, the Holy Spirit placed the life of Christ in us enabling us to live like Him. We became identified with Christ, which transferred the believer spiritually from being under the tyranny of sin to a new realm of life. However, the only way the new life can be effective in us, is that in our mind (the place of our thoughts), our will (the place of our decisions), and our heart (the place of our affections), we reckon (consider, regard, behave as if) the old life is dead. This reckoning (Greek: logizomai) can be very difficult for those who have never gone through the mental process of burying the old life.

Paul used the physical symbol of water baptism to illustrate what should take place in the mind of the believer. Baptism is the public identification with Christ, by which we identify with His death and burial of the old sinful life, and with His resurrection to a new life. The physical symbol helps us to maintain the picture of the mental process. It provides us with the location of the gravesite as a point of reference. Whenever we are tempted to act in accordance with our old life, whether in sexual lusts, pride, greed or hateful attitudes, we have to tell ourselves convincingly that the old life is dead. And we have the evidence of the burial as proof that we don't have to obey the promptings of the old nature. Why be ruled by what is supposed to be dead?

There are believers who claim salvation by grace without works, yet live under the rule of their old lifestyles that should have been dead. Our challenge is to live with a sense of closure on the old life by reckoning it to be dead, because we know the gravesite. We may not avoid the temptations, but we can resist them with our declaration that we will not be ruled by what is dead.

Lord, we thank You that our identification with You gives us the opportunity of resurrection to a new life. May we be so dominated by the new life that the old life will be rendered totally ineffective, for Jesus' sake.

January 4

MANNA SERIES: GOD'S RECKONING AND OUR RECKONING
WAS IT WORTH THE PAIN?

Reading Passage: Rom. 8:18-25
Main Text: Rom. 8:18 I consider that our present sufferings are not worth comparing with the glory that will be revealed in us. (NIV)

There will come a time in our lives when we are confronted with the question of whether the rewards of our endeavors were worth the pain suffered. It is the question that faces the soldier returning from the battlefield in a wheelchair, having lost both his legs, or the graduate whose job application was just rejected, and who is facing an enormous student loan balance, having completed years of rigorous studies. Parents also face the question when children in whom they invested their time and funds, abandon the principles of the home and lead a life of rebellion. Unfortunately, many times after answering the question in the negative, people live with the misery of regrets.

The truth is that there is a degree of suffering attached to every pursuit in life. In fact, as Paul explains, even the earth is going through the process of suffering (Rom. 8:22). So there is no way of avoiding suffering in this life, despite our best efforts. In order to minimize regrets, whenever possible, we should take into consideration the price to be paid before we pursue goals, to assess whether the rewards will be worth the pain.

There is a suffering attached to being identified with Jesus in order to share His identity as a Son, His inheritance, and His glory (Rom. 8:15-17).

For some of us, this suffering may involve the loss of friends, social standing or some pleasurable habit. For others, that suffering involves persecution such as family rejection, loss of employment, or even loss of life. Paul, who suffered great loss in pursuit of Christ stated that when he considered (Greek - logizomai) the suffering, it was insignificant compared with the glory that would be revealed by being identified with Christ. It would be more than worth the suffering.

What are you suffering for Christ's sake today? If you consider it too high a price, your calculations are wrong. You will one day come to appreciate that the surpassing glory of being identified as a child of God, and obtaining the rewards of everlasting life, and the Father's approval, far outweigh any suffering we may endure for Him. Consider the example of Christ who suffered on the cross, but afterward obtained the glory of being seated at the right hand of the Father. When you encounter any challenges today, remember Him.

Father, open our eyes to appreciate the glory that awaits us when we identify with Christ so we will be strengthened to withstand any suffering we have to endure for His sake.

January 5

MANNA SERIES: GOD'S RECKONING
AND OUR RECKONING
MY LOVE MUST EMBRACE YOUR SCRUPLES

Reading Passage: Rom. 14:12-21
Main Text: Rom. 14:14 As one who is in the Lord Jesus, I am fully convinced that no food is unclean in itself. But if anyone regards something as unclean, then for him it is unclean. (NIV)

As an individual and a Christian believer I have preferences, likes and dislikes regarding matters such as food, fashion, entertainment and recreation. These define my personality but may have nothing to do with my spirituality. In matters for which there is no New Testament instruction, I cannot be dogmatic; but I am guided by my scruples and what I believe the Lord requires of me.

Problems arise when I insist that others must share my preferences and see things from my perspective, or when I decide to ignore the scruples of a fellow believer and consider their preferences silly and unnecessary. Paul states that food is morally neutral, but people may place their own morality on it by the way they reckon or regard (Greek - logizomai) it. When I indulge my preference for food or any similar item, in the presence of a fellow believer who considers it 'immoral,' I may destroy his or her faith.

Far more important than my freedom to practice my convictions in these matters of Christian living, is that I portray Christian love. My love should be able to embrace the scruples and preferences of others that differ from mine. God accepts people because of their faith in Christ and not because of various non-core lifestyle matters. If Christ accepts them the way they are, we ought also to accept them as they are (Rom. 15:7), and our responsibility to our fellow believers is to love them.

Do you find that you tend to look for the differences between you and other believers in order to criticize and condemn, rather than to appreciate the variety of people that God includes in His kingdom? Do you feel a sense of superiority because of your brand of Christianity when compared with others? Are you reluctant to adjust your lifestyle to accommodate other believers in order to minimize the risk of offense? In all these cases we need to re-examine our love for those who Christ loves.

Lord, You have called us to exhibit the love of Christ, which means loving those who are different from us. May Your Spirit work in our lives that we will find it increasingly easy to embrace those who we previously excluded, for Jesus' sake.

January 6

MANNA SERIES: GOD'S RECKONING AND OUR RECKONING
THESE NO LONGER COUNT

Reading Passage:, 2Cor. 5:16-21
Main Text: 2Cor. 5:18-19 All this is from God, who reconciled us to himself through Christ and gave us the ministry of reconciliation: that God was reconciling the world to himself in Christ, not counting

men's sins against them. And he has committed to us the message of reconciliation. (NIV)

We often have a battle, in our minds and against people who know us, to maintain our new identity in Christ. Our memory of past sins and our current failures cause us to feel condemned and lead us to question the validity of our Christ identity. At those times we need to be reminded that our reconciliation to God is based on the fact of an event and must not be determined by our feelings.

Paul described the event as the act of reconciliation that occurred on the cross. While the God-man Jesus was dying, God was at work through Him reconciling the sinful world to Himself. Humanity became alienated from God because of sin, and we had no interest in a harmonious relationship with our Creator. However, God the Father took the initiative to reconcile mankind back to Himself by working through Jesus the mediator, who could perfectly represent both the Divine and mankind. Because of Jesus' sacrifice, God determined that sins would no longer be counted (Greek - logizomai) against us. To obtain this benefit, mankind would be required to come to God through Jesus Christ. Immediately this is done by an act of faith, the individual obtains a new identity; he is a new creation. God no longer sees the old person; He sees a new person with the identity of His Son. This is the good news of reconciliation.

It does not matter how we feel, what sins we have committed, how our acquaintances or the devil may try to harass our minds, God says these no longer count against us because of Christ. For this reason, our faith in Christ's sacrifice gives us the victory over all accusations and feelings of condemnation. You may find it helpful to read some passages that reinforce our faith, such as Psa. 103:10-12 (NIV),

> He does not treat us as our sins deserve or repay us according to our iniquities. For as high as the heavens are above the earth, so great is His love for those who fear Him; as far as the east is from the west, so far has He removed our transgressions from us.

Or as stated in Rom. 8:33-34 (NIV),

Who will bring any charge against those whom God has chosen? It is God who justifies. Who is he that condemns? Christ Jesus, Who died—more than that, Who was raised to life—is at the right hand of God and is also interceding for us.

Our justification is based on His reconciliation in Christ, which is available to everyone (2Cor. 5:17).

Father, thank You for the assurance provided by Your word. Help us as we seek to live by faith and not by feelings, in Jesus' name.

January 7

MANNA SERIES: GOD'S RECKONING AND OUR RECKONING
BE CHILD-LIKE NOT CHILDISH

Reading Passage: 1Cor. 13:1-12
Main Text: 1Cor. 13:11 When I was a child, I talked like a child, I thought like a child, I reasoned like a child. When I became a man, I put childish ways behind me. (NIV)

Growing up and becoming mature affects the way we reason, which determines the way we calculate in order to evaluate. The Greek term logizomai, which means to reckon or consider, is translated in this verse as to reason.

Childish reasoning is predominantly self-centered. Disregarding the needs of others, the child becomes the center of his universe and demands all the attention and the priority of his needs for food and rest, or else he will respond with a temper tantrum. Childish reasoning based on limited knowledge and exposure does not see consequences for actions. The child will insist on having his own way while disregarding the dangers of falling and harming himself. Childish reasoning requires toys for immediate entertainment, without thinking of more serious matters such as what he can contribute for the long-term benefit of others.

The implication from Paul's statement, "when I became a man I put childish ways behind me," is that there are many grown persons who are still childish in their reasoning. They still want to be the center of attention with priority given to their needs; they speak and act without thinking about the consequences, unconcerned about who they may hurt. Although they are supposed to be adults, they must be entertained or provided entertainment. Paul was writing in the context of spiritual gifts in the Corinthian church, and was indicating that the members were being childish in the use of these gifts, as if they were for self-glorification and for entertainment. When we become mature, our reasoning will be based on love and the benefit to others instead of gaining attention for ourselves and being spectacular (1Cor. 13-1-3).

God requires us to have the child-like attitude of innocence, simplicity and dependency that will cause us to recognize our need of the Heavenly Father. But in our relationship with each other we must become mature and put away childish reasoning. By doing this we will have an attitude of love for God and for others.

You may face situations today in which you may feel disrespected, overlooked or unrecognized. Are you willing to commit these situations to your Heavenly Father in child-like trust, confident that He knows when to honor His children? Or will you retaliate with a childish attitude of selfish ambition?

Father, we admit that we easily become blinded by childish desires for immediate attention and forget that You called us to demonstrate love that is long-suffering and kind. We seek to become mature in our trust so we will speak, think and reason as those who have put away childish ways, for the honor of Jesus.

January 8

MANNA SERIES: GOD'S RECKONING AND OUR RECKONING
BEING STRETCHED BEYOND OUR COMPETENCE

Reading Passage: 2Cor. 3:1-6
Main Text: 2Cor. 3:5-6 Not that we are competent in ourselves to claim anything for ourselves, but our competence comes from God. He has made

us competent as ministers of a new covenant—not of the letter but of the Spirit; for the letter kills, but the Spirit gives life. (NIV)

Normal life for most people involves study and practice in specific fields in order to develop competency to execute certain tasks successfully. The high achievers are those who perform to the best of their abilities or to the highest standards established. However, when God calls us to a task it is usually to accomplish something beyond our natural competencies, so we will be stretched beyond our reach to fulfill the call.

This has always been the pattern God used in calling various characters in the Bible. He called Noah, a farmer, to construct a large ship. He called David, a shepherd, to become the general of the army and the king of Israel. Jesus called several of His disciples who were fishermen and gave them the task of evangelizing the world. None of these people could claim to be competent for the task they were given. They were stretched beyond their competency and had to depend on the sufficiency that God provides. Paul considered the fact that the Corinthian believers were so transformed by his preaching, that it was as if the Spirit of God had written His instructions on their hearts. Paul did not credit his preaching for their transformation. Rather he stated, "not that we are competent in ourselves to claim (Greek - logizomai) anything for ourselves, but our competence comes from God," (NIV). God gets the glory when we have to rely on His sufficiency.

You may be facing a task today that you feel incompetent to tackle. It may just be that God wants to stretch you so you can depend on Him. You may be parenting a difficult child, or your business may be expanding more rapidly than your ability to control it. You may be required to manage a project that, despite the title before your name or the degrees behind it, you feel inadequate to perform.

If the task was within our competency, we would simply rely on our ability, and after completing it we could justifiably boast in our achievements. But when our abilities and resources are inadequate for the task, we are forced to seek God's help to perform it. We then discover the realm of possibilities when we are just instruments in His hands. As you approach these tasks, declare with Paul, "my sufficiency comes from God."

Lord, we don't want to be limited to the things that are just within our competency. We want to be used as Your instruments to perform tasks that will cause us to marvel. We rest in the assurance that we can do all things through Christ who gives us strength.

January 9

MANNA SERIES: GOD'S RECKONING AND OUR RECKONING
MAINTAINING A RESTRICTED IMAGE

Reading Passage:, 2Cor. 12:1-10
Main Text: 2Cor. 12:6 Even if I should choose to boast, I would not be a fool, because I would be speaking the truth. But I refrain, so no one will think more of me than is warranted by what I do or say. (NIV)

In trying to set up a page for printing an image we may be alerted to the fact that it falls outside of the document boundaries allowed for that page. Our options are to resize the image to fit within the boundaries, or print the image leaving the viewer to imagine the missing parts.

What people see in our lives and hear in our message allows them to form an impression of us. Frequently we want to expand the impression beyond their direct experience of us. Therefore we embellish our accomplishments in order to develop an image in their minds beyond the boundaries of what they observe. This boasting is always about our strengths and virtues, never about our weakness and failings. Why is it necessary to boast? To make people reckon (Greek: logizomai) or think more of us than is warranted? Are we so insecure and in need of their approval and applause that we try to boost our image in their eyes? If we find ourselves in that position, we will always be subject to what people think and live under their control. They will be able to control our state of peace and confidence as we worry over their impression of us.

What is the solution? Paul was writing to the church at Corinth where some members were impressed by men who claimed they were apostles, and who questioned his apostleship. He felt under pressure to prove his superior claims as an apostle and his priority claim on their affection. In so doing he found himself boasting and realized he was making a fool of himself. He decided to restrain himself in order to maintain a restricted image so they would not regard him beyond what they observed of him.

He also decided to boast of his weaknesses so they would no longer focus on him. Instead they would see Christ's power through his weakness.

If you feel you are under pressure to give an impression beyond the frame of what people can observe, practice restraint. When you determine to be accepted based only on what you let them observe, you will be more careful and honest in your behavior, and you will talk less. There will be less risk of exaggeration to boost your image and less fear of being found to be inconsistent or insincere. Seek to grow to the stage where you are not afraid to let your weaknesses be known because you trust that God's grace and strength will be manifested in your weaknesses.

Father, help us to focus only on You and Your approval so we will avoid the snare of people and their opinions.

January 10

MANNA SERIES: GOD'S RECKONING AND OUR RECKONING
ONLY THESE SHOULD PASS YOUR FILTERS

Reading Passage:, Phil. 4:4-9
Main Text: Phil. 4:8 Finally, brothers, whatever is true, whatever is noble, whatever is right, whatever is pure, whatever is lovely, whatever is admirable—if anything is excellent or praiseworthy—think about such things. (NIV)

Filters are designed to remove impurities or unwanted items, leaving behind the pure and beneficial. They are used for purifying water, air, light and even broadcast material. Paul urges us to apply filters over our thought-life in order to protect our hearts and minds, so they may be maintained in a state of joy and peace.

We are constantly exposed to news, information and conversations that contain things that may appeal to our curiosity yet may be injurious to our state of peace. The latest report on crimes or political maneuvering in the evening news can leave us depressed. We may be eager to listen to the latest gossip regarding our neighbors, but discover as a consequence, our inability to maintain a harmonious relationship with them. The solution is to filter out any item that does not meet the criteria of things that are of good quality, virtuous, righteous, and praiseworthy.

It will take discipline to diligently keep our thought-filters active to avoid thinking on anything we suspect is false and dishonest; dishonorable and undignified; anything unjust or unfair; impure or sexually explicit; anything unacceptable or ugly; destructive, negative or not commendable. We may not be able to avoid being exposed to some of these matters, but we can determine not to consider, regard or think on (Greek - logizomai) these things by applying thought filters.

To maintain the filter we may have to remove ourselves from certain conversations and avoid certain people who are poison-carriers. We may have to reduce the time spent discussing negative things that will burden our minds. But at the same time we must find wholesome, positive, constructive conversations and thoughts to replace the negative and destructive. Make this your challenge in this year. What we feed our minds on will ultimately determine our disposition and our happiness.

Father, thanks for giving us the power to choose what will occupy our minds, and consequently our state of peace and joy. Help us to diligently apply our thought-filters today, and to focus on things that are excellent and praiseworthy.

January 11

MANNA SERIES: GOD'S REQUIREMENTS FOR RIGHTEOUS LIVING
FAILINGS AT JUSTICE AFFECT OUR STANDING WITH GOD

Reading Passage:, Isa. 1:10-28
Main Text: Mic. 6:8 He has showed you, O man, what is good. And what does the LORD require of you? To act justly and to love mercy and to walk humbly with your God. (NIV)

Religion becomes ritualistic as we engage in the practices of trying to please God and gain His favor. We gladly offer our 'sacrifices' at church as we make financial contributions, become diligent in attending meetings, and enthusiastically participate in the worship activities. These are commendable, and acceptable by God as long as we don't overlook fulfilling our responsibilities to the people around us. The vertical relationship with God is meaningless if we don't meet His requirements for the horizontal relationship with others.

One of the foundations of God's kingdom is the practice of justice, which represents the very nature of a just God. Because we were created in the image of God, humanity has a sense of what is just, but this has been corrupted by our sinful nature. It was therefore necessary for God to provide His first kingdom- people, Israel, with regulations for justice in the Old Testament laws. When we read the writings of the prophets, we see that God's people ignored His commands to look out for the poor and weak, take care of the orphans and widows, meet the needs of the aliens and strangers in their midst, and punish all evil doers. To compensate for their failures, the Israelites tried to please the Lord by offering sacrifices.

We learn from the prophets that God pays attention to what we overlook, and He is disgusted by our attempts to cover our failings by sacrificing. God declared that instead of sacrificing to please Him and to impress our neighbors, we should first act justly to our neighbors. We find it easy to criticize the government for failing to address the social problems around us, but the question is: What are we doing about it? Can those who serve us attest to how fairly we treat them? Do we ignore the plight of those who are disenfranchised and seek to ensure provision is made for them? Are we known for our kindness to the sick and the weak? Do we take care of the children who have no protection? Can those with special-needs depend on us to provide them assistance?

This is what the Lord requires of us. "To do justly" means that we will demonstrate His desire to balance the scales of justice in the world. Through the prophet Isaiah, God told Israel that He was so tired of their sacrificial rituals that when they came to Him in prayer He hid from them (Isa. 1:14-15). He urged them to learn to do good, and seek justice for the oppressed, fatherless and widows (Isa. 1:17). Are we prepared to meet God's requirements?

Father, we have tried to serve You on our terms, while ignoring Your heart. Please forgive us and help us to seek first Your kingdom and righteousness.

January 12

MANNA SERIES: GOD'S REQUIREMENTS
FOR RIGHTEOUS LIVING
ANSWERING THE CRY FOR MERCY

Reading Passage: Luke 10:29-37
Main Text: Mic. 6:8 He has showed you, O man, what is good.
And what does the LORD require of you? To act justly and to love mercy
and to walk humbly with your God. (NIV)

'Mercy' is a cry we can find good reasons to ignore until it is our turn
to cry. "Why should we help when 'those people' seem lazy and do nothing
to help themselves?" "Surely they are getting what they deserve; if they did
the crime they must serve the time." "How many chances must we give
them? They will never change." Because we have all the reasons to deny
them, the supplicants direct their cry to God, "Lord have mercy!"

But God answers these cries through the acts of His righteous people.
He requires that His people not only subscribe to the idea of mercy, or offer
mercy, but also that they should love mercy. It must have such a place in
our hearts that we find it easy to disregard our reasonable arguments and
provide mercy when it is needed. It is not that we condone wrongdoing or
ignore justified demands for punishment; rather, as humans we recognize
that we all have our own failures and, at some time, we will be in need of
mercy. Indeed before God, we are all guilty sinners in need of mercy. Since
we have received it, we should be willing to give it. By offering mercy, we
represent the nature of God, who is full of compassion and rich in mercy.

One reason for our reluctance to offer mercy is that it usually costs
us to do so. We may have to surrender our rights to compensation, make
sacrifices to accommodate others, or decide not to insist on our standards
or principles for the sake of another. The parable of the Good Samaritan
provides a good illustration. The religious priest and the Levite would not
risk their convenience and reputation to help an injured man on the road.
So they passed on the other side. The Samaritan interrupted his journey,
offered medical care, and gave his funds to take care of someone who
would naturally despise him. Jesus said he proved to be a neighbor because
he showed mercy to the injured man.

Can God trust us to answer the call for mercy on His behalf? Do we love mercy, or do we offer it unwillingly or grudgingly? Unfortunately, as in the story of the Samaritan, some of the most religious people are also the most merciless people, who have no room to accommodate anyone who cannot maintain the standards they have set. Remember the blessing is not to those receiving, but to the ones giving mercy, because they in turn will obtain mercy when they cry.

Merciful God, we are thankful You have never withdrawn Your mercy despite our many failures. May we realize that You sent Jesus to prove that You desire mercy, because mercy will always triumph over judgment (Jam. 2:13).

January 13

MANNA SERIES: GOD'S REQUIREMENTS FOR RIGHTEOUS LIVING
UNLESS HE IS IN CONTROL

Reading Passage: James 4:1-10
Main Text: Mic. 6:8 He has showed you, O man, what is good. And what does the LORD require of you? To act justly and to love mercy and to walk humbly with your God. (NIV)

Learning to walk is a human quest for independence. A baby, having been taken around in the arms of caregivers for the early months of life, eventually desires the ability to walk and go wherever he or she pleases. Yet this concept of independence becomes an impediment in our ability to walk with God. Righteous living requires that we walk humbly with God.

Walking with God means we give up our right to determine where we go, when we go, and the manner of our walk. This requires humility on our part. It is an admission that we don't know what is best for us. We are in need, dependent on a power beyond ourselves. This is the direct opposite of what is expected of the modern, intelligent individual who has progressed so far in his evolutionary development that he is self-made and self-dependent. This proud, worldly person becomes his own god and makes himself the enemy of the Creator God. His lifestyle (his walk) is subject to his own rules, which are designed to help him satisfy his passions.

But it is precisely this proud, godless lifestyle that leads to quarrels, contentions and discontentment (James 4:1-2). Sadly, this profile does not belong only to unbelievers. Many of us who claim to be Christ's followers sometimes seek to declare our independence to do what we want, when we want, in the way that pleases us. God states that He opposes, resists and sets Himself against the proud, independent person, but gives grace to the humble (James 4:6). He refuses to walk with us unless He is in control.

God's righteous people should be identified by their lifestyle of humility and dependency on God. They never make decisions without prayer, and they admit their weaknesses and flaws, acknowledging their need of divine help to live righteously. They seek instruction from scripture, and the counsel of other believers to guide them through life. They have no difficulty in accepting God's will whether it means prosperity or adversity, whether they face stormy periods of sickness and loss, or the blessings of calm, peaceful times. Their contentment and serenity come from the awareness that they are walking with God, and where He leads they are willing to follow.

Father, our pride urges us to demonstrate our independence, but we realize we lose Your companionship in such a quest. We declare that we need You, so we humble ourselves and hand over the control of our lives to You. Please walk with us until You are ready to take us home, in Jesus' name.

January 14

MANNA SERIES: GOD'S REQUIREMENTS FOR RIGHTEOUS LIVING
IT IS FOR OUR OWN GOOD

Reading Passage: Deut. 10:12-22
Main Text: Deut. 10:12-13 And now, O Israel, what does the LORD your God ask of you but to fear the LORD your God, to walk in all his ways, to love him, to serve the LORD your God with all your heart and with

all your soul, and to observe the LORD'S commands and decrees that I am giving you today for your own good? (NIV)

We negotiate our way through life driven by our self-interest, therefore our first consideration for any decision is, "What's in it for me?" Many people walk away from God's requirements because they cannot see the immediate personal benefits whether tangible or intangible.

This benefit-based mentality keeps many wealthy people away from the kingdom of God. They think they have done well by their own efforts and there is nothing further to be gained by following God's rules for life. On the other hand, there are many in the kingdom who are disgruntled when they do not end up with material wealth, successful children, and all the lovely things in life. Why bother living righteously, following God's commands if the rewards are not immediately forthcoming?

No wonder so many think they are doing God a favor by doing His will or serving Him. They live to please themselves, then periodically make a sacrifice of giving an offering, contributing to a worthy cause, sometimes attending church, and hope this will compensate for ignoring God at other times. It is this attitude that causes God to declare that He hates our sacrifices. He doesn't need our sacrifices; He wants us. The only way to truly please God is to begin by loving Him without pre-conditions or desire for reward. Why love Him? Because He owns everything, even the highest heaven, and He could do without us, yet He chose us and placed His affection on us.

When we truly love Him, we will demonstrate His character without feeling it is a burden. He is just and merciful, so He defends the weak and the helpless and takes care of the fatherless and widows. When we love Him and walk in His ways, we will do the same without expecting a reward. Yet we will discover that these deeds are not done as a favor for Him; rather they are for our own good, so we may be a reflection of our Heavenly Father.

God requires this lifestyle from us as stated in Micah 6:8, and Deut. 10:12, but we will not be forced to produce it, nor will God accept it in the form of a sacrifice – for – reward deal. He is waiting for us to live for Him because we love Him.

Father, may the deeds of our lives truly represent our love for You, and may the constant cry of our hearts be, "More love to thee". This is our desire, in Jesus' name.

January 15

MANNA SERIES: WHEN KNOWING GOD MAKES THE DIFFERENCE
HIS PLANS FOR US EXCEED OUR EXPECTATIONS

Reading Passage: Gen. 12:1-9
Main Text: Psa. 139:17-18 How precious to me are your thoughts, O God! How vast is the sum of them! Were I to count them, they would outnumber the grains of sand. When I awake, I am still with you. (NIV)

"Nobody understands me like I do," is an axiom that could indicate why we may think no one but ourselves can provide a vision suitable for our lives. We fail to consider that God created us for a purpose, which we may not have yet discovered, and which we will only realize when we get to know God.

Abram may have thought he maximized the dream for his life after he acquired wealth while in the land of Ur. Living in a heathen culture of idol worship, perhaps he resigned himself to the fate of the gods that placed him in such a small family, but in a prosperous land near the great river. He was puzzled at the irony of his life, having a name that meant "father" yet being fatherless. But then, it was useless wasting his thoughts on these matters since he was growing old and had no power to change this situation. He considered bestowing his inheritance on his nephew Lot who was close to him, or on his faithful servant, Eliezer.

The limitation Abram placed on his life when he thought he knew what was best for him was suddenly disturbed by a vision in which he was told of God's plan for his future. This wonderful plan meant leaving his hometown, breaking loose from his small band of relatives and venturing into a future of new possibilities as revealed to him. He would get the opportunity to know by experience the God who gave the vision, while relying on Him for the journey to the unknown. This God changed his name to Abraham, befitting his status as the head of the great nation that he would produce despite his age. He was also promised to be the means of bringing blessing to all nations of the earth. These plans far exceeded anything he expected. Abraham's life demonstrated how the vision and goals of a person under God's direction could be expanded beyond expectations. Consequently, this God became known as 'the God of Abraham.'

Have you become contented with your achievements in life and have resisted the possibilities of further ventures? The fact that you were not productive in the past because of family, educational, financial or physical constraints might have caused you to place a limitation on your future usefulness. Have you discounted a vision received from the Lord as being impractical because it does not suit your personality? I challenge you to get to know the God of Abraham whose plans will exceed your expectations.

Father, how precious and amazing are Your thoughts concerning me, and how foolish of me to try to set limitations on what You would like to accomplish through me. Lord please forgive me.

January 16

MANNA SERIES: WHEN KNOWING GOD MAKES THE DIFFERENCE
IT BEGAN WITH A MIRACULOUS DELIVERANCE

Reading Passage: Psa. 78:42-55
Main Text: Ex. 15:11 "Who among the gods is like you, O LORD?
Who is like you—
majestic in holiness,
awesome in glory,
working wonders? (NIV)

In the panic of our latest crisis, walls seem impenetrable, mountains insurmountable, ditches bottomless, and chains unbreakable. We think the situation is the worst ever, and chances of escape or recovery are nearly impossible. These responses come from a short-term memory. If we could talk with an old friend, read some old entries in our journals, or spend some time in quiet reflection, we will soon realize we have been through equal or greater crises in the past, and God brought us through. Our challenge is to remember the God of our past deliverances.

The Hebrew people were living in slavery in Egypt with a vague knowledge of the God of their ancestors. God introduced Himself to them as a mighty deliverer, by awesome and miraculous deeds. He sent ten plagues on the powerful Egyptian nation that caused them to willingly release their slaves without compensation. When the Egyptian army tried to recapture the Hebrews by chasing them to the Red Sea, God miraculously made a path of escape through the Sea, and drowned the army in the waters. The nation of Israel came into existence with these demonstrations of God's mighty power. Why? That they would know their God as a mighty deliverer, and that no crisis they might face would be a match for the power of God. In every crisis they just needed to recall their beginnings as a nation.

Those of us who know Christ became followers because we experienced the mighty power of God, delivering us from the power of sin and Satan. It is important that we never forget the miracle of that supernatural deliverance, or allow it to appear as some ordinary event in our lives. It is the basis of our worship and adoration of our Lord. It allows us to put all the other crises of our lives in perspective. If God could free us from the bondage to our sinful nature, and captivity to the hellish destiny planned by Satan, then the challenges of our health problems, financial crisis or spousal infidelity, are all less significant. The God we met at the beginning of our spiritual journey will be the same powerful deliverer throughout our lives.

If you are in the midst of a crisis, shift your focus from the things that are burdening you and focus on your initial salvation. Then you will be able to worship God for His greatness as a deliverer, and place your circumstances in the proper perspective.

Lord, we are grateful that we know You as our deliverer. We are assured by Paul that since You did not spare Your own Son, but gave Him up for us all - will You not also, along with Him, graciously give us all things? (Rom. 8:32). *We rest in this assurance, in Jesus' name.*

MANNA SERIES: WHEN KNOWING GOD MAKES THE DIFFERENCE
THE KNOWLEDGE THAT GIVES COURAGE

Reading Passage: Dan. 1:8-20
Main Text: Dan. 11:32 Those who do wickedly against the covenant he shall corrupt with flattery; but the people who know their God shall be strong, and carry out *great exploits.* (NIV)

"Knowledge is power" is the popular quote from Francis Bacon. It implies that having information allows people to make decisions, pursue goals and control their response to situations. But the possession of information is not the same as possession of the character and courage to properly use the information.

Far more important than knowing facts is knowing the Person who is sovereign over everything in heaven and earth. Knowledge is obtained by notification, observation or by experience. Scripture provides information about God and His dealings with humanity. This historical notification must be supplemented by our general observation of God as He works in creation and in the lives of people around us. But our knowledge of God remains limited until we have experienced God for ourselves and can declare "He is my God." This is the knowledge that truly makes a difference in our lives and in our witness to the world.

In these days it appears that evil is triumphing over good and many who claim to know God seem to be afraid to take a stand for righteousness and truth. There is a need for people who not only know about God based on information received, but intimately know the God of truth who is able to give them power to display strength and take action in the form of great exploits. When the Hebrew named Daniel was taken captive to Babylon as a young man, he, along with his three friends made the courageous decision not to defile themselves with the Babylonian culture. They refused to eat the food and drink the wine of the palace despite the decree of the king. God vindicated their trust and caused the king to acknowledge that these Hebrews outshone the other youths who had submitted to the king's decree.

You may be facing situations that are making you fearful to speak out or to take a firm stand. If you know your God, don't be afraid. He will give you the courage to stand for righteousness regardless of the power and popularity of those who oppose you. He wants to use you to demonstrate the greatness of His power. Martin Luther King Jr. said, "The ultimate measure of a man is not where he stands in moments of comfort and convenience, but where he stands at times of challenge and controversy." Know your God, stand firm and take action.

Lord, we know that if we will stand up for You, You will stand with us and give us the victory. We admit our fears but we trust that You will grant us the courage to take a stand that will overwhelm our fears, for Jesus' sake.

January 18

MANNA SERIES: WHEN KNOWING GOD MAKES THE DIFFERENCE
KNOWING THE GOD OF CREATION

Reading Passage: Job 38:1-11
Main Text: Job 42:1-3 Then Job replied to the LORD:
"I know that you can do all things;
no plan of yours can be thwarted.
[You asked,] 'Who is this that obscures my counsel without knowledge?'
Surely I spoke of things I did not understand,
things too wonderful for me to know. (NIV)

"If only I could be certain that the events in my life that seem so painful, random, and pointless were under the control of an omnipotent, benevolent person who understands me." Indeed, after we have reasoned away God with our enlightened minds, or ignored Him as irrelevant to our busy lives, we have no way of making sense of the crises that occur in our lives.

Moses had the task of taking a large group of ex-slaves and establishing the Israelite nation with a common identity, knowledge of their God and also their special relationship with Him. For this purpose, He documented in the Genesis story that the earth was created out of nothing (ex nihilo) by the Most High God who rules over His creation. Moreover this God created man with the capacity to have a relationship with Himself. Moses knew the Israelites would encounter other false creation myths from Egyptian and Babylonian sources. He wanted them to be certain that they knew the true author and designer of life, and to understand they could trust His sovereign decisions. If we are wrong about the source of life, we will be uncertain about the control of life.

Based on this fundamental principle, we can understand God's response to Job's confused accusations against Him as being a God who acts capriciously and unfairly to His subjects. Job could not understand why he should suffer such great misfortunes and losses when he lived a righteous life. Instead of providing reasons for His actions, God reminded Job of His acts of wisdom in creation. He indicated that the wonder of creation, which is beyond the scope of man's understanding, illustrates the wisdom and sovereignty of God.

God does not owe us an explanation for anything He does or allows to happen to us. He is God and we are mere humans. While we may not understand the circumstances and misfortunes of our lives, we can know the God who created all things, who can do all things, and whose plans can never be thwarted. If He can create something out of nothing, no situation we may have is beyond His power to redeem. We are not victims of chance and time; rather we are in the hands of the Creator God who personally designed the path of our lives, and has a glorious future for us whether in this life or in the hereafter.

Almighty God, we rejoice at the fact that we know You as Creator and this makes a great difference in our lives. We trust Your wisdom, and rest in the assurance that You do all things well.

January 19

MANNA SERIES: WHEN KNOWING
GOD MAKES THE DIFFERENCE
HE NEVER GIVES UP ON ME

Reading Passage: Gen. 32:24-32
Main Text: Is. 43:1 But now, this is what the LORD says—
he who created you, O Jacob,
he who formed you, O Israel: "Fear not, for I have
redeemed you;
I have summoned you by name; you are mine. (NIV)

One of the tragedies of our times is the number of abandoned children in the world. It is difficult to understand how a child who was once the delight of parents, represented their contribution to the world, and carries their DNA and personality, could be left unprotected with no one to care for him or her. What could cause a parent to give up on a child?

There are times when parents cannot cope with the responsibilities of childrearing due to financial pressures, physical or mental disabilities, or war conditions which may render them unable to care for their children. But there are also cases when a child has lived in rebellion, spurned the love offered, and the parent simply gives up, weary of making further attempts to be responsible for him or her.

Knowing the rebellion of our hearts and the many times we resist the love of our Heavenly Father, failing to keep His commands or showing Him affection, He would be justified in abandoning us. The fear of wearying His patience by our repeated failures can lead to a sense of insecurity and our constant effort to try to win His love. Our perspective of our Heavenly Father needs to be corrected by getting to know Him better as He is revealed in the Bible.

God's relationship with Jacob provides one of the best illustrations of His faithfulness, long-suffering, and His refusal to cease loving His children. God chose Jacob before his birth, although he was not the firstborn, and possessed serious character flaws. His name Jacob described him as a cunning, untrustworthy deceiver. Having chosen him, God pursued him after he defrauded his older brother of his birthright and the related blessing.

He continued to pursue him as Jacob ran as a fugitive to a foreign country. He used his uncle Laban to discipline him hoping to change him. Finally, God confronted him directly at Peniel where He wrestled with him. Jacob admitted the flaws of his character when he declared, "I am Jacob." The injury he received in his hip was a constant reminder to Jacob of his struggle with God and the weakness of his character.

The value of the story is to show that God never gives up on His children, pursuing and disciplining them until He can change their nature from a 'Jacob' to an 'Israel.' He declares, "I have created you, redeemed you, you are mine." Do you know the God of Jacob as your refuge? This knowledge will give you the assurance that you will be pursued, disciplined, even wounded, but never abandoned.

Lord, we thank You for the assurance that You are the faithful One who keeps us, and You are determined to present us perfect at the end, for the glory of Jesus' name.

January 20

MANNA SERIES: WHEN KNOWING GOD MAKES THE DIFFERENCE
HE CARES ABOUT YOUR NEEDS

Reading Passage: Psa. 78:19-29
Main Text: Psa. 78:19-20 They spoke against God, saying,
"Can God spread a table in the desert?
When he struck the rock, water gushed out,
and streams flowed abundantly.
But can he also give us food?
Can he supply meat for his people?" (NIV)

We usually have no difficulty accepting the concept of a powerful, transcendent God who created all things and maintains the order of the universe. In fact, God easily becomes our default answer for complex matters of life that are beyond our understanding. But as one of billions of people occupying planet earth, each of us sometimes struggles with seeing this large CEO God as interested in our daily mundane concerns.

We observe in the story of the children of Israel, the struggle to understand the Almighty God who does marvelous acts in creation, as also being interested in their need for food and drink. They saw Him perform miracles, causing the sun to be darkened, locusts to appear, a river turned to blood, and a path made in the Red Sea. After celebrating the greatness of their powerful God, they found themselves in a wilderness without food or water. The excitement quickly died as reality hit. Could God do something about their daily needs? Could He 'spread a table in the desert?'

One of the reasons they had these doubts was because of their location and the logistics. In a wilderness, providing food and water for over a million people seemed impossible from a human perspective. What they learned is that God's resources transcend human sources. He provided manna for food, a mysterious substance that came like dew each morning. It was available, plentiful, nourishing and flexible for culinary preparation; never before known by humans, yet ideal for the wilderness. For water, He instructed Moses to strike a rock, and out of that flinty source God provided a stream that was able to sustain them. His power is not reserved for the 'major tasks' of the universe; it is also available to meet our minor mundane needs.

When we begin to ask, "Can God?" it indicates there are certain areas in which we have doubts as to whether He is willing to act for our benefit. Perhaps He is too busy controlling volcanos or managing hurricanes to be concerned. One of the blessings resulting from the revelation of Jesus Christ is that it helps us to understand that God cares about our needs. Jesus stated,

> If ... God clothes the grass of the field, which is here today and tomorrow is thrown into the fire, will He not much more clothe you, O you of little faith? So do not worry, saying, 'What shall we eat?' or 'What shall we drink?' or 'What shall we wear?' (Matt. 6:30-31 NIV).

If you are going through a dry wilderness-type experience, know that God cares about you, and He can furnish a table in the wilderness.

Father, we thank you for Jesus who made us understand Your concern for us. We therefore cast our cares on You and trust Your power to meet our needs, in Jesus' name.

January 21

MANNA SERIES: WHEN KNOWING
GOD MAKES THE DIFFERENCE
BLINDED BY MISTRUST

Reading Passage: Deut. 1:21-33
Main Text: Deut. 1:26-27 But you were unwilling to go up; you rebelled against the command of the LORD your God. You grumbled in your tents and said, "The LORD hates us; so he brought us out of Egypt to deliver us into the hands of the Amorites to destroy us. (NIV)

As a child my mother took me to the doctor after I sustained a nasty wound in an accident. He administered a painful injection. I could not understand why she allowed this man to add pain to my already hurting body, but I did not rebel, nor did I resent her for it. I trusted that she loved me and was looking out for my best interest. The trust factor enables us to accept what we may not understand, and gives us confidence that greater knowledge will confirm our trust. Where there is no trust there will always be the demand for proof of love. We can be so blinded by mistrust that deeds of love are misunderstood and motives questioned.

God introduced Himself to the Israelites as Yahweh (Lord), the God who fulfills covenant. His name represented His nature and He proved His love by saving them out of the misery of their bondage. He explained that the mighty deeds He performed in Egypt were to let them know that their Lord was the only true God (Deut. 4:33-35). But despite all the great miracles they saw, and marvelous provisions they enjoyed, they still mistrusted Him. When the people reached the border of Canaan, their promised inheritance, the rumors of giants occupying the land caused them to forget the past miracles and great victories won by the Lord. Blinded by mistrust they questioned His motives in taking them to a place of giants, completely ignoring the fact that these enemies provided opportunities for greater knowledge of the Lord. They concluded that 'The Lord hates us.'

If our relationship with God is not firmly based on a deep trust in His love, doubts will begin to surface when He leads us along certain paths where we see formidable 'giants.' In our suspicion we will be seeking another sign for God to prove to us that He is who He says He is. Our pursuit of God should never be for verification, rather it should be to deepen our intimacy with Him, confirming what we already accepted by faith. We may not understand what God is doing in our lives but we already know enough of His character that we can trust His love. As stated by St. Augustine of Hippo: "Understanding is the reward of faith. Therefore seek not to understand that you may believe, but believe that you may understand."

Lord, we trust Your love for us as demonstrated by the cross. We accept that You may lead us along a winding path, allow us to face affliction, or confront some giants, but we will never doubt that You are bringing us to a blessed inheritance of intimacy with You.

January 22

MANNA SERIES: WHEN KNOWING GOD MAKES THE DIFFERENCE
HE'S INTOLERANT OF INFIDELITY

Reading Passage: Deut. 6:10-15
Main Text: Deut. 4:24 For the LORD your God is a consuming fire, a jealous God. (NIV)

Jealousy is not usually considered a virtue and it is certainly not a characteristic we normally associate with our Holy God. But His self-description to Moses in Ex. 20:5 (NIV) is "...for I, the LORD your God, am a jealous God," and Moses later remarked in Ex. 34:14 (NIV) "Do not worship any other god, for the Lord, whose name is Jealous, is a jealous God." The word jealous describes someone who zealously guards and maintains a personal possession so it can be enjoyed exclusively.

Negatively, this characteristic produces a fear of loss that leads to suspicion of those considered rivals, and to aggressive action to enforce claims of ownership. Positively, it represents the extent of love bestowed that ethically demands a response of loyalty and faithfulness. It is amazing to think that the God of the universe who created us decided to leave us with the free choice as to our response to His love. However, once we know His love, we will also know the accompanying characteristic of His jealousy.

Since He is all-knowing, His jealousy is not based on suspicions or fears; rather He expects no rivals to His love and He does not tolerate infidelity.

The Old Testament mainly represents the story of God choosing a nation, making them the special object of His love, and warning them of His jealousy if they pursued other gods. Despite the warnings, Israel repeatedly fell into idolatry and the Lord in His jealousy punished them so they would return to Him. This explains why, along with the description of His jealousy, He is described as "a consuming fire." The Lord does not give up on the fickle objects of His love; rather He pursues them with fire to destroy all rivals, and to purge their nature of all tendency toward infidelity.

The good news for us is that God loves us and has chosen us as His exclusive possession. The bad news is that He is jealous and will tolerate no rivals. We risk taking His love for granted as we become enamored with the gods of wealth, popularity and pleasure. In reality, we construct gods in our own image, leading to our self-worship, while we forget the One who took us from the 'scrap heap' of the world and made us the object of His love. Eventually, we will appreciate that when the fire consumes the things we consider precious in our lives, it is a reminder that our lover is jealous and tolerates no rivals.

Lord, our prayer is expressed in the verse of the hymn, "O, to grace how great a debtor, daily I'm constrained to be. Let Thy goodness like a fetter bind my wandering heart to Thee. Prone to wander Lord I feel it, prone to leave the God I love. Here's my heart, O, take and seal it, seal it for Thy courts above."

January 23

MANNA SERIES: WHEN KNOWING GOD MAKES THE DIFFERENCE
DEVELOPING YOUR OWN EAR FOR GOD

Reading Passage: 1Sam. 3:1-14
Main Text: 1Sam. 3:7-8 Now Samuel did not yet know the LORD: The word of the LORD had not yet been revealed to him. The LORD called Samuel a third time, and Samuel got up and went to Eli and said, "Here I am; you called me." Then Eli realized that the LORD was calling the boy. (NIV)

Watching a baby grow and mature is an amazing and fascinating process. As the child becomes familiar with different voices and sounds, he connects them to certain persons, and that usually determines his reaction. A mother's voice usually brings a smile or other warm responses and sets hers apart from all other voices.

We will never develop a proper knowledge of God without developing the spiritual ability to hear His voice. Without the ability to discern God's voice for ourselves, we will be dependent on indirect means of learning His instructions and this will hamper our relationship with Him. God speaks to us primarily through revelation in His Word.

The story of the boy Samuel provides an interesting illustration. Samuel was the protégé of Eli, the high priest, at a time when the priesthood was under God's judgment. The lamp of the temple, signifying the enlightenment provided by God, had almost gone out. Eli's eyesight was growing dim, which was symbolic of his diminished contact with the Lord. Samuel usually slept in the tabernacle near the ark, which represented the presence of the Lord. But his familiarity with the ark and the priest failed to help him hear the voice of God. Furthermore, at that time, the Word of the Lord and visions from God were rare. All that Samuel should have relied on for an indirect word from God had become suspect. It was during this period that one night the Lord spoke directly to Samuel. But he could not recognize the voice because he 'did not yet know the Lord.'

Samuel may be excused as he was still very young. But many people through ignorance, indolence or negligence find themselves depending on traditions, religious symbols or other people to provide them with contact with God. He wants to speak to us directly, so we can have a personal relationship with Him.

To hear God directly you must respond as Samuel did in 3:10, with an open ear ("speak Lord") and a willing, humble heart ("your servant hears"). Perhaps one reason you may be getting bored with religious routine, or are being unnecessarily critical of Christian leadership, is that you have developed an unhealthy dependence on these means of hearing from God. Instead, you should study scripture and allow God to reveal His voice directly to you as you develop your own ear for God.

Lord, I now realize You have allowed the failure of other dependencies in my life so I will be forced to listen to You directly. Thank You for the reminder that Your sheep know Your voice and follow You.

MANNA SERIES: WHEN KNOWING GOD MAKES THE DIFFERENCE
THE RÉSUMÉ OF A GIANT KILLER,

Reading Passage: 1Sam. 17:32-50
Main Text: 1Sam. 17:46-47 This day the LORD will hand you over to me, and I'll strike you down and cut off your head. Today I will give the carcasses of the Philistine army to the birds of the air and the beasts of the earth, and the whole world will know that there is a God in Israel. All those gathered here will know that it is not by sword or spear that the LORD saves; for the battle is the LORD'S, and he will give all of you into our hands." (NIV)

It was a complete mismatch: A young boy versus a giant; one whose only experience was shepherding a small flock on the countryside versus an experienced, trained fighter representing the hopes of his country; the boy with basic shepherd's equipment of a sling and stones versus a fully equipped champion with the latest defensive and offensive gear.

The well- known story of David's victory over Goliath portrays the drama of a rank underdog beating the odds and becoming a giant killer. What made David confident to face the giant when the king and the armies were cowering in fear? What did he know that the others, like Goliath and Saul, didn't? He quickly recognized this was not an ordinary battle between opposing forces seeking territory or proving the better trained and equipped army. This was a battle involving cosmic forces and spiritual realities. The goal of these battles was to prove which spiritual power was more trustworthy in a crisis. Can your God give you victory?

The Philistines' hope for victory was centered in one person, Goliath. The victory or defeat of the whole army and country would be based on his success (17:8-9). Goliath's size was imposing but his greatest weapon was fear. David disregarded his size and ignored his threats; instead, he focused on his God. On his résumé he had sufficient evidence of what his God had done in the time of crisis. As he told Saul, "The LORD who delivered me from the paw of the lion and the paw of the bear will deliver me from the hand of this Philistine." (17:37). He knew his God was trustworthy in a crisis, so Goliath would be no problem to his God.

You may be facing a crisis in your life that torments your mind like a well- equipped and experienced giant, and you may feel inadequate to face it. Your God is greater than any giant; remember your résumé. What crises did the Lord deliver you out of in the past? If He gave you victory then, He can do it again. Give God the opportunity to add another victory to your résumé.

Father, help us not to be fearful when the odds are stacked against us; rather, help us to recognize that Your reputation is enhanced when You give us victory despite the mismatch.

January 25

MANNA SERIES: WHEN KNOWING GOD MAKES THE DIFFERENCE
LEAVING A VALUABLE LEGACY

Reading Passage: 1Chr. 28:1-10
Main Text: 1Chr. 28:9 "As for you, my son Solomon, know the God of your father, and serve Him with a loyal heart and with a willing mind; for the LORD searches all hearts and understands all the intent of the thoughts. If you seek Him, He will be found by you; but if you forsake Him, He will cast you off forever. (NKJV)

What can we leave behind when we depart this life that will be valuable to succeeding generations? This is a question that becomes more important to us as we enter the sunset years of our lives.

It is a question that can lead to despair. As described by the wise man in Ecclesiastes 2:18-23, an individual will work hard, sacrifice much, and accumulate wealth, then it dawns on him that he will die and leave all he has accumulated to someone who did not toil for it. Furthermore, he can't be certain whether that person is wise or a fool. There is no guarantee that his inheritance will be put to good use after he dies. Someone remarked on the irony that many businessmen spend so much time working, building an inheritance for their children, with little time invested in developing their character. Yet without character, the children will waste the inheritance.

King David was preparing for his departure and handed over the throne to his son Solomon. He also handed over the task of building a temple for the Lord, and provided Solomon with the plans and materials he had accumulated for the project. In his final speech to Solomon, David provided the key instruction that forms the basis of a lasting legacy. He said, "...know the God of your father and serve Him ..." This command implied that the father's life proved that his God was worth knowing; and the son would discover that this God was worth serving "with a loyal heart and willing mind." Consequently, God would provide wisdom to carry on the legacy that was bequeathed by David. He wanted Solomon to know the grace of his God that chose him when he was overlooked as the last child of his father, and elevated him to be the King of Israel with riches and power.

There is no more valuable legacy to leave to those following us than an appreciation of the God in whom we trust. We may not be able to leave much in the way of financial inheritance; but if they know our God who opens doors, creates opportunities, and provides wisdom to handle life, we have provided the key for a successful future. Do our lifestyles promote to our children, a God that is worth knowing and serving? Do we seek to leave a valuable legacy of faith in God that can influence future generations?

Lord, You have been good to us and we have benefitted from Your mercy and grace. We desire that our lifestyle and faith will become a legacy that influences our children and other observers to desire to know and serve You.

January 26

MANNA SERIES: WHEN KNOWING GOD MAKES THE DIFFERENCE
NEVER UNDERESTIMATE OUR GOD

Reading Passage: 1Kings 20:22-30a
Main Text: 1Kings 20:28 The man of God came up and told the king of Israel, "This is what the LORD says: 'Because the Arameans think the LORD is a god of the hills and not a god of the valleys, I will deliver this vast army into your hands, and you will know that I am the LORD.'" (NIV)

Whether in sports, business, or war, our opponents study our strengths and weaknesses in order to know where we are most vulnerable; or which conditions will give them an advantage over us. Our enemies may correctly identify our weaknesses, but they would be greatly mistaken if they made a similar evaluation of our God, who is our Helper, Protector and Provider.

A very weak Israelite army was at war against the mighty Syrian army. During the battle in the hills of Samaria, the Lord intervened to help Israel and they totally defeated the Syrian army. In analyzing their defeat, the Syrian King and his counselors concluded that Israel and her God were strong when fighting in the hills, but were vulnerable in the valleys. Therefore Syria planned the next battle for the valley. The Lord's response was to prove to both Israel and her opponent that His power was not limited to the hills. He was able to give them victory both in the hills and the valleys. Syria would learn, to her detriment, not to underestimate the God of Israel.

God's problem is not with our opponents but with His own people. Are we making the enemies' mistake in underestimating the power and ability of our God? We compartmentalize God and confidently trust Him in certain situations, but in others, we are fearfully and frantically searching for alternate sources of help, or admitting defeat. It is as if He is Lord of the hills when dealing with sickness of our friends, difficult people on the committee at church, or finances to meet the next month's rent. But when facing the valleys of a personal devastating diagnosis, an obnoxious manager at work, or finances to buy a house, these are out of our God's league and He is no longer able to give us victory.

We trust God for success in a strong economy but doubt Him in the valley of a recession. We have no problem being effective in a place where we have a friendly supportive organization, but fail to know the God who can make 'a root in a dry ground' grow into a productive plant. He wants to be known as the God of both the hills and the valleys. Trust Him today.

Father, we accept that life does not consist of a straight consistent experience, but is a combination of hills and valleys. Help us to appreciate You as our God for all seasons and circumstances of life. We never want to join our opponents in underestimating You.

January 27

MANNA SERIES: WHEN KNOWING
GOD MAKES THE DIFFERENCE
SOMETHING BOAST-WORTHY

Reading Passage: 1Cor. 1:26-31
Main Text: Jer. 9:23 This is what the Lord says:
"Let not the wise man boast of his wisdom
Or the strong man boast of his strength
Or the rich man boast of his riches,
But let him who boasts boast about this:
That he understands and knows me,
That I am the Lord, who exercises kindness,
Justice and righteousness on earth,
For in these I delight," declares the Lord. (NIV)

When people boast, they reveal much of their personality and inner thoughts. We discover what is important to their sense of identity, what motivates them, their areas of interest, or people they consider significant. It is natural for people to desire commendation for what they consider to be some great achievement in their lives. But we must place limitations on our boasting. The sound of our accomplishments when trumpeted by others can be beautiful, yet when played by ourselves can be jarring. Furthermore, there are some things that are not worthy of our boasting because they reveal our self-centeredness and our shallowness.

The Lord Himself declares that wisdom, might and riches are not boast-worthy. These are not achievements until they are used for the benefit of others. When they are so used, the boasting will not be in the tools employed, but in the improvement achieved in the lives of others. These tools must always be viewed as gifts bestowed on us, not because we are more deserving than others, but because God sovereignly selected us in a certain context to fulfill a specific role. This will lead us to seek to know and understand the Gift Giver so we can boast about Him.

As we grow in our knowledge of the Lord, we will see more of our unworthiness and find less in ourselves to boast about. At the same time we will discover more of what He delights in, namely: faithful love, justice and righteousness in the earth. Whenever we observe, or are able to participate in the demonstration of these qualities in the earth, we provide our Lord great delight. When we offer words of wisdom to help individuals to redirect their lives, or use our positions of power or finances to lift someone out of hardship, injustice or deprivation, we are being used by the Lord, and He gets the glory. In addition, we learn more about Him, and this is something boast-worthy.

Lord, we desire to know Your wisdom, power and riches so we will no longer spend our lives in trivial pursuits that cause us to boast about ourselves. We seek to boast in our God who delights in improving the lives of the peoples of the earth.

January 28 .

MANNA SERIES: WHEN KNOWING GOD MAKES THE DIFFERENCE
THAT'S WHY WE NEED THE HOLY SPIRIT

Reading Passage: Ezek. 36:22-32
Main Text: Ezek. 36:26-27 I will give you a new heart and put a new spirit in you; I will remove from you your heart of stone and give you a heart of flesh. And I will put my Spirit in you and move you to follow my decrees and be careful to keep my laws.
Jer. 31:33-34 "This is the covenant I will make with the house of Israel
After that time," declares the LORD. "I will put my law in their minds
And write it on their hearts. I will be their God,
And they will be my people. No longer will a man teach his neighbor,
Or a man his brother, saying, 'Know the LORD,'
Because they will all know me, from the least of them to the greatest,"
Declares the LORD. "For I will forgive their wickedness
And will remember their sins no more." (NIV)

Knowledge of God is crucial for humans to be able to live in accordance with His laws, to maintain a relationship with Him, and to represent Him in this world. This knowledge cannot be based on mere observation or information received. It must come from an intimate experience with Him. We must have a continuous personal relationship with God in which He can communicate His instructions, we can expose our hearts to Him, and we can be transformed into His image.

Our sinful nature is in rebellion against a Holy God, creating a barrier to knowledge of Him. So we observe the wonders of creation and attribute it to non-God sources. We study the Bible and regard it as great literature written by philosophical minds. Israel received God's laws, experienced His miracles and provisions, heard His prophets, yet the Lord made the painful lament in Isa. 1:2-3 (NKJV),

> Hear, O heavens, and give ear, O earth: for the LORD has spoken, I have nourished and brought up children, and they have rebelled against me. The ox knows its owner, and the donkey its master's crib; but Israel does not know, my people do not consider.

What was God's plan to get His rebellious people to turn to Him? The solution was the new covenant described in our text. In this new covenant they are given a new heart, forgiveness of sins, and the abiding presence of His Spirit. Our new hearts will desire Him, His laws will be in our hearts and minds, and His Spirit will be available to supply His nature in us. When this happens we will begin to know The Lord. There are several additional benefits to having the Spirit, such as assurance of salvation, and the operation of spiritual gifts in the church, but the fundamental purpose of the Spirit is to enable us to know God.

With the help of the Spirit we are able to communicate with God, understand what He desires in every situation, respond with His love, while basking in His joy and peace.

Spirit of the Living God fall afresh on me, break me, melt me, mold me, fill me; refine my nature until the beauty of Jesus is seen in me.

January 29

MANNA SERIES: WHEN KNOWING
GOD MAKES THE DIFFERENCE
THE INCOMPARABLE GOD

Reading Passage: Is. 40:10-31
Main Text: Is. 40:18 To whom, then, will you compare God?
What image will you compare him to?
Is. 40:25 "To whom will you compare me?
Or who is my equal?" says the Holy One. (NIV)

One of the means by which we gain a proper understanding of objects or ideas is to place them in their proper perspective. An object is presented in relationship to other objects so the size, distance etc. can be appreciated. Similarly, an idea is placed against the background of other ideas or facts to provide perspective. The problem arises when we are seeking to understand something to which there is nothing comparable.

Humanity has this challenge in trying to know and understand God. Since we are limited to time and space, how can we understand the One who is infinite and unlimited? We try to solve this problem by comparing God with objects or ideas familiar to our limited world. However any such attempts result in our demeaning God.

Isaiah's poetic presentation of the majesty of God in chapter 40, describes Him as being beyond our comprehension. He is so great that He measures all the waters of the universe in the hollow of His hand, and the span of His hand measures the breadth of the heavens (v 12). The nations are to Him, merely like dust on a scale when He weighs them (v 15). He created the heavens and all the stars, and He accounts for each of them, "so none is missing" (v 26). He is an awesome God. Yet some people try to capture this God by creating some idol (made from created material) to represent Him (vv. 19-20).

As He is incomparable, so He is incomprehensible. However we can still have a relationship with this awesome God because we know He cares about us. Isaiah describes this caring characteristic, "He tends to His flock like a shepherd, He gathers the lambs in His arms, and carries them close to His heart ..." (v 11).

When we are faced with difficulties and seemingly impossible situations, it is good to know that our God is so large and powerful that nothing is beyond His control. It is also reassuring to know that He is not only concerned about us but tenderly cares for us as His sheep. In fact, when life makes us so tired and weary that we begin to lose hope, we can remember that He gives strength to the weary and He will renew our strength. He will cause us to "run and not grow weary, and walk and not faint" (vv 29-31). How wonderful to have a relationship with such an amazing God.

Our Amazing and Incomparable God, although we can't comprehend You, we can know Your tender care and concern for us. As Your sheep we rest with confidence in the greatness of our Shepherd.

January 30

MANNA SERIES: WHEN KNOWING GOD MAKES THE DIFFERENCE
JESUS PROVIDES EXCLUSIVE ACCESS TO GOD

Reading Passage: John 14:1-11
Main Text: John 14:9 Jesus answered: "Don't you know me, Philip, even after I have been among you such a long time? Anyone who has seen me has seen the Father. How can you say, 'Show us the Father'? (NIV)

It is a great falsehood to state that all religions serve the same God. For some people God is a transcendent impersonal force that determines the fate of everything in the universe without the possibility of any human relationship or need for worship. Some religions believe in multiple gods with various powers and jurisdictions. Religions that are monotheistic accept the existence of a single, supreme, supernatural power, but there are vast differences in how various groups understand, and thus relate to, this supreme power.

The major monotheistic religions – Judaism, Christianity and Islam, have very different perspectives of their God. To the Jews, their connection to God is through the law, prophets and priests, and they keep looking for a Messiah who will represent their God-King. God, to an adherent of Islam, a Muslim, is completely apart from his followers and is represented by the Quran - his ethical code for living, delivered verbatim to his prophet Muhammad in the 7th century AD.

For a Christian, God is not just a moral code, a lawgiver or a judge. He became personal and relatable in the person of God's Son, Jesus Christ, who is both human and divine. Because Jesus represented God in human form, we have no need to be puzzled about how God thinks, acts or speaks. God recognized man's inability to keep the law or moral code because of sin, and sent Jesus to save man by His death on a cross so man can be brought into a love relationship with Him. Jesus reveals God as a relational Being, seeking a relationship with man, but also relational within Himself. Jesus' self-reference as a Son, recognized his relationship to a Father. The Father initiates, the Son executes and the Holy Spirit reveals this relationship to us. Yet they act in a complete loving unity as One God. This is the God of the Christian.

Jesus so fully represented God that He explained to His disciple, "If you have seen me, you have seen the Father." He further stated, 'No one comes to the Father except through me' (v 6). In order to know God, we don't need the word of a prophet, nor do we wait for a priest or messiah. Jesus has come as the only human revelation of God, providing exclusive access to Him. If Jesus is not God, and not the exclusive means of knowing God, He would be a liar and unworthy of our devotion and worship.

However, if we desire to know God, which is the major quest of humanity, God has facilitated our desire by providing access to Himself in human terms in Jesus Christ, and through the revelation of the Spirit. What a wonderful revelation.

Father, we thank You for sending Jesus to prove Your love for us, and providing the means by which we can know You. Our desire is to know, love and worship Him better, for Your Glory.

January 31

MANNA SERIES: WHEN KNOWING GOD MAKES THE DIFFERENCE
PAUL'S QUEST, NOT A TRIVIAL PURSUIT

Reading Passage: Phil. 3:1-14
Main Text: Phil. 3:10-11 I want to know Christ and the power of his resurrection and the fellowship of sharing in his sufferings, becoming like him in his death, and so, somehow, to attain to the resurrection from the dead. (NIV)

Trivial Pursuit is a game in which the players demonstrate their knowledge of facts, many of which are of little value or importance. It is an interesting game that reveals how much meaningless information we have accumulated about diverse matters. Sometimes the pursuit of knowledge provides the basis on which great discoveries are made in fields of science or human behavior, yet most times the knowledge has no impact on the lifestyle or destiny of the pursuer in the context of eternity. Because of the lack of value attached to spiritual life, this pursuit may also be ultimately classified as a trivial pursuit.

The search for meaning in our brief human existence drives us to inquire into the source of life and the divine purpose for life. These answers far outweigh any other knowledge that mankind can gain. These answers can never be found in scientific or philosophical investigation. Instead, we have to turn to God for the answer. This desire to know God was the quest of the apostle Paul. In his passion to find an answer, he became devoted to his native Jewish religion. He describes in Phil. 3:1-14 how his pursuit of the Jewish religion was futile until he discovered Christ. After this discovery, he sacrificed all things that were valuable to him as a Jew and disregarded all that he had achieved, in order to gain knowledge of Christ.

Why was knowing Christ so valuable to Paul? Because this knowledge provided him with a transformation of his immediate life, and gave him a new destiny beyond the grave. Like Paul, with this knowledge, we discover that Christ provides resurrection life, which has power over anything that could impede or nullify righteousness in this life. Our righteousness is not dependent on our ability to live in accordance with God's demands; rather, our righteousness comes from a relationship with Christ. We also discover that our life does not end with death; instead, resurrected life continues beyond the grave. The pursuit of this knowledge is not a trivial pursuit.

This knowledge of Christ does not occur in a quick, one-off incident. In fact, it is the result of a continuous, lifelong, growing relationship with Him, whereby He becomes the most valuable aspect of our lives and He gradually transforms us into His image. We will never enlist in this pursuit until we recognize how valuable Christ is to us. And we will never succeed in the pursuit until we are willing to sacrifice everything in the quest.

Do we have Paul's goal and his passion, to know Christ?

Lord, give us the revelation of the transformative value of knowing Christ, and help us to be so focused on gaining this knowledge that all other things in our lives will lose their attraction, for Jesus' sake.

February 1

MANNA SERIES: WHEN KNOWING GOD MAKES THE DIFFERENCE
THE SEARCH FOR THE TRUE GOD

Reading Passage: Acts 17:16-33

Main Text: Acts 17:23 For as I walked around and looked carefully at your objects of worship, I even found an altar with this inscription: TO AN UNKNOWN GOD. Now what you worship as something unknown I am going to proclaim to you.

Acts 17:27-28 God did this so that men would seek him and perhaps reach out for him and find him, though he is not far from each one of us. 'For in him we live and move and have our being.' As some of your own poets have said, 'We are his offspring.' (NIV)

The question we face regarding the search for God is: "How does the Unknown become Known?" Most humans, regardless of ethnicity, geographic location or cultural background, have an innate sense of the existence of a god, a transcendent being. Our challenge is getting to know this seemingly unknown God. It is easy to become frustrated, and concede that this reportedly impossible search for hidden treasure should not be attempted, or should be abandoned. Indeed, it has become popular to believe that it makes no difference to our lives whether or not we get to know the True God.

The passage describes the occasion when Paul visited the Areopagus in Greece where many famous Grecian philosophers frequently gathered to debate ideas. In delivering his notable address to this audience, Paul highlighted the fact that he saw among the many idols representing their gods, an idol to 'An Unknown God.' This idol symbolized the fact that these intellectuals were worshipping what was unknown to them. They were worshipping in ignorance because they failed to find what they were searching for.

Paul proceeded to proclaim that the unknown can become known if we follow the clues God has provided, and forsake the limitations of our vain imaginations. First, since God is the creator of everything and gives life to everything, He cannot be limited to anything created by man, such as temples or idols (vv. 24-25). Second, there is the commonality of humanity: God created all humans of all nations with the limitation of time and space but with a spiritual sensitivity. As a result, mankind would instinctively seek after God with the hope of sensing Him by experience. God is not an intellectual idea; He is someone we relate to spiritually. Third, although God seems beyond us as Creator and Sustainer, yet He is close and accessible to each of us because we are His offspring. We will discover that our very existence is dependent on Him.

Finding and having a relationship with God is as significant as the relationship of a branch to a tree. Without the connection, we will be spiritually dead. Without knowing where we came from and the purpose of our lives, we will live empty lives with a fear of facing God as Judge at the end of life.

Why should we live in futility without God when He has made Himself available and accessible to us?

Lord, we are challenged by Paul's sermon to consider how easily we settle for futility and idolatry, when You have designed us for Yourself. We thank You for drawing close to us, so that through Jesus, the Unknown can become Known.

February 2

MANNA SERIES: THOUGHTS ON THE TOPIC OF LOVE
HOW DEEP IS GOD'S LOVE?

Reading Passage: Rom. 5:1-11
Main Text: John 3:16 For God so loved the world that he gave his one and only Son, that whoever believes in him shall not perish but have eternal life. (NIV)

We recall the words of the popular song by the Bee Gees in the 1980's that has the following refrain:

> How deep is your love
> I really need to learn
> Cause we're living in a world of fools
> Breaking us down
> When they all should let us be

This is the cry from human hearts seeking to know whether the love to which they have been attracted, and on which they are dependent has a limit. Is there a defect in our character, deficiency in our behavior, or demand by our needy lives that will exhaust this love? With respect to the love of God, we know how frequently we fail to live up to the standards He requires. Sometimes we are blatant in our disobedience, at other times we are indifferent, or spurn His love. Will we be rejected at the end?

Why are our foolish hearts so worried? Are we ignorant of the words of our Sovereign Lord? He loved the world – everyone - without respect to nationality, ethnicity, intelligence or background. The extent of His love is extremely wide; it cannot be measured. His love includes the vilest sinner and the most self-righteous Pharisee. It is extremely deep. But what proof do we have of this love? God gave the most valuable prize of heaven, His one and only Son to be sacrificed on our behalf. This is a historical fact, and not based on my subjective feelings.

Since the Son represented the essence of Himself, we can state that God sacrificed Himself for the world, which is comprised of people who rebelled and sinned against Him. But the whole world does not benefit from the gift, only those who believe on the Son. This belief is not merely mental assent or casual acknowledgment; rather, it is placing our trust in the Son. Much like strapping ourselves in an airplane seat and trusting the mechanics of the airplane, which we don't understand, and the pilots whom we don't know, to take us safely to our destination. How does God respond to this trust? He gives us eternal life, an unending life of bliss that cannot be interrupted even by death.

Do you know His love? Do you trust His love? Or are you trying to offer God some of your goodness to justify His love? This would be as if we are attempting to fly the airplane when we should be resting. It is by trusting in Christ that we experience and learn the depth of God's love.

Lord, I cannot comprehend the gift of Your unconditional love when I have done nothing to deserve it. But I stand assured in Your Word that there is nothing I can do to cause You to cease loving me, so all I can say is, Thanks.

February 3

MANNA SERIES: THOUGHTS ON THE TOPIC OF LOVE
THE THREE-LEGGED DOG

Reading Passage: 1John 4:7-21
Main Text: 1John 4:19 We love because he first loved us. (NIV)

As the relatives sorrowfully moved around the house awaiting the arrival of the undertakers, they were aware that Tom's dog refused to leave his bedside. Tom's son, Steve, explained that he made several attempts to coax away the beloved three-legged dog. But he was unsuccessful, despite placing food in her feeding bowl at the normal feeding time.

The story behind the strong bond between Tom and the three-legged dog began four years before when Tom wished to replace his pet dog who had died of old age. At the local dog shelter Tom was immediately drawn to the three-legged puppy that had been abandoned at birth. The likelihood of her being adopted was slim because of the deformity. The shelter had planned to put down the puppy later that day. Tom was saddened as he thought of her imminent death. To the surprise of the shelter's owner, he overlooked the other normal, beautiful dogs and chose the three-legged puppy. As the years passed, Tom lovingly cared for this dog, taking her with him everywhere, and they became inseparable. He was rewarded with the loyalty and devotion of his three-legged companion who rarely left the room during Tom's recent illness. What a great response to love.

What should be our response to the love of God who so loved us that He took the initiative to come to our rescue when we were deformed by sin and destined for eternal death? The response to love is love, loyalty and devotion. We sometimes act as if we are doing God a favor by our devotion in worship, time spent in prayer and study of His word, fellowship within the church, and service to the people of the world in His name. Our response to God must be based on gratitude for His love to us when we were undeserving. He first loved us; therefore we had done nothing to cause Him to love us. And His love for us is not dependent on anything we can do. For this reason, our love for God must never be based on what we desire to receive from Him as if we are making a bargain: "I will love You if You meet this request."

May we never forget that we were just like a three-legged dog in a shelter: abnormal, abandoned and unloved, until God by His grace loved us first. We must now love Him in return. What is the state of our love for God today? Do we show indifference or delinquency in our love by our lack of devotion and service for Him? Do we act as if we are in a love bargain with God so our love is dependent on what we expect to receive from Him?

Father, although we can never repay our debt of love, help us to demonstrate by acts of loyalty and devotion, a full expression of our gratitude for Your love, Amen.

February 4

MANNA SERIES: THOUGHTS ON THE TOPIC OF LOVE
LOVE'S OBLIGATORY EXPRESSION

Reading Passage: 1John 4:7-21
Main Text: 1John 4:11 Beloved, if God so loved us, we also ought to love one another. No one has seen God at any time; if we love one another, God abides in us, and His love is perfected in us. (NIV)

"These people are just not my type; I find most of them so judgmental and hypocritical." "I never would have chosen them for my companions as they are not of my social class." "They are much too boring to be engaging; a few hours on a Sunday is the most I can bear to be around them." These are some of the comments we hear regarding the community of believers coming from others who consider themselves Christians, members of the body of Christ. It makes us wonder how Jesus must view those who make these claims that conflict with His teachings. They claim to be members of the body of Christ and yet are intolerant of the other members.

John declared the unconditional nature of God's love for us stating, "In this is love, not that we loved God, but that He loved us and sent His Son to be the propitiation for our sins." Then he stated love's obligation, "...we also ought to love one another" (4:10-11 NIV). We usually have no difficulty understanding the concept that love received, demands a response. However, we may think that our response should be to love only the God who loves us. But John raises the question, 'How do we express love to God?' No one has seen God at any time, so one way to express love to the unseen God is to love those who represent Him around us: namely members of His body, the Church.

We have no right to determine who God chooses to represent Him, therefore we don't get to choose those we are obligated to love in order to prove our love for God. When we ask why God includes in the church certain persons we find incompatible with us, the same question could be posed about us, "Why did He choose me?" When we overcome the difficult challenge of loving persons whom we consider unlovable, we discover that God abides in us, enables us to love, and His love is perfected in us.

Father, we understand from scripture that Your goal for loving us is that You might live in us and Your love might be expressed through us. Keep us from being so self-focused with our preferences for certain personalities, that we miss Your desire to broaden our perspectives and appreciate the nature of Your love. Help us to see every person we meet today as an opportunity to express our love for You by the way we treat each of them, for Jesus' sake.

MANNA SERIES: THOUGHTS ON THE TOPIC OF LOVE
WHEN GOD USES OUR ADDRESS

Reading Passage: 1John 4:7-21
Main Text: 1John 4:16 We have come to know and have believed the love which God has for us. God is love, and the one who abides in love abides in God, and God abides in him. (NIV)

The post office sorting clerk looked quizzically at the envelope addressed to "God, c/o Heaven". He took it to his supervisor to ask what should be done with the letter. Opening the envelope they read a letter scrawled by a six year old girl asking God to heal her little brother who was seriously ill.

This story discloses a dilemma in the mind of a child that is also a puzzle for many adults. We know God as the omnipresent, all-knowing Spirit who is identified with a heavenly abode. But how does He respond 'locally'? There are times He acts supernaturally, intervening in nature and circumstances to answer prayers, but most times He answers using people just like us.

In his epistle, John explains that the very nature of God is love. Therefore anyone who abides in love, making love the center of the environment in which he or she chooses to exist, and the basis of his or her decision making, is demonstrating the very essence of God. In order to live in love, we start by knowing and believing that God looked beyond our weaknesses and imperfections and loved us. He gives us His strength to compensate for our weaknesses, forgives our failures, and develops our lives toward perfection.

Knowing what God, by His love, is doing in us, we, in turn, begin to do the same to those around us. That is when we discover that God begins to use our address, working through our lives to impact others. People no longer need to search for God in heaven to find examples of love, forgiveness and reconciliation; they will recognize us as God's representatives. We should live with this awareness that when we meet someone suffering from guilt because of bad choices, we can offer them the gospel of God's forgiveness through Jesus Christ. Or, if someone needs comfort because of the pain caused by circumstances of life, we can offer the touch of God and the consolation of His words. This is in contrast to the usual human behavior of emphasizing the weaknesses and sins of others, in an effort to ensure they pay for past wrongs, while pointing out our superior virtues.

Are we convinced of God's love to us to the extent we can become models of His love to others? God needs to use our address to reach people in our community, so let's fly the flag of love to identify His residence.

Lord, while we celebrate the knowledge and awareness of Your love to us, we desire to accept our responsibility as Christ's ambassadors working to reconcile people to God. May we be bold in representing you, for Jesus' sake.

February 6

MANNA SERIES: THOUGHTS ON THE TOPIC OF LOVE
KNOWING HIM AS A LOVER FIRST

Reading Passage: 1John 4:7-21
Main Text: 1John 4:17-18 By this, love is perfected with us, so that we may have confidence in the day of judgment; because as He is, so also are we in this world. There is no fear in love; but perfect love casts out fear, because fear involves punishment, and the one who fears is not perfected in love. (NIV)

There is a certain vulnerability that comes with being in love. We expose ourselves to our lover fully aware that such exposure of our faults, weaknesses, warts and all, could lead to our abuse, yet trusting the love of our covenant partner to keep us safe and make us whole.

When we trusted Jesus as our Savior, He became our Lover. He knows all our faults and still continues to love us. As this type of love develops, fear is gradually replaced by trust. Perfect love casts out fear. Fear only resurfaces when there is a deficiency in our love; when we are failing to trust the promise of Jesus' sacrifice to cover our sins.

At the end of our lives, we all will face the judgment. Knowing our imperfections, it is natural for us to be apprehensive about facing the Judge of all the earth who knows not only our actions but our very thoughts. But when we know that the expected Judge is also our Lover with whom we have a relationship, and whom we are trusting to cover our sins, we have no need to fear the judgment. Our goal in life is not a perfect moral record but a perfect love based on trust. This removes the fear of death and the judgment, and gives us confidence to face the Judge who is our Lover.

We should continuously evaluate the level of our love, not by our religious exercises but by our appreciation of the finished work on the cross and by the quality of the daily relationship with our Lover. When we begin to be fearful of the judgment, it is time to renew our love commitment. Remember Jesus' message in Rev. 2:4 (NKJV) to the church in Ephesus, "Nevertheless I have this against you, that you have left your first love." When we know Him as a lover first, we have no fear of facing Him as judge.

Lord, we confess that we are sometimes tormented at the thought of facing the judgment. We seek to develop our love relationship with You to such an extent that it will eliminate our fear of You as our Judge.

February 7

MANNA SERIES: THOUGHTS ON THE TOPIC OF LOVE
LOVE'S DUTY

Reading Passage: John 14:15-24
Main Text: John 14:15 "If you love me, you will obey what I command." (NIV)

"I ... take thee ... to have and to hold ... to love, honor and obey ..." We recall these words from the traditional wedding vows. In recent times these vows have been revised or customized to represent, what some believe, are commitments more relevant to our modern times.

The greatest objection to the traditional wording of the vows is the inclusion of the word 'obey.' To the modern mind it seems unfair that one party in a marriage would commit herself to obey the other party. What makes the traditional practice appear especially appalling is that the responsibility to obey is placed on the wife which seems to place her in a subservient role to her husband.

There is subservience when obedience is demanded of an unwilling partner, or obedience is offered in exchange for compensation. When obedience is offered willingly as a grateful response for the commitment by the husband to care for and to protect his wife, we recognize a direct relationship between love and obedience. Obedience becomes not servitude but evidence of love. Jesus stated, "If you love Me, you will obey what I command" (v.15); "Whoever has my commands and obeys them, he is the one who loves me" (v. 21); "He who does not love me will not obey my teaching" (v. 24).

God's relationship with man always included commandments or laws given to man: He commanded Adam not to eat of the fruit of a certain tree, He commanded Abraham to leave his country and relatives, He commanded the Israelites to obey the laws given through Moses. The test of their love was always in the obedience to His command.

Through Jesus, God has commanded us to go into the world and be witnesses, baptizing and teaching (Matt 28:19), to love our enemies and pray for those who persecute us (Matt 5:44), and to be holy in our lifestyle (1Pet 1:15). We do find many of these commands difficult and contrary to our own desires, but we obey as evidence of our love for Him. And in loving Him we trust that He knows what is best for us.

How can we say we love Him and refuse to obey Him or try to appease Him by other religious sacrifices? When there is rebellion in a marriage, attempts to compensate without seeking forgiveness do not repair the spiritual love-gap created by disobedience. It may be old fashioned but it is still the truth that the evidence of true love is obedience and this is our duty to Jesus.

Father, You know the natural rebellion of our hearts that causes us to believe we know what is best for us. Therefore, we limit our obedience to only Your commands that suit us. Give us the grace and love that will always respond in obedience to You. Even when it is difficult we will still trust You as the Lover of our souls. Amen.

February 8

MANNA SERIES: THOUGHTS ON THE TOPIC OF LOVE
WHAT IS LOVE'S REWARD?

Reading Passage: 1Cor. 13:1-13
Main Text: 1Cor. 13:1-3 If I speak in the tongues of men and of angels, but have not love, I am only a resounding gong or a clanging cymbal. If I have the gift of prophecy and can fathom all mysteries and all knowledge, and if I have a faith that can move mountains, but have not love, I am nothing. If I give all I possess to the poor and surrender my body to the flames, but have not love, I gain nothing. (NIV)

In these verses, at first glance it appears Paul is describing either the superiority of love over spiritual gifts, or how essential love is to the effectual operation of these gifts. However, the closing statement of each stanza describes the negative consequences of exercising spiritual gifts without love: "I have become an empty noise maker (a resounding gong or a clanging cymbal)," "I am nothing," "I gain nothing." My performance may benefit others but when done without love it leaves me empty. My giftedness and résumé may appear impressive and valuable, but when not matched with the inward desire to love, I end up worthless. My sacrifice of time and money may appear extreme and compelling and may be helpful to many, but this sacrificial investment unaccompanied by love provides no improvement to my life. Since there is no reward for a person exercising his or her spiritual gifts without love, what then is the reward to persons when their actions are motivated by sincere love?

We face this question when we have sacrificed and given our all in rearing children then experience rejection and even abandonment by them. We held back nothing in a relationship; always willing to go the extra mile for the benefit of the other party, yet we are later dumped from the relationship. We have given stellar service in building a church fellowship, only to be overlooked when the accolades are given. What is my reward for loving sincerely and wholeheartedly? Paul does not appear to answer this question directly in this chapter, but there is the clear implication that love is its own reward. As we love we become ... more full of love (lovely), because love is transformational. Our love develops greater integrity (authenticity), intensity (actions done in love are more impactful) and our capacity to love increases. When Jesus sees us producing fruit, He prunes us so we may produce more of the same fruit, such as love. Growth in love leads us to more God-likeness, because the nature of God is love.

Though challenged by hate and rejection, let us keep on loving, because the rewards are divine and the world needs it. As Stevle Wonder sings, "Love's in need of love today, don't delay, send yours right away."

Holy Spirit, I get so disheartened when my love seems unrewarded. Help me to value the fact that my practice of love makes me more fulfilled and helps me become more like Jesus, for His name's sake.

February 9

MANNA SERIES: THOUGHTS ON THE TOPIC OF LOVE
KNOW THE COUNTERFEITS, AVOID DECEPTION

Reading Passage: 1Cor. 13:1-13
Main Text: 1Cor. 13:4 Love is patient, love is kind. It does not envy, it does not boast, it is not proud. (NIV)

We learn from the website of the International Anti-Counterfeiting Coalition that counterfeiting is a US$600 billion per year business. To counterfeit is to imitate something with the intention to deceive. In the marketplace, various merchandise are counterfeited, such as jewelry, luxury bags and accessories, clothing, perfume, art, automobile parts, even pharmaceutical products. Purchasing a counterfeit product provides a person with the appearance of having something valuable, at a bargain price. The fact is, the counterfeit is inferior and may even be harmful.

Unfortunately spiritual gifts can be counterfeited as well, and love, which should be the foundation of these gifts, can also be imitated. The devil who seeks to oppose and undermine anything established by Jesus, is the master deceiver. The Corinthian church was obsessed with spiritual gifts. Paul instructed that they should ensure that these gifts had the proper foundation of love, and that the love was genuine, not a counterfeit. In 1Cor 13:4-7 he presents a description of genuine love with seven positive characteristics and seven negative indicators. He begins in verse 4 with two positive characteristics followed by the negative indicators, so we would have an initial picture of what genuine love is before seeing what it is not.

To state love is patient means that love is willing to endure the weaknesses and failings of another for a long time while waiting for a change. Ironically, the gifted church members at Corinth were not about to wait on each other even to eat the communion meal together (1Cor 11:33). When we consider how patient God has been with us, waiting for us to learn to stop sinning and to develop maturity, why are we so impatient with fellow believers or our relatives? In the same way that God is using the process of time for our development, we should be able to offer love while waiting for the development of others.

Love is kind. Love always offers a helping hand with gentleness. As we patiently wait for God to complete His work in the lives of others, love must become active in extending help to them. Kindness should not only be demonstrated by our actions but also in our attitudes and words. The world does not care about our gifts until it can experience our love as shown by our kindness.

Can I be described as someone who is patient and kind; if not, how genuine is my declaration of love?

Lord, we confess we find it so much easier to talk about love or pretend that we have love, than to demonstrate it by the way we treat people. Transform our hearts by your Spirit so that those around us may appreciate your authentic love by our actions, for Christ's sake.

February 10

MANNA SERIES: THOUGHTS ON THE TOPIC OF LOVE
BREAKING THE SPELL OF EGOCENTRISM

Reading Passage: 1Cor. 13:1-13
Main Text: 1Cor. 13:4-5 Love ... is not jealous; love does not brag and is not arrogant, does not act unbecomingly; it does not seek its own. (NASB)

In the fairy tale of Snow White, her wicked step-mother practiced going before a magic mirror asking, "Mirror, mirror on the wall, who is the fairest of all?" Her behavior illustrates the classic case of people so obsessed with themselves that they constantly need the affirmation of others and the massaging of their egos. But these actions of self- promotion also reveal their inner fears of others being esteemed better than themselves.

When we are under the spell of egocentrism, we are jealous, arrogant, boastful, and undignified or rude. The Greek term translated "jealous" in NASB could also be translated as "envious" (NIV, NKJV, ESV), and the root of the term means to be zealous. When we portray this characteristic, we strongly desire to protect our successes or advantages from others, or we envy the success of others. We cannot acknowledge the achievements of others without boasting of our contributions to their success. No opportunity is missed to ensure we are the center of attention and our contributions are acknowledged. When we are not readily recognized we withhold our participation or seek to undermine the program.

We may easily point the finger when we recognize this behavior in popular celebrities, politicians and business leaders, but if we are honest, we have to acknowledge its occurrence also in church leaders and in ourselves. How many disputes have occurred in churches, even leading to splits, because of self-centered behavior? How many times were we unable to honestly celebrate the achievements of fellow believers because we were secretly checking with the mirror on the wall? How many eager and talented persons have found an impenetrable glass ceiling constructed by us to ensure they would never surpass us in accomplishments?

What is the 'potion' that can break this spell of egocentrism? A good dose of authentic love. The basic nature of love is that it is 'other-person' centered, seeking the best for others even at the expense of ourselves. When love becomes the driving force in our lives, we will esteem others above ourselves, and our gifts will no longer be tools for self-promotion but for service. We will genuinely celebrate the successes of others and be willing to sacrifice to aid them in their achievements.

Father, our competitive world squeezes us into the mold of self-glorification, and this delights our sinful nature. Give us a true heart of love. May the Spirit find fertile ground in our hearts to produce fruits that will counteract our natural tendency toward selfishness, for Christ's sake.

February 11

MANNA SERIES: THOUGHTS ON THE TOPIC OF LOVE
LOVE ELIMINATES THE SCORECARD

Reading Passage: 1Cor. 13:1-13
Main Text: 1Cor. 13:5-6 … it is not self-seeking, it is not easily angered, it keeps no record of wrongs. Love does not delight in evil but rejoices with the truth. (NIV)

We are familiar with the use of scorecards in various sports, such as golf and boxing, for the purpose of determining a winner. What is not so apparent are the scorecards kept in our relationships for the purpose of ensuring we do not lose out to another party. This self-seeking attitude has been the cause of much of the disagreements, divisions and dissensions in our relationships.

Consider the scorecards of the following statements or thoughts: "We visited with your family four times last year and only twice with mine"; "When I paid for lunch the bill was US$50 and the bill you are offering to pay is only US$35"; "You received the greater share of the assets in our parent's will"; "You have been the featured speaker at the conference twice compared to my once"; "This is the fifth time you have embarrassed me before my mother-in-law." What is even more divisive is when one party is very sensitive or easily provoked and so makes entries on the scorecard, while the other party remains oblivious to the offense. The basic motivation for this behavior is that one party is seeking to be victorious or unblemished in what has become a competitive relationship. We think that we have to look out for ourselves or we may be taken advantage of.

When love becomes the foundation of the relationship, we seek the advantage of the other person and need no scorecard. This love is best illustrated by a mother's love for her children. There is no extent to her sacrifice and no cost to her love. Having risked her life to give birth to her child, she wins when her child succeeds. This type of love shuns bad news about others, (admittedly sometimes living in denial), because we choose only to rejoice with truth, even if it is not yet reality.

God has called us to this type of love that eliminates scorecards, reduces sensitivities, and rejects news that portrays people in a bad light. Do you find yourself nursing hurts and holding resentments because you feel you were treated unfairly in past relationships? Do you find it easy to recall and enumerate the various instances where your loving deeds were not acknowledged, or reciprocated? Despite the satisfaction you may have in announcing your superior 'virtue' as shown by your scorecard, you will lose the joy of sacrificial love in contributing to the lives of others.

Father, we fall short of this type of love because we are busy seeking our own success at the expense of others. Help us to follow Jesus whose only scorecard reflected the wounds in His hands and side that He bore for us.

February 12

MANNA SERIES: THOUGHTS ON THE TOPIC OF LOVE
LOVE'S OPTIMISM

Reading Passage: 1Cor. 13:1-13
Main Text: 1Cor. 13:7 (love) ... bears all things, believes all things, hopes all things, endures all things. (NIV)

What is it that energizes love to bear all things, believe all things, and endure all things? It must be the expectation of the fulfillment of dreams for the one we love. The journey to the fulfillment is filled with many difficulties, detours and disappointments that have the potential to undermine love. But love is always optimistic.

The term used for "bears" all things could also be translated, cover, conceal or endure. When we love we will be exposed to many aspects of someone's life that we may find objectionable or repulsive. We shouldn't withdraw love at such times. Instead, because we believe in our dreams for that person, we should offer a covering of protection while we continue to hope for the fulfillment of the dream. While we cover and conceal loved ones from public dishonor and disgrace (not for the purpose of condoning wrongdoing), we endure the burden and cost of helping them conquer their 'demons' and overcome their deficiencies. We see this type of optimism in a farmer who plants his crop, and endures through times of drought and crop diseases. He keeps tending his farm, bearing the cost of fertilizers and pesticides, and seeking water through the disappointment of drought, because he believes in the crop and he is hopeful for the harvest.

Unlike a crop planted in a field, we choose to love people who have their unique dispositions, minds and wills that are beyond our control. That is why love encompasses "all things." We can never anticipate the things we will encounter when we choose to love someone, but love covers a "multitude of sins." This optimistic love enabled a father to keep going to the brow of the hill each day looking for the return of his rebellious son who ran off to a 'far country.' It caused Jesus to journey to Bethany to the house of Lazarus who had been dead for four days and say, "Show me the grave," although by this time the body was stinking. It moved the resurrected Jesus to visit the lake in Galilee where the disciples were fishing, so He could meet Peter who had openly denied Him. He did this in order to restore him to his destiny.

We may currently be going through difficulties, detours and disappointments in our relationships, but we cannot allow our love to be defeated, nor should we seek to withdraw our love. Let us renew our love in hope, so we will continue to bear all things, believe in the dreams we have for others, and endure the challenges that present themselves.

Father, what a challenge this is to my heart because of my inclination to give up easily on people. My weak love is in need of Your strength, and I need Your grace to empower me to endure the challenges that accompany my relationships at church, the workplace and at home, for Christ's sake.

February 13

MANNA SERIES: THOUGHTS ON THE TOPIC OF LOVE
PRESENT POSSESSION OF AN ETERNAL VIRTUE

Reading Passage: 1Cor. 13:1-13
Main Text: 1Cor. 13:8 Love never fails ... 1Cor. 13:13 But now faith, hope, love, abide these three; but the greatest of these is love. (NIV)

Paul began this hymn by explaining that pursuing the virtue of love is the superior way of building up the church, in contrast to the pursuit of spiritual gifts. He brings the hymn to a climatic conclusion by explaining why possessing love is not only superior to possessing spiritual gifts, but is also superior to the possession of any other virtue.

In the Corinthian church, great emphasis was placed on the exercise of spiritual gifts, yet the church suffered from spiritual dysfunctionality. Paul explained that the pursuit of love provides the proper foundation for the effective use of spiritual gifts. Therefore, the emphasis in the assembly should not be on activities that were spectacular and impressive, yet divisive and giving rise to spiritual pride. In his conclusion, he stated that love never fails, meaning it will never cease to be effective. It also means love will remain an eternal possession, whereas there is a time limit to the possession of certain spiritual gifts. Prophecies and knowledge will be done away, and tongues will cease (1Cor. 13:8). On the other hand, He listed three virtues that will never cease to be effective during this life: "faith, hope and love abide."

Faith (even faith to move mountains) is worthless without love, and hope has no noble objective without love. Therefore love is greater in worth than either of these other virtues. In addition, in the eternal state when we see the Lord, all will be explained and clearly understood. So there will be no further need for faith, and hope will then be fully realized. But our relationship with our Lord will continue to be based on love throughout eternity. This explains the eternal worth of love.

Why would we give priority to the temporary over the eternal? Love is the only thing we can possess in this life that we can continue to possess for eternity. We can begin using the currency of eternity in this present life. No pursuit of any temporal gift or virtue can ever be compared with the pursuit of love. And this is available to all. No special spiritual qualification is necessary, no special anointing is required; just the yielding of ourselves to the Holy Spirit, allowing Him to pour love in our lives, and produce His fruit in us.

Father, we are amazed at the privilege afforded us to participate in eternal things while in this earthly life. Our hearts are so easily seduced by the spectacular and the temporary things that exalt us in the eyes of man, instead of what makes us true servants to people. May Your love possess us until we become possessors of love, for Christ's sake.

MANNA SERIES: THOUGHTS ON THE TOPIC OF LOVE
LOVE MY NEIGHBOR; DO I HAVE A CHOICE?

Reading Passage: Luke 10:25-37
Main Text: Luke 10:27-28 He answered: " 'Love the Lord your God with all your heart and with all your soul and with all your strength and with all your mind'; and, 'Love your neighbor as yourself.'" "You have answered correctly," Jesus replied, "Do this and you will live." (NIV)

It would be so much easier to obey God's command to love if we were given the choice of the people to be used as proof of our obedience. If love is defined as the giving of ourselves unconditionally for the good of another, surely I can prove I have that love for the people I select, such as my family and friends. Love to my selected group does not need much divine assistance. As stated by Jesus, even the pagans meet this qualification of love (Matt 5:46-47). But to demonstrate the divine type of love that should flow from us to everyone, it has to be proven with people whom we would normally exclude.

The background to our text was the encounter between Jesus and a brilliant lawyer who was not just an expert professor in law, but also a highly moral person. The lawyer sought to test Jesus by asking Him the requirement for eternal life. When Jesus challenged him to keep the law, the lawyer wanted to know Jesus' definition of loving one's neighbor so he could prove he was in full compliance. Jesus told the story popularly known as The Good Samaritan. His explanation completely revolutionized the understanding of who a neighbor is, and made us understand that the required love is nothing that can be achieved without divine assistance.

The lesson from the story is that (a) a neighbor is not someone I choose but someone who needs my help, and (b) a neighbor appears on the path I happen to travel, not in a place and a condition in which I plan to meet him. We do not determine who becomes our neighbor; rather, we prove that we are neighborly by how we respond to the one we find in our path who is in need of help. The irony of the story is that the one who proved to be the genuine neighbor was a Samaritan. These people were considered by the Jews to be outcasts. The religious Jews who were walking on the same path as the Samaritan didn't provide the help required by the victim. Who has God placed in our path that may be in need of help? They may not be from our neighborhood, from our race, social class or educational background. However, they may become the means of proving whether we have love or not. In fact, they may even despise us, but they are in our path and in need.

Father, this teaching of Jesus causes us to wonder if what appears to be accidental or casual encounters in life are not your divine appointments so we can prove the quality of our love. Help us to love the "neighbors" you place in our path today, as we love ourselves, for Christ's sake.

February 15

MANNA SERIES: THOUGHTS ON THE TOPIC OF LOVE
LOVE SETS A HIGH STANDARD
FOR TREATING OTHERS

Reading Passage: Luke 10:25-37
Main Text: Luke 10:27-28 He answered: "'Love the Lord your God with all your heart and with all your soul and with all your strength and with all your mind'; and, 'Love your neighbor as yourself.' "You have answered correctly," Jesus replied. "Do this and you will live." (NIV)

Jesus agreed with the reduction (summary) of all the commandments and laws into the two commandments in our text. The second, "Love your neighbor as yourself" appears so simplistic that we often overlook the wisdom of the statement and the guidance it provides for loving, interpersonal relationships.

The first principle implied by the command is that we are unable to properly love our neighbor (any person in our path and in need) if we don't love ourselves. This is clearly not the promotion of obsessive self-love, which enters into relationships for the purpose of gaining personal advantage. The principle is that a person who loves and cares for himself or herself has a standard to use for caring for someone else (cf. Eph. 5:24-25).

Never entrust yourself to people who have low standards of caring for themselves.

The next principle taught by the command is that love demands we treat others the way we wish to be treated. Think about how this would alter our behavior in all our interaction with people. For example, how many times have we been annoyed with or disrespectful to a waiter because of delays in processing our order? At such times we need to consider how we would like to be treated if the roles were reversed. Have we ever made a deal knowing we were taking advantage of the other party? We certainly would not be pleased if we knew someone was deliberately giving us a bad deal. Think about how we abuse our employer's time and resources. Is this how we would like to be treated by our employees if we owned the business?

Let this command be the basis of our interaction with others today, whether it is the cashier at the store, the little boys begging on the street, siblings who demand too much of us, or those in our neighborhood who offend us. Before acting, we should always ask ourselves, "How would I wish to be treated if our roles were reversed?" Jesus said, "Do this and you will live." Although our salvation depends on our faith in Christ, Christians are expected to demonstrate their love for God by their love for neighbors.

Father, this command is so difficult that I wish it was just a suggestion. Then it would allow me some options. But I know Your desire is that Your people live in love in order to reflect Your heart. Grant me the power of Your love so I will be able to fulfill this command, and truly live, for Jesus' glory, Amen.

February 16

MANNA SERIES: THOUGHTS ON THE TOPIC OF LOVE
LOVE'S WILD EXPRESSIONS

Reading Passage: Luke 7:36-50
Main Text: Luke 7:47 Therefore, I tell you, her many sins have been forgiven—for she loved much. But he who has been forgiven little loves little. (NIV)

We struggle to know the most appropriate way to communicate our love. Love demands expression so that our loved ones may enter into the secrets of our heart. Many poems and songs have been written and many sacrificial gifts given, all in an attempt to find the appropriate language to express our feelings of love. Sometimes the regular and usual gestures appear too mundane and weak to convey the depth of love we wish to express. So we 'step it up' and make the expressions more wild and creative, and more memorable. For example, at a recent ballgame in the presence of thousands, an excited lover arranged to propose to his girlfriend on the large screen at half-time.

The background to our text is the occasion when a woman with a known sinful lifestyle barged into the house of a Pharisee where Jesus was attending a dinner party. The woman evaded the security and ignored the angry stares of the host and other guests. She went directly to Jesus and began to wash His feet with her tears and dry them with her hair. She then poured very expensive perfume over His feet while rubbing and kissing them. When the host questioned this wild display, Jesus explained that the woman loved much because she was forgiven much. Although the Pharisee didn't understand it, Jesus clearly appreciated the sincere uninhibited expression of her love in response to what He had done for her.

This event challenges us who claim to love Jesus, and who say we appreciate His sacrifice for our sins. Do our expressions of love for our Lord cost us something so significant that others think we are crazy and wasteful? Or are we content with a routine, non-sacrificial, cheap and superficial pretense of love? When King David was offered cost-free, a site for building an altar, he refused. He declared that he would not make offerings to God, which cost him nothing (2Sam 24:24). In the eyes of onlookers, are our careers, our social status, or our finances off-limits for expressing our love for Jesus? Do our expressions of love get Jesus' attention so He can say of us that we love much? Remember, our expressions of love are reflective of how much we believe we have been forgiven.

Father, I realize that there was no limit in Your expression of love for me, in that You sacrificed Jesus, the best of heaven, for me. The limited expressions of my love must be so disappointing to You. Keep reminding me of my sinfulness, so I will never forget Your great forgiveness. Give me the courage to ignore the disapproval of those around me as I give full expression of my love, whether in worshipping, in giving, in witnessing or in serving as You command. I pray in the name of Jesus.

February 17

MANNA SERIES: THOUGHTS ON THE TOPIC OF LOVE
LOVE VS LAW

Reading Passage: Rom. 13:8-14
Main Text: Rom. 13:10 Love does no wrong to a neighbor; therefore love is the fulfillment of the law. (NIV)

In implementing goal-setting strategies, it is important to ensure the goals are measurable, reasonable, and have target completion dates. This allows for assessment of the progress in achieving goals, and provides an expected end for the project. While such strategies may be applicable and necessary for certain aspects of life, it is redundant in the area of loving human relationships. How do we measure the progress of love? When can we celebrate the completion of a love project?

God provided the law as an indication of His righteous standards for relationships among mankind and with Himself. It was a means by which failure to measure up to God's requirements (sin), might be known (Rom 4:15, 5:13, 7:7). However, the law was inadequate as a measure of the love required for human relationships, because while it might stipulate an action it could not specify attitude; while it may describe a deed it could not determine motive. The law, as an external document, provided mankind with a code of conduct but was powerless to initiate the desire to live by it.

All that the law was seeking to achieve would be accomplished if mankind had a heart of love. The external law becomes unnecessary when the law is present in the heart. Paul's statement, "love is the fulfillment of the law," repeats a principle taught by Jesus that all the law is completed and its goal achieved when we love. The attempt to keep rules without the motivation of love in our hearts makes us hypocrites and the effort burdensome. We may be able to tick off items on the checklist of accomplishments in our relationship, and while that may feed our pride it may not be any indication of our love. Jesus beautifully summarized the Ten Commandments and the additional 613 laws, in two commandments centered on the one four-letter word, LOVE (Mark 12:30-31). Paul explains that love for our neighbor is a debt that can never be eliminated and a virtue that completes all the law. Although we may produce tokens that represent our love, the only true measurement of love is the state of our hearts.

Do you approach relationships with predetermined guidelines of how much your love will tolerate, or how long it will last? Love's simple but sincere declaration to neighbors is, "I will do you no wrong" or "I will always do what is right for you." The love response is never conditional on my neighbor's attitude or actions toward me, just on my desire to please God.

Father, I now realize that Your judgment of me will not be based on the number of rules I try to keep, but on the state of my heart toward my neighbor. I desire a sincere heart of love for all people You bring into my sphere of relationship, so my life will be pleasing to You, for Christ's sake.

February 18

MANNA SERIES: THOUGHTS ON THE TOPIC OF LOVE
IT'S ALL A LOVE STORY

Reading Passage: Rev. 21:1-27
Main Text: Rev. 19:6-8 Then I heard what sounded like a great multitude, like the roar of rushing waters and like loud peals of thunder, shouting: "Hallelujah! For our Lord God Almighty reigns. Let us rejoice and be glad and give him glory! For the wedding of the Lamb has come, and his bride has made herself ready. Fine linen, bright and clean, was given her to wear." (NIV)

There are various opinions regarding the overall theme of the Bible. One theme we cannot overlook is that of a love story involving God and mankind, with a Satanic antagonist, and an earthly paradise in which the lovers will ultimately live and reign.

For what purpose did God create man and place him in the earthly paradise He made? So that the supreme Creator could have a love affair with His human creation, and that this love affair could be consummated in marriage. God's relationship with humans was interrupted after the Satanic antagonist entered the story in Genesis 3 and won the affections of the first couple. The Bible is a record of the divine Husband seeking to recover His expected bride.

Following the Middle Eastern practice, a man engages his expected bride in a covenant relationship that will be later consummated in marriage at the time of the wedding feast. Throughout the Bible we see the language of love and the picture of God's pursuit of His bride. First, the bride was comprised of people of just one nation, Israel, whom God wanted to use as the means of expanding His program to the whole world. God introduced Himself to Israel as her Redeemer (the Exodus story). In His dealing with the nation we learn about the character of God. He is compassionate, merciful, and abounding in love and faithfulness (Ex 34:6-7). God used this nation to produce the husband in human form, namely Jesus Christ. Through Jesus' sacrificial death and victory over Satan, He selects His bride, the Church, from all nations and peoples. He is now waiting for the final act, the ceremony, when He will consummate the marriage to His bride. Our text in the book of Revelation describes this final marriage celebration.

This brief overview of the Bible not only confirms the theme as a love story, but also presents the Bible as a unique book. It is unusual for a book to have the readers as participants in the dramatic story; one that describes an ending yet to be fulfilled. The text explains that during the current period in history, the bride is making herself ready for the wedding by adorning herself in garments (her lifestyle) that are bright and clean (attractive and holy) to please her Husband. We can determine our role in the dramatic conclusion. Are you included in the Church, the great multitude representing the bride, by preparing yourself for your divine Husband? This is our highest pursuit and nothing else in this world is as important.

Father, we thank You for giving us such a comprehensive record of the purpose of our lives and what You expect of us as we await Jesus' return. Please help us to remain committed to the task of making ourselves ready for our Lover, in fulfillment of our covenant to Jesus, our Redeemer.

February 19

MANNA SERIES: GREAT REVERSALS IN THE BIBLE
FROM BARRENNESS TO BLESSEDNESS

Reading Passage: 1Sam. 1:1-20
Main Text: 1Sam. 2:5-8 Those who were full hire themselves out for food,
but those who were hungry hunger no more. She who was
barren has borne seven children,
but she who has had many sons pines away.
"The LORD brings death and makes alive;
he brings down to the grave and raises up.
The LORD sends poverty and wealth;
he humbles and he exalts.
He raises the poor from the dust
and lifts the needy from the ash heap;
he seats them with princes
and has them inherit a throne of honor.
"For the foundations of the earth are the LORD'S;
upon them he has set the world. (NIV)

Our faith in God provides us with hope, which causes us to look beyond our existing status or the problems that confront us. We can be confident that our God is able to change our circumstances so that our tomorrows can be better than our todays. This knowledge of God is obtained from reading the history of His dealings with many people in the Bible. There we observe several examples where God intervenes providentially to bring about a reversal, placing those who were in adversity in a place of prosperity and vice versa.

In the story of the birth of Samuel (1Sam. 1), we are presented with a man named Elkanah who had two wives. Hannah, the wife he loved, was barren, whereas the other wife, Peninnah, had children. In those days, barrenness was regarded as a curse. The social stigma, and the spousal rivalry caused by Peninnah's taunts, made Hannah's life miserable. The annual pilgrimage to the place of worship for sacrifice was particularly painful for Hannah, but she used the opportunity to cry out to God in her distress. Eventually she made a vow that if God blessed her with a son she would give him back to God for the rest of his life. God answered her prayer and gave her a son named Samuel.

Having the child caused Hannah to learn that no condition is final when we have God on our side; even barrenness can be reversed to abundance. Furthermore, our adversaries who taunt us today can be the ones to envy us tomorrow. Our God is able to "raise the poor from the dust, and lift the needy from the ash heap," and "seat them with princes" so they "inherit a throne of honor."

We don't have to let the adverse situations we find ourselves in today drive us to despair. There is no condition that is too entrenched, no enemy too formidable, no circumstance so impossible that our God cannot intervene and bring about a reversal that is beyond our comprehension. Trust Him today.

Father, help us to believe like Hannah that "the foundations of the earth are the Lord's," and You can establish whatever You please thereon. We will not allow ourselves to be driven to despair, but we will put our faith in Our Sovereign Lord who can bring about Divine Reversals for Christ's glory.

February 20

MANNA SERIES: GREAT REVERSALS IN THE BIBLE
RECOVERY FROM DISADVANTAGE DUE TO DISRESPECT

Reading Passage: Gen. 13:1-13; 19:12-17
Main Text: Gen. 19:28-29 He looked down toward Sodom and Gomorrah, toward all the land of the plain, and he saw dense smoke rising from the land, like smoke from a furnace. So when God destroyed the cities of the plain, he remembered Abraham, and he brought Lot out of the catastrophe that overthrew the cities where Lot had lived. (NIV)

There is a hurt we feel when people in whom we have invested love and goodness disrespect us. This hurt cannot be healed until God vindicates us. Many times we receive this vindication only after God intervenes to cause a reversal in the circumstances, and places us in a position to help those who disrespected us.

God promised Abraham the land of Canaan as an inheritance for his offspring. Abraham was childless at the time he received the promise, and he took his nephew Lot on the journey to Canaan. He raised Lot as a son after the death of his father. Both Abraham and Lot grew wealthy in livestock, silver and gold. Eventually the area where they lived became too small for them and this resulted in conflicts between their servants. To solve this problem, Abraham proposed that he and Lot should move to separate locations. He gave Lot the first choice of the land for a new settlement. Because Lot should have regarded himself as a son, and the promise of land had been given to Abraham, Lot should have ensured that Abraham receive the more fertile land. Instead Lot selfishly chose the best land for himself. Abraham must have felt disrespected, but he graciously parted from Lot and accepted the inferior land.

What Lot did not realize was that the fertile land was located among the cities of Sodom, occupied by people whom God regarded as wicked. Eventually the wickedness of the people became so great that God decided to destroy all the cities of Sodom. Before God destroyed the cities, He informed Abraham. Abraham interceded with God, seeking to prevent the destruction of Sodom because Lot was dwelling there. He was unsuccessful in his intercession, but for Uncle Abraham's sake, God rescued Lot from the cities before He destroyed them. In the end the location with the rich, fertile land was destroyed, while Abraham's portion of the land was unaffected. Lot, who was disrespectful, lost all his possessions, while the disrespected Abraham had to petition for Lot's deliverance. This reversal vindicated Abraham.

There is often a temptation to seek to vindicate ourselves when we feel we have not been respected or we are taken advantage of. It is always best to leave the vindication to God, who is able to reverse the circumstances and elevate us in the eyes of men. When we humble ourselves He will exalt us at the proper time. Let us trust the God who says, "Vengeance is mine; I will repay."

Father, we admit that we sometimes struggle to accept the hurt caused by disrespect from people we have helped. Help us to trust You to vindicate us so we can keep on helping and being merciful despite any rejection. This we pray in Jesus' name.

February 21

MANNA SERIES: GREAT REVERSALS IN THE BIBLE
PROSPERITY DESPITE ABUSIVE SITUATIONS

Reading Passage: Gen. 30:25-43

Main Text: Gen. 31:6-9 You know that I've worked for your father with all my strength, yet your father has cheated me by changing my wages ten times. However, God has not allowed him to harm me. If he said, 'The speckled ones will be your wages,' then all the flocks gave birth to speckled young; and if he said, 'The streaked ones will be your wages,' then all the flocks bore streaked young. So God has taken away your father's livestock and has given them to me. (NIV)

Abusive situations must be avoided, vigorously opposed, and every effort made to rescue victims from them. It may be a marriage where the spouse has been suffering physical abuse, yet is dependent on the abuser for financial support. Or the victim could be illegally residing in a country, so an employer keeps him or her in a state of virtual slavery. Sometimes the abusive situation is caused by someone being unsuspectingly tied to a contract with terms that place that person at a great disadvantage, but there is no easy way to avoid the contract. Christians should be known as people who champion the cause of those suffering under abusive situations. However, we also know that God is able to cause reversals that allow victims to be victorious, and prosper in these abusive situations.

When Jacob was living with his uncle Laban in Paddan-aram, he found himself in an abusive situation. He had fallen in love with Laban's daughter, Rachel. After he gave seven years of servant-labor as dowry for his bride, Laban tricked him and gave him Rachel's sister as his bride. Jacob had to agree to work an additional seven years in order to marry Rachel. When Jacob completed the fourteen years of service and wanted to return home with his family, Laban insisted on an additional period of service for wages. Jacob's wages would be any speckled and spotted sheep and goats, while all the solid colored animals would belong to Laban. Once they made this agreement, Laban and his sons quietly removed all the speckled and spotted animals from the flock leaving Jacob with only solid colored animals to use for breeding. Yet God intervened and caused the solid colored animals to produce mostly speckled and spotted animals, thereby increasing Jacob's portion of the flock. In fact, Laban changed the terms of Jacob's wages ten times intending to disadvantage him. But God caused Jacob to prosper despite Laban's abusive actions, while Laban suffered significant loss.

This story in the life of Jacob illustrates why we can trust God in any situation we find ourselves. Although we should work for changes in adverse situations, if there seems to be little or no progress, we should not despair since God is able to cause us to prosper even in these situations.

Father, we are thankful that You are Lord over all our circumstances. We trust that You will protect us until You are ready to deliver us, and You will bless us despite the plans of our enemies.

February 22

MANNA SERIES: GREAT REVERSALS IN THE BIBLE
FROM ABANDONMENT TO ENTHRONEMENT

Reading Passage: Gen. 50:15-21
Main Text: Gen. 50:20-21 "…You intended to harm me, but God intended it for good to accomplish what is now being done, the saving of many lives. So then, don't be afraid. I will provide for you and your children." And he reassured them and spoke kindly to them. (NIV)

The family is our place of refuge when the challenges and the antagonism of the outside world become too much for us to handle. But to whom should we turn when our families become the source of our pain?

In the well-known story of Joseph, the son of Jacob, we see the antagonism of his brothers leading to his abandonment by them. Jacob gave Joseph a special robe, openly showing his favoritism of him, and this caused his brothers to hate him. This hatred increased after Joseph told the family his dreams in which they were bowing down to him. They plotted to get rid of him. They abandoned him in a pit, and later sold him to slave traders who took him to Egypt. Joseph found favor with Potiphar, his master in Egypt, who was an officer in the army. Later Potiphar's wife lied about Joseph, which resulted in his being placed in prison. While in prison, God showed Joseph favor and he was promoted to be in charge of all the prisoners. He was supervising two officers who had been imprisoned by Pharaoh, when they told him their dreams. The cupbearer's dream was later fulfilled, and he was released and reinstated, just as interpreted by Joseph. Contrary to Joseph's request, however, the newly restored cupbearer did not advocate for him. Joseph was forgotten; abandoned in the prison for two more years.

One day Pharaoh had a dream that troubled him, and he couldn't find anyone to interpret it. At that time the cupbearer remembered Joseph and told Pharaoh of his ability to interpret dreams. As a result of the interpretation of the dream, Pharaoh released Joseph from prison, and promoted him to be the chief minister in Egypt, next in status to the Pharaoh. The dream was of a coming famine over that entire region. Joseph proposed a plan whereby food would be stored in Egypt that would allow them to survive the famine and make the Pharaoh prosperous. More significantly, the plan would allow Jacob and his family to find food in Egypt, with Joseph there to give them special favor. God used the abandonment of Joseph to enable his positioning in Egypt for the benefit of his family. He providentially worked through their plan for evil to bring about their deliverance.

You may be feeling rejected and abandoned even by your family. The story of Joseph teaches us that God can use these situations to work out His purpose for our eventual good, and to serve as a blessing to our antagonists. Even in the darkness of our abandonment we can hope in God's reversals.

Father, we do get feelings of dejection during our periods of abandonment. Help us to believe that You are at work during these times to accomplish Your purposes.

February 23

MANNA SERIES: GREAT REVERSALS IN THE BIBLE
TRUSTING GOD'S TIMING FOR REVERSALS

Reading Passage: Ex. 11:1-9
Main Text: Ex. 12:30 Pharaoh and all his officials and all the Egyptians got up during the night, and there was loud wailing in Egypt, for there was not a house without someone dead. (NIV)

We usually think we know the best time for God to intervene in our affairs, bringing about changes that would relieve us of our adversaries. It is humbling to acknowledge, after a review of our lives, that God's timing was so much better than ours. However, this has never diminished our desire to be in control of the schedule of the events of our lives.

At the time when Moses was born, the Pharaoh had become fearful of the numerical growth of the Hebrew people in Egypt so he wanted to restrict their proliferation. He gave the edict to the Hebrew midwives that they should kill all male newborns. To avoid the killing of baby Moses, his parents placed him in a basket in the Nile. He was rescued by Pharaoh's daughter, who fell in love with him and took him as her own child. As a result, Moses, a Hebrew boy, was grown in the palace of Pharaoh as a member of the royal household. At around age forty, Moses observed an Egyptian abusing a Hebrew. Being angry at the suffering of his Hebrew people, he took control of matters, attacked the Egyptian and killed him. When he realized that Pharaoh was aware of his act of murder and was seeking to kill him, Moses escaped to the land of Midian.

Moses' act against the Egyptian could be viewed as avenging the mistreatment of the Hebrews by the Egyptians; he was intervening since God had not yet intervened. He could have justified his action based on the fact that the Pharaoh had killed so many of the Hebrew boys, and he was just fortunate to have escaped the infanticide. But this was not yet God's timing for an intervention.

Forty years later when God decided to intervene, he sent Moses on a mission to Pharaoh requesting the release of the Hebrew slaves. When Pharaoh refused, God sent ten plagues against the people of Egypt culminating in the death of every firstborn in the country.

Moses' timing of revenge killed only one Egyptian, but when God acted every household was affected. Moses wanted to be an avenger, God wanted to use him as a deliverer for the nation. When Moses acted prematurely, he hoped to become a hero to the Hebrews (and he was unsuccessful), but God wanted to make him "great in the land of Egypt, in the sight of Pharaoh, and in the sight of the people" (Ex.11:3 NKJV). God's intervention is much more effective against our enemies, and rewarding for us. Let us be willing to wait on the Lord because the timing of His reversals is always best.

Father, in our impatience for relief or for a change in what seems to be wrong in the world, we are tempted to act without waiting on

You. Help us to be confident in Your timing, so we will humbly wait for Your intervention. This we ask in Jesus' name.

February 24

MANNA SERIES: GREAT REVERSALS IN THE BIBLE
PLUNDERING THE SLAVE MASTER

Reading Passage: Ex. 12:29-36
Main Text: Ex. 12:35-36 The Israelites did as Moses instructed and asked the Egyptians for articles of silver and gold and for clothing. The LORD had made the Egyptians favorably disposed toward the people, and they gave them what they asked for; so they plundered the Egyptians. (NIV)

One reason we have such difficulty trusting God to bring about a reversal in our circumstances is that the process for the change is beyond our natural minds or wildest imagination. This is the case even when we know God's promises for our ultimate liberation and blessing.

In Gen. 15:13-14 God told Abraham that his offspring would be afflicted for four hundred years in a foreign land, after which they would come out with great possessions. When God called and commissioned Moses to approach Pharaoh to demand the release of the Israelites, He stated that the people would not leave empty handed, but they would plunder the Egyptians (Ex. 3:21). We can understand how difficult it was for these people, who were enslaved for four hundred years and who suffered great affliction and abuse, to believe in the possibility of deliverance. It was even more difficult to believe that they would leave with great possessions. But God has numerous and creative ways to bring about a great reversal.

After Pharaoh's stubbornness resulted in God inflicting plagues on Egypt, the people were anxious for the Israelites to leave the country, for fear of further destruction. Following Moses' instructions, the Israelites asked the Egyptians for gold, silver and articles of clothing. In addition, God moved the hearts of the Egyptians so they were favorably disposed to the Israelites. Whatever the Israelites wanted they got. Consequently they plundered the Egyptians, collecting compensation for four hundred years of slavery, and leaving their captivity with wealth. The Israelites could never have conceived of such an occurrence, in that their only contribution to obtaining the deliverance and the wealth, was in being obedient to God's instructions to ask for the goods. The reversal was all God's doing. These were acts of grace.

We are sometimes in the same position as the Israelites, suffering hardship and so accustomed to the enslavement of our circumstances that we are unable to believe that God can accomplish His promise to bring about a reversal in our lives. God does not only want to deliver us, but also to cause us to plunder the enemy in order to take back whatever we were deprived of. He wants to set us free with the love, joy and peace that are gifts of His grace. Even when we find it difficult to imagine how it will be done, let us continue to believe that God is able to do immeasurably more than we are able to ask or think.

Father, we are in awe of Your methods, but we are thankful for Your amazing power to accomplish Your purposes in our lives. Help us not to become enslaved in our minds so we fail to believe Your goodness toward us, for Christ's sake.

February 25

MANNA SERIES: GREAT REVERSALS IN THE BIBLE
CURSES TRANSFORMED TO BLESSINGS

Reading Passage: Num. 22:2-35
Main Text: Num. 23:7-8 Then Balaam uttered his oracle:
"Balak brought me from Aram,
the king of Moab from the eastern mountains.
'Come,' he said, 'curse Jacob for me;
Come, denounce Israel.'
How can I curse those whom God has not cursed?
How can I denounce those whom the LORD has not
denounced?" (NIV)

There is a great divergence of opinion as to the reality and effect of curses pronounced on people. There are those who claim power to impose evil on the lives of selected people. Others dismiss these claims stating it is just a matter that belief "kills or cures." Regardless, it is disturbing to think that the events of our lives could be affected by what another individual has determined for us, and we are powerless to influence the outcome. Many people have lived with great fear, or have spent much of their resources in an attempt to overcome perceived 'evil spells' imposed on them.

Scripture acknowledges the existence of curses. It states that the Lord will curse those who fail to obey the commandments of the Lord. The question we face is, Can a believer suffer from an evil curse? The story of the Israelites' encounter with Balaam is instructive.

The Israelites were on their journey to Canaan, and came to the country of Moab. Balak, the King of Moab was fearful of the Israelites, especially after hearing how they conquered the Amorites. He engaged the services of Balaam, a diviner from Pethor, known for the effect of his curses. Balak wanted him to curse Israel. Before he could go to pronounce curses on Israel, God spoke to Balaam and told him not to go, "... You must not put a curse on those people, because they are blessed" (Num. 22:12 NIV). Balaam resisted this instruction, and eventually God allowed him to go but told him he could only speak what the Lord instructed.

Later, whenever Balaam attempted to speak against Israel, instead of a curse he spoke blessings. God reversed the plan of the King of Moab and caused Balaam to record some of the most impressive words of blessing upon the young nation, Israel. This became the confidence booster they needed before beginning the conquest of Canaan. Balaam explained his inability to fulfill his assignment in Moab by stating, "How can I curse those whom God has not cursed?" (Num. 23:8 NIV).

As Christians our faith in Jesus assures us that in Him we are blessed. The Lord's statement to Balaam applies to us, "You must not put a curse on those people, because they are blessed." Let us not live in fear of curses; rather let us be assured by our faith, that once we are in Christ, no one can curse us.

Father, it is reassuring to know that in Christ we are protected from the curses of men. Help us to resist any attempts of the enemy to tell us otherwise. For we know if God is for us, no one can be against us.

February 26

MANNA SERIES: GREAT REVERSALS IN THE BIBLE
IS THERE RECOVERY FROM DISGRACE?

Reading Passage: Judg. 16:18-30
Main Text: Judg. 16:28,30 Then Samson prayed to the LORD, "O Sovereign LORD, remember me. O God, please strengthen me just once more, and let me with one blow get revenge on the Philistines for my two eyes." ... Samson said, "Let me die with the Philistines!" Then he pushed with all his might, and down came the temple on the rulers and all the people in it. Thus he killed many more when he died than while he lived. (NIV)

We are familiar with the sensational stories, especially in the world of athletics. The gifted star athlete broke most of the records and had become the main attraction for the sport. Then there was the news that he was caught doing drugs. Suddenly he is banned from the sport, and becomes the poster boy for all that is wrong with modern sports. Usually there is no hope of redemption for such a personality.

Is the outcome in this story the same as in the Kingdom of God? If God called and gifted someone for a particular purpose, and that person falls in disgrace, are the purposes of God for that person thwarted? Is there any possibility of recovery for this individual, or does the disgrace mean absolute disqualification?

Samson was born under miraculous circumstances, while Israel was under forty years of oppression by the Philistines. Before he was born, the Lord told his parents he was being sent for the purpose of saving Israel from the oppression of the Philistines. He would be endowed with amazing strength whenever the Spirit of the Lord came upon him, as long as he kept his vow to the Lord. The symbol of this vow was his uncut hair. Samson demonstrated his strength on several occasions, which resulted in him killing many Philistines. However while Samson had great physical strength he also had a great weakness for Philistine women.

Eventually he fell in love with Delilah who conspired with the Lords of the Philistines to ascertain the secret to Samson's strength. She nagged him until he revealed that if his hair was cut off he would become as weak as any other man. She lured him to sleep and arranged for his hair to be cut off. The Philistines not only captured him but they gouged out his eyes and placed him in prison in shackles. This hero of Israel spent his days in disgrace grinding at the mill in prison, and as the object of Philistine taunts. However, after a while his hair began to grow again.

One day when the Lords of the Philistines gathered for sacrifice to their gods, they called for Samson to provide entertainment. While entertaining them Samson cried out to God to restore his strength so he would be able take revenge against the Philistines. He took hold of the pillars of the temple and brought down the house killing everybody gathered there, including himself. He killed many more in his death than while he lived. God restored Samson to his purpose when he reversed the plans of the Philistine lords.

We can be encouraged that God can cause us to recover and fulfill our purpose, even if we have to suffer the consequences for our failures.

Father, thank You for never giving up on us, but always giving us the chance of recovery from disgrace when we call to You in repentance, for the glory of Christ.

February 27

MANNA SERIES: GREAT REVERSALS IN THE BIBLE
WINNING AGAINST THE ODDS

Reading Passage: 1Sam. 17:41-54
Main Text: 1Sam. 17:50-51…So David triumphed over the Philistine with a sling and a stone; without a sword in his hand he struck down the Philistine and killed him. David ran and stood over him. He took hold of the Philistine's sword and drew it from the scabbard. After he killed him, he cut off his head with the sword. When the Philistines saw that their hero was dead, they turned and ran. (NIV)

You know the odds are against you when the prospective employer, while reading your application, asks whether you are sure you read the requirements for the requested position; when the loan officer looking at your application remarks that collateral means items that have value; or the doctor tells you that medical researchers are interested in people with your condition.

When we are faced with these challenges, they have the effect of causing us to see our opponents as giants and ourselves as inadequate. The easiest thing to do is to ask ourselves, " Why bother? Why not just accept things as they are, and learn to live with the taunts of the giants of impossibilities in our lives?" But God does not get any glory from such an attitude of complacency. On the contrary, He delights in manifesting Himself where the odds are stacked against us.

David faced the giant Goliath when the Israelite army was content to camp across from the Philistines in the Valley of Elah and listen to the daily taunts of their champion. No one tried to attack Goliath, nor did Israel try to negotiate some peace treaty. King Saul only offered an incentive to anyone who would kill Goliath. We might think David was naive or impetuous when he offered to fight the giant. But he saw Goliath as an uncultured outcast ('an unworthy Philistine'), and his taunts as an attack against the armies of the Lord (17:26, 36). Goliath had the advantage of size (he was nearly 10 feet tall), and armament (he wore a bronze helmet, had a coat of heavy armor, carried a bronze javelin and a long spear with an iron tip); while little David had no weapons but a sling and stones. David never considered the odds, because he came to the battle in the 'name of the Lord of hosts, the God of the armies of Israel.'

How we view the challenge will determine how we approach the battle. Do we see a giant or an opponent of the Lord? Do we approach the battle in our own strength, with our resume, and shrewdness, or do we approach it with the help and guidance of the Lord (in the name of the Lord)? Like David, when we face the challenges with God's strength, we can be assured of winning against the odds, and bringing glory to Him.

Father, we know that You are bigger than all our enemies and challenges. Nothing and no one can withstand Your power. Help us to face each battle as an opportunity for You to be glorified, for Jesus' sake.

MANNA SERIES: GREAT REVERSALS IN THE BIBLE
WHEN THE ALLIANCE SELF-DESTRUCTS

Reading Passage: 2Chr. 20:1-25
Main Text: 2Chr. 20:22-23 As they began to sing and praise, the LORD set ambushes against the men of Ammon and Moab and Mount Seir who were invading Judah, and they were defeated. The men of Ammon and Moab rose up against the men from Mount Seir to destroy and annihilate them. After they finished slaughtering the men from Seir, they helped to destroy one another. (NIV)

There are some challenges we feel capable of managing. In fact, it is possible we can recall having conquered these challenges previously. We usually get worried when it seems various challenges come at us all at the same time, as if there was a conspiracy to combine forces to attack us. For example, we discover a serious medical condition at the same time we lose our job and medical insurance coverage. As we are confronting these situations, one of our children asks for emotional support while dealing with a marriage breakup. The triple blow seems just too much to manage, and we lose any pretense of calm and self - sufficiency. It is at these times we realize that we cannot survive without God's help. Yet once we become God-dependent, He allows us to observe His ability to turn around situations in such a manner that we are amazed how easily our enemies self-destruct.

King Jehoshaphat of Judea had restored good order and the worship of the Lord in his country. Immediately thereafter he was confronted with the alliance of three foreign enemies who planned to attack Judea. The situation caused Jehoshaphat to realize his inadequacy and hence his dependence on God. He declared, "We are powerless against this horde ... we don't know what to do, but our eyes are on You." He discovered that with such an attitude God gladly accepted the responsibility and the challenge, by declaring, "The battle is not yours, but God's."

The only task for Jehoshaphat and his people, was to worship and praise God, celebrating the faithfulness of His covenant love. "When they began to sing and praise," God caused confusion among the enemies who began to attack each other, until they had fully self-destructed. The people of Judah moved from worry to worship, and to observing the war among the alliance, and then to collecting the spoils of the war. Only God could orchestrate such a reversal.

This opportunity for God's glory does not occur until we are in a position where we acknowledge our powerlessness against a formidable foe, and our dependence on God. In such a posture of humility, we can clearly hear His instruction, and become willing to place the battle in His hand. We can know this transfer is made when we find our fears begin turning to praise and worship. If you are facing an alliance of challenges today, remember God is waiting for you to turn the battle over to Him.

Father, we are so foolish in trying to fight in our own might when we know our foes are too formidable for us. We also know You are waiting to fight on our behalf. Help us to humbly seek Your help and trust You to turn around the battle for Your glory.

February 29

MANNA SERIES: GREAT REVERSALS IN THE BIBLE
GOD RESPONDS TO HIS ACCUSERS

Reading Passage: Isa. 37:10-29, 33-38
Main Text: Is. 37:14-15 Hezekiah received the letter from the messengers and read it. Then he went up to the temple of the LORD and spread it out before the LORD. And Hezekiah prayed to the LORD: (NIV)

We frequently face ridicule regarding our belief in God and a life of faith. We are told that faith in God is an old-fashioned practice by people who lack confidence in their own intelligence, and are trapped by superstitions. We easily begin to take the accusations personally and shrink away in embarrassment or strike back at our accusers. Many of these attacks are really indirect attacks against our God and should not be taken personally. However there are times when the accusers disregard the diplomatic language and 'political correctness', and direct their attacks pointedly against the Lord. We know that God is able to defend himself and humble the boastful accusers.

The Assyrian army had conquered the Northern tribes of Israel and taken the people into exile. Their sights were now set on the Southern tribe of Judea hoping to capture the capital, Jerusalem. After capturing some key cities of Judea, the Assyrian army laid siege around Jerusalem, and appealed to King Hezekiah of Judea to surrender. When that appeal failed, King Sennacherib of Assyria decided to appeal directly to the inhabitants of Jerusalem to revolt against the leadership. He told them it was useless to trust in the Lord, because the gods of other countries had been unable to protect them against the Assyrian assault (36:18-20; 37:10-13).

The words of the Assyrian messengers were recorded in a letter to King Hezekiah. On reading the letter, Hezekiah took it to the house of the Lord, spread it out before the Lord and prayed. He told the Lord that many of the claims in the letter were true, but since He was the only true God, he was asking the Lord to save His people and prove that He is the true God. In spreading out the letter to God, Hezekiah was saying, "Lord this is your letter, Please respond." God responded through Isaiah the prophet, explaining that the attack against the inhabitants of Jerusalem was really an attack against "the Holy One of Israel." So the Lord's response to Assyria would be direct and devastating. The Assyrians would not enter the city or shoot an arrow there, because God would defend it. That night, the angel of the Lord went through the Assyrian camp and killed 185,000 soldiers. As a result the boastful King Sennacherib and the vaunted Assyrians hurried home to their country, in defeat. Later his own sons assassinated him.

Don't be dismayed by the criticism of our accusers, redirect them to the Lord. Our God is able to defend Himself. When He decides to take action, He is able to humble any proud accuser and reverse them in their course. He told Sennacharib, "Because you rage against me and because your insolence has reached my ears, I will put my hook in your nose and my bit in your mouth, and I will make you return by the way you came." (37:29 NIV).

Father, we want to have the right response to those who challenge our faith in You. Help us to understand that we don't have to fight against these accusers. We can present them to You and trust Your response.

March 1

MANNA SERIES: GREAT REVERSALS IN THE BIBLE
A SOURCE THAT PROVIDES
SURPRISING RESULTS

Reading Passage: Dan. 1:1-20
Main Text: Dan. 1:19-20 The king talked with them, and he found none equal to Daniel, Hananiah, Mishael and Azariah; so they entered the king's service. In every matter of wisdom and understanding about which the king questioned them, he found them ten times better than all the magicians and enchanters in his whole kingdom. (NIV)

Whenever we begin to have doubts as to whether we can succeed in life without relying on unethical, 'worldly wise' methods that are employed by many 'prosperous' people, we have to confront the question of who or what is the source for our lives? The answer to this question will determine whether we are dependent on natural or supernatural means for our existence. When we depend on God, He sometimes uses unconventional means to provide surprising results. When the Israelites were journeying through the wilderness, He provided 'manna,' a new food source, which sustained over two million people for forty years without any reports of malnutrition and sickness among them.

After Nebuchadnezzar conquered Jerusalem, he requested the capture of a group of the Jewish young men of the aristocracy to be taken to Babylon and groomed for leadership. These were youths who were very intelligent, with the aptitude for palace service. They were to be educated for three years in the Babylonian literature, customs and language. During this period they were to be provided with an exquisite diet of royal food and wine in preparation for their interview with the king at the end of the three years. Notable among these young men were Daniel and his three friends.

But even at that young age, Daniel and his friends resolved that they would not defile themselves with anything that was contrary to the requirements of Jewish law, such as the king's food and wine. Daniel asked the supervisor to supply them with vegetables and water instead. When the supervisor refused because he feared for his life if the king noticed that the boys under his care became emaciated, Daniel suggested a test run of ten days. At the end of that time, Daniel and his friends were better in appearance than the other youths who ate the king's food.

In addition to providing for their health, God also provided for their education (1:17). At the end of the three years, the king noticed that Daniel and his friends surpassed all the other youths in every way, and they were ten times superior to the wise men in the kingdom of Babylon. Although they were in the environment of the pagan prestigious Babylonian college, Daniel and his friends depended on the Lord for their sustenance. And they had a superior outcome, which was surprising to the kingdom of Babylon.

On what are you depending? Is it a job, a professional certification, or a track record of achievements? God is able to cause you to surpass the outcome of any natural qualifications to prove that dependency on Him is always the highest qualification to possess.

Father, we confess that we sometimes struggle with doubts that Your ways and means are best for us. Thank You for the examples like Daniel who prove that when You are our source we will not be in lack.

March 2

MANNA SERIES: GREAT REVERSALS IN THE BIBLE
A SURPRISING PATH TO A PROMOTION

Reading Passage: Dan. 3:1-30
Main Text: Dan. 3:28 Then Nebuchadnezzar said, "Praise be to the God of Shadrach, Meshach and Abednego, who has sent his angel and rescued his servants! They trusted in him and defied the king's command and were willing to give up their lives rather than serve or worship any god except their own God."
Dan. 3:30 Then the king promoted Shadrach, Meshach and Abednego in the province of Babylon. (NIV)

Promotion in the Kingdom of God is not achieved by a straight, smooth, predictable path; instead we have to follow a path that includes surprising twists and turns, with some unpredictable hardships and difficulties. Yet afterward, we can look back and appreciate that God was interested in far more than our promotional success. He was either seeking to develop our character or He wanted to use our testimony to impact a wider audience.

When the kingdom of Babylon was rapidly expanding, King Nebuchadnezzar needed to unify the empire and consolidate his rule. He erected a massive image to represent the greatness of his kingdom, and demanded that everyone in the kingdom bow down and worship the image at the sound of orchestrated music. The penalty for failing to comply with this ruling was that the guilty party would be cast in a burning fiery furnace. There were three Hebrew men, Shadrach, Meshach and Abednego, who were leaders in the kingdom, and they were accused of failing to bow and worship the image. The men were brought before the King who verified their refusal to bow. The King announced the penalty of death by the fiery furnace and stated that there was no god who could deliver them from the deadly punishment. In response, the men told Nebuchadnezzar that they were confident their God could deliver them, but even if He did not, they were determined not to serve his gods or bow to the image.

The King angrily instructed that the furnace be heated seven times hotter than normal, and the men be thrown in. The fire was so hot that the flames killed the servants who threw them in. But the Hebrew men were unharmed, and not even their hair was singed. More amazingly, the King observed the figure of another man in the fire with them, while they freely moved around in the fire that was powerless against them. When the King called the men out of the fire, he had a total reversal of his decree. He declared that the God of the Hebrew men was the only God to be worshipped because of His power to deliver His followers out of the fire. In addition, he promoted Shadrach, Meshach and Abednego to a higher office in Babylon.

Their path to promotion led through a defiant stand for God at the risk of their lives, facing the wrath of the King, and going into a fiery furnace so they could discover the presence of the Lord in the fire. Which of these stages would we seek to avoid? In seeking our self-preservation we would deprive God of the opportunity of turning around the mind of the King, and deprive ourselves of the promotion that comes through the fire. Let us follow our Lord even in the fires we have to face so He can be glorified through us.

Father, we don't want to avoid anything You have designed to improve our lives or provide a testimony to Your enemies. We pray for Your grace and strength, in Jesus' name.

March 3

MANNA SERIES: GREAT REVERSALS IN THE BIBLE
PURIM: THE MEMORIAL OF A GREAT REVERSAL

Reading Passage: Esth. 9:1-28

Main Text: Esth. 9:1 On the thirteenth day of the twelfth month, the month of Adar, the edict commanded by the king was to be carried out. On this day the enemies of the Jews had hoped to overpower them, but now the tables were turned and the Jews got the upper hand over those who hated them.

9:26 (Therefore these days were called Purim, from the word pur.) Because of everything written in this letter and because of what they had seen and what had happened to them, (NIV)

The Book of Esther is unique in that it is the only book in the Bible in which the name of God is not mentioned. The book records the origin of the Jewish Feast of Purim. This is the celebration of the time when the enemies of the Jews planned to destroy them, but the tables were turned and the Jews took revenge and destroyed their enemies. The word Purim came from the term "pur" which describes the lot that was cast to determine the date when the Jews should have been annihilated (3:7). But behind these chance-based decisions, we observe the hand of providence in bringing about a God-determined outcome.

Xerxes was the king of Persia, the ruling empire. He appeared to be a cavalier, impulsive ruler, who was easily manipulated by Haman, an egotistical, power-hungry deputy, who hated the Jews. Haman especially despised Mordecai, the Jew who once saved Xerxes from an assassination plot, because Mordecai failed to bow down to him. The unseen hand of God must have been behind the significant events in the intriguing story. King Xerxes, in a drunken state at one of his banquets, decided to dispose of Queen Vashti. Esther, an obscure Jewish beauty won the contest to replace Queen Vashti, and became the king's favorite wife. Esther was under the guardianship of her cousin Mordecai, but hid her Jewish ethnicity from those in the palace.

Haman was able to convince the king to annihilate all the Jews in the kingdom because of their laws which made them a distinct people. When Mordecai became aware of the proclamation against the Jews, he requested that Esther use her position in the palace to petition the king to halt this evil against her people. Haman planned the killing of the Jews and the confiscation of their wealth on the date determined by the pur.

By a sequence of events, which included the sleeplessness of the king so he could be reminded that Mordecai helped to save his life, Haman was instructed to arrange for the honoring of Mordecai. Eventually Haman was hanged on the gallows he built for hanging Mordecai. The king issued a contradicting edict that authorized the Jews to kill all their enemies and confiscate their goods. On the very day the Jews should have been killed, they were celebrating the death of their enemies.

Purim was established as a time to remember that regardless of what men may plan against His people, God is in control of the outcome. He is able to turn the tables so that the instruments for our destruction become the means for destroying our enemies. All God's people can celebrate that there are no chance events in our lives that God cannot use for our blessing and His glory. "The lot is cast into the lap, but its every decision is from the LORD" (Prov. 16:33 NIV)

Father, we are thankful that even when we do not recognize Your activity in our lives, You are still behind every event to ensure Your will is being accomplished for our benefit.

March 4

MANNA SERIES: GREAT REVERSALS IN THE BIBLE
GOLGOTHA, THE PLACE OF THE GREATEST REVERSAL

Reading Passage: John 12:20-32
Main Text: John 12:32 "But I, when I am lifted up from the earth, will draw all men to myself." (NIV)

The names Waterloo, Normandy, Dunkirk, Stalingrad, and Iwo Jima are immediately recognizable as places of significant battles. They tell a story, evoke memories, and stir emotions even without any personal experience of the wars. In these battles, numerous soldiers died for a cause, significant reversals occurred in the course of a war, formidable enemies were defeated, and the future of many people and nations was significantly altered. Although we hate the horrible human cost of wars, they are often necessary in order to defeat evil and ensure the progress of mankind.

However, the greatest battle since creation that had the most significant impact on humanity was fought at Golgotha, also known as Calvary. After the fall of the first man Adam, God devised a plan to defeat Satan. Throughout the Old Testament history, the main goal of Satan was to prevent the Son of God from coming to earth to execute the plan for his destruction. When Jesus came into the world, He knew His path was leading to the time and place of the great battle. Although there were many people or groups who were used by Satan to try to influence the build-up of the battle in his favor, Jesus remained in control of the war environment.

In John's gospel this control was illustrated by Jesus' reference to the 'time or hour.' For example, John 7:30 NIV states, "... at this they tried to seize him, but no one laid a hand on him, because his time had not yet come" (cf. 12:23, 12:27, 13:1, 17:1). The enemy could not attack Him before He determined the 'hour' of the battle. When He was ready, the powers of darkness were prepared to unleash the full impact of their demonic forces on Him, in collaboration with the Jewish and Roman authorities. When the soldiers came for Him in the garden of Gethsemane, He remarked, "Every day I was with you in the temple courts, and you did not lay a hand on me. But this is your hour—when darkness reigns" (Luke 22:53 NIV). In this battle Jesus was crucified on the cross at Golgotha, but this was His means of gaining the victory over the enemy.

Jesus recognized that His death, like that of a grain of wheat, would be the means of producing much fruit (12:24). What seemed to be the time of His humiliation, was in fact, His moment of glorification (12:27-28), so when He was lifted up by crucifixion on the cross, it was the time He began drawing all people to Himself (12:32). This amazing reversal in the battle, defeated Satan, and provided the opportunity for the release of his prisoners into the kingdom of the Son of God.

He died that we might be forgiven, He died to set us free. He is the mighty conqueror over death and the Devil, Hallelujah!

Lord, we glorify You for the plan of salvation, by which You suffered and died in our place in order to defeat our enemy and set us free. May we forever praise You for Your victory at Golgotha.

March 5

CAREER CHANGE FOR FULFILLMENT OF PURPOSE

Reading Passage: John 21:1-19
Main Text: John 21:3 "I'm going out to fish," Simon Peter told them, and they said, "We'll go with you." So they went out and got into the boat, but that night they caught nothing.
John 21:15 When they had finished eating, Jesus said to Simon Peter, "Simon son of John, do you truly love me more than these?" "Yes, Lord," he said, "you know that I love you." Jesus said, "Feed my lambs." (NIV)

It was interesting how quickly Randy answered my questions and smoothly redirected the conversation to promoting qualities of the car he was selling. I remarked, "You are such a gifted salesman. How did you choose this career?" After a brief pause he responded, "I did not choose a career in sales; the career chose me." I had to agree with Randy that some people seem so suited to a career, it is as if the career chose them. However, there are times when some significant intervention causes a career change that results in an individual discovering a new purpose that must be fulfilled.

Simon Peter was introduced in the Gospels as a fisherman. In common with many men in that area of Galilee, this was likely a career that was passed down to him and his brother Andrew from their father. He was successful at fishing and owned his own boat. However, one day Jesus went by the Sea of Galilee as Peter was casting his net, and commanded him, "Come follow me ....and I will make you fishers of men" (Matt. 4:18-19 NIV). Peter had a career change and reversed his course in life from pursuing fish to being a disciple reaching people.

Peter was disappointed as he observed his master being captured by the Jewish authorities, then subjected to humiliation and death by the

Roman soldiers. He eventually denied he even knew Jesus, whom he had followed for three years, and for whom he was very vocal in his love and devotion. Now that Jesus was planning to meet with him and the other disciples in Galilee after His resurrection, Peter perhaps had doubts whether he would be accepted because of his betrayal. He reverted to his old career in which he felt secure and said, "I am going fishing." Just as He did when He first called Peter, Jesus had to demonstrate that He was able to miraculously provide fish, even when the experienced fishermen were unsuccessful at the task (John 21:5-6, cf. Luke 5:1-11). He was challenging Peter to believe that there was no need to revert to the old career since He could meet those needs.

Meeting individually with Peter He asked, "Do you love me more than these? … then feed my lambs." Although Peter was naturally disposed to fishing, Jesus' call was to fulfill a higher purpose - from catching fish to feeding lambs. The change of roles was divinely ordained and nothing Peter pursued would be as fulfilling to him or glorifying to God.

Once you have heard the call of God, don't let disappointment with events or failure on the journey cause you to revert from the purpose God has for your life. He is able to supply what you were seeking in your "old career", and you will never be fulfilled outside of His purpose for your life.

Lord, we don't want our failures or our doubts to keep us from pursuing Your purpose for our lives. We want to be so motivated by love for You that we will be obedient to Your call.

March 6

MANNA SERIES: GREAT REVERSALS IN THE BIBLE
TODAY'S MANNA: THE TRANSFORMATION OF A ZEALOT

Reading Passage: Acts 26:1-20
Main Text: Acts 26:15-16 "Then I asked, 'Who are you, Lord?' 'I am Jesus, whom you are persecuting,' the Lord replied. 'Now get up and stand on your feet. I have appeared to you to appoint you as a servant and as a witness of what you have seen of me and what I will show you." (NIV)

In dealing with criminals, what society desires is more than merely having them arrested and incarcerated; they would like to see them transformed. When someone has been transformed, there is a total reversal in his or her conduct and behavior. What one previously believed was good is now accepted as bad, and what was considered bad is believed to be good.

Saul of Tarsus, later known as Paul the Apostle, described his transformation in his testimony to King Agrippa in Acts 26. He was educated in Judaism, and belonged to the strictest Jewish party, the Pharisees. He was so passionate about this religion that he strongly opposed anything concerning the name of Jesus of Nazareth. In his extreme zeal to destroy the followers of Jesus, he placed some of the saints in prison, persecuted many of them, and even voted for the execution of a number of them. It was while he was on a campaign to persecute the saints in Damascus that he had a personal encounter with Jesus. He was knocked off his horse by a bright light from heaven, then he heard Jesus speaking to him. This was an astonishing revelation, because he thought Jesus was dead, and His followers deceived for thinking otherwise.

The awareness that Jesus was indeed alive was transformative. Paul willingly accepted a new assignment to preach about the resurrection of Jesus so that the eyes of unbelievers might be opened and they might receive salvation. Paul had left Jerusalem, traveling to Damascus, as a persecutor of the followers of Jesus, but arrived there as a servant and a witness of the resurrected Jesus.

Not all transformations will be as sudden, dramatic or astonishing as Paul's. However, many times we meet people we think are too warped in their convictions, too militant in their opposition to Christ, or so indifferent to the gospel, that we conclude that it is nearly impossible for them to have a reversal in their mindset. Paul's story reminds us that nobody is too difficult for the Lord to transform. We have a duty to faithfully witness to the salvation of Jesus so the Spirit of God may marvelously transform errant lives.

Lord, we know that You are able to transform the lives of others as You did for Paul and for us. Help us never to doubt Your power for salvation, so we may witness even to people we consider "difficult," so that Your name may be glorified.

MANNA SERIES: PRINCIPLES FROM THE PARABLES
TODAY'S MANNA: IDENTIFYING WINNERS AND LOSERS

Reading Passage: Matt 13:10-17
Main Text: Matt. 13:12-13 Whoever has will be given more, and he will have an abundance. Whoever does not have, even what he has will be taken from him. This is why I speak to them in parables: Though seeing, they do not see; though hearing, they do not hear or understand. (NIV)

As several people stood around the gallery discussing their impressions of the paintings displayed by the famous artist, some comments were very critical of the collection. When someone asked the curator his opinion, he remarked that the comments were not a reflection of the art or the artist; rather they identified the level of discernment of the observer. This remark by the curator is similar to the reason Jesus gave for teaching in parables.

A parable is a method of teaching that uses known everyday illustrations to describe unknown or obscure principles. The result of teaching through parables is that those who are interested, even a simple uneducated person, may easily grasp the underlying lesson being taught. But those who are uninterested because of unbelief, even though highly educated, will be left unenlightened or further puzzled by the parable. It is interesting to note that Jesus began using the parabolic method of teaching only after he was accused by the Jewish religious leaders of performing miracles by demonic powers (Matt 12:24). This led to his rejection by many in the nation. Jesus decided to teach in such a manner that the hearers' response would identify who they were, whether a winner or loser. After hearing, winners gain more knowledge and enlightenment so they will have abundance. On the other hand, losers, after hearing, become more confused and the meaning becomes more obscured so they lose what little understanding they previously possessed.

In the same way that stepping on a scale reveals our weight category, our response to Jesus' words reveals to us God's view of our identity. Jesus told his disciples they were privileged to be included with those who know the secrets of the kingdom, but losers were excluded. Indeed, the words of Jesus will be the witness against us at the judgment. This challenges us to examine our attitude to the Word of God since our response identifies who we are.

Do we treat the Word of God as unimportant, irrelevant or ridiculous? Or do we have an appetite for the Word that drives us to explore its meaning and apply its truth? Our attitude will indicate whether we are winners or losers.

Lord, we know you speak to us through your Word, and because we want to be winners, we desire to hear and heed all that you say to us. Keep us from becoming negligent or indifferent to your Word.

March 8

MANNA SERIES: PRINCIPLES FROM THE PARABLES
THE WORD NOT ROOTED IN
THE HEART IS LOST

Reading Passage: Matt 13:3-9
Main Text: Matt. 13:4 As he was scattering the seed, some fell along the path, and the birds came and ate it up.
Matt. 13:19 When anyone hears the message about the kingdom and does not understand it, the evil one comes and snatches away what was sown in his heart. This is the seed sown along the path. (NIV)

Fay was sure she got a fantastic deal at the auction. With her knowledge of the antiques market she knew that the old chair she purchased only needed minor refurbishing to become something valuable. When she got home she left the chair by the side of the driveway intending to find a secure place for it. However, by the following day the chair was stolen. Someone else saw its potential and capitalized on the owner's carelessness. It is careless to leave valuables unsecured because of the possibility of theft.

We are just as careless in the way we treat the valuable Word of God. By making the effort to attend church or read the Bible or a devotional, we hear the Word. But often our attitude is to tick off the completion of another item on our duty list, before pursuing what we consider, more important or entertaining tasks. We spend no time to ensure we understand the Word we heard; no meditation to see how God wants us to apply that Word to our lives; and we don't make any attempt to practice what we heard in order that it will take root so we can obtain value from it. We carelessly leave the Word along the "path" unprotected – undigested and unapplied, as if it has little value, or think we will be able to recover it any time we wish.

The parable of the Sower informs us that we have an enemy who wants to deprive us of the value of the Word. When we take no steps to let it take root in our hearts, it will be "stolen" by the enemy. If, on the other hand, we let the Word take root, securing its value, it will begin to multiply and we will have the benefit of abundance of fruit in our lives. We will be winners.

Do we value the Word we hear so that we take the necessary steps to protect it from the enemy? Are we diligent to ensure we understand, apply and practice it?

Lord, we don't want to be careless hearers, depriving ourselves of the benefits You want us to get from the Word. Help us to appreciate that the Word is Your communication with us, which makes it the most valuable thing in the world.

March 9

MANNA SERIES: PRINCIPLES FROM THE PARABLES
SUPERFICIAL PROFESSION
WILL NOT SURVIVE

Reading Passage: Matt 13:3-9; 20-21
Main Text: Matt. 13:5 Some fell on rocky places, where it did not have much soil. It sprang up quickly, because the soil was shallow.
Matt. 13:21 But since he has no root, he lasts only a short time. When trouble or persecution comes because of the word, he quickly falls away. (NIV)

A beautiful grass cover on a field can give the false impression of fertile soil. But after a brief period of intense heat or severe drought the grass quickly withers and dies. The thin layer of soil masks the underlying rocky ground that prevents plants from developing healthy roots. For plants to survive adverse weather conditions and thrive to become productive, they require healthy roots that have been properly developed over time. Sometimes quick growth may indicate undeveloped roots.

In the parable of the Sower, Jesus first describes careless hearers of the Word who allow indifference to rob them of its value. He next describes the hearers whose lives are filled with beliefs and practices that are hostile to the Word; the rocky soil. This attitude is not immediately apparent because the Word is initially received with joy. They hear the Word and it causes excitement because it confirms their own perspective on life. These are the ones who are usually rejoicing in the songs and sermons about the love and blessings of God, and quickly quote scripture about their prosperity. They "spring up quickly" in the worship services making a big impression, but are usually missing from prayer meetings and Bible studies where the work of root development takes place.

Jesus explained that the Word would attract tribulation and persecution to our lives. Inner tribulation occurs when we find something in the Word offensive to our reasoning. Think of our reaction to passages such as: "If someone forces you to go one mile, go with him two miles." (Matt. 5:41 NIV); or "Do not be yoked together with unbelievers. For what do righteousness and wickedness have in common? Or what fellowship can light have with darkness?" (2Cor. 6:14 NIV). These passages might not cause us to jump and shout, but If we cannot overcome the resistance in our hearts we will never allow the Word to take root in us. For some, the Word will cause their families to forsake them or their social circle to reject them as being too simple minded by believing the Bible. It is our response to the inner challenges and outward persecutions that will reveal whether our hearts are rocky or receptive to the Word of God.

How is your heart responding to the Word?

Lord, we recognize that Your Word comes to test us to reveal the type of soil of our hearts. We want to allow the Word to develop roots in our heart so we will become productive. Help us to remove the rocks that are resistant to the Word, in Jesus' name.

MANNA SERIES: PRINCIPLES FROM THE PARABLES
THE SUBTLE SUFFOCATION OF THE WORD

Reading Passage: Matt 13:3-9; 22
Main Text: Matt. 13:22 The one who received the seed that fell among the thorns is the man who hears the word, but the worries of this life and the deceitfulness of wealth choke it, making it unfruitful. (NIV)

It is far easier to fight an enemy we have identified because he has declared war against us, has a reputation for destruction, and has disclosed his plan to destroy us. Our difficulty is with an enemy that appears harmless or even good and attractive, but is ultimately destructive. The effect of salt in our diet makes food very palatable; therefore we do not wage war against it. However, the uncontrolled use of this item can result in destructive health conditions. We have to be on guard against lethal enemies that are disguised.

The parable of the sower reveals our attitudes that are clearly opposed to the Word of God, such as careless indifference (the wayside), and rebellion (rocky ground). However, there are less obvious conditions we must guard against. We may consider it acceptable and responsible to be concerned about the affairs of life, but the desire to be in control of life's affairs can lead to worry, and this becomes destructive to the Word of God in our lives. It is normal and noble for someone to have ambition to achieve wealth for self and for family. Yet this ambition can quickly become an obsession, entrapping a person into constant thoughts of ways and means to gain wealth with no end to the pursuit, or sense of contentment. The desire for riches is a deceitful and deadly trap (1Tim. 6:9-10, 17).

Jesus compared this mental occupation with worry and wealth to thorns in the soil of our hearts. No one plants thorns; they grow naturally. But if they are not removed and the soil vigorously monitored to prevent their re-invasion, they will always grow faster than any plant that is sown. Thorns will overwhelm the good plants, eventually suffocating and killing them. When our minds are overburdened with worries over the affairs of life, or obsessed with gaining riches, the Word of God cannot thrive or even survive in that environment. We may spend time reading the Bible or listening to a sermon but the nourishment from the Word is soon overtaken by thoughts of worry and wealth. Whatever dominates our thoughts will determine our destiny.

Is the Word being suffocated in your life by an environment of worry or an obsessive desire for wealth?

Lord, it is frightening to realize how easily we become spiritually malnourished because we allow thorns to occupy our minds and choke the Word of God. Help us to fight against the subtle enemies that appear appealing but are lethal.

March 11

MANNA SERIES: PRINCIPLES FROM THE PARABLES
FOCUS ON SOIL PREPARATION

Reading Passage: Matt 13:3-9; 23
Main Text: Matt. 13:8 Still other seed fell on good soil, where it produced a crop—a hundred, sixty or thirty times what was sown.
Matt. 13:23 But the one who received the seed that fell on good soil is the man who hears the word and understands it. He produces a crop, yielding a hundred, sixty or thirty times what was sown. (NIV)

In the 1992 USA presidential election, the Clinton campaign team effectively used the slogan, "It's the economy, stupid." This meant that although the country had serious concerns about the war effort in Iraq, and a great diversity of opinion over social policies, there was nothing that could be compared to the public's concern over the economy. So that was the focus of the campaign.

Millions of dollars are spent in researching and improving the seed stock in agriculture, and there is great interest in the genetic modification of seeds to increase production and resist diseases. Yet all these efforts are futile if there is no good soil for planting. "It's the soil, stupid!" In this parable, known as "The Parable of the Sower", the focus is really on the soil. The seed and sower remained constant, but the soil was different in each phase of the parable. The soil represents our hearts, or our disposition to hearing the Word of God.

The seed is the constant, inerrant, powerful Word of God that is full of potential, is able to create new life, can transform human nature, and make even simple people, wise. Although we may quibble and complain about the sower because we have our preferences in presenters, the job of the sower is simply to scatter the seed. As a mere role player he cannot affect the seed. But we have control over that most significant area of crop production, which is the soil. Since some seed will fall on good soil we must ensure our hearts are prepared to be that good soil.

We prepare the soil of our hearts by ensuring we remove any attitudes that are in rebellion to God's Word (rocks), and we fight against tendencies to worry over the affairs of life or the desires for riches (thorns). But the most important step for preparing good soil is diligence in hearing the Word with open hearts. This involves investigating and meditating on the Word to ensure we understand what it is saying to us. We cannot apply what we don't understand, but once we put the Word in practice, God will make us fruitful.

When you are tempted to blame the society, family environment or church conditions for your spiritual barrenness, remember it is the soil preparation that determines fruitfulness.

Lord, although we desire to understand the Word so we may apply it, we frequently encounter passages that we find difficult. Help us not to give up in the struggle to understand, and may the Holy Spirit come to our aid so we don't miss anything you designed for our fruitfulness.

March 12

MANNA SERIES: PRINCIPLES FROM THE PARABLES
LIVING WITH WEEDS

Reading Passage: Matt 13:24-30, 37-43.
Main Text: Matt. 13:30 "Let both grow together until the harvest. At that time, I will tell the harvesters: First collect the weeds and tie them in bundles to be burned; then gather the wheat and bring it into my barn." (NIV)

No one cultivates weeds, yet no cultivated field is devoid of weeds. A farmer spends much effort and money trying to control weeds because of the adverse effect they can have on the growth of the cultivation.

In this parable Jesus made a surprising declaration regarding the weeds growing in the field. He stated, "Let both grow together until the harvest." He was alluding to a common reality of a Near Eastern wheat farm and comparing it to the kingdom of heaven, which comprises saved people (kingdom of God) and the unsaved. There is a type of weed, *zizanium*, which closely resembles wheat and usually appears in the wheat field. The weed causes a problem for the farmer in three areas: its introduction, its intertwining, and its identity, being indistinguishable from wheat.

After the farmer has removed weeds from his field, he knows the ground can easily be recontaminated in various unexpected ways. Similarly, unconverted, contaminated individuals can enter in among the believers while profiling as genuine believers. Jesus said the introduction of the weeds is the work of the enemy (13:25), who is seeking to undermine and frustrate what God is seeking to cultivate on the earth. He refers to the good seeds as the sons of the kingdom and the weeds as the sons of the evil one, the devil (13:38). In fact, the weeds are so intertwined with the root of the wheat that any attempt to extract the weeds may damage or extract the wheat prematurely. Furthermore, because weeds are so indistinguishable in appearance from wheat, the work of identifying them for extraction cannot be done by Jesus' earthly servants. He has reserved this work for angels at the end of the age (13:41).

We may be unable to prevent the devil from planting weeds in our communities, and our efforts to extract the weeds may damage the good grain. Therefore, we have to learn to live with weeds until the harvest at the end. Jesus did not try to prevent the planting of Judas or try to get rid of him. However, just as the farmer can identify the zizanium when it begins to produce by seeing its black grain, in contrast to the white grain of wheat, so we can identify the weeds among us by their fruit.

Let us concentrate on proving that we are good plants by our fruit, while leaving the sorting out of weeds to the Lord of the harvest.

Lord, save us from the futile effort of trying to do Your job of separating weeds from wheat, when we should be ensuring our fruit proves we are the sons of the kingdom. We desire your grace to do this, in Jesus' name.

March 13

MANNA SERIES: PRINCIPLES FROM THE PARABLES
SEED SIZE DOES NOT DETERMINE GROWTH POTENTIAL

Reading Passage: Matt 13:31-32

Main Text: Matt. 13:31-32 He told them another parable: "The kingdom of heaven is like a mustard seed, which a man took and planted in his field. Though it is the smallest of all your seeds, yet when it grows, it is the largest of garden plants and becomes a tree, so that the birds of the air come and perch in its branches." (NIV)

The amazing thing about a seed is that it is impossible to assess its potential from its appearance. God so designed life that all plant, animal and human life begin in the form of a seed. The seed contains all elements of the final product in miniature, but there is no indication of the final product, except by knowledge of the nature of the seed. An orange seed has no resemblance to an orange tree or an orange, nor does a fertilized human egg resemble a human being. The seed principle teaches us never to disregard small things; rather we should focus on their growth potential.

In the parable in our text, Jesus used the example of a mustard seed, which is so small it could be easily overlooked. Yet that small seed contains a mustard plant which grows into the largest of the garden plants. He knew his message regarding the kingdom of heaven was being heard by a skeptical audience that looked at the small loose band of disciples in the obscure villages around Galilee, with an unknown leader, and they were shaking their heads in disbelief. This so-called kingdom could not be compared with the massive kingdom of Rome or the ancient kingdom of Greece.

The parable was an encouragement to the disciples that they should not be concerned about the present small size of the kingdom, as they were just seeing a seed. But this seed being planted by Jesus has the nature of the heavenly product and its potential is unlimited. Eventually it will be so large that people of every type will seek refuge in it, like birds of the air finding refuge in the tree branches.

You may be investing in a small business, a small church or a small child.

Don't despise the smallness of what you are working with. Begin to regard it as seed and visualize the potential for growth. Don't be discouraged. All "big things" in life started as a seed but by diligent work they grew. The product depends not on the size, but on the nature of the seed.

Lord, it is so easy to become disillusioned when we don't see early results for our efforts. Help us to remember the parable of the mustard seed and keep the vision of the principle of the seed.

March 14

MANNA SERIES: PRINCIPLES FROM THE PARABLES
DON'T UNDERESTIMATE THE POWER OF YOUR SPIRITUAL INFLUENCE

Reading Passage: Matt 13:33
Main Text: Matt. 13:33 He told them still another parable: "The kingdom of heaven is like yeast that a woman took and mixed into a large amount of flour until it worked all through the dough." (NIV)

The task seems enormous and daunting. We have been mandated to be salt and light in our communities. But these communities appear very dark and tasteless as very few are interested in spiritual matters, and our message is rejected. We wonder if it makes any sense to try to make an impact and promote the kingdom of God. Perhaps it is easier to go with the flow and fit in with the prevailing culture.

What appears to be an almost impossible task to us in the 21st century was even more daunting to Jesus' disciples in the 1st century. Jesus gave them this parable of the yeast (leaven) to instruct them not to underestimate the power of their spiritual influence. The woman mixed a large amount of dough in order to make bread for over 100 people. To the large mixture she added a little yeast. Such a small amount of yeast appeared as if it would be overwhelmed by the large quantity of the dough. But after applying it, the yeast permeated all the dough causing it to rise. Jesus explained that his kingdom was like the yeast. Once it is introduced into the surrounding dark, tasteless community, a process of influence is initiated that cannot be stopped.

God knows that many people in our communities are suffering from the emptiness arising from the pursuit of materialism and worthless pleasures, or they are just driven to despair by the challenges of life. Or they encounter various crises in their health or family relations that drive them to seek help. At those times our spiritual light becomes a place of refuge for them. Although we are not responsible for their crises, we must be diligent to provide the spiritual influence that will point them to God who can enable them to rise out of their gloom and despair.

The principle of this parable is that we should not fear the challenge presented by the size of the task. We must keep shining and providing spiritual flavor, and leave the process of transforming those around us, to God. We will be surprised who will approach us asking for prayers. It just proves the influence is working.

Lord, You have called us and placed us in the communities You selected for our influence. Help us to fearlessly do our part and trust You to make an impact through us, for Jesus' sake.

March 15

MANNA SERIES: PRINCIPLES FROM THE PARABLES
HOW MUCH IS IT WORTH TO YOU?

Reading Passage: Matt 13:44-46
Main Text: Matt. 13:44-46 "The kingdom of heaven is like treasure hidden in a field. When a man found it, he hid it again, and then in his joy went and sold all he had and bought that field. "Again, the kingdom of heaven is like a merchant looking for fine pearls. When he found one of great value, he went away and sold everything he had and bought it." (NIV)

How much is it worth to me? This is a question we pose whenever we are deciding on a purchase. We buy, if the asking price for an item or service is equal to or less than its worth to us, if not we walk away. Worth is determined by the combination of the value of the product, and our need of it. A US$10 floating device may be worthless to us in our normal daily lives, but if we are overboard at sea about to drown we would be willing to give all our life's savings to purchase it. When we have a full stomach, we have no interest in a US$3 hamburger, but on the verge of starvation in a prison camp, we would sell our rights to an inheritance for a life-saving meal.

Jesus presented two examples of men who were willing to sacrifice everything to obtain the inheritance of the heavenly kingdom. It was worth that much to them because they realized how desperately their lives needed it. In the first example, the man discovered the treasure quite accidentally because it was hidden. He was like someone living in a spiritually dark culture where it is normal to think of death as a hopeless end, then he discovers there is a Savior who provides salvation from sin and death. Thinking this is too valuable a discovery to lose, he hides it until he can pay the price to fully enjoy it. The cost to him means sacrificing his culture and family relations.

In the second example, there was a religious seeker who tried various religions without satisfaction. One day he heard the gospel news that God was seeking him by sending Christ. This pearl was so valuable to him he was willing to sacrifice his merchant moneymaking career to possess and proclaim this heavenly inheritance.

These parables challenge us to consider how much the good news of salvation in Christ is worth to us. The fact common to both stories is that the treasure finder was willing to sacrifice everything to obtain it. Sometimes we find it difficult to sacrifice time, relationships or material things for the sake of Christ. But if we truly recognized our need as sinners, and appreciated Jesus' sacrifice to save us, and the blessing of a heavenly inheritance, we would be willing to sacrifice everything for this treasure.

Lord, without You my life would have no meaning and there would be no hope for the future. May my sacrifice for You demonstrate Your worth to me.

March 16

MANNA SERIES: PRINCIPLES FROM THE PARABLES
POLLUTION - ITS SYMPTOMS AND SOURCE

Reading Passage: Matt 15:1-20
Main Text: Matt. 15:10-11 Jesus called the crowd to him and said, "Listen and understand. What goes into a man's mouth does not make him

'unclean,' but what comes out of his mouth, that is what makes him 'unclean.'" (NIV)

How do we avoid becoming polluted in a world that is polluted? This question was a challenge to the religious people in Jesus' day, and is still the challenge for us today. The Pharisees, who were known as the Separated Ones, had many rules, and adopted behavior that would make them distinct from the non-religious crowd. They emphasized rules of the Sabbath, dietary laws and hygienic practices. They hoped by these practices to avoid the society's pollution, and highlight their righteousness.

Jesus explained that the intake of food is a poor confirmation of someone's state of pollution or purity. A proper functioning body is so structured to extract nutrients from food and eliminate what may be harmful. Therefore the pollution that Jesus referred to is not in the physical realm. By emphasizing the physical external, the Pharisees were overlooking a person's real source of pollution. The purity or pollution of people is determined by what they produce out of their hearts. Although we cannot see their hearts, we can see the symptoms, "for out of the heart come evil thoughts, murder, adultery, sexual immorality, theft, false testimony, slander" (15:19 NIV).

Like the Pharisees, we tend to judge purity by activities that simulate righteousness, such as church attendance or public prayers. While these practices are commendable and helpful, they can be done merely to conform to tradition or done with the wrong motive. Individuals can engage in appropriate religious activities while their hearts are polluted. As Jesus said of the Pharisees, they worshipped God with their lips but their hearts were far from Him (15:8). We condemn others because of their attire, their recreation or their associations that are not acceptable to us, even though these may not be explicitly contrary to the Word of God.

The parable on the source of pollution demands that we focus our attention on symptoms produced by the heart, many of which we try to disguise. In monitoring the 'health of our hearts,' we must be quick to condemn evil thoughts instead of entertaining them. We must avoid inappropriate sexual images that could corrupt our thoughts, and we should never seek to justify sinful activities.

Since the heart is the primary source of our purity or pollution, we must keep vigilant watch and guard our hearts (Prov. 4:23)

Lord, we desire to have pure hearts and not simulated behavior, so help us to diligently monitor our hearts, since it is the true source of our purity or pollution.

March 17

MANNA SERIES: PRINCIPLES FROM THE PARABLES
WHO'S WHO IN THE NET

Reading Passage: Matt 13:47-50
Main Text: Matt. 13:47-48 "Once again, the kingdom of heaven is like a net that was let down into the lake and caught all kinds of fish. When it was full, the fishermen pulled it up on the shore. Then they sat down and collected the good fish in baskets, but threw the bad away." (NIV)

Community organizations in some cities have developed directories to assist visitors or prospective business people in identifying key personalities of the city. Titled "Who's Who in the City" the directories provide a profile of these personalities and detail their achievements and significance to the city. Many people clamor to be included, but many are excluded because they are not regarded as significant.

In contrast, the kingdom of heaven invites all to come into its net. However, not all who are there are genuine in their faith. Indeed, there are many who make an outward profession without an inward conversion. In the parable of the net, Jesus referred to the usual practice of fishermen by the Sea of Galilee to illustrate the nature of the existing manifestation of the kingdom of heaven. The net is cast covering a wide expanse, and various fish without restriction enter it. When it is full the fisherman pulls the net to shore to sort out the fish.

We are currently living in the time when the net of the kingdom is still collecting fish, but it is not yet full. However, "at the end of the age" it will be gathered and the sorting will begin. Sorting means separation, and it is important to prevent evil people, "bad fish," from entering into the blessing of the righteous. Although we may find the idea of separation disturbing, the parable indicates that it is necessary so that punishment on evil may be accomplished. Those who reject salvation in Jesus face judgment of a fiery furnace (13:49-50).

We learn from the parable that our task at the present time is to keep inviting people into the net, and leave the sorting out of "who's who" to the angels at the end of the age. No one is considered too insignificant to God, once they put their trust in the Lord Jesus Christ. Let us not get distracted from our task in the kingdom.

Father, we are thankful that we don't have the task of sorting the good fish from the evil, so we can focus on ensuring our faith is firmly anchored in Jesus, and do our best to welcome others into the net.

March 18

MANNA SERIES: PRINCIPLES FROM THE PARABLES
WHY THE OLD WON'T MIX WITH THE NEW

Reading Passage: Luke 5:27-39
Main Text: Luke 5:36-37 He told them this parable: "No one tears a patch from a new garment and sews it on an old one. If he does, he will have torn the new garment, and the patch from the new will not match the old. And no one pours new wine into old wineskins. If he does, the new wine will burst the skins, the wine will run out and the wineskins will be ruined." (NIV)

Oil and water are both liquid but can never be mixed. Both are useful, but one is never the substitute for the other.

In the text, Jesus used a parable to describe items that should not be mixed since it would cause the destruction of one or both items. The attempt to patch an old garment with a piece of a new garment destroys both. Putting new wine into old wine skins will destroy the wine skins while wasting the new wine. In these illustrations Jesus was not stating that the old was better than the new, or vice versa. Rather he was emphasizing that the old and new were so incompatible that trying to combine them would render both useless.

The background to this parable was the attempts by the Pharisees to get Him to conform to their prescription for righteousness and salvation. The Pharisees believed that by doing, one became righteous. Righteousness was based on keeping the commandments, observing certain religious rituals such as fasting, praying and dietary practices, and avoiding the company of sinners. Jesus came preaching that no one was righteous, but that we are all sinners in need of salvation. By believing in Him and His salvation, individuals became righteous, and because they are righteous they will begin doing righteous deeds. There was such a marked difference between the Pharisees' and Jesus' path to salvation, it rendered them incompatible. To try to accommodate the Pharisees' works-based salvation with Jesus' faith-based salvation was as ridiculous as attempting to fast while attending a wedding feast. The old and new cannot be mixed.

Many professing Christians and churches are constantly trying to marry these incompatible prescriptions. They state that salvation is by grace through faith when we acknowledge we are sinners and trust Christ's sacrifice. But in addition they insist certain "works" are necessary for salvation, such as the sacraments or certain religious traditions.

Let us ensure that the only basis for our salvation is our trust in what Christ has done for us. This faith is expressed in the words of the hymn by Eliza Hewitt.

> *My faith has found a resting place, Not in device nor creed;*
> *I trust the Ever-living One, His wounds for me shall plead.*
> *I need no other argument; I need no other plea;*
> *It is enough that Jesus died, and that He died for me.*

March 19

MANNA SERIES: PRINCIPLES FROM THE PARABLES
WE CAN'T DEFY GRAVITY
WITHOUT ASSISTANCE

Reading Passage: Luke 14:7-11
Main Text: Luke 14:10 But when you are invited, take the lowest place, so that when your host comes, he will say to you, 'Friend, move up to a better place.' Then you will be honored in the presence of all your fellow guests. (NIV)

Gravity is the force exerted on any object that pulls it towards the earth. It causes any object that has weight to be kept earth bound. It is possible for objects to defy gravity when a counteracting force acts on the object. An airplane is able to get airborne when powered by an engine that creates a force greater than gravity. A balloon will remain airborne while it is filled with a gas lighter than air, thus defying gravity. There is no object of weight on earth that can defy gravity without assistance. This principle also applies in the realm of social relationships.

Jesus noticed how people had a tendency for self-promotion because of self-importance. For example, at a wedding feast they were seeking the most important seats, so they would possibly be noticed and acclaimed. Jesus remarked that this attitude carried the risk of public humiliation. If an individual in a prominent seat is moved to a lower one in order to be replaced by someone of greater honor, this could be very humiliating. He suggested we should always seek out the lowest seat for ourselves to avoid embarrassment, and to provide the opportunity for promotion at the discretion of the host. Our efforts for self-promotion will never defy gravity. Although we may be elevated for a while we will be brought down eventually in embarrassment. He said, "For everyone who exalts himself will be humbled, and he who humbles himself will be exalted" (Luke 14:11 NIV). The statement was absolute, "everyone ... will be," indicating there are no exceptions to the force of social gravity.

When we can humbly accept our own "earthiness" as not being better than others and not deserving of any privileges, we will be exalted. When someone else elevates us and we realize our dependency on this support, forces that defy the "pull of gravity" will support us. This is precisely what happens to us in salvation. We humbly acknowledge our sinfulness and unworthiness, and God elevates us in Christ to a heavenly position. Supported by his power, we are no longer subject to the gravity of sin. We must let the salvation principle of humility before exaltation govern every aspect of our social relationships. It will certainly save us from embarrassment.

Lord, we admit our struggle with pride that causes us to seek to exalt ourselves. Help us to remember that You oppose the proud but You give grace to the humble, and You have promised to exalt the humble. We need Your grace in Jesus' name.

March 20

MANNA SERIES: PRINCIPLES FROM THE PARABLES
ARE WE REALLY THIS VALUABLE TO GOD?

Reading Passage: Luke 15:1-32
Main Text: Luke 15:2-3 But the Pharisees and the teachers of the law muttered, "This man welcomes sinners and eats with them." Then Jesus told them this parable:
Luke 15:10 "In the same way, I tell you, there is rejoicing in the presence of the angels of God over one sinner who repents." (NIV)

We never usually appreciate the value of things or people until we lose them. Suddenly, we begin a frantic search for things we previously took for granted. We are willing to suspend our normal agenda, make great sacrifices, or offer valuable compensation to recover an estranged spouse, an art piece, or a pet. The cost and effort made for the recovery demonstrates the value of the lost item or person to us, and we want everyone to share our joy at the time of recovery.

Therefore, it is not surprising that Jesus used parables of lostness to illustrate the value God places on us. We are His by creation, but we became lost to Him when we decided to give our allegiance to the Devil. But He did not give up on us. The search began from the time He asked Adam, "Where are you?" and continued until He gave His only Son as a sacrifice to redeem us.

Jesus provided three parables to illustrate the search process and result. All three included something owned, which became lost, and resulted in a great celebration of the recovery. The big difference is the way by which each became lost. The sheep wandered astray, the coin was out of place, and the son rebelled and went missing. These describe the various states in which sinners find themselves. Some simply get lost by foolishly wandering after the wrong crowds; some find themselves out of place because of the country and culture in which they are socialized. Others have the proper knowledge and exposure, and simply rebel. God goes seeking after all types of sinners because we are all valuable to Him.

These parables were told in response to the observation by the scribes and Pharisees that Jesus was associating with sinners, by even eating with them. Jesus' parabolic response was that He valued sinners so much, He came from heaven to seek them. We learn from these parables that no condition of the sinner, no cause of their sinfulness, no accusation from religious observers should keep us from seeking to recover them for God.

Let us imitate our Lord and view people as being so valuable to God that we make every effort to reach them for Jesus?

Lord, may Your love for us motivate us to be willing to associate with all categories of sinners, whether atheists, Christ-haters, murderers, homosexuals, adulterers, or any other type, because we are all equally valuable to God. I am thankful that Jesus did not come to call the righteous, but sinners, which included me.

March 21

MANNA SERIES: PRINCIPLES FROM THE PARABLES
THE POWER OF FAITH IS IN ITS PERSEVERANCE

Reading Passage: Luke 18:1-8
Main Text: Luke 18:1 Then Jesus told his disciples a parable to show them that they should always pray and not give up. (NIV)

One of the primary factors in our relationship with God is faith. Heb. 11:6 NIV states, "And without faith it is impossible to please God, because anyone who comes to him must believe that he exists and that he rewards those who earnestly seek him." Our faith is in His existence and His response to us. We begin losing faith when we have doubts that He will respond, and consequently we stop seeking God. Perseverance demonstrates our faith, and the evidence of perseverance is endurance through delay and disappointment. The reason we endure is because of our confidence in the character of our God. He is faithful to His promises, and He is a God of love.

Jesus told a parable about an importunate widow to teach His disciples the importance of perseverance in prayer. The widow petitioned a corrupt city judge for legal protection. The judge ignored her pleas, perhaps hoping for a bribe. But the widow kept harassing him until he became tired of her constant pleas and honored her request. Jesus' point was that if the stubbornness of a corrupt judge could be broken down by the perseverance of the widow, consider how our loving Heavenly Father will quickly respond to the prayers of his children. Do we show sufficient perseverance in prayer to give evidence of faith? The question posed by Jesus (18:8) gives a picture of Jesus looking and listening, and seeing people give up praying for certain matters after a brief period.

One of the reasons we give up is because we stop believing Jesus is able or interested in answering our prayers. Such thoughts reveal our doubts regarding the existence or faithfulness of God. Are there unanswered items on our prayer list at the beginning of the year that we have stopped praying about? Unless we sense God has denied our requests, why have we given up? We may not understand why it seems our prayers are unanswered, but we must believe that He has a loving reason for the delay, including the development of our faith.

He is not corrupt and He loves his children, so keep on praying. Ask, and keep on asking; seek, and keep on seeking; knock, and keep on knocking, for the power of our faith is in its perseverance.

Father, help us to demonstrate our trust in You by our perseverance in prayer. We don't want You to be disappointed in us because we have given up our faith in you. We trust Your love and faithfulness, through Jesus Christ.

March 22

MANNA SERIES: PRINCIPLES FROM THE PARABLES
WHAT IS YOUR ATTITUDE IN PRAYER?

Reading Passage: Luke 18:9-14
Main Text: Luke 18:9 To some who were confident of their own righteousness and looked down on everybody else, Jesus told this parable. (NIV)

Prayer is basically our communication with God. And since the definition of the verb 'to pray' means making a request, our prayers usually consist of petitions. However, our attitude in prayer reveals our perception of God and of ourselves.

There are times our prayers are full of complaints because we see ourselves as the center of the universe, and we think that God is not doing a good job of responding to our needs. Because of certain incidents in our lives or in our world, we have doubts whether God really knows what He is doing. At such times our prayers become instructional sessions, directing and correcting God on what He ought to be doing. This attitude indicates we view God as being our servant, taking orders from us.

Jesus told a parable including the words used by two men in prayer, to illustrate how our prayers can disclose our wrong perceptions of God and ourselves. The Pharisee's words, boasting of his virtues and his superior spirituality, are typical of our prayers when we think too much ourselves. We use words and phrases that sound profound, that will make an impression on the audience. Perhaps we expect a heavenly applause at the end of the prayer, or we will settle for one from our earthly audience. The tax collector had no such pretensions. He knew the public already viewed him as a sinner, but more importantly he knew that before God he was just an undeserving petitioner. Rather than approaching God as if he was on equal spiritual terms, he bowed his head in humility to the One who knew his sins and failures, and he begged for mercy.

What attitude do you have in prayer? First, do we recognize that God is the only person we are addressing, whether we are praying in public or in private? Remember Jesus said, when we pray we should enter into a closet, a private place, and shut the door. Secondly, do we realize that the most important thing in prayer is not our desires or our needs, but that God's will might be done and His reputation glorified? Until our prayers reflect these priorities we will never be justified (right with God) in our prayers, regardless of how much we have impressed our audience or ourselves.

Our approach to God will determine His response to us.

Lord, help us to remember that the pattern of prayer You gave the disciples began with an attitude of a child to a father, and it gave priority to the honor of Your name: "Our Father in heaven, hallowed be Your name, may Your kingdom come and Your will be done." We pray in Jesus' name, Amen.

March 23

MANNA SERIES: MISSING PERSONS REGISTER
DEALING WITH ADAMIC 'LOSTNESS'

Reading Passage: Gen 3:1-19
Main Text: Gen. 3:9-10 But the LORD God called to the man, "Where are you?" He answered, "I heard you in the garden, and I was afraid because I was naked; so I hid." (NIV).

We frequently observe news reports on missing persons, especially children. When a person is missing, a void is created, an expectation is not met, and there will always be the feeling of incompleteness. Like a jigsaw puzzle with one missing piece or a mouth with a missing tooth, there is no feeling of wholeness, no shalom.

The first Biblical account of a missing person was in the case of Adam in Gen 3. God came down to have daily fellowship with the man He created in His image for the purpose of relationship. When Adam disobeyed God by yielding to the temptation from Satan, he broke fellowship with God and went missing. God went searching for him and asked the first question recorded in scripture, "Where are you?" This question was not asked to provide information to an All-Knowing God, but to reveal to man his state of 'lostness'.

In this state of 'lostness', Adam became aware of his nakedness, as if his inner inadequacies and fears were exposed to all. To compensate, he made fig leaves to cover himself. When we are in a state of 'lostness', we wonder what others think about us, whether we measure up to people's expectations, whether we are truly loved, whether our lives will be significant at the end, or whether God will accept us as we are. Very often we use the fig leaves of material possessions, over-indulgence in pleasure, or a passion for power, to cover our inadequacies. We also use the fig leaves of aggressiveness in relationships, dependency on narcotics and misuse of other toxic substances, to cover our inner fears.

What then is the solution to this state of Adamic 'lostness'? Return home to our creator God who is searching for us. He will forgive us of our rebellion and provide us with the proper covering for our sin. Jesus died to provide this covering through His blood shed for us. We then can experience a relationship with God, and enjoy the sense of wholeness with Him.

Have you responded to the seeking God by coming home to Him in repentance? Are you ready to give up the fig leaves and accept the covering provided by Jesus Christ? Will you accept His covering for inner inadequacies and fears? Take steps to get off the missing persons register and find inner peace.

Father, I truly appreciate the fact that You not only revealed the cause of my inner restlessness but provided the means of my restoration in Jesus Christ. I now can sing "Amazing grace! How sweet the sound that saved a wretch like me, I once was lost, but now am found, was blind but now I see."

March 24

MANNA SERIES: MISSING PERSONS REGISTER
MY BROTHER, MY RESPONSIBILITY

Reading Passage: Gen 4:1-13
Main Text: Gen. 4:8-9 Now Cain said to his brother Abel, "Let's go out to the field." And while they were in the field, Cain attacked his brother Abel and killed him. Then the LORD said to Cain, "Where is your brother Abel?" "I don't know," he replied. "Am I my brother's keeper?" (NIV).

Recently a local newspaper reported the discovery of the body of a pregnant fourteen-year-old girl in the river of a rural community. Police investigation revealed that her killer was a prominent businessman who was married with a family, and well respected in the community. He was known to be providing financial assistance to the girl and her poor family headed by a single mother. The man who was expected to be her protector became her assailant. When we fail to recognize our responsibilities to our brothers and sisters, we may contribute to their disappearance from our lives.

The text tells the story of Cain and Abel, offspring of the first couple on earth. As brothers, it was expected they would provide the pattern of mankind living in brotherly love. Because of the sin of the first man,

Adam, in Gen 3, all mankind is now born with a sinful nature. The sinful nature is the cause of all the attitudes and behavior that make it difficult for humanity to live in unity. When each brother, in obedience to God, offered a sacrifice, God accepted Abel's sacrifice but not Cain's. Cain was offended and became jealous of his brother. He no longer viewed his brother as his responsibility to protect and cherish because his ego and self-esteem were more important to him. His brother was now a threat to the priority of his self-hood, so brotherhood had to be sacrificed.

In most broken relationships there is a common thread. Someone is getting more attention, more wealth, a better position, or greater favor, than I am. Therefore to boost my ego and self-esteem, or to fulfill my selfish desires, I change from being the protector of my brother or sister to being an assailant. Jesus said whoever is angry with his brother is guilty before the court, like a murderer (Matt 5:21-22). When our brother or sister goes missing from our lives because of actions and/or attitudes intended to promote ourselves, we suffer loss of completeness, but more significantly God holds us responsible. He is asking, "Where is your brother or sister?"

Who is missing from our lives today because we have failed to be their "keeper?" What can we do to reconcile with our missing brother or sister? Are we pretending to be concerned when we are, in reality, the unsuspected murderers? The song written by Bobby Scot and Bob Russell describes our responsibility.

> The road is long, with many a winding turn
> That leads us to who knows where
> But I'm strong, Strong enough to carry him
> He ain't heavy, he's my brother.

March 25

MANNA SERIES: MISSING PERSONS REGISTER
MISSING TO FORGE A NEW FUTURE

Reading Passage: Gen 31:17-55
Main Text: Gen. 31:48-49 Laban said, "This heap is a witness between you and me today." That is why it was called Galeed. It was also called

Mizpah, because he said, "May the LORD keep watch between you and me when we are away from each other." (NIV).

There are times when the separation created by a missing person is necessary and beneficial in order to facilitate a new future based on new relationships. When a human limb is injured and becomes infected there is the risk that the infection in that part of the body could spread and infect the whole body risking the life of the person. The solution is to surgically remove the infected limb so that the whole body may benefit. Similarly, when our past associations become toxic, or perhaps the season for them is over, we need to be willing to cut them loose so they will not be a hindrance to a better future.

In the story of the text, Jacob became a missing person after spending 20 years working for his uncle Laban. During that time, he married Laban's two daughters and built a family. Laban made every effort to keep Jacob in poverty so he would continue working for him, yet God miraculously provided for Jacob and made him prosperous. Finally, God instructed Jacob to leave his uncle's employment, taking his family and possessions, and to return to his own country where he could settle and build a new future. The separation was hard for Laban, but was necessary and beneficial to Jacob. More importantly, this was what the Lord had ordered for Jacob.

Are there situations in our lives requiring a separation, but we delay making the move because we are more concerned about the pain of separation than about God's plan for our future? Beware of sentimental attachment to our past relationships, past achievements, or past lifestyles. Holding on to the past when we should make a complete break can lead to a weakened and toxic life that has no benefit to ourselves or anyone around us. Make the decision for a clean break. This decision is even more important if the past associations are preventing us from developing our relationship with the Lord.

Lord, we recognize that Your call to us to make a clean break from our past is a call to a better future. We admit we are fearful to venture into the unknown and leave behind the known, the tried and the proven. Grant us the faith, the courage and the vision to make the move. Also assure us of Your accompanying presence as we forge a new future.

March 26

MANNA SERIES: MISSING PERSONS REGISTER
MISSING GOD WHILE MOURNING

Reading Passage: Gen 42:8-38
Main Text: Gen. 42:36 Their father Jacob said to them, "You have deprived me of my children. Joseph is no more and Simeon is no more, and now you want to take Benjamin. Everything is against me!" (NIV).

The story of Joseph is one of the most dramatic in the Bible. He was the favorite son of his father Jacob, and in addition, he kept telling his family his dreams, in which they bowed in submission to him. His brothers were jealous and sought to get rid of him. Eventually they sold him to passing merchants and lied to their father, explaining that a wild animal had killed their missing brother. Many years later, through a sequence of intriguing events, Joseph ended up in Egypt where he became the Prime Minister. At that time some of Joseph's brothers happened to appear before him hoping to purchase food, because Jacob and his family were suffering from the famine in Canaan. While Joseph recognized his brothers as they were bowing before him, they did not recognize him. He devised a plan to try to get them to reunite him with his favorite brother Benjamin, and eventually with his beloved father.

The brothers reported to Jacob that the Prime Minister of Egypt demanded they bring Benjamin to him before he would allow them to purchase any more food. On hearing this, Jacob was overwhelmed with sorrow. Thinking he would lose another son he cried, "Everything is against me." While he was mourning his life that seemed like 'everything' was against him, the events were actually developing in his favor. He was on the verge of being reunited with his missing son whom he considered dead. Instead of famine he was about to have available to him all the food reserves of Egypt. Instead of facing a sorrowful end to his life, he would be able to die in peace and honor. But the sorrow of his loss blinded him to the possibility that God could be working out these events for his good.

There are times in our lives when our mourning over what we think we have lost, keeps us from looking to God who is sovereign over our lives.

He knows all the events we encounter, and He knows the pain we endure because of losses. But He is the God who provides grace for every trial, and He is able to cause what the Devil intended for our harm to turn out for our good. Don't become so overwhelmed with your loss that you miss what God is doing. As the line from George Matteson's hymn states, His love enables us to, "...trace the rainbow through the rain, and feel the promise is not vain that morn shall tearless be."

Father, increase our faith so we may trust You when we are confronted with the pain of loss. May we never allow our sorrow at these times to prevent us from believing that You are good and You are able to work out all the circumstances of our lives for our good, for the glory of Christ.

March 27

MANNA SERIES: MISSING PERSONS REGISTER
MISSING BY CHOICE

Reading Passage: Ex. 2:1-15
Main Text: Ex. 2:15 When Pharaoh heard of this, he tried to kill Moses, but Moses fled from Pharaoh and went to live in Midian, where he sat down by a well. (NIV).

What cause people to decide to go missing? There was the case of a woman in England whose husband left home one evening for the grocery store and she never saw him again for 10 years. The story behind his disappearance was that, on his way to the store, he met some of his old drinking buddies and went to the local bar. While there, he met a girl, struck up a relationship, accompanied her home and settled down with her for a new life. It is reasonable to assume his life at home was not attractive, making it easy for him to forsake the matrimonial home and pursue another woman without thinking of the hurt he would cause by suddenly going missing.

The story of Moses provides an example of someone choosing to abandon a privileged and comfortable home. Born as a Hebrew, he was adopted by Pharaoh's daughter and grew up as a part of the royal household. But when a dispute between an Egyptian and a Hebrew slave led him to the awareness of his identity as a Hebrew, and resulted in his killing the Egyptian, he knew he would never be comfortable again in the palace. He chose to abandon the grand lifestyle of an Egyptian prince and accept his real identity as a slave, even though it meant suffering hardship as a fugitive. This is a choice based on identity. The Bible states concerning Moses,

> By faith Moses, when he had grown up, refused to be known as the son of Pharaoh's daughter. He chose to be mistreated along with the people of God rather than to enjoy the pleasures of sin for a short time. He regarded disgrace for the sake of Christ as of greater value than the treasures of Egypt, because he was looking ahead to his reward, Heb. 11:24-26 NIV.

Living as Christians in a world hostile to Christianity, we are constantly faced with the same choice of identity faced by Moses. Do we belong to the worldly kingdom or the heavenly kingdom? The worldly kingdom promises us a life of enjoyable, sinful pleasures and acceptance by the majority, whereas the heavenly kingdom promises a life of ridicule, rejection, and sometimes mistreatment. Our choice will be based on our real identity - Are we children of this world or born-again children of God? Once we make the choice to be identified with the children of God, we will be missing from many of the activities, social settings, and crowds in this world. We will be missing by choice because we consider life with the people of God of eternal worth, compared with the temporal worth of life with the people of this world.

Lord, we recognize the difficulty of living with values that are different from the majority, and which cause us to appear strange. Help us to be secure in the choice of our heavenly identity and to keep our eyes on our future reward, for Christ's sake.

March 28

MANNA SERIES: MISSING PERSONS REGISTER
GOD IS NEVER MISSING

Reading Passage: Ex. 32:1-10
Main Text: Ex. 24:18 Then Moses entered the cloud as he went on up the mountain. And he stayed on the mountain forty days and forty nights.
Ex. 32:1 When the people saw that Moses was so long in coming down from the mountain, they gathered around Aaron and said, "Come, make us gods who will go before us. As for this fellow Moses who brought us up out of Egypt, we don't know what has happened to him." (NIV).

Moses was missing and the people were perplexed. He was the one who spoke to them on behalf of God while they were slaves in Egypt. He led them to the Red Sea, then he stretched his rod over the waters and a path through the waters was created. He led them to the foot of Mount Horeb and caused them to hear the voice of God. But now he had been missing for 40 days after he told them he was going to get instructions from God in the mountain. The Israelites were filled with uncertainty as to who would lead them, so they asked Aaron to make them gods to lead them. Moses so fully represented God to them that when Moses was missing they thought God was also missing. Because these people had grown up in an Egyptian culture where God was always represented by some image, they had difficulty following a god without seeing a physical representation.

We sometimes experience a predicament similar to that of the Israelites. We express our belief in God, but we yearn for physical manifestations of God that conform to our imagination. For some, this manifestation may be a godly parent, a pastor, the physical structure of the church, or the sacraments such as the communion cup and bread. What happens when these manifestations are missing? Do we feel as if God is missing from our lives? We need to develop a concept of God, and a relationship with Him that requires no tangible manifestations.

Whether or not He shows up in circumstances, provides any special sensation, or gives any confirmation, we must still have a conviction that God is with us. He never goes missing. "And without faith it is impossible to please God, because anyone who comes to him must believe that he exists and that he rewards those who earnestly seek him." Heb. 11:6 NIV. The lesson from this event in the history of Israel is that when people think that God is missing from their lives, they are likely to seek substitutes for Him. This might explain why some people need some spiritual charm, or crystals, and some become dependent on horoscopes, or fortunetellers. Even Christians sometimes become dependent on spiritual experiences or special messengers of God. Remember He rewards those who diligently seek Him, not in conjunction with other media or representations.

Father, how easily our souls become corrupted by false concepts of You, and become dependent on idols which are false representations of You. May our hearts rest in the knowledge that You are never missing, and You will never leave nor forsake us. We will only seek You. You only will be our desire and our fulfillment.

March 29

MANNA SERIES: MISSING PERSONS REGISTER
GODLY MAN GONE MISSING

Reading Passage: Gen. 5:18-24
Main Text: Gen. 5:23-24 Altogether, Enoch lived 365 years. Enoch walked with God; then he was no more, because God took him away. (NIV)

The creation account in Genesis stated God made man a living being by breathing His breath or spirit into him. Therefore mankind was created with an eternal nature that was dependent on its connection with God. After sin caused the Fall, this connection was severed. Mankind, facing inevitable death, still has a yearning for eternity, seeking every way to avoid death.

What is the answer to the desire for eternity in the human heart? The Bible provides an early example of the solution to this problem in the life of Enoch. For seven generations from the time of Adam, all people died even after living for a very long time. Then along came Enoch who lived and never died; he just went missing. He was living at a time of great evil, among many ungodly men (Jude 14-16), but Enoch denounced these men and lived in constant fellowship with God. "He walked with God and God took him." Enoch had a lifestyle of faith, living to please someone who is unseen. He was always conscious of God's presence, talking with Him and believing that God would enable him to overcome death (Heb. 11:5). The fact that Enoch could live in this way, before God was manifested in human form in the person of Jesus, showed the magnitude of his faith. When he disappeared, he left a testimony, even to the rebellious crowd, that his life pleased God.

The path to eternal life is much easier for us than it was for Enoch. Jesus came to show us that even though we may not avoid death, we can overcome death by believing in Him (John 3:16). Faith in Jesus is demonstrated by a lifestyle of constant fellowship with God, seeking to please Him, and having a testimony to that fact. This is similar to the lifestyle of Enoch. Jesus declared that when we believe in Him we are born again, and a new eternal life begins in us. This new life initiated by the Holy Spirit, is created for fellowship with God, and cannot die. Though the old nature (the flesh) still exists and is destined for death, the godly man has an eternal nature also. When the new nature is dominating, the godly man will be missing from the ungodly crowds because of his fellowship with God.

Do you live with a fear of death? Have you accepted God's solution to the problem of death by trusting Jesus as your Savior, and gaining eternal life? Have you made the new nature your dominant life? When this happens, we, like Enoch, will live in fellowship with God, seek to please God, and provide a testimony of Christ to this world.

Thank You, Father, that You provided a solution to the destiny of death caused by our sinful nature. Thank You for Jesus and the opportunity for a new birth. Help us, as we seek to make the new life dominant, and maintain constant fellowship with You.

March 30

MANNA SERIES: MISSING PERSONS REGISTER
MISSING DUE TO INFERIORITY COMPLEX

Reading Passage: 1Sam. 10:1-8, 17-24.
Main Text: 1Sam. 10:21-23 Then he brought forward the tribe of Benjamin, clan by clan, and Matri's clan was chosen. Finally, Saul son of

Kish was chosen. But when they looked for him, he was not to be found. So they inquired further of the LORD, "Has the man come here yet?" And the LORD said, "Yes, he has hidden himself among the baggage." They ran and brought him out, and as he stood among the people he was a head taller than any of the others. (NIV)

There are few factors that have a greater influence on our success or failure in any venture than our self-perception. Low self-esteem results in a lack of confidence in approaching a task, and as Marcus Garvey said, "If you have no confidence in self, you are twice defeated in the race of life." Frequently a leader lacking self-confidence, either over-compensates by acting with aggression and arrogance or becomes a people pleaser.

Saul, the first king of Israel, provides an illustration of a person with an inferiority complex. The prophet Samuel wanted to anoint Saul publicly as king, after privately informing him that he was God's choice. But Saul went missing by hiding himself among the baggage. What made Saul want to hide when all the people were waiting on him, and when he had such an impressive stature (he stood tall, head and shoulders above all others (v. 23)? The answer is found in Samuel's statement after God terminated Saul's kingship. Samuel said, "Although you were once small in your own eyes, did you not become the head of the tribes of Israel? The LORD anointed you king over Israel," (1Sam. 15:17 NIV). Saul's low self-esteem caused him to go missing when he was called to present himself for leadership.

Saul's limitations did not prevent God from appointing him king. Neither should our limitations keep us from confidently tackling any task. Instead this should force us to humbly seek to access a source of strength outside of ourselves. The example of this is David, the anti-hero to Saul, who constantly stated that his strength came from his dependence on the Lord. He affirmed that "the Lord is the strength of my life" (Ps. 27:1 NKJV). Reliance on the Lord makes Him the source of our strength and the basis of our confidence. With this reliance, our limitations will not result in low self-esteem. We don't have to suffer from an inferiority complex and go missing when duty calls, or the need arises.

Are you facing a situation where people are calling for you to lead? Are you aware of a need for someone to fill a leadership role, but think your inadequacies make you unqualified? Don't go missing. Put your confidence in God and trust Him to help you to respond for his glory.

Father, like the Psalmist we declare that our help comes from the Lord who makes heaven and earth, and in You we place our trust. With Your help we make ourselves available for all situations, and all opportunities that You place before us, for Christ's sake.

March 31

MANNA SERIES: MISSING PERSONS REGISTER
WHEN GOD USED A MISSING MAN

Reading Passage: 1Sam. 13:16-14:23
Main Text: 1Sam. 14:17 Then Saul said to the men who were with him, "Muster the forces and see who has left us." When they did, it was Jonathan and his armor-bearer who were not there. (NIV)

There are times in our lives when circumstances become so bleak and hopeless that we feel the need of a respite to think clearly or gain a different perspective. It may be the dark cloud of acute illness, family crisis, financial disaster, or a toxic relationship. When we take ourselves away from the immediate surroundings, mentally or physically, the intention may not be to go missing, but to seek the strength to face the situation with confidence. Sometimes these periods of absence are just what we need for our faith in God to be renewed, and to understand our role in one of His miracles.

There was a time when King Saul and the armies of Israel faced a crisis in their battle against the Philistines. The Philistines came to the area close to the camp of Israel with a very large army including 30,000 chariots and 6,000 horsemen. Israel had only 600 men. At that time the only weapons like a sword or spear, available in Israel belonged to Saul and his son Jonathan. If they needed any other metal weapons they would have to obtain them in the land of the Philistines. Furthermore, most of the fighting men of Israel were so terrified that those who had not deserted the army were hiding in caves.

It was at that bleak time when all odds were stacked against them, Jonathan decided to take his armor bearer and secretly leave the camp, not as a deserter but to see whether God would perform a miracle for Israel. Perhaps he thought he needed a break from the stifling atmosphere of fear and doubt so he could breathe the fresh air of faith in the miracle-working God of Israel. The Lord did not require conventional means like a large army or the weapons of war to gain victory for His people. God responded by allowing Jonathan and his assistant to begin a slaughter of the Philistines that led to the enemies killing each other. The scene ended with the large Philistine army fleeing, and the revived and surprised Israel army giving chase.

Do you feel under siege by your circumstances because it appears all odds are stacked against you? Perhaps this is a time to take a break from the naysayers, negative talkers, and doubters around. It may just be the time when God wants to perform a miracle in your circumstances that will amaze both you and those around. You will have no doubt that God has used you to create new opportunities for everyone.

Lord, I am so glad I know your track record of miracles in my past experience, and in the record of scripture. I will not let circumstances overwhelm me so I get lost in despair. Rather I will take the time out to focus on You and Your will for me. I am willing to be used by You for a miracle, for Christ's glory.

April 1

MANNA SERIES: MISSING PERSONS REGISTER
THE MESSAGE OF AN EMPTY SEAT

Reading Passage: 1Sam. 20:1-42
Main Text: 1Sam. 20:17-18 And Jonathan had David reaffirm his oath out of love for him, because he loved him as he loved himself. Then Jonathan said to David: "Tomorrow is the New Moon festival. You will be missed, because your seat will be empty." (NIV)

An essential aspect of being a Christian is the recognition that we have been made a part of a community of believers. We are saved individually to be a part of the Church. The Church is expressed both as the spiritual universal group of all believers, and the local assembly of believers. Paul portrayed the relationship between believers as being joined together in a body, similar to the connection between the various parts of the human body (1Cor. 12:12-27). Therefore, consider what it means to the body of a local church when one member is missing for a while for whatever reason?

An incident in the story of King Saul and David provides a vivid illustration of such a scene. David had become an adopted member of Saul's household; he had already been privately informed that he would be replacing Saul as king. Saul sensing God's favor on David was suspicious of him, so he planned to kill him. To add to the intrigue, Saul's son Jonathan, who was the natural heir to the throne, loved David "as he loved himself" and vowed to protect him.

David usually joined Saul's household at the table for all the major feasts. But after Saul made several public attempts on his life, David was worried about sitting at the table at an upcoming New Moon feast. So he planned to be absent. He asked Jonathan to cover for him and to report on Saul's reaction to his absence. Jonathan replied, "You will be missed because your seat will be empty."

When there is a bond of love, an empty chair will sometimes convey the message that something is not quite right. We can't be comfortable or complacent when one member of our group is missing. For the loving local Church, it means we must make every effort to seek out the missing person, meet the needs of that person, provide healing and reconciliation where necessary, so the empty chair will be filled. We should never be comfortable or complacent until this is done because the Church exists for the purpose of serving, developing and caring for its members, regardless of their status in society. Each member should know that his or her absence creates a void that affects the whole body. In a world suffering from lack of community and care of people, and a world filled with lonely people, Jesus desires that his Church represent the ideal human community.

Have we made ourselves a part of a local Church so we can play our part in serving and caring for our fellow believers? If your seat has been empty, remember the whole body is affected by your absence.

Lord, forgive us for our selfish tendency to take actions to please ourselves without considering how our behavior affects Your Church. We don't want to grieve Your heart and send the wrong message by our empty seats.

April 2

MANNA SERIES: MISSING PERSONS REGISTER
MISSING FROM THE BATTLE LEADS TO SIN

Reading Passage: 2Sam. 11:1-18
Main Text: 2Sam. 11:1 In the spring, at the time when kings go off to war, David sent Joab out with the king's men and the whole Israelite army. They destroyed the Ammonites and besieged Rabbah. But David remained in Jerusalem. (NIV)

War has been described as a most cruel, devastating and excruciating human experience by several renowned and celebrated army generals. Most people would agree that every effort should be made to avoid war. But there is also a danger if we are disengaged from war when we should be fighting. Our enemies will not cease their attacks because of our complacency.

Israel was at war against the Ammonites. Usually the king leads the armies into the battle, but on this occasion David instructed General Joab to lead the army while he stayed at home. No reason was given for David's decision. Was he weary after many years of fighting? Or perhaps he thought this was such an easy battle, he could spare himself the effort. Whatever the reason, it resulted in a disastrous turning point for the Davidic reign. While relaxing at home, he happened to walk on the balcony of his house and saw a woman having a bath next-door 'al fresco'. The sight of the woman captivated him and this led to his committing adultery with Bathsheba, Uriah's wife. He avoided the battle with the army, but lost the war against his lustful nature. Missing, when he should be fighting resulted in his being unprepared for another type of attack.

This is the great danger of complacency. When we have times of peace in our circumstances, when things are going well in our relationships, there are no problems with our finances, and we are in good health, it is easy to feel little need for divine help. Therefore we don't spend much time in prayer, and meditation on scripture seems redundant. Yet it is at these times we may be most vulnerable to a stealth attack by the Devil that could devastate our lives. At such times of calm in our lives, we should be busy equipping ourselves defensively, and praying about our weaknesses and sinful tendencies. We can therefore understand Jesus' frequent warnings to his disciples to be alert because we don't know the time of attack by our enemy, or the time of accounting by our Lord.

We keep alert for battle by our preparation in prayer, Luke 21:36. Eph. 6:18. Col. 4:6. Never be missing in the battle of prayer where we wage war against the Devil on our knees, or else he will trap us when we least expect him.

Father, we know how difficult it is to pray when we are not aware of any problems in our lives or expected threats. Help us to avoid the trap of complacency, falling asleep like Peter (Matt. 26:40) when we should be alert and praying in preparation for the unseen trial ahead of us.

April 3

MANNA SERIES: MISSING PERSONS REGISTER
WHEN THE DISCIPLES ARE MISSING

Reading Passage: Matt. 26:31-56
Main Text: Matt. 26:56 ...Then all the disciples deserted him and fled. (NIV)

It is a tragedy to live without a friend. As Helen Keller said, "I would rather walk with a friend in the dark than alone in the light." But a greater tragedy is to be in trouble and find that all our trusted friends are missing, having deserted us. This was the experience of Jesus in His agony when facing the trials leading to His crucifixion.

In Matthew's account of the last night before His crucifixion, we observe that Jesus warned the disciples that one of them would betray Him (v. 21). This prediction was later fulfilled when Judas kissed Him in order to hand Him over to the chief priests and elders. Jesus also predicted that all the disciples would forsake Him when He said to them, "You will all fall away because of Me this night, for it is written, 'I will strike the shepherd, and the sheep of the flock will be scattered' " (v. 31 NIV).

When Peter stated in protest that Jesus could count on Him, Jesus predicted Peter would deny Him three times before the rooster crowed that night. Later, Jesus asked His three closest disciples to keep awake and support Him while He agonized in prayer in preparation for bearing the sin of the world. But each time He checked, the disciples were sleeping, so He was alone. When the soldiers came with weapons to arrest Him, instead of defending or standing with Him, all the disciples deserted Him and fled (26:56). The assignment of being the sin offering for the world was very burdensome, but Jesus must have been heartbroken over the fact that the disciples whom He chose, who lived and learned from Him for three years, and who promised to be loyal to Him, all deserted Him in His moment of crisis.

The words of Martin Luther King are relevant: "In the end we will remember not the words of our enemies but the silence of our friends." Psalm 88 records the suffering of someone facing affliction and death, and in a scenario similar to the disciples' desertion of Jesus, he stated, "You have taken my companions and loved ones from me; the darkness is my closest friend" (88:18 NIV). Jesus suffered great emotional pain on our behalf.

Are we faithful when our Lord is depending on us to take a stand for Him against those who oppose and ridicule Him in our world? Does He still find us missing when we should be supporting? Are we deserting when we should be defending? Are we betraying when we should be loving Him? When Jesus was brought for trial before the tribunal of the high priest, scribes and elders, Matthew reported that Peter followed at a distance, and then sat with the accusing crowd (26:58). How we follow the Lord will influence how we respond with regard to Him in the time of crisis. Let us follow closely.

Lord, our hearts have become sensitized to Your suffering caused by our sins and also by the desertion of Your friends. We know You are still being opposed, tried and condemned in our world. Help us to follow You so closely that we will suffer with You. You promised that if we suffer with You, we will reign with You.

April 4

MANNA SERIES: MISSING PERSONS REGISTER
AN EMPTY TOMB, THE MISSING OCCUPANT

Reading Passage: Luke 23:50-24:12
Main Text: Luke 24:2-3 They found the stone rolled away from the tomb, but when they entered, they did not find the body of the Lord Jesus. (NIV)

The women who visited the tomb on that Easter Sunday morning were disciples of Jesus having followed Him from Galilee. They saw the tomb where His body was placed after He was taken down from the cross (23:55). But they now found the stone rolled away from the entrance of the tomb and Jesus' body missing. Did someone steal His body? And why would anyone be interested in a dead body?

The two angelic beings that suddenly appeared to the women indicated that the tomb was the wrong place to be looking for Jesus. "Why are you seeking the living among the dead?" This must have been puzzling for the women. We naturally expect the living ultimately to end up dead, and the dead to remain dead. Jesus came to change the destiny of humanity and show us that death is no longer terminal. This is fantastic news, because after the first man Adam, all mankind lives under the fearful tyranny of death. Regardless of our success in life and the pleasure, power and prestige we achieve, it all ends in death. We are all victims of the tomb.

But there is One who has triumphed over the tomb. The apostle Paul commenting on this event stated that in Adam all died (all offspring of Adam), so also in Christ all shall be made alive (all offspring of Christ), (1Cor. 15:22). He referred to Jesus as the "last Adam" (1Cor. 15:45), the last of humanity for whom death is their destiny. What happened on that Easter Sunday morning made a cataclysmic shift in the destiny of humanity. When the women observed the stone rolled away from the tomb, little did they realize that this act signified that the enemy of mankind (death) had been conquered, the tomb lost its power over its occupants, and a new Order was established.

We have the option of becoming the offspring of Christ. We become His offspring by placing our faith in Him. The scripture states that this is accomplished when we make a verbal confession of our acceptance of

Jesus as our Savior, and believe in our hearts that God raised Him from the dead (Rom. 10:9-10).

Have you taken the steps to become the offspring of Christ and secure your victory over the tomb?

Lord, we thank You for entering our world for the purpose of ending the old Adamic Order of death and establishing a new Order of life after death. You have removed our fear of death and given us hope beyond the grave. May this truth revolutionize our lives as we live in appreciation of your resurrection power.

April 5

MANNA SERIES: MISSING PERSONS REGISTER
MISSING HIS SPECIAL APPEARANCE

Reading Passage: John 20:19-29
Main Text: John 20:24-25 But Thomas, one of the twelve, called Didymus, was not with them when Jesus came. So the other disciples were saying to him, "We have seen the Lord!" But he said to them, "Unless I see in His hands the imprint of the nails, and put my finger into the place of the nails, and put my hand into His side, I will not believe." (NIV)

What did I miss when I went missing? Sometimes when we ask this question we have an idea of what was to be expected at a performance or event while we were absent. Like a soldier on the battlefield during the birth of his child at home, or someone suddenly hospitalized at the time of his or her graduation ceremony. But there are times when our absence causes us to miss a special surprise and even deprives us of a blessing. The Gospel writers provide us with such an exciting account of Jesus' earthly ministry that it seems no one wanted to be missing from His presence.

But He died and was buried. The disciples were scattered, and there was no longer any sense of expectation for the presence of Jesus. Before He died He requested that the disciples meet Him in Galilee after His resurrection (Matt. 26:32). After His resurrection He told the women at the tomb to meet Him in Galilee (Matt. 28:10). Yet, when the disciples did gather in Galilee after the resurrection, one of them, Thomas was missing. There was no explicit explanation for the cause of his absence, but his subsequent statements implied that he did not believe Jesus was resurrected and would be present at the gathering. What did he miss at that Sunday meeting? He missed the joy and excitement of the disciples at this first general appearance of the resurrected Lord. He also missed the commissioning of the disciples, with the endowment of the Spirit and message of forgiveness of sins (20:21-23).

Unbelief kept Thomas from enjoying this experience for eight days, until Jesus graciously provided him with a repeat performance the following Sunday. By being absent from the gathering, Thomas not only missed the blessings of the first Sunday, he was deprived of the opportunity for the removal of doubts that clouded his heart. If we were sure Jesus would be appearing in the assembly of the believers, would we risk being absent and deprive ourselves of a blessing? HIs resurrection means that He is available to manifest His presence wherever and whenever the believers are assembled (Matt. 18:20). Whenever He is present we will have joy (Ps. 16:11), we will be commissioned for ministry, and we will be renewed in faith.

If we truly believe that our Lord is alive and desires to meet with us, let us take every opportunity to celebrate our resurrected Lord together and be blessed.

Our Resurrected Lord, we thank You for the community of believers where You choose to manifest Your presence in a unique way. Help us not to neglect gathering together, even when doubts enter our hearts. We know that You will appear to strengthen our faith and renew our hopes, in Jesus' name.

April 6

MANNA SERIES: MISSING PERSONS REGISTER
THE PAIN CAUSED BY A MISSING REBEL

Reading Passage: 2Sam. 13:20-39
Main Text: 2Sam. 13:38-39 After Absalom fled and went to Geshur, he stayed there three years. And the spirit of the king longed to go to Absalom, for he was consoled concerning Amnon's death. (NIV)

What a painful and conflicted position David was in! As a father he was missing his son Absalom, but as King he knew Absalom was a murderer and a fugitive who should be brought to justice. David's pain was made worse by the knowledge of his contribution to his son's rebellion. The Lord had told David that one of the punishments for his sin of adultery with Bathsheba and murder of her husband was that there would be disaster within his own family (2Sam 12:10-11).

Absalom was frustrated with his father's inaction regarding justice for the rape of his sister, so he decided to take matters in his own hands. He killed Amnon, his brother, who was the rapist, then he fled to Geshur. Because his sin and negligence contributed to Absalom's behavior, it was possible David saw Absalom's escape to Geshur as a relief, so he could avoid bringing Absalom to justice for murder. But after getting over the sorrow for the murder of his first born, David's heart was yearning for his missing son whom he loved.

This dramatic account reminds us of the challenges we sometimes face as parents. There are times when some of our children go missing, and we can justify not making any attempts to pursue them because they are in rebellion against us. Perhaps they rejected our religious, moral or lifestyle standards, or they may have disregarded and broken the rules of the home. Our feeling is that they should remain missing until they apologize and seek reconciliation with us. However, our hearts can become conflicted with our heads because of our love for the missing children. We hope they will pay a price for their rebellion, but we realize that as parents we are paying a greater price by their absence.

Furthermore, we recognize, with shame, where our own behavior contributed to their rebellion. We were not sufficiently patient, we were too demanding, we missed many occasions to affirm and encourage them, we failed to let them know how much we loved them, and because of pride we never apologized for our injustices against them. The only solution is we must be prepared to substitute our sense of justice with our desire to offer mercy, and pursue the return of the missing rebel. This was what David had to do.

Is our pride, or our sense of justice keeping us from pursuing someone who has been missing from our lives? It could be a child, a parent, a sibling, or an old friend. Let us have hearts of love that seek reconciliation and offer mercy and forgiveness. Blessed are the merciful for they shall obtain mercy.

Father, we are so thankful You do not hold our sins against us, but because of Your love You pursue us to bring us back home to Yourself. Help us to have a heart like Yours so we will always seek to be reconciled to others.

April 7

MANNA SERIES: MISSING PERSONS REGISTER
GOD'S RELENTLESS PURSUIT OF A MISSING PROPHET

Reading Passage: Jonah 1:1-3:3

Main Text: Jonah 1:1-3 The word of the LORD came to Jonah, son of Amittai: "Go to the great city of Nineveh and preach against it, because its wickedness has come up before me." But Jonah ran away from the LORD and headed for Tarshish. He went down to Joppa, where he found a ship bound for that port. After paying the fare, he went aboard and sailed for Tarshish to flee from the LORD. (NIV)

There are various opinions as to the main theme of the story of Jonah. Was it God's mercy to a non-Israelite, heathen nation? Or, was it the triumph of God's purpose in the life of Jonah? The Bible provides us with many examples of God calling prophets to the very difficult task of announcing His judgment against a country, for example, Elijah to King Ahab, or Jeremiah to the kingdom of Judah. The story of Jonah details the rebellion of the prophet who disagreed with his assignment. God sent him to Nineveh but he headed to Tarshish, which was in the exact opposite direction.

If the main theme of the story were God's mercy to the Ninevites, it would be easy for God to ignore His rebellious prophet and select another to accomplish the task. Instead the story provides an interesting and miraculous account of how God pursued His missing prophet until he delivered the message in Nineveh. God sent a storm against the boat taking Jonah to Tarshish away from Nineveh, and then He sent a large fish to swallow Jonah and deliver him to his assigned destination. While in the belly of the fish, Jonah became convinced he had no choice but to obey God.

Many of us can testify from personal experiences that God does not give up His call on our lives. He is patient and long-suffering but He does not relent in His pursuit to ensure we fulfill the purpose He has for us. He is never content to let us go missing in action. One author referred to God as "the hound of heaven." We may have sensed the call of God to serve in a certain capacity, to be committed to a ministry or to develop our talents for the purpose of meeting certain needs. Over the years we may have tried to ignore or suppress these promptings by God. We may even have tried to become fully occupied with other tasks so our lives would have no room for God's plans for us. But our voyage to 'Tarshish' is no obstacle to God; He is in control of all our life's circumstances.

God will have His way, and we will pay the price for our rebellion and the delay in responding to Him. Let us be wise and immediately answer the Lord when He calls.

Lord, I don't know why I tend to doubt Your plans for me and think they will cause me pain or unhappiness. I want to trust Your love so I will delight in Your will for my life. Help me to know that I will never be truly fulfilled until I accept Your purpose for me.

April 8

MANNA SERIES: MISSING PERSONS REGISTER
MISSING EVIDENCE DOES NOT REMOVE GUILT

Reading Passage: Gen. 38:1-30
Main Text: Gen. 38:22-23. So he went back to Judah and said, "I didn't find her, besides, the men who lived there said, 'There hasn't been any shrine prostitute here.'" Then Judah said, "Let her keep what she has, or we will become a laughingstock. After all, I did send her this young goat, but you didn't find her." (NIV)

Quite often our response to our sins and the resulting guilt is to seek to cover or deny them so that we maintain our good reputation. We are even more boldly hypocritical when we think there is no evidence to expose our sinful actions. But the lack of evidence can never vindicate us or assuage our guilty consciences.

The story of Judah in Genesis 38 provides a sordid and fascinating illustration. After the death of Judah's first son, he gave his widowed daughter-in-law, Tamar, to his son Onan so she could produce an heir. This was the custom of that culture. When Onan died without producing an offspring, Judah promised her his third and last son Shelah, in marriage. But he asked her to return to her father's home until Shelah was grown. Judah failed to keep the promise. Later, when Tamar learned that Judah would be on business to Timnah, she dressed up as a prostitute and deliberately went to the area to await him.

In the celebration and anonymity of the sheep-shearing activities, Judah engaged the services of a prostitute not knowing she was his very own daughter-in-law. He promised to send her a young goat as payment, but she demanded certain personal items including his seal, as collateral. Judah later sent his friend to find the prostitute to give her the young goat as payment and to recover his personal belongings. But the prostitute was now missing because Tamar had reverted to being a widow awaiting the fulfillment of the promise by her father-in-law. In the meantime, Judah accepted the loss of his valuables thinking there was no evidence of his indiscretions, so his reputation was intact.

When Judah eventually heard that Tamar was pregnant as a result of working as a prostitute, he was incensed and demanded that she appear before him to be killed. She showed up with his personal items and told him she was pregnant for their owner. Shocked, Judah had to acknowledge his sin and stated, "She is more righteous than I."

How hypocritically self-righteous Judah was when the evidence of his sin was missing? How easily we condemn the teenager, pregnant as a result of promiscuity, while hiding the fact that we engaged in similar activities. Perhaps our sin was not discovered as the evidence was missing because of good fortune, contraception, or an abortion; but our honor was gone, our valuables were in the hand of another, and we live with the guilt.

The proper way to deal with our sins is to acknowledge that we are flawed, sinful beings in need of forgiveness, and confess our sins to God. After receiving His forgiveness, we may even need to confront the "Tamars" in our lives and ask forgiveness. The good news is that God redeems these situations. It was from Tamar that Judah received the grandsons who would carry on his name, one of whom became the progenitor of David and ultimately Jesus.

Lord, help us to confront sin in our lives and believe Your word that if we cover our sins we will not prosper, but if we confess and forsake them we will find mercy.

April 9

MANNA SERIES: MISSING PERSONS REGISTER
MISSING GOD'S PURPOSE FOR MINISTRY

Reading Passage: 2Kings 5:1-27
Main Text: 2Kings 5:25-26 Then he went in and stood before his master Elisha. "Where have you been, Gehazi?" Elisha asked. "Your servant didn't go anywhere," Gehazi answered. But Elisha said to him, "Was not my spirit with you when the man got down from his chariot to meet you? Is this the time to take money, or to accept clothes, olive groves, vineyards, flocks, herds, or menservants and maidservants?" (NIV)

One of the challenges we face when we are involved in Christian ministry is to be able to resist the desire for personal rewards and trust God to take care of us. Our desire for personal gain can corrupt God's purpose for ministry, and cause us to miss God's timing for rewarding us.

Naaman, the captain of the army in Aram and a prominent citizen, suffered from the embarrassing disease of leprosy. With the assistance of the king of Aram, he arranged to visit the prophet Elisha in Israel to receive his healing. Initially he rejected the prophet's instructions, but eventually he obeyed and was completely healed of his leprosy. Naaman was so humbled by the miracle that he acknowledged the supremacy of the God of Israel. Then he begged Elisha to accept his gifts of silver, gold and clothes in gratitude for the prophet's services. Elisha flatly refused the gifts.

However, Elisha's servant Gehazi, thought his master was missing an opportunity for a personal blessing. When Naaman departed, Gehazi sneaked away and followed Naaman's entourage. Catching up with Naaman, he concocted a story that Elisha had changed his mind and wanted some of the goods to give to some needy people. Gehazi's desire for reward caused him to miss what God wanted to achieve by Elisha's ministry to Naaman. When he returned and was asked by Elisha why he had been missing, he denied going anywhere. The prophet challenged

Gehazi's story and asked whether that was the proper time to go missing in pursuit of material things.

Elisha's response implies that there will be a time for rewards, but not when we should be focused on ministry and God's purposes. God knows when to provide the rewards, whether in wealth, health, or acclaim. When we pursue our own agenda while we should be ministering, it is likely we will miss God's purpose and diminish His glory. Because Gehazi was missing the purpose of God by chasing personal reward, Elisha told him the leprosy of Naaman "would cling to him and his family."

We have seen where greed has produced shame and embarrassment in the lives of many servants of God, similar to the effect of the shameful disease of leprosy. Our work for God should be motivated by our love for Him and desire for His glory, and never by our desire for personal compensation.

Lord, we receive this word of warning as we examine our hearts and our motives. We don't want to be missing, chasing our own rewards when we should be ministering,. Help us to be fully devoted to Your purposes in ministry, and trust Your timing for our rewards, whether in this life or in the next.

April 10

MANNA SERIES: MISSING PERSONS REGISTER
WHEN OUR MENTOR IS MISSING

Reading Passage: 2Kings 2:1-18
Main Text: 2Kings 2:16-17 "Look," they said, "we your servants have fifty able men. Let them go and look for your master. Perhaps the Spirit of the LORD has picked him up and set him down on some mountain or in some valley." "No," Elisha replied, "do not send them." But they persisted until he was too ashamed to refuse. So he said, "Send them." And they sent fifty men, who searched for three days but did not find him. (NIV)

Many of us have benefitted from being mentored or coached by people who poured their lives into us. They guided, instructed and modeled for us without compensation, for the sole purpose that we might receive the knowledge they gained from their experience of traveling the path ahead of us. The mentor may have been a parent, a schoolteacher, a pastor, a coach, a boss, or just an older friend. How should we respond when that mentor goes missing due to change of residence or employment, graduation or death?

Elisha, the servant of Elijah, faced this question when Elijah was taken away by a whirlwind into heaven. After Elijah personally selected him as a disciple, Elisha faithfully served his master. When Elijah became aware that God was about to take him away, he sought to separate himself from Elisha. He moved from place to place intending to sneak away from Elisha, but Elisha resolutely declared, "As the Lord lives ... I will not leave you." Finally, Elijah came to the Jordan, used his mantle to part the waters of the river, and they both crossed to the other side. Knowing his master was about to depart, Elisha requested a double-portion of Elijah's spirit, which was the inheritance of his power and authority. While they were talking, a fiery chariot appeared and separated them. Elijah was then taken away to heaven in a whirlwind. This was illustrative of a divine separation.

Elisha left the scene and traveled to the Jordan. He used the cloak that fell from the departing Elijah to part the waters of the Jordan. By replicating Elijah's miracle he proved Elijah's power had been transferred to him. No mentorship is intended to last forever. The goal of mentorship is to develop the disciple to replace his or her mentor. We have an understandable fear of losing a mentor, but this challenges us to change our role in life, and assume the responsibility to mentor others. This is the cycle of life. What we receive we are responsible to pass on; what was developed in us, we must develop in others.

Sometimes it may take divine action to separate us from our mentor, but we must respond to the missing mentor by realizing a responsibility has been passed to us. When we begin to act with this new sense of responsibility, we may just be amazed to see how well we repeat the miracles of our mentors, or recognize their personalities in our actions. Instead of mourning our loss, are we grasping the opportunity to carry on our mentor's legacy?

Father, we admit our fear of losing someone we regard as a mentor in our lives. Yet we realize that oftentimes this loss provides the opportunities for our growth. Help us to learn well the lessons received from our mentors as we prepare for our new responsibilities in life.

April 11

MANNA SERIES: MISSING PERSONS REGISTER
"WHERE ARE YOU, LORD?"

Reading Passage: Job 23:1-15
Main Text: Job 23:3-4 If only I knew where to find him;
if only I could go to his dwelling! I would state my case before him and
fill my mouth with arguments. (NIV)

When does it appear as if God has gone missing from our lives? It
is not when life is going smoothly, our needs are being met, and we have
much to celebrate. Nor even when we face adverse circumstances, once
we can provide some explanation for the adversity (even if our explanation
is based on a false philosophy). What really challenges us is when we
experience or observe suffering or injustice, and these are contrary to
our expectation of a benevolent Sovereign God. When we seek for an
explanation, God seems to provide no answer. These are the times we
question the existence of God or we doubt whether He cares about us.

We can appreciate the story of Job because it portrays the struggle of a
man confronted with extreme adversities and the difficulty of reconciling
his expectation of God with the experience of his circumstances. Unlike
most of us, Job could claim that he was a righteous man. Therefore, he
expected his blameless life would be rewarded with blessing and not
adversity. When his friends made the accusation that his wickedness must
have been the source of his trouble, he yearned for an opportunity to plead
his case before God. His dilemma was that God, as Spirit, was inaccessible
for a face-to-face dialogue.

Job said, "But if I go to the east, He is not there, if I go to the west
I do not find Him. When He is at work in the north, I do not see Him;
when He turns to the south, I catch no glimpse of Him" Job 23:8-9 NIV.
What should we do at those times when God seems absent and offers no
explanation that could provide us with comfort? We sometimes make
sacrifices helping people, and instead of gratitude we receive slander and
cursing. Or, while engaged in Christian ministry, we are diagnosed with
a malignant tumor. Perhaps our loved ones who have given their lives in
service for the Lord are killed in a motor vehicle accident.

If we choose to deny the existence of God, we have to accept that we are victims of random chance or bad luck. If this is the case we will have a fearful existence, enduring pain and suffering without purpose.

The fact that we can't find God doesn't mean He is not with us; the fact that what happens to us makes no sense, doesn't mean we are wiser than He is. The fact that He appears to be asleep while our lives are in jeopardy doesn't mean He doesn't care for us, or has no power over the circumstances of our lives. It is at these times we have to learn to walk by faith and believe He has a purpose for every event in our lives. He is still in control and loves us even when He seems to be missing.

Lord, we have learned that our faith, which is developed during times of adversity and darkness, is more valuable than our peace and comfort. Please increase our faith so that we will trust You even when You seem to be missing.

April 12

MANNA SERIES: MISSING PERSONS REGISTER
WHY ARE YOU SEEKING FOR JESUS?

Reading Passage: John 6:1-15, 48-58.
Main Text: John 6:24-26 Once the crowd realized that neither Jesus nor his disciples were there, they got into the boats and went to Capernaum in search of Jesus. When they found him on the other side of the lake, they asked him, "Rabbi, when did you get here?" Jesus answered, "I tell you the truth, you are looking for me, not because you saw miraculous signs but because you ate the loaves and had your fill." (NIV)

We struggle to maintain the proper motives for seeking God. We are introduced to God as the One who can supply all our needs. We therefore seek Him for the purpose of obtaining material blessings. But God's provision of blessings is a means to His greater objective, which is that we are brought into full relationship with Him, becoming one with Him (John 17:21). This is similar to a man, who provides a woman with gifts with the goal of winning her affections and making her his bride,

At the beginning of John 6, Jesus performed the miracle of feeding over

5,000 people with five barley loaves and two fish. The crowd was so impressed with this miracle that they forcibly wanted to make Him their King. So Jesus hid from the crowds. When they finally found their missing food supplier, Jesus exposed their selfish, lustful motive for seeking Him. They were not interested in Him as a person, or for His purposes; they were only interested in what He could provide for their benefit. When Jesus challenged them to seek Him for more than physical bread by partaking of His life, they rejected Him. They had no interest in becoming united with Him by believing in Him.

How are we different from the crowds that were seeking Jesus? We seek Him for help with our finances, healing for our bodies, taking care of our children, and getting us out of difficulties. But do we seek Him just for who He is, to sense what is on His heart, and to learn His ways? Our selfish, lustful motives for seeking God cause Him to go missing from us so He can expose our bread and fish mentality. He wants more than to see us blessed; He wants our hearts in order that we may develop a love relationship with Him. A recurring theme of scripture is, if we seek the Lord we will find Him when we search for Him with all our hearts (Deut. 4:29, 2 Chron. 15:4, Jer. 29:13). God will allow us to go through certain trials to transform our hearts from being 'spiritual gold diggers.'

Let us examine our motives for seeking the Lord, and ensure we are motivated by love.

Father, so often we miss the purpose of our relationship with You, and we seek You only to obtain blessings that meet our needs. A review of our past prayers reveals our bread and fish mentality. Please forgive us of our selfishness and help us to see that You want to be the only desire of our hearts.

April 13

MANNA SERIES: GLEANINGS FROM THE PSALMS
THE LIFESTYLE OF THE BLESSED I

Reading Passage: Psalm 1
Main Text: Psa. 1:1-2 Blessed is the man who does not walk in the
counsel of the wicked
Or stand in the way of sinners

Or sit in the seat of mockers. But his delight is in the law of the LORD,

And on his law he meditates day and night. (NIV)

We do not live our lives in isolation; in fact we are always subjected to external influences. God placed the Hebrew people in a land where they were surrounded by alien and hostile peoples who exerted their influence on them. Before placing them in the land, He gave them His instructions on how they should live, in the form of laws, commandments and statutes. He emphasized through Moses that the path to blessing was through obedience to His Word, but disobedience or following any other path would result in destruction.

The Book of Psalms includes many verses that celebrate the significance of the Word of the Lord in the lives of these Hebrews. This first Psalm provides a thematic foundation for the whole book. It begins with a trilogy of expressions describing the lifestyle to be avoided by a person desiring to be blessed. He does not walk - stand - sit, which describes a growing state of adaptation leading to full accommodation of the lifestyle of the ungodly.

Walking in the counsel of the wicked means taking advice from those who are godless in their thoughts and lifestyles. When we stand in the way of sinners, we have accepted their godless advice and have begun to adapt and defend their sinful philosophies and behavior. When we sit in the seat of mockers, we have arrived at the stage where we are comfortable in the company of the very ones who not only promote a sinful lifestyle but attack and mock the godly. They deride those who adhere to the Word of the Lord, and denounce them as being fools. It is not sufficient for the blessed person to avoid association with the godless, mocking sinners. He also has to take positive action and focus his attention on the law of the Lord. When we desire to be blessed, we will take the time to learn and meditate on the Word of the Lord until His instructions become our delight. Then we will have no difficulty obeying and living in accordance with these instructions.

Like the Hebrews, we are living in an alien and hostile environment with the godless mockers around us seeking to influence our lifestyles. If we desire to live blessed lives we have to counteract the influence of the world that comes through books, magazines, television and other media, by spending time learning and meditating on the Word of God.

What is the main influence for our lifestyles, and from whom do we take counsel? God's guidance comes through His Word, our direction comes from our meditation on it, and our blessing comes from ordering our lives accordingly.

Father, we are thankful that You never left us without direction for our lives in this godless world. We desire to live the life of the blessed, so help us to have the discipline to make Your Word a lamp to our feet and a light to our path.

April 14

MANNA SERIES: GLEANINGS FROM THE PSALMS
THE LIFESTYLE OF THE BLESSED II

Reading Passage: Psalm 1
Main Text: Psa. 1:3 He is like a tree planted by streams of water,
Which yields its fruit in season and whose leaf does not wither.
Whatever he does prospers. (NIV)

The term "blessed" is sometimes translated "happy", not in the sense of hilarity caused by amusing incidents, but as a state of existence providing peace, security and fulfillment. Such a state of blessedness is not the result of receiving material things or special favors. The psalm indicates the state of blessedness is achieved when we adopt the prescribed lifestyle of delighting in and obeying the instructions of the Lord recorded in the Bible.

The Psalmist uses the analogy of a tree in a location with an abundant supply of water, to describe the lifestyle of the blessed. We mistakenly assume the blessed lifestyle means all our needs are met, we have no struggles, and there is nothing disturbing our minds. Yes, the blessed person has abundance, but this is not personal wealth or a problem-free life. It is constant access to the source that can provide what is required as needed, like a tree beside the streams of waters.

The text states two functions of the tree with a constant flowing supply of water. First it produces fruit in its season. The blessed person will always be fruitful at the proper time in order to be a blessing to those needing fruit. Our blessing is not for ourselves; rather we are blessed so we may meet the needs of others. The need in the season may be a word of encouragement, a hug of compassion, guidance for solving a problem or financial support. If we are living the life of the blessed, God expects us to produce the appropriate fruit as required.

The other function of the tree with abundant supply of water is to remain luxuriant despite the surrounding weather conditions. The life dependent on receiving blessings will wither and become dry when facing the drought of material things, or the heat of adverse circumstances. But the person living the blessed life will remain peaceful, secure and joyful, seemingly unaffected by these external difficulties. Many of the psalms echo the theme of praising God and rejoicing even when facing life's difficulties. The reason we are able to rejoice at these times is because of where the trees of our lives are planted. The streams that water our tree come from a divine, unending and abundant source.

The verse concludes with the amazing observation that whatever the blessed person does, prospers. This may be interpreted that blessed persons succeed in everything they attempt, or they cause everything they become involved in to prosper. In the former they themselves become prosperous, in the latter interpretation, they convey prosperity. Regardless, blessed persons are associated with prosperity, enhancing the lives of others, and they are fulfilled, resulting in happiness. This lifestyle of fruitfulness, resilience and fulfillment is available to us when we choose to delight in following the Word of God and avoid the influence of the ungodly world.

Father, You desire to make our lives effective and enjoyable. But so many people have been deceived by the Devil to believe that following You will cause them to be bored and unhappy. Deliver us from the lies of the Devil so we will delight in following You.

April 15

MANNA SERIES: GLEANINGS FROM THE PSALMS
DECLARATIONS ABOUT GOD
WHILE IN DANGER

Reading Passage: Psalm 3
Main Text: Psa. 3:3 But you are a shield around me, O LORD;
You bestow glory on me and lift up my head. (NIV)

Our understanding of God adapts to suit our situations. It is not that God changes in His nature but that we expand our knowledge of God as we see His involvement in various phases of our lives.

David already knew God as sovereign when as the last child in an obscure family, he was chosen and promoted to be the ruler of Israel. After reigning for many years and being guided by the Lord in conquering most of his enemies, David now faced one of his greatest challenges. His son, Absalom, undermined his authority, led a successful coup against him and deposed him. David and his supporters had to flee the palace and Jerusalem because Absalom and his army were intent on destroying them.

David had lost his throne and the honor of the kingship. He was hurt and embarrassed at the fact that he was overthrown by his own son, and taunted by his enemies. Knowing that he was in imminent danger of being captured and killed by Absalom's army, David's enemies told him God would never deliver him, and that God had abandoned him. How did David respond to this crisis? Was his faith sufficiently strong to believe God would deliver him out of his fear and despair?

David's faith was demonstrated by his declarations. He said of the Lord, "You are my shield, my glory, and the One who lifts my head." As his shield, David saw the Lord surrounding him for his protection. He was so confident in his divine shield that he declared that he would not be afraid of the ten thousand enemies who were attacking him from every side (3:6). Although he was not enjoying the glory of the throne while in exile, he found his glory in the Lord who brought him honor. The situation he was in could have made him downcast, but the Lord caused his head to be held high. His faith enabled him to see the Lord as his means of countering all his difficulties.

We may not be able to avoid devastating experiences in life. The lesson we learn from David's experience is that we must possess a faith that leads us to see God as larger than any situation we will encounter. Without the confidence that God is able to protect, deliver, and provide us with honor, or lift our spirits, we will live fearful and anxious lives. After he knew the Lord heard his cry for help, David was able to sleep in confidence, trusting God's protection.

What keeps us awake at nights? What declarations do we make about God in our moments of crisis?

Lord, we are thankful that You will not abandon us to life's

circumstances, but You are able to deliver us. May we never allow the dark difficulties we encounter to cause us to lose faith in You. We want to be able to sleep even when enemies surround us. Amen.

April 16

MANNA SERIES: GLEANINGS FROM THE PSALMS
MAN: GOD'S CHOICE FOR HIS GLORY I

Reading Passage: Psalm 8
Main Text: Psa. 8:4-5 "What is man that you are mindful of him,
The son of man that you care for him?
You made him a little lower than the heavenly beings
And crowned him with glory and honor." (NIV)

The news is not good. Because we are constantly reminded of our flawed human nature, it is difficult to recall God's original design for man. When we hear of the latest acts of violence, the latest practice of debauchery, man's plans for inflicting terror on his fellowman, we lose hope of any ultimate goodness for this fallen creature.

In this text the Psalmist takes us back to creation to paint a completely different picture of mankind. God wanted His glory to be seen in creation. Creation with the beauty of the mountains, flowers and trees, and the variety of animals and birds, would advertise the excellence of His nature. These cause us to be in awe of God and declare with the Psalmist, "How excellent is Your name in all the earth." But God wanted a glory that surpassed the physical creation and animal life, so He made man. In making man superior, God created him with a copy of His own nature: "the image of God." The Psalmist declares, "You made him a little lower than the heavenly beings (in Hebrew text, "god"), and crowned him with glory and honor."

The nature God placed in man provided him with an independent intellect and will, allowing him freedom to choose to obey or disobey God. He wanted to prove to all the heavenly beings and to Satan himself that man, in independence and honor, would choose to love and serve God just because of the excellence and greatness of His character. This would provide the greatest glory to God.

God made man His delegated ruler in charge of creation, with authority over even the most powerful animals. But man sinned and failed to fulfill his role in the plan. When man fell, the image of God in him was defaced, the glory and honor was gone, and his authority over creation was diminished. How would God fulfill His original desire, which was to obtain His glory from mankind? He decided to offer Himself as the new man to accomplish the goals of the first man, and to restore those who believe in Jesus to their original design.

Heb. 2:9-11 NIV states,

> But we see Jesus, who was made a little lower than the angels, now crowned with glory and honor because he suffered death, so that by the grace of God he might taste death for everyone. In bringing many sons to glory, it was fitting that God, for whom and through whom everything exists, should make the author of their salvation perfect through suffering. Both the one who makes men holy and those who are made holy are of the same family. So Jesus is not ashamed to call them brothers.

The good news is that man's glory has been restored through Jesus.

Father, we are thankful that You never gave up on us, but devised a plan to restore us to the place where we can give You glory. Thank You for Jesus. We commit our lives to following Him and inviting others to surrender to His rule, in order to make Your name great in the earth, Amen.

April 17

MANNA SERIES: GLEANINGS FROM THE PSALMS
MAN: GOD'S CHOICE FOR HIS GLORY II

Reading Passage: Psalm 8
Main Text: Psa. 8:2 From the lips of children and infants you have ordained praise Because of your enemies, to silence the foe and the avenger. (NIV)

The thought that man was God's choice to provide His highest praise seemed to fascinate and mystify David and other psalmists.

In a passage similar to Psalm 8, David wondered why God would consider man as significant when his life is as flimsy as breath, and his days are as fleeting as a shadow (Psa. 144:3-4). Another psalmist describes in Psa. 148 how creation praises the Lord. The heavens, the angels, sun and moon, and the seas, the mountains, even the trees, all give praise to the Lord their Creator. When we consider the majesty and permanence of mountains, the splendor and enduring value of the sun and moon, man seems trivial in comparison. Yet God has chosen man as the source of His highest praise. Of all created things and beings, only man truly represents His nature. Only man was created to communicate and have a relationship with Him. There is no other being in all creation that Satan, God's enemy, seeks to own so he can obtain worship and devotion in competition with the Lord. Therefore David declares, "From the lips of children and infants you have ordained praise ... to silence the foe and the avenger."

God established in man's nature an instinct to respond to Him in praise and adoration. The Hebrew term used in this verse suggests that God builds a wall of strength in man through praise that acts as a weapon against God's enemies. In establishing this defensive wall, His purpose is to silence the enemies, causing them to cease their attacks. To prove that this praise is innate and instinctive to man, He demonstrates it in children and infants. It is usually only after we become older, with greater exposure to the devil and his worldly systems, that we begin to exercise our independence from the Creator and cease to praise Him. We do not seem to realize that by ceasing to praise the Lord, we empower the weapons of the enemy.

Jesus provided a great illustration of this instinctive nature in children, in contrast to the developed behavior of mature, cynical and worldly people. When He entered Jerusalem, the children began to shout praises to Him, " Hosanna to the Son of David." The chief priests and the Jewish leaders became indignant at the behavior of the children. In response, Jesus quoted Psa. 8:2. With this awareness of what God established in us, and His purpose in having us praise Him, let us not fail to silence the enemy with our praise to the Lord. As the Psalmist declares, "May the praise of God be in their mouths and a double-edged sword in their hands, to inflict vengeance on the nations and punishment on the peoples" Psa. 149:6-7 NIV. If you have become too 'intelligent', 'mature' and 'sophisticated' to offer generous praise to God, you are failing to fulfill His purpose in creating us, and you are empowering God's enemies.

We praise You, Lord, because we were created for Your praise. We praise You more abundantly because You have redeemed our lives and saved us from the kingdom of Your enemy. May Your praise be always in our mouths so we will be able to shut the mouth of the enemy.

April 18

MANNA SERIES: GLEANINGS FROM THE PSALMS
JOURNEYING THROUGH LIFE'S TUNNELS

Reading Passage: Psalm 13
Main Text: Psa. 13:1-2 How long, O LORD? Will you forget me forever? How long will you hide your face from me? How long must I wrestle with my thoughts and every day have sorrow in my heart?
How long will my enemy triumph over me? (NIV)

While going through a tunnel, time becomes distorted and the hours of darkness seem like an eternity. Recall the moments in pain while waiting for the doctor, the time spent waiting to hear the phone ring with an update on a loved one who was in an accident, the moments following the slamming of a door by a spouse who announced he or she is leaving. It was during those long dark times we wondered if God had forgotten or forsaken us.

The Psalms record many of David's tunnel-like experiences. In the above passage David asked the question "how long?" four times. His feelings of abandonment are palpable. The period of his struggle and sorrow with no help from God seemed unending. In verse 5 of the passage we observe the turning point in David's struggle; he decided to trust in what he knew of God's faithfulness. How could he revert to trusting in the One he believed had abandoned him?

Very likely David realized that God was still his only hope of deliverance. He began to reflect on his past crises when the Lord came through for him. A ray of hope began to penetrate the darkness of the tunnel. He moves from despair to hope of deliverance, and, as he thinks of this possibility, he begins to rejoice in anticipation of the Lord's intervention. He ends with a strong statement of confidence in the Lord, "I will sing to the Lord, for He has been good to me." The goodness or bountiful blessings that David was rejoicing about were both the past deliverances he recalled, and the deliverance he was expecting in this particular situation.

David provides us with the formula to begin to see light at the end of our tunnels. In those long dark hours that seem like an eternity, we need to remember God's past goodness to us. When we begin to give thanks and celebrate the times when God intervened and delivered us in the past, it will change our perspective of the present difficulty. We will begin to believe that there is no situation that is beyond God's ability to change. Instead of wondering in despair "How long?", we will begin to sing and rejoice in our expected exit from the tunnel.

What situations are you currently facing that cause you to feel as if you are in an endless dark tunnel? Don't despair! God has not forsaken you. Begin singing! Your exit may be just around the corner.

Lord, while we know we will not escape the dark times of difficulties in our lives, we know You are faithful and You will deliver us. Help us never to lose faith in Your ability to give us the victory. We want to be able to sing of Your goodness even in the midst of dark experiences.

April 19

MANNA SERIES: GLEANINGS FROM THE PSALMS
THE PRIVILEGE OF KNOWING HIS NAME

Reading Passage: Psalm 9
Main Text: Psa. 9:9-10 The LORD is a refuge for the oppressed,
A stronghold in times of trouble.
Those who know your name will trust in you,
For you, LORD, have never forsaken those who seek you. (NIV)

What is the hope of the oppressed? To be oppressed describes a state of being crushed by a burden beyond our ability to bear it. The burden may be caused by the powerful who take advantage of the weak, or those in authority who ignore the cry of the helpless. The burdensome state may also be applied to someone under a spiritual attack by demonic forces, or circumstances over which we have no control.

David referred to his experiences when enemies too powerful confronted him. He saw where powerful enemies were overthrown and ceased to exist after the Lord intervened on his behalf. He concluded that the Lord sits in judgment at a place higher than any earthly power or authority, and furthermore, the Lord will outlast any enemy, "He abides forever." Consequently, David declared, "The Lord is a refuge for the oppressed." The term refuge describes a place of high elevation that is secure, allowing the occupants to observe the movement of the enemy, and to find safety in the defenses of the stronghold. David was familiar with this type of stronghold through his experience in the caves of Engedi. Only those who knew the location and the way to get there could enjoy the protection of the stronghold.

The Lord, as our place of refuge from oppression, can only be enjoyed by those who know His name. Knowing the name of the Lord is a Hebrew idiom that describes those who are in relationship with Him, recognize His authority, and become His followers. It is a great privilege to know the name of the Lord, in order that we may find refuge in the stronghold of His protection whenever we are oppressed. David further states that the Lord has never forsaken those who seek Him for the purpose of trusting in Him.

It seems such a simple act for the oppressed to trust the Lord in the time of trouble and find Him a place of refuge from oppression. Yet this is not the usual path taken by the oppressed. The default position of most people facing times of trouble is to seek frantically and vainly for their own solutions, or worry about their helpless state. Unless they previously knew Him, it is unlikely someone will begin to genuinely trust the Lord at the time of trouble. It is better that we develop trust before times of trouble by taking time to learn about Him and entering into a relationship with Him.

Have you prepared for your time of trouble and oppression? Have you developed such a relationship with the Lord that will allow you to declare that you know His name? Don't disregard the opportunity to have a place of refuge.

Father, we are thankful that You are a place of refuge for our oppressed souls. We commit ourselves to know You in prayer and study of the Word so we will increase our trust in You. We rest confidently in the fact that You will never forsake those who trust in You.

April 20

MANNA SERIES: GLEANINGS FROM THE PSALMS
GOD PERSONALIZED

Reading Passage: Psalm 18
Main Text: Psa. 18:30-31 As for God, his way is perfect;
The word of the LORD is flawless. He is a shield
For all who take refuge in him. For who is God besides the LORD?
And who is the Rock except our God? (NIV)

David raised a question in the passage for which everyone who is a believer should seek to provide his or her own answer: "Who is God?" (v. 31) Description of the nature and characteristics of God has been provided by Scripture, theologians, and the testimony of other believers. But these descriptions, though substantial, truthful and logical, are ineffective for personal conviction and for sincere worship.

The most effective descriptions of God are those derived from personal experience, and those that are consistent with Scripture. Psalm 18 is described as a song David wrote after God had delivered him from all his enemies, presumably in the latter years of his life (note its placement in 2 Sam. 22). By this time, David had a personal knowledge of God based on his experiences. His descriptions were not merely those of the God received by tradition. First, he identified God as the Lord, Yahweh (Greek, Jehovah), the One who made covenant with Israel, becoming their personal deity, not some generic, supreme, impersonal force. The Lord was his rock, his fortress, his deliverer, his refuge, his shield, and his stronghold (v. 2). There was an incident in his life that pointed to each of these characteristics in God. Because of these experiences with God, David began by declaring, "I love you, O Lord, my strength" (v. 1). We cannot love a God whom we have not personally experienced, a God who is a literary figure, or a figment of our imagination.

The God I know, love and serve has been my comfort in times of loss and grief: during the sudden loss of my parents. He has been my companion in times of loneliness: when I was alone in foreign countries having no one with whom to share my joys or unburden my hurts. He has been my wisdom when I did not know which choice to make or in which direction to go; in Jesus, He was my Savior when I became aware of my sin that separated me from God. This is my God, and I love Him because I have proven that He is worthy to be praised.

The character of my God is fully supported by Scripture, and although I may not be able to explain Him, I am fully convinced of His reality in my life. Therefore, like David I will declare,

> The LORD lives! Praise be to my Rock!
> Exalted be God my Savior! (v. 46)
> Therefore, I will praise You among the nations, O LORD;
> I will sing praises to Your name. (v. 49)

Do you have a description of God based on a personal relationship with Him? Unless you are able to have this description, your worship will consist of empty platitudes, and you will be unable to have a love relationship with Him.

Lord, I am so glad that I know You personally and that I can declare that You are my God.

April 21

MANNA SERIES: GLEANINGS FROM THE PSALMS
SENSITIVITY TO SIN

Reading Passage: Psalm 19
Main Text: Psa. 19:12-13 Who can discern his errors?
> Forgive my hidden faults. Keep your servant also from willful sins;
> May they not rule over me.
> Then will I be blameless, innocent of great transgression. (NIV)

Sin disrupts fellowship between God and us, and sin is always significant in the eyes of God. To avoid grieving the heart of God and causing disruptions in our fellowship, we must remain sensitive to sin. We may be watchful to avoid acts and attitudes that are generally regarded as sinful by the society, such as sexual sins, drunkenness, or stealing. But the challenge is avoiding sins that are acceptable to society but offensive to God, or those known by us but hidden from others, or those we are unaware of.

David, desiring to be sensitive to sin, raised the question, "Who can discern his errors?" Since there are sins we commit that we might not be aware of, yet they grieve God's heart, how may we avoid them, or what should we do about them? David noted in this Psalm that just as creation reveals God to all mankind regardless of race or language, the requirements of the Lord are revealed in his laws, statutes, precepts and commandments. These are recorded in the Word of God - in scripture, and these are able to restore the soul to its proper condition, and give wisdom to the ignorant (v.7). The Word of God keeps us from sin, and also warns us when we sin (v.11). The only way we may remain sensitive to sin and avoid grieving the Lord is by exposing ourselves constantly to His words in scripture.

We cannot trust culture, others, or even ourselves to provide guidance on what is sinful to God. We have to keep the Word of God in our hearts so we will not sin against God. As stated in Heb. 4:12-13 NIV,

> For the Word of God is living and active, sharper than any double-edged sword, it penetrates even to dividing soul and spirit, joints and marrow; it judges the thoughts and attitudes of the heart. Nothing in all creation is hidden from God's sight. Everything is uncovered and laid bare before the eyes of Him to whom we must give account.

David's desire was that his spoken words, and also the thoughts of his heart would comprise an acceptable offering to the Lord at all times (v.14).

Are we so desirous of fellowship with God that we will remain sensitive to sin, and like David, seek to have our words and thoughts acceptable to the Lord? The way to remain sensitive is for us to constantly examine our lives by the Word of God, and be willing to repent and make the adjustments disclosed to us.

Father, we admit the difficulty of knowing the many ways in which we sin against You. Help us to remain sensitive to sin by always being guided by Your Word. We desire to maintain our fellowship with You, for Christ's sake. Amen.

April 22

MANNA SERIES: GLEANINGS FROM THE PSALMS
AN UNNATURAL WAY TO STAND FIRM

Reading Passage: Psalm 20
Main Text: Psa. 20:7-8 Some trust in chariots and some in horses,
But we trust in the name of the LORD our God.
They are brought to their knees and fall,
But we rise up and stand firm. (NIV)

We strive to guarantee success in life by following certain generally accepted patterns. To gain a reasonable standard of living, we try to obtain a good education that would lead to a lucrative job. To have a healthy body, we practice eating a balanced diet and engaging in regular physical exercise. In preparation for retirement, we try to save and invest wisely hoping to have a future source of income. Yet there is no guarantee to the outcomes of these normal patterns in life. We know of many examples where the poorly educated have exceeded the financial success of the well educated, or the disciplined, healthy–lifestyle practitioner has died prematurely leaving behind those that ignored all the rules for healthy living. We learn that we are not in control of all the factors to provide success in life.

King David in this Psalm was preparing to lead his army in a battle against his enemies. The natural pattern in preparing for warfare is to ensure there is adequate offensive equipment, but David's men knew that their King did not rely on the usual implements of war. So the Psalm describes their prayer for the king in preparation for battle. After hearing their petitions to God on his behalf, David, full of confidence declared, "Now I know the Lord will deliver His anointed King and answer him from His holy heaven" (v.6). While the enemies trusted the natural equipment for war, like chariots and horses, he was choosing to trust in the name of the Lord.

This would appear to be an unnatural way to enter into battle, but David knew from experience that those trusting in normal, generally accepted means for success frequently end up fallen and disappointed. "Chariots will rust, and horses will pull up lame, but those trusting the Lord will rise up and stand firm" (Message Bible). This does not mean they may never fall, but even if they fall, they will rise again, and ultimately they will be left standing. From the time that he was a young boy facing the strength, might and weaponry of Goliath, David learned that conventional means of engagement would never triumph over trust in the Lord. He was victorious against the well-equipped Goliath with just a slingshot and stones.

We do not deny the importance of following the normal patterns in life that are available to us. We must take the maximum advantages of what God has made available to us of educational, employment or medical opportunities. But we must never place our trust in these natural things. Faith in God is the most important preparation for every aspect of our lives if we want God's success.

Father, we so easily neglect the confidence you provide and seek to rely on the normal, man-made means of "chariots and horses" for success. We want to place our confidence only in You, so we will stand only in Your strength. Amen.

April 23

MANNA SERIES: GLEANINGS FROM THE PSALMS
BEING PURSUED BY FAVOR

Reading Passage: Psalm 23
Main Text: Psa. 23:6 Surely goodness and love
Will follow me all the days of my life,
And I will dwell in the house of the LORD forever. (NIV)

Imagine being pursued not by enemies or misfortune, but by divine favor expressed as goodness and loving-kindness for your entire life.

This conclusion to David's most well- known psalm is a great expression of assurance of the blessing that will result from an intimate relationship with the Lord. But how did David become so confident of divine favor when his life had an abundance of unfavorable circumstances? He saw himself as a dependent sheep under the care of a faithful shepherd, and as an honored guest at the table of a gracious host. Once David committed himself to the care of the shepherd, he gave up the right to choose the places and sources of sustenance, or the paths he should walk. And even when he mistakenly strayed into the dangerous territory of the "valley of the shadow," he didn't seek his own escape, but waited on the protection and deliverance of the shepherd.

We would love to have this assurance of divine favor, but we have difficulty in accepting the role of dependent sheep. We have already decided where we should feed, so we object if the Lord is not providing the job and salary we are demanding. When He would direct us to quiet streams, we run away in search of the excitement of the crowds. David discovered that sheep have no right of determination; their only obligation is to stay near to the shepherd and listen to His voice.

As the honored guest at a feast, David did not have a choice as to the identity of the other guests. With respect to our enemies we urge the Lord to destroy them so we can enjoy an undisturbed life. But instead of destroying them, the Lord sometimes decides to provide a feast for us while the enemies are watching, so they can observe our special relationship with Him. He causes our cups to overflow so we will be able to share with the surrounding enemies the abundant joy we experience through His provision and anointing oil. We no longer fear the enemies; instead we are offering to assist them.

The clear lesson from David's experience is that our relationship with the Lord is adversely affected when we are the independent, self-determined, chest-beating, successful personality the world usually adores. However, as dependent sheep and His invited guests we can have assurance of His favor and His presence for our entire lives. Are you prepared to adjust your attitude so you can say with confidence, "The Lord is my shepherd, I shall not want?"

Lord, we tend to resist becoming selfless, helpless sheep because we believe we know what is best for us. Help us to be willing to yield

to You as the Good Shepherd so we can confidently enjoy Your favor and Your presence, for Jesus' sake, Amen.

April 24

GUIDANCE IN CHOICES

Reading Passage: Psalm 25
Main Text: Psa. 25:12-13 Who, then, is the man that fears the LORD?
He will instruct him in the way chosen for him.
He will spend his days in prosperity,
And his descendants will inherit the land. (NIV)

Yogi Berra, the American baseball coach famous for his humorous quotations said, "If you come to a fork in the road, take it." We all experience the challenge of not knowing which choice to make when presented with alternatives. It doesn't help that as finite beings, the consequences attached to each choice are not usually very clear to us, especially in the long term. If only we did not have the burden of decision making, or we had someone to guide us in the direction that is best for us. Followers of Christ have come to believe that our all-knowing Lord has a path for our lives that leads to success.

David had to make numerous crucial decisions as a naive youngster in Saul's household, then as a fugitive hunted by Saul himself, and later as a king. In Psalm 25 he explains that because the Lord is good and fair, He teaches sinful people the right way to live, He shows those who are humble what is right, and teaches them His way (vv.8-9). If the Lord is willing to provide us with guidance, why are we not accepting His instructions when we are puzzled concerning matters such as career choices, marital relationships, investment decisions, or church affiliation? David states that those who accept guidance are those who fear the Lord. He instructs them in the way they should choose, which is God's designed way for them.

When someone fears the Lord, he or she honors Him in attitude and conduct, and submits to Him in desires and decision-making. There is no resistance or rebellion when His will is contrary to our desires. This implies that the greatest hindrance to receiving God's guidance is our unwillingness to be obedient to His instructions when they are contrary to our plans. Once we fear Him, we don't need a dramatic notification from Him or a prophetic word, although these may be provided. Instead, we remain open to Him when reading scripture, petitioning in prayer, or listening to a fellow believer, so that when we take any action we are conscious that His hand is on the steering wheel of our lives. His instructions come by a prompting in our spirit, or the arrangement of our circumstances. And after responding, we will sense His peace.

Do you desire to find the pre-ordained path for your life? Are you willing to be open to God's guidance, without insisting on your own preferences? We have a willing guide, but do we show that we fear Him by becoming willing followers?

Lord, we are so grateful that although we are sinful by nature and limited in knowledge, You are willing to provide us guidance in the way we should go. Help us to resist every inclination to lose our fear of You.

April 25

MANNA SERIES: GLEANINGS FROM THE PSALMS
FEELING GOD-FORSAKEN? THERE'S COMFORT

Reading Passage: Psalm 22
Main Text: Psa. 22:1-2 My God, my God, why have you forsaken me?
Why are you so far from saving me,
So far from the words of my groaning?
O my God, I cry out by day, but you do not answer,
By night, and am not silent. (NIV)

The ultimate human state of despair is to feel forsaken by God. We can endure any adverse circumstance in life once we know we have hope of deliverance by a powerful, loving, supreme Being. But life becomes unbearable if it seems that there is no hope of help even from God.

David graphically described the adversity he faced, as being scorned by men and despised by people who mocked and hurled insults at him

(vv. 6-7). His enemies appeared like encircling strong bulls and roaring lions ready to destroy him (vv.12-13), while physically he was exhausted with his strength poured out like water and his bones out of joint (v.14). His enemies pierced his hands and feet (v.16), divided his garments and cast lots for them (v.18). To compound the suffering, when he called out he received no answer from God who seemed far from saving him. Understandably, he cried, "My God, why have you forsaken me?" After a while there was a change in David's circumstances and he realized he was not actually forsaken. In fact, he was able to celebrate that God "has not hidden His face, but has listened to his cry for help" (v.24).

On the cross, Jesus endured the extreme of human suffering as He bore the sin of all humanity. In describing what He endured, the gospel writers employed several lines from Psalm 22 to describe Jesus' agony. His suffering was climaxed with the cry of despair, "My God, my God, why have you forsaken me?" (Matt. 27:46 NIV). There is much we cannot understand in this mysterious cry. How can God forsake God? or the all-knowing God ask the question, Why? But we can learn from the agony of God the Son, that He experienced the ultimate of human suffering. Furthermore, unlike in David's experience, this was not a poetic imagined abandonment but a real experience by our Lord, which He suffered on account of our sins. On the cross there was an interruption in the eternal relationship between Father and Son so that the sin sacrifice could be offered and the penalty of sin of all humanity might be paid.

The Lord's suffering is a comfort to us when we go through our times of adversity. When we are under attack by enemies, or become physically exhausted, and feel God-forsaken, He knows how we feel because He experienced it. We have a God who can identify with us so He is able to comfort us. Moreover, He has paid the penalty for our sin, so we can be assured we will never actually be forsaken by our Father God.

Father, while we don't understand the mystery of Your divine nature and all that happened on the cross, we are comforted in knowing that You are personally acquainted with all our suffering, and that You have borne our sins. We are assured that once we are in Christ we can never be God-forsaken.

April 26

MANNA SERIES: GLEANINGS FROM THE PSALMS
THE WEIGHT OF WAITING

Reading Passage: Psalm 27
Main Text: Psa. 27:13-14 I am still confident of this:
I will see the goodness of the LORD
In the land of the living. Wait for the LORD;
Be strong and take heart and wait for the LORD. (NIV)

Waiting is not easy. The deadline approaches but no solution is in sight. I am in desperate need of help; I pray but there is no indication of an answer from God. Is it that God has forsaken me, or that my need is not significant to Him? The burden of the uncertainty of not knowing if or when He will respond is sometimes unbearable.

On the other hand, could it be that I am impatiently expecting God to respond according to my schedule, and in a manner according to my preference? My impatience could indicate my lack of trust in the Lord. We have to be so convinced that the Lord is our only means of direction and deliverance, and the very source of strength of our lives (27:1), that we become blinded to any alternatives to Him. This means we must remain confident in God even if the circumstances seem like they are about to destroy us, or we are forsaken by those on whom we normally rely, such as close friends. Our confidence is not in our predetermined solutions; our confidence is in the Lord.

David's prescription for dealing with the burden of waiting for a desired response is to worship the Lord for who He is. He says, "One thing I ask of the Lord, this is what I seek: that I may dwell in the house of the Lord ... to gaze upon the beauty of the Lord" (v. 4). When we begin to admire the beauty of His character, it changes our perspective of our troubles and of the power of the adversaries that oppose us. Worship causes us to be confident that we will see the goodness of the Lord in our circumstances; He will come through for us.

As a result, our hearts will gain strength, we will be relieved of the burden of the wait, and in fact we will begin to sing His praises while we are waiting.

Lord, please help us to worship You when anxiety and fear would overwhelm us because it seems You are delayed in delivering us. We want to be able to recall the beauty of Your character in Your past deliverances, so our confidence in You might be strengthened, in the name of our Great Savior, Amen.

April 27

MANNA SERIES: GLEANINGS FROM THE PSALMS
HE REWARDS OUR PRAISE

Reading Passage: Psalm 29
Main Text: Psa. 29:1-2 Ascribe to the LORD, O mighty ones,
Ascribe to the LORD glory and strength.
Ascribe to the LORD the glory due his name;
Worship the LORD in the splendor of his holiness. (NIV)

Praising the Lord is not flattery by which we insincerely exaggerate His attributes hoping this will lead to receiving blessings in return. It is useless to seek to bribe the God who knows our motives completely. Just as a woman reveals the level of her knowledge of fine art by her expressions of appreciation of a certain artist, our praises reveal our knowledge of God. We cannot sincerely praise beyond what we know and appreciate.

David in this psalm appeals to the sons of God (literal translation), who sometimes are identified as angels, but could also refer to anyone who truly knows Him, to ascribe glory to the Lord for His awesome works. We ascribe glory by speech and behavior. We talk with adoration about His accomplishments; we stand in awe as we consider His greatness. Once we know Him and have considered the awesomeness of our God, we respond with powerful, and sometimes conflicting emotions. There are times we erupt in verbal expressions of praise in songs or declarations, at other times we are silently "lost in wonder, love and praise."

David considered the power of God in a thunderstorm, which he refers to as "the voice of the Lord." He observed God's power as it thundered loudly across the Palestinian valley, as it stirred up the waters of the sea, as it destroyed the majestic cedar trees of Lebanon, as it shook the mountains, and sent lightning bolts into the forest. In awe at this demonstration, he said everyone in the temple responded with a shout of "Glory" (v.9). If we have seen and appreciated God's power in nature or in people's lives, we too will join in with shouts of "Glory!"

While we respond with expressions of praise in appreciation of who He is and not for reward, there is yet a reward to our praise. When we acknowledge the strength of the Lord, by glorifying Him, He in turn strengthens us and blesses us with peace (shalom) (v.11). It is as if the power we acknowledge in Him becomes appropriated to us; His glorious might in nature is made available to us. With our praise providing awareness and confirmation that He is able to do exceedingly abundantly above all we may ask or think, we receive strength to face any obstacle. Thus we have peace. Take the time to consider the greatness of God and praise Him today.

Father, what a lesson we have learned about the power of praise. We praise You not because You demand it or You are dependent on it, but because You are worthy of it. It is the "glory due to your name." May our praise properly indicate how much we appreciate You, and we look forward to Your strength and peace in return. May the name of Jesus be glorified, Amen.

April 28

MANNA SERIES: GLEANINGS FROM THE PSALMS
TAKING THE LORD'S FAVOR FOR GRANTED

Reading Passage: Psalm 30
Main Text: Psa. 30:6-7 When I felt secure, I said,
"I will never be shaken." O LORD, when you favored me,
You made my mountain stand firm;
But when you hid your face, I was dismayed. (NIV)

It is so easy to take the Lord's favor for granted. When we have no financial challenges, no breakdown in our relationships, and there are no medical complaints, we can be tempted to believe that we are entitled to a prosperous, problem-free life. David declared, "When things were going great I crowed, 'I've got it made'. " (v. 6, The Message Bible). At these times we are in danger of becoming self-centered, proudly thinking about what makes us so special, and not appreciating grace that provides favor at certain seasons.

The Lord knows when to strike the balance in our lives to keep us dependent on Him. He simply hides His face for a season. Suddenly, we discover that the season of prosperity was not permanent, and the favor was not because we were special. We can never fully appreciate the mountaintop of favor until we experience the valleys of despair. Our job situation has become tenuous, just when bills are escalating, or there are new worrying changes in our health, or friends we depended on are suddenly acting strangely. At such times we may experience a spiritual revival; God and prayer now become important, "To you, O LORD, I called; to the Lord I cried for mercy" (v. 8).

The unfavorable season is not to cause us to despair; instead it's for us to learn the lesson that God is faithful in all seasons of life. "Weeping may remain for a night, but rejoicing comes in the morning" (v. 5b). The season of adversity is not permanent. We will come out of adversity with greater appreciation for the Lord, who is in control of our lives. If our lives were merely subject to the randomness of fate, we would be unable to enjoy the seasons of prosperity. We would live with the fear of not knowing when the hand of fate will change our fortunes. But we trust the loving heart of our Father who controls the change of seasons for our good. When we understand this we can join David with the following celebration:

> You turned my wailing into dancing;
> You removed my sackcloth and clothed me with joy,
> That my heart may sing to you and not be silent.
> O LORD my God, I will give you thanks forever.
> (vv.11-12)

Lord, we are thankful that we are always in Your loving care whether we enjoy blessings or endure adversities. We trust You through the changing seasons of our lives, because You always know what is best for us. We remain dependent on You, in Jesus' name.

April 29

MANNA SERIES: GLEANINGS FROM THE PSALMS
THE BLESSINGS OF BEING UNMASKED

Reading Passage: Psalm 32
Main Text: Psa. 32:1-2 Blessed is he whose transgressions are forgiven,
Whose sins are covered. Blessed is the man
Whose sin the LORD does not count against him
And in whose spirit is no deceit. (NIV)

Silence about sin causes suffering. This is the lesson of Psalm 32, and we can confirm it from our own experiences. David wrote this psalm in the aftermath of being confronted about his sin of adultery and murder that ruined his relationship with the Lord and nearly destroyed his kingship. He described the physical torture and mental anguish he suffered during the time "he kept silent" concerning his sin (vv. 3-4).

The question facing us is: Why do we choose to keep silent about sin and suffer? The reality is, we are always seeking to project an image before people to protect our egos. So the king can't allow his subjects to know that he is a sinner, neither the parent before the children, or the pastor before the congregation, or friends before each other. To protect our image we wear masks so the real self will not be known. We avoid relationships where we may have to risk exposing ourselves. But while we are content that the world around us sees a false portrait because the flawed self is masked, we are suffering in silence. What is ironic is that since everyone plays the same game, we already suspect others of being as sinful as we are, and we keep waiting for an accident that will cause their masks to fall. Perhaps this explains the world's interest in tabloid news.

The Lord provided a path out of the misery of living falsely into the freedom of the blessed life. We begin by taking the step of removing the mask and acknowledging that we are sinners. He in turn covers our sin, forgives us (v.5), hides us (v.7), and instructs us on how to live (v.8). The problem in the Church is that we think this process occurred only when we initially trusted Christ for salvation, and so we try to disguise our continuous battle with sin by maintaining our masks. Our churches are filled with masked, suffering people who are too scared to let anyone know of their struggles.

The only solution to this problem is to continuously and deliberately practice removing our masks. When we practice being honest before God in prayer, it will become easier to be honest about our weaknesses before our families, and our fellow church members. We will then trust the Lord to keep covering and forgiving us, while transforming us. More importantly, we will experience the freedom of not worrying about the mask, and accepting the protection from the One who covers us. What a blessing!

Why should you continue suffering because of unconfessed sin, when you can enjoy the freedom of the blessed life because you have removed your masks?

Lord, help us to fight the temptation of making ourselves saints to impress people. Give us the courage to be honest as to who we are, so we can trust Your process of transformation. We thank You for your grace to do this, in Jesus' name.

April 30

MANNA SERIES: GLEANINGS FROM THE PSALMS
THE ESSENTIALS FOR LIFE

Reading Passage: Psalm 36
Main Text: Psa. 36:8-9 They (mankind) feast on the abundance of your house;
> You give them drink from your river of delights.
> For with you is the fountain of life;
> In your light we see light. (NIV)

When we think of the elements that are essential for physical life, water and light are usually included at the top of the list. There may be a greater debate over the essentials for the non-physical life. Some have argued convincingly that freedom and the pursuit of happiness must be near the top of any such list. In this psalm David provides his reasons why the only essential for life is a relationship with the Lord.

He identified the Lord as the God whose main characteristic is lovingkindness, which means He is bound by His nature to give love, mercy and goodness to those who are in relationship with Him. Imagine living with the fearful thought that the God who is in control of nature and the circumstances of our lives is against us or indifferent to what happens to us? With all the tragedies and dangers that surround us, life is only worth living when we believe it is undergirded by a loving God. We seek security against the uncertainties of life, and this is why mankind "finds refuge in the shadow of your (the Lord's) wings" (v. 7).

When we rely on God we obtain satisfaction and revelation - two essential elements for which He is the only true source. Our money, intellect and friends may provide resources on which we can draw, but they can never provide satisfaction (read the Ecclesiastes of King Solomon). On the other hand, God who works on us from the inside enables us to be satisfied as we feed on the abundance of His house, and drink from the river of His delights (v.8). We are able to lift our thoughts above the negative and mundane issues of our earthly circumstances and enjoy the delights of a heavenly perspective that He provides.

God also provides us with revelation, giving us understanding on how we should live. Where does the ungodly find guidance on how to live? They seek it from their own reasoning or from earthly 'experts' with limited knowledge. David argued that the heart of the ungodly is so sinful that it naturally pursues a path of transgression and wickedness (vv.1-3). In contrast, God provides us with 'light', which is instruction for our understanding and guidance for life. When He lives in us we no longer walk in the darkness of our sinful nature.

When we have the Lord, we are assured of divine love, spiritual water and light, which provide all we need for enjoyment and guidance for life. Nothing else matters. Do not attempt life's journey without the essential ingredient of a relationship with the Lord.

Lord, with the knowledge of this truth, we pray like David, continue to pour out Your lovingkindness upon those who know You (v.10).

May 1

MANNA SERIES: GLEANINGS FROM THE PSALMS
THE TRUE PATH OF LIFE

Reading Passage: Psalm 16
Main Text: Psa. 16:11 You have made known to me the path of life;
You will fill me with joy in your presence,
With eternal pleasures at your right hand. (NIV)

What is the true path of life - the lifestyle that we were designed to live that will result in true happiness and contentment? This is the question that has troubled humanity. The wealthy and successful end up wondering in frustration, "Is this all there is to life?" The poor and disenfranchised question which of their needs should be prioritized. Many religious people, after performing their routines, remain concerned whether they have accomplished anything worthwhile.

King David provides his answer to this crucial question based on his experience. He had achieved great military success; he had the wealth and power of the throne of Israel, yet he concluded that nothing in life compares with having access to the presence of the Lord. He regarded the presence of the Lord as a personal possession, in that he knew its location, was confident he could gain unlimited access when he so desired, and there was no restriction on how long he would be allowed to reside there. He states in verse 2: "You are my Lord, my only source of well being," and in vv. 5 and 6: "My choice is you, God, first and only. And now I find I'm your choice! You set me up with a house and yard. And then you made me your heir!" (The Message Bible).

David discovered this path of life was a contrast to the usual human path of death that ends with the body decaying in the grave (vv. 9-10). Possessing the presence of the Lord provides a future hope of resurrection that conquers death. In addition, it provides absolute joy in this life, and the assurance of eternal pleasure. This is the path of life, the way the Creator designed for us to live. Not surprisingly, David made every effort to obtain and maintain his portion of the presence of the Lord (cf. Psa. 27:4).

If the King had this passion, why are we so negligent in pursuing this path of life? We spend so much time and expend so much effort and expense pursuing alternate paths to fulfillment, joy and pleasure, only to end up frustrated. We will get to the stage of life where material things no longer bring us pleasure, or we may be unable to find human companionship that satisfies. Yet throughout all phases and changes we can be sustained, and we can enjoy the presence of the Lord. Let us learn from David's life and passionately pursue the true path of life.

Lord, we are thankful You did not leave us clueless as to how we were designed to live. Learning that the path to life is the Creator God himself, we are delighted and grateful You made Yourself available for our possession. We will passionately pursue You.

May 2

MANNA SERIES: GLEANINGS FROM THE PSALMS
DELIGHT DETERMINES DESIRE

Reading Passage: Psalm 37
Main Text: Psa. 37:4 Delight yourself in the LORD
And he will give you the desires of your heart. (NIV)

In popular culture we can quickly know the current pop idol by observing the fashion trends of the youth. Their desires in clothing and hairstyles reflect the style of the artist that provides them delight. As we discover in most areas of life, delight determines desire.

Today's text has been frequently quoted without the precondition "Delight yourself in the Lord." This misquotation results in the misinterpretation that God has provided a carte blanche promise to provide His children with whatever their hearts desire unconditionally. Such an application would be ridiculous for an earthly parent, and even more absurd for our Heavenly Father who desires to build character in His naturally lustful children. Our desires, influenced by the world, the flesh and the devil, are usually for material things that impress those around us, or the things that provide satisfaction to our appetites. When we delight ourselves in the Lord our desires are restricted and re-orientated to the things that please Him. When we ask, He is willing and eager to give us the things that are pleasing to Him.

We may be quick to dismiss the verse as not providing a useful promise for our lives in the real world, because it is restricted to those things that are pleasing to the Lord. But the things that are pleasing to the Lord include the virtues that are enduring, and that provide true pleasure in life. These include peace, joy, security and love. In the context of this psalm where David was contrasting the life status of the wicked with that of the righteous, he recognized the tendency for the righteous to envy the wicked, and fret about not matching their successes. He reassured the righteous that there was no need for worry or envy, since the prosperity and successes of the wicked are shallow and short-lived. In contrast, what the Lord provides is truly valuable and long lasting, allowing us to really enjoy our lives on earth. Wealth is useless if we can't live long enough to use it; having many possessions become redundant if our mental stress prevents us from enjoying them.

What is significant is that when we delight ourselves in the Lord, we lose the appetite for the things that are considered important in this world but are not truly valuable. So while we gain what the Lord provides, we do not feel we are losing anything the world offers. When we find ourselves concerned with the successes and possessions of the ungodly, this could indicate our need to assess our desires.

Are we delighting ourselves in the Lord?

Lord, help us to remember the contrast of lifestyles provided in this psalm. We seek to delight in You so our desires might be altered to those which are pleasing to You, for Jesus' sake.

May 3

MANNA SERIES: GLEANINGS FROM THE PSALMS
STEPPING WITH ASSURANCE

Reading Passage: Psalm 37
Main Text: Psa. 37:23-24 If the LORD delights in a man's way,
He makes his steps firm; though he stumbles, he will not fall,
For the LORD upholds him with his hand. (NIV)

The journey of life is sometimes like walking in a minefield, and trying to choose the correct path for our feet. We are surrounded by dangers and if we make a mistake in our steps we risk injury that may lead to our demise. We know of lives that have been destroyed by the wrong decision with respect to friendships (sometimes causing even guilt by association), marital partners, career moves, and even religious pursuits where people have ended up in cults. How can we step with assurance when the risks are so great and our knowledge so limited?

In this Psalm in which David contrasted the lifestyle of the righteous and the wicked, he highlights this benefit for the righteous: "When the Lord delights in someone's lifestyle, He makes his steps firm." This is a person who pursues a path of life that finds favor with the Lord, or whose behavior He finds commendable. As described by David, this righteous person will not have to worry or be tentative when he walks. Other Psalms describe people with firm steps as having feet like a deer so they can walk without difficulty on the dangerous high places (18:33); or feet that are enlarged under them to avoid slippage (18:36).

David portrays firm feet as those that may sometimes stumble; yet we will not fall because the Lord will intervene to uphold us with His supporting hand. Great security is provided to the righteous. Therefore, our focus should not be on the possible dangers that surround a decision we have to make; rather our focus should be on whether or not we are living in a way that pleases the Lord. Once we sense that we please Him, we can trust Him to guide us in our decision-making. In verse 4 of this Psalm, David states that when we delight ourselves in the Lord, He gives us the desires of our hearts. Here in verse 23, he explains that when the Lord delights in us, we will walk with assurance.

Lord, on the basis of this promise, I desire to live in a way that is pleasing to you, so you may order my steps. In the midst of the uncertainties and dangers we face daily, we want to walk with confidence knowing we have your support.

May 4

MANNA SERIES: GLEANINGS FROM THE PSALMS
MAXIMIZING LIMITED STAGE TIME

Reading Passage: Psalm 39
Main Text: Psa. 39:4 "Show me, O LORD, my life's end
And the number of my days;
Let me know how fleeting is my life." (NIV)

How differently would we live if we knew this was the last week of our lives? It is interesting to read about the lives of people on death row and how they prioritize their time. They have knowledge of their life's end, but no freedom to do as they wish in the remaining time.

On the other hand, we have freedom but no knowledge of the extent of our lives. We naturally try to live without thinking about the possibility of the end of life, perhaps because such morbid thoughts would diminish present enjoyment. However there are times we are shocked into the realization that 'this party' will end. Sometimes we are driven to these thoughts by the news of the sudden passing of an acquaintance in our age group, or by the sober reflection at a funeral service.

Sometimes we may be involved in an accident or a physical incident that reminds us of the fragility of life. We are then challenged by questions such as: "Does my accumulation of possessions reflect my status as a transient?" "Am I speaking words that I wish to be remembered by after I depart?" "Am I making the investment in the lives of people that represent a proper legacy of my contribution to their lives?" "Am I using all the gifts and talents supplied to me, to ensure they are exhausted in this life?" "Am I taking all the opportunities presented to me to enjoy God's creation, and the people around me?" "Am I taking all the necessary steps to add value to my life by gaining knowledge and improving my health?" "Am I investing in the future life by giving the proper attention to my spiritual life?"

These and many other similar questions take on greater significance when we recognize that we have limited time on the stage of life, and while we don't know when our act will end, we know we have been allotted only one scene. Let us adopt the life principle stated in the lines of the hymn, to "give every flying minute, something to keep in store. Work for the night is coming, when man works no more."

Father, our prayer is captured in the words of Psa. 90:12 "Teach us to number our days aright, that we may gain a heart of wisdom." Help us to live with the awareness that our days on earth are limited, so we will be careful not to waste the valuable hours allotted to us. This we ask in Jesus' precious name.

May 5

MANNA SERIES: GLEANINGS FROM THE PSALMS
RESPONDING TO TAUNTS ABOUT GOD

Reading Passage: Psalm 42
Main Text: Psa. 42:11 Why are you downcast, O my soul?
Why so disturbed within me? Put your hope in God,
For I will yet praise him, my Savior and my God. (NIV)

We are familiar with times in life when it seems that God has disappointed us because He has not delivered when we expected. We trusted Him when others were advising otherwise. We confidently boasted that we would not suffer loss or injury; our jobs would be secure; our children would be protected. We expected that our devotion to the Lord, our attendance at church, our diligence in paying our tithe, would provide us some insurance against the things that affect people who are not as devoted. But now, we are suffering and it appears that God is not even answering our requests for an explanation. To add to the pain, we have to listen to the taunts of others saying, "Where is the God in whom you trusted?" (vv. 3 &10) Honestly, we have to admit that our own souls have been asking the same question, and the disappointment is leading to depression.

In response to this internal turmoil, I need to have a conversation with my soul: "Why are you disturbed within me?" I must remind myself of the past faithfulness of God, the times He delivered me when my back was against the wall. I must remember the times when I used to celebrate with others the blessings of the Lord (v. 4). I may not be in the best state of mind (not in Mount Zion), but I can still reflect on the past goodness of the Lord while being in a less than ideal state (Mount Mizar) (v. 6). After spending this time in reflection, my hope in God is restored. If He was my helper in the past, I know He will help me again; if I enjoyed His presence in the past, I know I will enjoy His presence again. My present disappointment will be replaced by hope, "For I will yet praise Him, my Savior and my God."

Are you currently facing some disappointment that has made you think that God has abandoned you? This is the time to respond with reflection on God's past faithfulness.

Father, I don't want to be paralyzed by my present disappointment. Help me to take control of my thoughts and reflect on Your past goodness, so I will be able to respond to the taunts, externally and internally. You are still my Savior and God.

May 6

MANNA SERIES: GLEANINGS FROM THE PSALMS
OUR STRIVING PREVENTS US FROM RECOGNIZING HIM

Reading Passage: Psalm 46
Main Text: Psa. 46:10 "Be still, and know that I am God;
I will be exalted among the nations,
I will be exalted in the earth." (NIV)

Like a drowning man hopelessly thrashing about, expending his energy and not recognizing the attempts being made to rescue him, so we waste our time needlessly striving when we should be still.

There may be chaos around us similar to the scene described in the Psalm. The earthquakes are causing mountains to be moved out of their place, and the seas roar and foam (vv. 2–3). There is a dislodging and shifting of the things that previously seemed stable and dependable. The traditional values of the family, decent and honorable behavior in society, the status of the church, and the role of government, all seem to be tossed about by the eruption of "new philosophies."

The chaos is not only in nature but also in the peoples of the earth: "Nations are in an uproar, kingdoms fall" (v. 6). There are changes in the attitude of people around us; those who we thought were our supporters are now fighting against us. In the midst of the chaos we begin to wonder if God has lost control of the world. Since He is not doing anything, we surely have to do something. However, what we have discovered is that instead of solving the problems and bringing settlement to situations, our interventions have intensified the chaos, and our efforts have led to greater frustrations.

The solution is to be still, to cease our striving, and let go of our proud attempts to fix what is too big for us. When we stop striving we begin to recognize that God is still in control, "He lifts His voice and the earth melts" (v. 6b); "He makes wars to cease to the ends of the earth" (v. 9). He is the Creator God that brought order out of chaos in the Genesis; He is still able to use the chaos in society and in our lives for His own purpose and for our good. Let us cease panicking and doubting and recognize Him in the midst of the storm. Remember the waves are under His feet, and when He comes into 'our boat', the storm ceases (Mark 6:49-51). His challenge is not the chaos of the world; His challenge is us. Will we be still and trust Him? He will be exalted among the nations – the people who oppose us; He will be exalted in the earth – over every situation that opposes Him. God is our refuge and strength, therefore we will not fear the chaos (vv. 1-2).

> *Be still, my soul: Thy God doth undertake*
> *To guide the future as He has the past.*
> *Thy hope, thy confidence let nothing shake;*
> *All now mysterious shall be bright at last.*
> *Be still, my soul: The waves and winds still know*
> *His voice, who ruled them while He dwelt below.*

May 7

MANNA SERIES: GLEANINGS FROM THE PSALMS
HOW VALUABLE IS MY LIFE?

Reading Passage: Psalm 49
Main Text: Psa. 49:8-9 the ransom for a life is costly,
No payment is ever enough—that he should live on forever
And not see decay. (NIV)

The businessman was relieved when the police rescued him from his kidnappers, but became incensed when he learned the small amount of money that was being asked for his ransom. It is said that one of the greatest advantages of being a poor, unknown and insignificant person in society is that there is no need to fear being kidnapped.

While kidnappers may discriminate based on the money they hope to get as compensation for a victim, death does not discriminate. There is no difference between the death of the wealthy and intellectually brilliant, and that of the poor and illiterate. What is the price to redeem someone from the penalty of the grave? The Psalmist states that the ransom price is so costly, it is futile to even attempt to make a payment. Despite the futility, we keep trying to negotiate for a way to avoid the power of the grave because of our primal desire for a long life. Consider the state of denial people experience when a doctor informs them that their sickness is terminal, or the pleas to someone attempting to murder them.

The hope of resurrection is the priceless possession of the believer, when he or she can declare with confidence, "...but God will redeem my life from the grave; He will surely take me to Himself" (v. 15). Our faith is in the fact that we are so valuable to God individually that He paid the price to redeem us from the grave. He demonstrated the payment of the price when Jesus, the Son of God, gave His life on the cross as a redemption price for us. And He proved the power of His redemption when He rose from the dead, showing that the grip of the grave has been loosed.

The price of redemption was the same for the wealthy as for the poor, for the wise as for the simple. Since we are all equally valuable to God, we cannot discriminate. We must regard the lives of everyone with equal value. Since redemption was paid for us and we couldn't pay it ourselves, we cannot boast. Instead, let us be grateful to God who redeemed us.

Let us practice viewing our lives and the lives of others with the value that God has placed on us.

Lord, we thank You for redemption from the power of the grave, and for the hope we received by Jesus' resurrection. Help us to see people from Your perspective, with lives equally valuable to You, and needing to accept the redemption purchased for them.

May 8

MANNA SERIES: GLEANINGS FROM THE PSALMS
THE SACRIFICES THAT QUALIFY

Reading Passage: Psalm 50
Main Text: Psa. 50:5 "Gather to me my consecrated ones,
Who made a covenant with me by sacrifice." (NIV)

God's relationship with humanity is always based on a covenant. By the terms of the covenant, we know what God has committed to do for us, and what is expected of us. In the Old Testament, Israel's obligation under the covenant was illustrated by the various sacrifices that were offered at designated times, and these are detailed in the Book of Leviticus. These sacrifices were intended to represent the sincere desire of the people to approach a Holy God, hence, the sin or trespass offerings; or to express gratitude for the blessings provided by God, hence, the thanksgiving offerings.

What happened over time was that the sacrifices became an external routine without any genuine commitment in the heart of the people. Sacrificing became superficial. This is very similar to what frequently occurs in our Christian life. We attend church services, give offerings, and indulge in devotional exercises out of routine. We may go through the motions, but there is no giving of ourselves in heart and mind as an act of sincere sacrifice to God.

In this Psalm, God has to remind us that He doesn't really need the things we offer, "I have no need for a bull from your stall, or of goats from your pen." We need to remember that the time we think we are offering as a sacrifice to Him is time that He gives us; and the money we offer was provided by Him. Furthermore, as the all-knowing Judge, He sees our hearts and knows whether we are acting sincerely. What then are the acceptable sacrifices that make us qualified, so we may be identified as His covenant people in relationship with Him? He declares: "Sacrifice thank offerings to God, fulfill your vows to the Most High," (v. 14). Our offerings of thanksgiving, done with a sincere heart of gratitude indicate we appreciate that God has been good to us, and we do not deserve His favor. We pay our vows by our obedience to Him in recognition of His sovereignty over us. This is the sacrifice that pleases Him and brings His reward.

"He who sacrifices thank offerings honors me, and he
prepares the way
So that I may show him the salvation of God." (v. 23)

Does our worship consist of empty rituals that are performed outwardly without any sincere heart sacrifice? Let us ensure our sacrifices are expressions of gratitude acceptable by the One who is examining our hearts.

Lord, forgive us for taking You for granted and acting as if you should be satisfied with the scraps of our time and devotion. You deserve our best because You have given us Your best. We commit to renewing our covenant with You to serve You in sincerity and complete obedience, so that our sacrifices will be pleasing to You. Amen.

May 9

MANNA SERIES: GLEANINGS FROM THE PSALMS
THE REJOICING OF CRUSHED BONES

Reading Passage: Psalm 51
Main Text: Psa. 51:8 Let me hear joy and gladness;
Let the bones you have crushed rejoice. (NIV)

Several mental images are captured by the phrase 'crushed bones.' One is that of an overwhelming weight placed on the human frame that becomes unbearable, so the person lies broken under the weight. Another is of bones broken into fragments and scattered so that any hope of restoration of the order and structure seems lost. This must have been a description of David's feelings under the weight of guilt arising from his sin of adultery and murder. The mental pressure of knowing the hurt he caused the heart of God was unbearable. He was giving the impression on the outside that he was okay while on the inside he was in turmoil because of his deceit. This began to take a physical toll on him. He acknowledged his crushed condition and wondered if there was any hope of restoration

When we come to God in penitence and humility, we will always find the basis for hope because of His love and compassion. When we acknowledge our sin, ask for cleansing, and express a desire for a clean heart, God will respond with forgiveness. This forgiveness is not just a sterile legal act; it is a sense that God re-gathers the fragments of our lives that were scattered and disorganized because of sin. After repairing the damaged pieces of our lives, He provides the news that our sins have been forgiven and we are once more accepted in His presence, which is like music to our ears.

It is almost impossible to avoid an emotional response to the miracle of restoration. While tears of joy will flow, we discover that crushed bones begin to rejoice. David's desire for celebrating forgiveness is unmistakable in this psalm. "Let me hear joy and gladness" (v. 8), "restore to me the joy of your salvation" (v. 12), "my tongue will sing of your righteousness" (v. 14b). This begs the question: Why would anyone delay coming to the Lord for forgiveness to seek relief from the burden of guilt? Why would we allow our pride to confine us to the misery of crushed bones with a hopeless outlook?

Let us quickly turn to a merciful God for relief and restoration.

Father, we know You want us to be truthful and genuine in our inner lives, so help us to be honest before You. We don't want to be crushed by guilt. Instead we want to hear the joyful sound of forgiveness and acceptance. Keep us humble and open to the work of Your Spirit in us.

May 10

MANNA SERIES: GLEANINGS FROM THE PSALMS
AN INVITATION TO UNLOAD

Reading Passage: Psalm 55
Main Text: Psa. 55:22 Cast your cares on the LORD
And he will sustain you; he will never let the righteous fall.
(NIV)

She was mockingly called "Bundle" because she was always carrying a load on her shoulder as she went around begging on the streets. When the social services agency decided to relocate her from the streets to a shelter, their efforts to rid her of the bundle were met with violent resistance. What would cause someone to be so attached to dirty old towels and crumpled newspapers? Interestingly, we allow certain burdens in our lives to become bundles and ultimately they identify us. We carry around the burden of childhood abandonment, or maybe the effects of racial discrimination, sexual abuse, or betrayal by a romantic partner. These burdens then become crutches that define our lives; in effect they hamper our progress into new areas of exciting opportunities.

David had some hurtful experiences that scarred his life. In this Psalm he described the pressure he endured because of enemies who hated him (vv. 3-8). But what he found especially difficult to deal with was the fact that a friend with whom he had close fellowship and who accompanied him to worship had betrayed him (vv. 13-14). He risked letting this burden become his bundle. Instead he decided to pour out his burden to the Lord, and he trusted Him to hear his prayer, give him peace and deal with the problem (vv. 17-19).

Using his experience as an example, David exhorts us to "cast our burdens upon the Lord, and he will sustain us." The term "cast" also means to throw away, or to fling. The message is clear. Don't try to hang on to our burdens, or to just drop them within reach so we can recover them. Instead fling them on the Lord in such a way that we are completely divorced from them. When we follow these instructions we will experience His strength to lift us above the situation that created our burdens.

Are there burdens we are hanging on to that identify us? These may be matters that have been the subject of our prayers for years, always mentioned in most of our conversations, or have constantly affected our sleep. It is time to accept David's recommendation to unload these burdens on the Lord. We have His promise, " He will not permit the godly to slip and fall." (NLT)

Lord, there are some past hurts that have scarred us and we are struggling to rise above the people or the occasion that caused them. Give us the strength and the faith to cast those burdens on You, and grant us relief from these bundles that are hindering our lives. We trust Your promises, through Jesus Christ, Amen.

MANNA SERIES: GLEANINGS FROM THE PSALMS
PRAISE, IN SPITE OF ...

Reading Passage: Psalm 57
Main Text: Psa. 57:7 My heart is steadfast, O God, my heart is steadfast; I will sing and make music. (NIV)

If we are honest, there are times when praising the Lord seems justified, and other times when offering praise appears inappropriate, irrational and fanatical. It appears appropriate to praise the Lord when the sun is shining for our outdoor activities, when we feel healthy and mentally alert, when we have received notice of a big bonus at work, or the family is happy and successful. But what about the times when we are falsely accused; are harassed by haters; when we fail an exam or get fired from the job? This challenges us to consider the reasons for praising the Lord.

We praise Him not for what He does, but for who He is. Our adverse circumstances do not change His character or His worth. He is still worthy to be praised in spite of what happens to us, or how we feel.

David demonstrates how we should offer praise during the difficult times. In v. 4 he describes his circumstances as being in the midst of lions, and among ravenous beasts, and in v. 6 he explains that these enemies had set a net to trap him. But between these verses he paused to give praise, "Be exalted, O God above the heavens" (v. 5). The reason he could intersperse praise in the midst of his complaining was because his heart was steadfast, firmly established on the character of his God. Regardless of the malevolent plans of his enemies and his own misadventures, God's love is still great, reaching to the heavens, and His faithfulness to the skies (v. 10). Admittedly, it was not easy for David to shift his mind from his distress to consider the glory of God, but since his heart was steadfast, he willed himself to refocus: "Awake my soul, awake musical instruments," it is time to sing about our glorious Lord.

When we refocus and sing, our distress will diminish against the background of the might of our glorious Lord, and we will be lifted to a place of victory: "Be exalted, O God, above the heavens; let your glory be over all the earth" (v. 11). Like David, Job was able to bless the Lord, in spite of tremendous loss. The following verses from a song by Matt Redman captures the steadfast heart of Job, which should also be our determination

> Blessed be Your name
> On the road marked with suffering
> Though there's pain in the offering
> Blessed be Your name

Lord, we glory in You as Our Faithful God, who is unchangeable. We know You reign over our circumstances, and will provide us with relief from the things that cause us distress. Therefore we praise You in spite of our circumstances. Amen.

May 12

MANNA SERIES: GLEANINGS FROM THE PSALMS
GAINING A PASSION FOR GOD

Reading Passage: Psalm 63
Main Text: Psa. 63:2-4 I have seen you in the sanctuary
And beheld your power and your glory.
Because your love is better than life,
My lips will glorify you. I will praise you as long as I live,
And in your name I will lift up my hands. (NIV)

It is difficult to identify the triggers for certain passions in life. What causes someone to develop a passion for music, fine art or culinary skills, as against an interest in sports or mechanical things? What we do know is that we do not naturally develop a passion for God. In fact, we reluctantly acknowledge the existence of a supreme being who is in control of our lives, and to whom we owe worship. But when we have a genuine encounter with the Almighty and discover that He wants to have a love relationship with us, it is a transformative event. Following such an encounter, nothing else in the world is significant, because He becomes our consuming passion.

This was David's experience after he saw the Lord's power and glory in the sanctuary. We can't be sure what he saw or when, but it is apparent the experience so transformed his desires that he declared that having God's love was better than having life. David wrote this psalm while he was in the dry parched wilderness. Although he was thirsty, he found his desire for the presence of God, symbolized by the tabernacle with the ark, was greater than his physical desire for water.

We are blessed today in that the presence of God is not localized to a temple or church, because God as Spirit is always available to anyone who seeks Him. We can have an experience with the Holy Spirit that will fill us with an awareness of God's love. This love reveals our true identity in Christ and the meaning of life. Living becomes centered on our relationship with Jesus who is the essence of our lives. Paul recognized this when he declared, "For me, living means living for Christ, and dying is even better" (Phil 1:21 NLT).

Have we had an experience with God that has transformed our desires so we recognize Him as our supreme passion? When this happens, we will live a life of constant praise, "I will praise You as long as I live." Such a passion cannot be obtained by joining an organization, cannot be worked up by following a set of rules, or be developed by imitating anyone. It is the natural result of a personal experience with God. May we seek God for such a revelation of His power and glory that our desires will be permanently transformed, making Him our life's passion.

Father, You have promised to reward the diligent seeker. Please cause us to experience You, and to know Your love that is better than life. This is our prayer through Jesus Christ our Lord, Amen.

May 13

MANNA SERIES: GLEANINGS FROM THE PSALMS
WHERE WILL YOU RUN?

Reading Passage: Psalm 71
Main Text: Psa. 71:3 Be my rock of refuge,
To which I can always go;
Give the command to save me,
For you are my rock and my fortress. (NIV)

I observe the lizards moving around in the yard seeking food. They have no physical defenses against attacks by predators or fearful humans. To compensate for their vulnerability they use the rocks and foliage to provide shelter. Whenever they are in danger they quickly run to a place of refuge. Some even have the ability to change into the color of their surrounding as a camouflage.

The unknown author of this psalm was asking the Lord to be his refuge, and to be always available when he needs to escape. He acknowledged that he frequently faced various threats from enemies who were trying to destroy him. At those times he found the Lord to be his reliable defense. The Lord protected him when he was vulnerable at birth (v. 6). Now that he was facing the vulnerable stage of old age (vv. 9,18) he was asking the Lord to remain his refuge.

We can identify with the Psalmist's plea, for we have discovered that life is filled with various perils. Sometimes these are in the form of incapacitating illnesses, or they may appear as envious people who have become our enemies. At least these are discernible dangers that confront us. However, there are also spiritual attacks that are difficult to discern, which play havoc with our minds and our circumstances.

As we grow older, life itself becomes more burdensome with the deterioration of our bodies, the reduction in our resources and our need of assistance. In view of these challenges, where can we run to find reliable help and security? We observe many, who have no spiritual support, in despair because the things they previously relied on, like their investments or their associations, have become useless or unreliable. That's when we appreciate the privilege we have to be able to cry to the Lord like the Psalmist, "be my rock of refuge to which I can always run, be there to give the command to save me."

Do you have the Lord as your place of refuge? Assurance of this place of refuge depends on our relationship with Him.

Lord, we recognize our vulnerability in the challenges we face, so we admit our need of a refuge. We thank You for being always available as our rock and fortress. We hide in You in the midst of our storm, confident in the protection You provide. This is our prayer in the name of Jesus.

May 14

MANNA SERIES: GLEANINGS FROM THE PSALMS
RECOVERY FROM SLIPPAGE

Reading Passage: Psalm 73
Main Text: Psa. 73:2-3 But as for me, my feet had almost slipped;
I had nearly lost my foothold. For I envied the arrogant
When I saw the prosperity of the wicked. (NIV)

We usually have great difficulty avoiding the tendency to compare our lives with others. We can't help noticing the success or failures of our neighbors in accumulating assets, in receiving acclaim from the community, in raising their families, or even in establishing Christian ministries. The danger arises when we misuse the information gathered. Does it lead to pride in thinking we are better than others, or does it lead to envy, making us dissatisfied with what we have, and desiring what others have?

In Psalm 73, the Psalmist gives an honest account of his feelings when he observed the success and prosperity of some people he regarded as wicked. These people were arrogant and ungodly, yet they did not seem to suffer from health problems, or have any hardships, and they increased in wealth. When he compared their lives with his life of hardship and struggles, he admitted that he envied them. The more he considered the matter, the more it disturbed him. Perhaps he believed the popular doctrine that material prosperity must be the result of a life dedicated to the Lord. But what he was seeing contradicted this conviction.

Consequently, his "feet began to slip," – he was losing his spiritual stability. He was no longer sure of his faith concerning the goodness of God; he had doubts about the value of living a godly life. Why bother when there are no obvious rewards? This oppressive, miserable, doubting condition continued until he entered the "sanctuary of God;" a place signifying the presence of God. There he received a revelation on the true state of the ungodly, and the privilege of the godly. He learned that what we observe as the prosperity of the ungodly was just a temporary bloom God allowed them to have before He removed them in judgment (vv.18-19); whereas, the godly have the continuous presence of the Lord, His guidance in this life, and a place of honor afterward (v. 24).

What we learn from the Psalmist's experience is that we will always slip in our faith when we begin to envy the prosperity of others, because we will overestimate their blessings and underestimate our own. There is nothing in this life that can be compared with the privilege of having the presence of the Lord. What is the source of our discontentment? Do we feel God has failed to bless us as He should? Perhaps He is teaching us to learn to be content, knowing we have His presence and guidance in life.

Father, we are grateful to you for allowing us to recover from slippage in our faith by causing us to see how blessed we are to have Your presence. Instead of being distracted by the prosperity of others, we declare, "God has been good to us ... He is the strength of our hearts and our portion forever."

May 15

MANNA SERIES: GLEANINGS FROM THE PSALMS
WATER FROM UNEXPECTED SOURCES

Reading Passage: Psalm 78:1-20
Main Text: Psa. 78:15-16 He split the rocks in the desert
And gave them water as abundant as the seas;
He brought streams out of a rocky crag
And made water flow down like rivers. (NIV)

In this psalm, Asaph provided a review of the history of God's dealings with Israel. He was writing to a new generation that had come out of Babylonian captivity, and he wanted to ensure that they would not forget God's amazing miracles for the nation. One of the miracles mentioned was the provision of water out of a rock to satisfy the thirst of the multitude. Consider the facts surrounding this incident. A large number of Israelites, possibly in excess of 1,000,000 people, left Egypt to journey to Canaan. With water being so essential to life, there was no way they could survive for more than 2-3 days without it, yet they were traveling for 40 years. The multitude was traveling through a barren wilderness without any rivers and with very little rainfall. There seemed to be no possible human solution to this problem, and the Lord did not intervene until the people recognized their desperate situation and cried to Him.

God's response was to instruct Moses to strike a rock. It would have been plausible had God told Moses to dig in the sand and locate subterranean water that could possibly supply a well. However this would be useless for people on a journey. There is nothing about a rock in a wilderness that is remotely associated with water. Yet when Moses struck the rock, a stream of water gushed out and the people were able to drink abundantly. In addition, the water flowed like a river with an unlimited supply that ran in the direction of their path to Canaan (cf. 1Cor. 10: 4). It was continuously available as they journeyed. The water was from an unexpected source but was adequate for their needs and was sufficient for their journey.

Perhaps, we can recall times in our past when we were in desperate need of God's help. We saw no hope of financial assistance, no friend to provide comfort and companionship, or no medical relief for our sickness. But in response to our cry, the Lord intervened and provided our deliverance from some unexpected source that was adequate for our need and sufficient for our journey. Furthermore, when we realized our need of deliverance from sin, God intervened and provided personal salvation through His Son, our Savior Jesus Christ.

You may now be facing a problem for which you see no human solution. Don't despair; instead remember the past miracles when God provided you with 'water from unexpected sources.' He is awaiting your desperate cry to prove He is the same yesterday, today and forever.

Father, we realize that You bring us to the times when we are unable to help ourselves so we can put our trust in You. Help us to remember that You are God, and You are not restricted to normal resources or procedures. We can trust you for the unexpected, for the glory of Jesus, Amen.

May 16

MANNA SERIES: GLEANINGS FROM THE PSALMS
CAN THE LORD RELY ON US?

Reading Passage: Psalm 78:54-64
Main Text: Psa. 78:56 But they put God to the test
And rebelled against the Most High;
They did not keep his statutes.
Like their fathers they were disloyal and faithless,
As unreliable as a faulty bow. (NIV)

The archer identifies his prey, selects his arrow, takes aim and releases it. The arrow goes far off target, the prey escapes, and the archer is disappointed. The failure was not due to a lack of preparation by the archer or his lack of skill; the problem was the bow. It was faulty or unreliable. While it appeared to be straight and had a proper string, when put to the test, the archer discovered that it was not properly aligned, so it produced an inaccurate result.

The Psalmist, Asaph, used this analogy to describe the behavior of the Israelites. They were chosen by God to be His special people in the earth, and to represent His rulership. They were to be the means by which all other nations would be brought under the dominion of the Lord. Psalm 78 describes how the Lord redeemed the nation, guided them, and provided for them. Yet they failed to keep His covenant, and they pursued the gods of the surrounding heathen nations. God brought judgment on them by destroying all the older generation in the wilderness, and began to nurture the younger generation. He hoped they would learn from the tragedy of their fathers, and would be faithful to the Lord. But they proved to be just as unreliable as their fathers because they rebelled against the Most High.

Having been presented with this example in the life of Israel, we are challenged to examine our lives to see if the Lord can rely on us. Can He rely on us to provide an example to the world of how those He has blessed demonstrate their loyalty and gratitude? Or do we rather complain about what we do not have and where we think the Lord has failed us? Can He rely on us to witness to the world of the transforming power of salvation? Or do we live such inconsistently moral lives that they wonder if there is any value to salvation? Can He rely on us to use our resources to improve the lives of the poor and deprived, and fight for social justice for the disadvantaged and abused? Or do we join the crowd looking out only for ourselves and criticizing those who fail in the rat race of life?

The Lord has not discarded us because of our failures. He still desires to use us. We need to rededicate ourselves to Him in response to His mercy in forgiving us of our past failures, and His continued confidence in us.

Father, we desire to prove that Your confidence in us is not misplaced. Please help us to be reliable weapons in Your hands to accomplish Your purposes in the world.

May 17

MANNA SERIES: GLEANINGS FROM THE PSALMS
DON'T WASTE YOUR ADVERSITIES

Reading Passage: Psalm 84
Main Text: Psa. 84:6 As they pass through the Valley of Baca,
They make it a place of springs;
The autumn rains also cover it with pools. (NIV)

Life neither follows a straight path, nor consists of only one type of experience. It is a mixture of good times and bad, periods of prosperity and adversity. Usually we are so anxious to get past the hard times in our lives that we risk losing their lessons, and waste the opportunity of using them for our future development and the benefit of others.

In the beautiful lyrics of Psalm 84, the Psalmist describes the life of a Hebrew pilgrim who has a strong desire to attend the festival at the temple in Jerusalem. The journey takes him through the Valley of Baca before making the climb up the mount to Jerusalem. The valley was called Baca, which may be a name derived from the balsam trees located there. However, Baca may also be a reference to a derivative from the verb meaning to weep, which illustrates the sound made by the wind in the trees. While going through the place of weeping, the pilgrim begins to dig in the dry ground trying to locate a spring to provide water to sustain him on his journey.

This is a picture of life in the time of adversity when we encounter the hot winds of trouble and there is no one to provide refreshing words of comfort. At these times we should dig deep in our memories for the springs of the memorized words of God to inspire us, or recall the past experiences with God that can encourage us. Like the pilgrim we will discover that when we do the hard work of digging for springs in the valley, God responds by sending rain to fill the holes we have dug. There would be no spiritual refreshment from the Lord if we did not make the effort to seek divine help during our times of adversity.

After the pilgrim creates these pools of water, others following in that path will benefit from the water already provided. Similarly, the lessons we learn during our adversity will be useful to others facing similar adversities. Many have benefitted from the testimonies, songs and poems written by people who recorded the blessings they received during their times of trouble. David's psalms are examples of these.

What springs have you discovered during your period of pain? Are you leaving a testimony of these lessons for the benefit of those following your path? Let us not waste these times of adversity, as they may be the source of blessings to others following us.

Father, while we don't ask for times of trouble, we realize that You use these experiences to provide us with invaluable lessons for our lives. Help us not to forget these lessons, so we may use them for our future development and for the benefit of others.

May 18

MANNA SERIES: GLEANINGS FROM THE PSALMS
LEAVING A LEGACY THAT ENDURES

Reading Passage: Psalm 90
Main Text: Psa. 90:17 May the favor of the Lord our God rest upon us;
Establish the work of our hands for us—
Yes, establish the work of our hands. (NIV)

The tornado swept across Oklahoma destroying buildings, uprooting trees, destroying vehicles, and killing people. In minutes, things that took nearly a lifetime to acquire or develop were destroyed. At these times when everything seems so temporary, we wonder at the purpose and meaning of life. There is a Jewish saying that states, "Should a wise man wish to leave something that outlives him, he should have a son, write a book or plant a tree."

In Psalm 90, the author contemplates the brevity of life: "In the morning it springs up new, by evening it is dry and withered" (vv. 5-6). He states that man's normal lifespan is 70 years, which is sometimes extended to 80, but these quickly pass (v. 10). It is unsettling to think that once we pass age 35 we begin the descent toward the end of our normal lifespan. With such a limited time on earth, the Psalmist desires to make the best use of it, so he appeals to the Lord: "Teach us to consider our mortality so that we might live wisely" (v. 12).

Some people live to seek pleasure, fame or fortune for themselves. But they are left unfulfilled because we were all born with an innate desire for eternity. There is a basic instinct to produce something that will outlast us. This desire is sometimes expressed in the establishment of structures or institutions designed for permanence. However, in order to give meaning to our brief earthly life we should invest our lives in things that are in harmony with what God is doing in the world. Therefore, the Psalmist prays, "Let your deeds be shown to your servants" (v. 16).

When we join with what God is doing, we can be assured that these ventures will outlast us, because we are contributing to what the everlasting God will continue. Jesus advised, "Seek first the kingdom of God," because when everything else is destroyed His kingdom will continue. His kingdom work involves showing people the salvation that is in Jesus Christ, building up the spiritual lives of people, working at matters of social justice, bringing hope to the underprivileged, and spreading the love of God to those in need. When we work in these areas, we are assured the favor of God will rest on us, and He will confirm and make permanent "the work of our hands" (v. 17). In the busyness of our lives, are we ensuring that we leave a lasting legacy?

Father, please reveal to us what and where You desire us to work, and lead us to join in these programs, so You may establish the works of our hands, through the grace of our Lord Jesus.

May 19

MANNA SERIES: GLEANINGS FROM THE PSALMS
CHOOSING A SECURE REFUGE

Reading Passage: Psalm 91
Main Text: Psa. 91:1-2 He who dwells in the shelter of the Most High Will rest in the shadow of the Almighty. I will say of the LORD, "He is my refuge and my fortress, my God, in whom I trust." (NIV)

Living in a dangerous world in which we encounter various attacks on our bodies and our minds, we must be careful to choose a secure refuge. Our choice of a refuge will determine the level of protection we will enjoy. The author of Psalm 91 lived in a culture where people had several gods for various purposes, such as the provision of fertility, or victory in war. In verse 1 he introduced the theme of the psalm. Having chosen a place of shelter provided by "the Most High God," he discovered he was protected by the God who is Almighty, which means He has power over everything. To avoid any doubt regarding who his God was, the Psalmist identified his protector as "the Lord" or Yahweh, the God of Israel. The remainder of the psalm describes the level of protection provided by the Lord.

The lesson we learn from this psalm is that we may wisely select the best medical facility available and have the best health insurance policy, but these may not be sufficient to protect us from "deadly pestilence" that may invade our world. We may have the most robust burglar bars against our doors and windows, vicious attack dogs, and the most expensive alarm system on the house, but it may be useless against the "terror by night or the arrow that flies by day." The protection provided by the Lord, keeps the plague far from our dwellings, makes angels available to guard us in all our ways, and nullifies the attacks of the lion and the serpent.

Although the imagery employed in the psalm may appear exaggerated for effect, the lesson is clear: no natural security we may choose can be compared with the divine security provided by the Lord. We are left with the options: What will we choose? Where do we want to dwell? It is interesting to note that the term used for "shelter" in verse 1 also means "secret place" derived from the verb "to hide." We will never know the hiding place provided by the Lord until we are in an intimate relationship with Him. In this relationship, He leads us to the private, personal, "secret" place where we can find shelter, feel secure and know we are in His protective care.

Father, we are often tempted to rely on securities we can see, that appear reasonable to the human mind, yet we end up feeling insecure in them. Help us to be mindful of the lesson of this psalm so we will seek intimacy with You and discover the security that only You can provide.

May 20

MANNA SERIES: GLEANINGS FROM THE PSALMS
A CONDITION GOD WON'T CURE

Reading Passage: Psalm 95
Main Text: Psa. 95:6-8 Come, let us bow down in worship,
Let us kneel before the LORD our Maker;
For he is our God and we are the people of his pasture,
The flock under his care.
Today, if you hear his voice,
Do not harden your hearts as you did at Meribah,
As you did that day at Massah in the desert, (NIV)

God revealed Himself to the Israelites as the Almighty God by the performance of many miracles that demonstrated His power over nature, demons and diseases. He began these demonstrations through Moses before Pharaoh and the Egyptians. After the death of their firstborn sons, the Egyptians released the enslaved Israelites so they could depart to the Promised Land. Later, the Lord made a path for them through the Red Sea, while the Egyptian army was drowned when they attempted to follow in pursuit. The Lord further revealed His miraculous power by providing daily manna for them in the wilderness. The Israelites were the sheep of His pasture and He cared for them in a powerful way.

Yet despite all they had seen and experienced, when they were without water on two occasions (at the beginning of the journey Ex.17:1-7, and at the border of Canaan Num. 20:1-13) they were angry with God, and wished they were back in Egypt. The Lord referred to these incidents as

Meribah, meaning place of strife, and Massah, meaning place of testing. What these incidents revealed was that the miracles the Israelites saw were ineffective in moving their hearts to a state of believing in God. They refused to believe God because their hearts were hardened.

The Psalmist wrote these words as a warning to a new generation so they would not harden their hearts as their ancestors did. God created humans with a free will that He refuses to violate. When people determine not to believe God despite the evidence provided, this is a condition He will not cure. We must freely respond to His care and goodness by acknowledging that the Lord is our maker and we are the people of His care. Regardless of the difficulties of our circumstances, let us never fail to worship and acknowledge His supremacy so we will avoid a heart of unbelief. The more we question His goodness and rebel against His authority over our lives, is the more we begin to develop the condition of unbelief. God speaks to us through His amazing miracles, and He also speaks through our difficulties and deprivations. The question is: Are we listening or rebelling?

May we always be responsive to His voice, as sheep to the shepherd's voice. We don't want to strive against, or test our Lord.

Father, we acknowledge the times when we have murmured and complained because You did not give us what we desired, or You allowed conditions we did not like. Please forgive our petulance and rebellion. You are still our Lord, and our hearts are open to Your voice.

May 21

MANNA SERIES: GLEANINGS FROM THE PSALMS
YOUR ORIGIN SHOULD
INDICATE YOUR OWNER

Reading Passage: Psalm 100
Main Text: Psa. 100:3 Know that the LORD is God.
　　　　It is he who made us, and we are his;
　　　　We are his people, the sheep of his pasture. (NIV)

The recognition of our origin is not an insignificant matter. In the biological realm, identifying one's parents provides genetic information that indicates possible predisposition to illnesses. In the social realm the environment in which we were nurtured establishes the base from which we develop our educational and religious values. There have been various theories or convictions on the origin of human life, and these have a significant influence on how mankind views the worth, accountability and the destiny of life.

Some believe that human life is an accident of nature, the result of random events that led to an evolutionary process by which the superior specie survived. With such a view, there cannot be any authority source outside of ourselves who determines our existence, to whom we are accountable, and whom we should worship. For these people, the path of life is based on self-determination; and morals are limited to what is suitable for their own pleasure and survival without causing harm to others. Since this is the philosophy of so many in the secular world, it is not surprising they view religion as primitive practices by undeveloped people.

The Psalmist declares to Israel, there is a God who is the Lord, and it is He who made us. We are not the result of an accident of nature, nor of any evolutionary process. Our Lord determined when, where and how we would exist, so He owns us. "We are His people, the sheep of His pasture." Consequently, we are accountable to Him for what we do with our lives, and we are obligated to worship Him because He made us to fulfill His purpose and pleasure. With this perspective, the main goal of our lives is to ensure that we are fully acquainted with our Maker, and we should seek to fulfill His purpose for us. In so doing, we will discover that the Lord is good, His love endures forever, and His faithfulness continues through all generations. He is worthy to be praised.

Have you acknowledged the Lord as your Maker and your God?

Lord, we are so thankful that a good and loving God owns us, and that our lives are not subject to the randomness of fate. We joyfully praise and worship You as our God.

May 22

MANNA SERIES: GLEANINGS FROM THE PSALMS
GRATEFUL FOR AN UNFAIR REWARD

Reading Passage: Psalm 103
Main Text: Psa. 103:9-10 He does not always accuse,
And does not stay angry.
He does not deal with us as our sins deserve;
He does not repay us as our misdeeds deserve. (NIV)

We are usually sensitive to unfair treatment. We are often quick to request compensation when our rewards are less than our efforts deserve, especially in comparison to rewards given to others. But with respect to our sins we should be grateful we are not rewarded according to what we deserve. First, we need to appreciate that sins are not merely actions and attitudes against our fellow humans. All sins are violations of God's righteous standards and a rejection of His rule over our lives. Therefore, all sins deserve to be punished by death, which is separation from God ("the wages of sin is death..." Rom 6:23).

Although we may suffer many natural and legal consequences for our sinful acts, our immediate punishment is never rejection by God. He is always available to hear our prayers of repentance, and He remains ready to receive us when we turn to Him. Because of this access to God, our punishment is less than we deserve. To atone for sin, even the smallest act of sin, it required the sacrifice of the Son of God on the cross. His suffering on the cross when He was identified with our sin resulted in a brief separation from His Father.

When we receive a punishment less than we deserve, we experience God's mercy whereby He withholds the full extent of His wrath in dealing with us. God gave the first indication of His mercy when Cain, of the first generation of sinners, killed His brother Abel. God declared His judgment against Cain, which included his being cast out from the presence of God. This caused Cain to protest that the punishment was too great. God responded with mercy by placing a mark on Cain to protect him from attack by enemies that he deserved (Gen 4:10-15).

The Psalmist, in response to the mercy of God, blessed the Lord ....

"Who forgives his sins, heals his body and delivers his life from the pit" (vv. 3-4). Because of His mercy, the Lord does not always accuse us, although we have done things worthy of accusation. He does not remain angry with us even when our behavior should keep Him angry. Owing to His great mercy, we can honestly acknowledge that we have not been punished to the extent that our sins deserve.

At those times when we are tempted to complain that the Lord has not given us blessings we expected, let us take a moment to think how He has not punished us as we deserved. This should lead us to praise Him for His mercies.

Lord, we are grateful for Your mercy in not rewarding us according to our sins. Like the Psalmist we say, "Bless the Lord, O my soul and all that is within me bless His holy name."

May 23

MANNA SERIES: GLEANINGS FROM THE PSALMS
FACING THE REALITY OF OUR FRAME

Reading Passage: Psalm 103
Main Text: Psa. 103:13-14 As a father has compassion on his children,
So the LORD has compassion on those who fear him;
For he knows how we are formed,
He remembers that we are dust. (NIV)

People who exhibit certain behaviors, traits or characteristics are often uniquely described. The late British Prime Minister, Margaret Thatcher, was described as the Iron Lady because of her toughness in dealing with the Russians and the British unions. The late United States president, Ronald Reagan, was described as the Teflon president because he gave the appearance of not being affected by various accusations leveled against his administration.

We are very conscious of the public perception of our character or our moral fiber, so we strive to give the impression that we are stronger than we really are. In our pride we resist any inclination to disclose our internal struggles with purity, honesty and truth. The strain of maintaining this public image sometimes can be overwhelming, and we long for a time and place where we can be open and honest with our failures, our struggles and our doubts. Unfortunately, we rarely can find such a safe place, even among fellow struggling believers. However, we are assured we will always find a safe retreat when we come to the Lord in humble prayer.

The Psalmist described our relationship to the Lord as one where we come before a Father who cares about His children. Rather than being punitive with His children because of their failures, our Father, with compassion, seeks to correct and restore them. The reason our Father can be so compassionate is that He knows what we are made of, since He was the One who made us. He created us from dirt. Regardless of how much we have developed physically, with strong muscles and beautiful skin, and have adorned ourselves with lovely clothes to cover our frame, yet at the core we are still dust. Others may admire us as being outstanding persons with great personality, but when the external pressure becomes too great, the internal, unseen dirt frame is at risk of crumbling. No one may understand us at such times except the Father who knows us intimately.

Those around us may forget we are human by the way they abuse us or take us for granted. We may forget our weaknesses by accepting more responsibilities than we are capable of fulfilling. But may we never forget that we have a compassionate Father who remembers who we really are, and He is willing to forgive, to refresh and strengthen us. With the assurance of His love, let us confidently seek the security of His presence through prayer.

Father, we look to You at this time when we find the pressures of life too great for us. Please send Your angels to minister to us so we can face the tasks before us today with Your divine strength. This we pray in Jesus' name, Amen.

May 24

MANNA SERIES: GLEANINGS FROM THE PSALMS
APPRECIATING THE BOUNDARIES

Reading Passage: Psalm 104:1-26
Main Text: Psa. 104:7 But at your rebuke the waters fled,
At the sound of your thunder they took to flight;
They flowed over the mountains,

They went down into the valleys,
To the place you assigned for them.
You set a boundary they cannot cross;
Never again will they cover the earth. (NIV)

Standing on the shore of a popular surfing beach, we observed large powerful waves approaching the land. Just when we thought the water would come ashore and wreak havoc, it suddenly lost its power, became a mild current against the beach and quickly returned to the sea. What caused the dramatic change from the state of potential destruction? The Psalmist, recalling the story of the Noahic flood when the waters covered the land, explained that God rebuked the waters so they returned to the place assigned for them. Then He set a boundary they cannot cross. Regardless of the power and hostility of the waves of the sea, when they come to the boundary they subside and become a mild current.

While some may provide a geophysical explanation for this marvelous occurrence, we can recognize a spiritual parallel in our lives. We are under the constant threat of Satanic and natural forces that appear designed to wreak havoc in our lives. These may be manifested in a sequence of adverse events, physical illnesses or mental harassment. Just when we think we cannot survive the assault, suddenly we experience the subsiding of the adversity, and we are now able to deal with the minimized challenges. Then we realize that there was a boundary set around our lives that the large waves of adversity could not cross, because the Master had 'rebuked the waters.'

Sometimes we experience the same struggle that Jesus' disciples experienced when their boat was in the stormy sea and they were convinced they would perish. Can we believe that God is in charge of the elements of our lives and that He has set a boundary, which they cannot cross? When He is ready He will command the storm to cease, and there will be a calm. What storms and waves are you facing today? Remember that even Satan is under God's command and he has to obtain God's permission to cross the boundary (cf. Job 1:6-12).

Let us not be anxious or fearful despite the intense appearance of the assault against us; remember that our Lord is in control of the elements that come against us.

Father, we admit our fears when facing seemingly uncontrollable, powerful circumstances that can devastate us. Grant us the faith to believe that You are in control of all circumstances and You have set a boundary they cannot cross to harm us. For this we are grateful.

May 25

OBSERVING GOD'S WISDOM IN HIS WORKS

Reading Passage: Psalm 104:1-31
Main Text: Psa. 104:24 How many are your works, O LORD!
In wisdom you made them all;
The earth is full of your creatures. (NIV)

Observing the wonders of Earth, the Psalmist concluded that the planet is full of creatures God has made, and He exhibited great skill in making them. He noticed the vast number and variety of the creatures, and the way in which they were beautifully adapted to their physical environment.

He further noticed the provision made for their sustenance and the fact that their ultimate dependency is on their Creator. God causes streams to flow in the valleys so the animals in the field, and the wild donkeys can quench their thirst. He sends rain for the growth of the cedars He planted in Lebanon, which allows the birds to make their nests in them. He even causes nights to be dark, so beasts of the field may prowl around seeking for their food. But they sleep in the day when man goes to work. The message of the Psalm is that God cares for His creatures and they all wait on Him to provide food as required (v. 28).

Neither our existence nor the environment we are placed in, is accidental. God designed us for our location and will ensure the availability and adequacy of our provision there. The difference between us and the animals is, whereas they depend on God without worry or complaint, we, the "superior beings" consider ourselves independent of God, and end up worrying and complaining. When God looks down on the splendor of His creation, He longs to find pleasure in the things He made (v. 31). Do we provide the Lord with pleasure by the way we respond to Him?

The Psalmist resolved that his life would not fail to provide the Lord with pleasure. So he declared:

I will sing to the LORD all my life;
I will sing praise to my God as long as I live.
May my meditation be pleasing to Him,
As I rejoice in the LORD. (vv. 33-34 NIV)

Does your life provide pleasure for the Lord, or does He only hear grumbling and complaints from you?

Father, when I consider how fearfully and wonderfully I have been made, and the way You have provided for me, I want to give You pleasure. I pray that my complaining will be replaced with a song that will celebrate You, for the glory of Your great name.

May 26

MANNA SERIES: GLEANINGS FROM THE PSALMS
GOD'S PUZZLING PATH TO DELIVERANCE

Reading Passage: Psalm 105:23-38
Main Text: Psa. 105:24-25 The LORD made his people very fruitful;
He made them too numerous for their foes,
Whose hearts he turned to hate his people,
To conspire against his servants. (NIV)

When we attempt to interpret our immediate circumstances without considering God's overall plan for our lives, we will always have difficulty understanding God's purpose in these circumstances.

The experience of the Israelites in Egypt vividly illustrates this point. God told them that Canaan was their promised land, yet He caused them to dwell in Egypt for 400 years. The length of their residency in Egypt, and the fact that they became prosperous and powerful caused them to lose sight of God's original plan. New generations came along who no longer thought about Canaan; instead they considered Egypt home. They thought that if God made them so comfortable and successful, He must have changed His plan for them. Afterwards, God caused the Egyptians to hate the Israelites, and the prosperous people became extremely uncomfortable.

With this change in their circumstances, they could not understand why God did not protect and defend them from the hardship inflicted by the Egyptians. It was puzzling that God authorized both their prosperity and their adversity. God used the adversity as an opportunity to arrange their deliverance from Egypt so they could proceed to their destiny (v. 37).

Our challenge is to avoid thinking that the prosperity and success we currently enjoy indicates that we have arrived at our destination in life, or that God has ordained this as our permanent status. We must never misunderstand that our experiences in this life are preparation for a bigger purpose: to be transformed in order to represent Christ. When circumstances change and we are hated and become uncomfortable, we must believe that God has not abandoned us. He causes the change to keep us from becoming complacent and missing His plan for our lives.

If you are facing adversity today, don't despair. Your adversity may be God's way of arranging for your deliverance into your destiny. Let us enjoy the good times and be hopeful in the bad times, but remember God has allowed these circumstances as stages in His overall plan for our lives.

Father, we need Your grace to keep our focus in every state of our lives so we will clearly see Your hand and Your purpose behind all our circumstances. We desire to fulfill the goal that Christ be manifested in our lives, for the glory of Jesus, Amen.

May 27

MANNA SERIES: GLEANINGS FROM THE PSALMS
APPRECIATION LEADS TO OBLIGATION

Reading Passage: Psalm 116
Main Text: Psa. 116:12 How can I repay the LORD
For all his goodness to me?
I will lift up the cup of salvation
And call on the name of the LORD. (NIV)

How much do we appreciate many of the blessings we receive from the Lord? Oftentimes, it takes a crisis in our lives to jolt us to the realization that we are enjoying blessings for which we never paused to express appreciation. Multiple times daily we go through the process of desiring food, enjoying the taste, digesting, and excreting the waste matter. When an illness disrupts any of these functions, we suddenly begin to value what we previously took for granted. We appreciate the sun much more after a long dark winter; and acknowledge the joy of life after a near death experience. Once we realize the blessings we enjoy are God's acts of kindness to us, which we did not deserve, we instinctively know we should offer a response. What is the appropriate response to the Lord for these blessings?

The Psalmist had been delivered from death, his eyes from tears, and his feet from stumbling (116:8). His question was, "How can I repay the Lord?" He resolved to celebrate his deliverance, and fulfill publicly everything he promised God he would do.

When we recognize some blessing we previously overlooked, do we stop to celebrate our Lord with thanksgiving? We will have very little to complain about when we begin to count our blessings and "call upon the name of the Lord." This goes beyond the brief, sometimes thoughtless "grace" before a meal. The Psalmist's other resolution recognizes that while in a crisis, we tend to make promises to the Lord: "If you will heal my body, or give me the job, or bring my child back home, I will...." After the crisis, when life returns to normality, we often forget the promises made to the Lord. The Psalmist resolved to pay these obligations publicly so others would hold him accountable, and they would also learn to be faithful in keeping their promises to the Lord.

While God's love is not conditioned on our faithfulness in showing our appreciation, He still looks for hearts that demonstrate gratitude. Jesus keeps asking, "Were not all ten cleansed? Where are the other nine?" (Luke 17:17)

Father, we confess that we sometimes overlook the many blessing we enjoy and focus instead on benefits we think we are missing. This causes us to fail to fulfill our obligations to You. Help us to be aware that You are waiting for us to express our gratitude as a demonstration of our appreciation.

May 28

MANNA SERIES: GLEANINGS FROM THE PSALMS
HELP! MY EYES ARE FAILING ME

Reading Passage: Psalm 119:17-24
Main Text: Psa. 119:18 Open my eyes that I may see
Wonderful things in your law
Psa. 119:37 Turn my eyes away from worthless things;
Preserve my life according to your word. (NIV)

What we focus on determines how we live. Unfortunately our eyes are prone to observing and appreciating vanity, things that have no worth, and making these the pursuit of our lives. Solomon, in the Book of Ecclesiastes, takes us on his reflective journey as he searched for meaning in life. After pursuing pleasure, wealth, and success, he was disappointed and declared these things made life empty. The first humans in the Genesis story were deceived when they followed what their eyes observed as being good for making them wise, and providing them with divine powers. Similarly, our eyes can lead us astray. This explains the Psalmist's plea in the verses of the text. In 119:37 he begged the Lord: "Turn away my eyes from vanity (worthless things)," and in 119:18 he pleaded: "Open my eyes to see wonderful thing in your law." Because our eyes are mis-focused and unreliable, we need the Lord to fix them.

First, we need the Lord to keep our eyes from looking at his Word as something that is archaic and irrelevant to our lives in the 21st century. We should stop regarding Scripture as just another book of philosophy or just interesting literature. Rather we need to see it as representing the very wisdom of God, containing the power to transform the lives of anyone who believes it, and to condemn those who reject it (Heb. 4:12). Secondly, our eyes need to be able to discern things such as popularity, power and materialism that are so appealing in our world, as being ultimately worthless. Just as we would reject fake jewelry that soon loses its appeal, we need to be able to turn away from false values. Instead, we need God to help us to turn our eyes to the Word of God, which has the power to preserve our lives.

We will never make this petition until we appreciate the great danger in trying to depend on eyes that are mis-focused and unreliable.

Lord, we don't want to be like Solomon and get near to the end of our time before realizing we spent our lives pursuing vanity. We want to live with the wisdom, power and discernment that can only be obtained through Your Word. So please open and refocus our eyes, through the mercy of our Redeemer, Jesus Christ.

May 29

MANNA SERIES: GLEANINGS FROM THE PSALMS
LESSONS LEARNED THE HARD WAY

Reading Passage: Psalm 119:65-72
Main Text: Psa. 119:67 Before I was afflicted I went astray,
But now I obey your word.
Psa. 119: 71 It was good for me to be afflicted
So that I might learn your decrees. (NIV)

My parents disagreed with my decision and warned me of the consequences, but I wanted to determine my own path. After all, what do they know? I can think for myself and I know what is best for me. By rejecting their advice, I disregarded the benefit of their own painful experience and chose to repeat their failures before gaining the lessons they learned. How unfortunate, that we do not gain many lessons in life by humbly heeding instruction. Instead, these lessons have to be etched into our consciousness by painful experiences.

The Psalmist explained that we respond to God's instructions in the same way we responded to our parents' instructions. He states that before he was disciplined by a painful experience, he wandered astray; but "now I follow instructions" (119:67). This is the sort of training commonly used on animals, like the case of a shepherd who has to break the leg of a sheep who rebels against instruction. When the pain is over and the discipline is established, we no longer have a problem obediently following instructions. Maybe it took the hardship of being without food and shelter, abuse by a "so-called" friend or partner, or a terrible illness, to finally break our rebellion, counteract our pride, and cause us to learn the instructions of the Lord.

We now begin to appreciate that the instructions were not intended to deprive us of excitement or pleasure; rather they were intended to keep us from permanent harm. It was the fatherly love of the Lord that made Him discipline us and inflict pain, "because the Lord disciplines those he loves" (Heb. 12:6 NIV). We know we have matured in God when we can view the discipline of the Lord with gratitude, and say "it was good for me to be afflicted." It was through the affliction that we appreciated the wisdom of God's instructions, realized how proud and foolish we were, and learned how much the Lord loved us.

Are you enduring some painful experience today? Don't miss the lessons that we can learn through pain and sorrow. One day we may be able to look back with appreciation on these experiences.

Father, we thank You for your plan for our lives and the patience you demonstrated in redeeming us from our rebellion. We now celebrate Your laws and declare that they are precious to us, and we love them.

May 30

MANNA SERIES: GLEANINGS FROM THE PSALMS
CHOOSING THE BEST LIFE PRESERVER

Reading Passage: Psalm 121
Main Text: Psa. 121:7 The LORD will keep you from all harm—
He will watch over your life;
The LORD will watch over your coming and going
Both now and forevermore. (NIV)

We were discussing items vandalized at the swimming pool and the high cost of replacing the life preserver. Someone suggested we could purchase a discounted but inferior brand, which would result in some savings for the budget. I couldn't help wondering about the risk people will take by not choosing the best means of preserving themselves from the uncertainties of life.

This might have been the thought occupying the mind of the Psalmist as he journeyed with Jews from various regions of Judea on a pilgrimage to Jerusalem for one of the religious celebrations. As they approached their destination, their eyes were focused on the hills of Zion. These Jewish pilgrims believed that the desire to worship at this location mysteriously provided them with protection, collectively and personally, as they faced the dangers of pilgrimage. After stating, "I lift up my eyes to the hills," he asked the question, "Where does my help come from?" (v. 1).

Did they receive divine help because of a religious exercise, or by being in a religious location? These visible practices and symbols often have useful value, but only to the extent that they aid us in getting to the real source. Unfortunately, many people settle for the religious symbols: a church membership, a cross pendant, "special" water or oils, a strategically placed, unread Bible, or their preference for gospel music. When we focus on the 'hills' without finding the Source, we are settling for the inferior item. We want to avoid the price of the authentic product, which is the cost of a relationship with God.

Our help does not come from a place, but from a person. The Lord made the heaven and the earth, including the hills. He is such a diligent guide that He takes no rest from the task of preserving us from dangerous falls. He personally becomes our protection from the heat of the sun by day, or the dangers associated with the night. He watches over our lives whether we are coming home, or going out, leaving the safety of home. He is the best life preserver and He is the One who watches over my life, keeping me from all harm.

What are you looking at as your life preserver? Are you looking to the Source, or taking a risk by depending on a bargain substitute?

Lord, I am glad for the faith that allows me to know with assurance where my help comes from. My trust is not in earthly defenses, religious practices, medical science or governmental power. My help comes from You, the Source of my security.

MANNA SERIES: GLEANINGS FROM THE PSALMS
AVOIDING FAMILY LIFE FUTILITY

Reading Passage: Psalm 127
Main Text: Psa. 127:1 Unless the LORD builds the house,
Its builders labor in vain.
Unless the LORD watches over the city,
The watchmen stand guard in vain. (NIV)

A house under construction provides a good illustration of a project that should not be attempted by a novice, without seeking professional advice. We have heard the complaints of many who were excited at the prospect; they began the project with great enthusiasm, only to end up with disastrous results. Poorly prepared building plans, underestimated costs, and/or dishonest, inefficient workmen, ultimately lead to unforeseen problems and costs. The solution needed to avoid the futility and frustration of a botched construction project is to rely on experts who, by education and experience, provide the necessary guidance and assistance.

Who can provide the expertise for the development of a family? This requires someone who knows the nature of the various members, the challenges that they will face in life, and the resources necessary for their development and protection. The Psalmist declares that only the Lord is qualified to meet this need. And if He is not involved in the development of the family, we all are working in vain. We may invest time, finances and emotional resources in the family, but these are useless without the Lord's involvement. With the Lord's help, we will be able to develop the family without being overworked and over-stressed.

Because we are depending on Him, He allows us to rest while He supplies the resources we are unable to supply. We are too ignorant of the strategies planned against our families by the enemy to be able to successfully protect them by our own efforts. The alternative is to leave the watchman duties to the Lord who is more powerful than any enemy, and who is always on guard. When we do this, we are able to rest while relying on His care and abilities. Unfortunately, we tend to take on responsibilities for which we are not qualified and perform family duties that will end up in futility, while we ignore the help that the Lord is willing and able to provide. Since our offspring are a heritage from the Lord, we can trust Him to care for those He has entrusted to us.

Are you feeling stressed trying to build family life? Why not trust the promises of the Lord to help you in the building-project of the lives of our families?

Father, we realize that our problem is that we think we are wise and strong enough so we can replace You. Help us not to wait until we are frustrated by the mess we have made, in attempting to develop the family, before seeking Your help. This we pray in the name of our Lord Jesus Christ.

June 1

MANNA SERIES: DEVELOPING MOUTH CONTROL
MALADIES REVEALED BY THE MOUTH

Reading Passage: Luke 6:39-45
Main Text: Luke 6:45 The good man brings good things out of the good stored up in his heart, and the evil man brings evil things out of the evil stored up in his heart. For out of the overflow of his heart his mouth speaks. (NIV)

"Many sicknesses in the body are manifested in the mouth." I was surprised when I heard this statement from my dentist as he was examining, not just my teeth, but also various areas of my mouth. He continued to explain that his examinations have resulted in the confirmation of systemic diseases (e.g. cancer) in some of his patients. I could not help seeing the parallel application of this statement in the realm of our spiritual life and behavior.

In this series of "Developing Mouth Control", we will observe that the reason the mouth is a critical organ for revealing the spiritual and moral health of a person, is that the mouth gives outward expression to the hidden inner life. The biblical term for describing the inner life is 'heart,' meaning the central core of a person. What Jesus explains in our text today is that, who people are, whether good or evil, is reflective of what they keep stored in their hearts. What is 'stored,' is regarded as treasure, which is the meaning of the Greek term 'thesaurus,' used in the main text.

We are constantly exposed to information, lifestyles, and personality traits. We have a choice as to what we will dump as unacceptable garbage and what we will keep as treasure. Once we make that choice to retain what seems valuable, we have no control over the consequences. When the human body fails to expel any poisons ingested, the whole body eventually becomes infected. Similarly, the ungodly lifestyles, personality traits and data that are treasured, corrupt the heart. Soon, these spiritual moral maladies will be exposed by our speech. That's why Jesus declared that by our words we would be justified or condemned, for it is out of whatever fills the heart that the mouth speaks.

This understanding challenges us to listen carefully to what comes out of our mouths. This is not just regarding its effect on others, but also to give us insight on what we have been treasuring. We also need to assess how the treasure in our hearts compares with what God has instructed in His Word. The Word of God is always the most important scale against which we should measure what God expects us to consider as good or evil. What disorders of our hearts have been disclosed by our speech recently?

Father, we once more acknowledge the challenge of choosing the correct treasure for our hearts. But we thank You for Jesus as our model, the Word of God as our guide, and the Holy Spirit as our Helper, as we deal with the maladies revealed by our mouths. Help us as we undertake this spiritual check-up, in the name of Jesus.

June 2

MANNA SERIES: DEVELOPING MOUTH CONTROL
PAINFUL MOUTH CLEANSING

Reading Passage: Isaiah 6
Main Text: Is. 6:6-7 Then one of the seraphs flew to me with a live coal in his hand, which he had taken with tongs from the altar. With it he touched my mouth and said, "See, this has touched your lips; your guilt is taken away and your sin atoned for." (NIV)

My mother heard that I was using words learned from the boys on the street that were unacceptable in our house. After urging me never again to use expletives, she added the threat that if I continued the practice she would scrub my mouth with a powerful detergent. She was hoping I would learn from her threat how important it is to clean up my language. But all I thought about was the pain I would suffer by her proposed action.

Isaiah, the prophet, actually experienced the pain. When the Lord wanted to use him to proclaim His message to the Jewish nation, He needed to purify the prophet before commissioning him. Isaiah saw the glory of the Lord in a vision and immediately acknowledged that he had "unclean lips." Since the mouth usually expresses the spiritual and moral state of a life, the cleansing of Isaiah's life had to begin with the cleansing of his lips. A live coal was taken from the altar and applied to his lips. This painful process resulted in the removal of his guilt, and his readiness for ministry.

We will not achieve the cleansing of our lives and language without some painful experiences. For us to acknowledge we are wrong in our opinions or behavior, or for us to apologize for hurts we have caused, is like applying hot coals to our proud lips. But we will never be free from guilt and be useable by the Lord until we have experienced the painful process. Our salvation experience begins with the acknowledgment that we are sinners deserving of God's judgment, and the verbal confession that we accept Jesus' sacrifice for our salvation (Rom 10:9-10). Many people reject salvation solely to avoid a verbal confession, considering this too painful a process for their pride.

We naturally resist the painful process of a mouth cleansing. But when we get a glimpse of God's glory, and become aware of the unsavory words that frequently come from our mouths, and when we appreciate how much God wants to use us, we will humbly submit to the process. Our changed speech will be indicative of the extent of God's glory that we have seen.

Lord, we desire mouths that will declare Your salvation and express Your praise. Keep applying hot coals to our lips until we are cleansed from everything that will detract from utterances that glorify Your name. We offer this prayer through Jesus Christ our Lord.

June 3

MANNA SERIES: DEVELOPING MOUTH CONTROL
WHAT IS THE DESIGN BEHIND
THE DELIVERY?

Reading Passage: James 3:1-12
Main Text: James 3:9-11 With the tongue we praise our Lord and Father, and with it we curse men, who have been made in God's likeness. Out of the same mouth come praise and cursing. My brothers, this should not be. Can both fresh water and salt water flow from the same spring? (NIV)

In the world of sports a ball can be delivered in different ways with the intention of achieving specific results. A ball from your tennis coach may be designed to develop your hand to eye coordination, but when delivered by an opponent it is intended to defeat you. The difference is in the motive behind the delivery. In speech, the differences are more subtle. A coach on one occasion may berate his players during a game accusing them of weakness and a lackadaisical performance, seeking to motivate them to raise their level of performance. Yet, at the end of the game, he offers words of compassion and comfort to the team after their loss, in order to prevent despair and provide hope for the future. Ultimately, the effect of words depends on the motive of the speaker. "Out of the same mouth (can) come praise and cursing."

While we can appreciate the difference in speech by the coach to achieve specific objectives, there is a problem when we are known as individuals who have words of cursing for others, while we are filled with words of praise to God. Generally words spoken are intended to help or hinder, to hurt or heal. Our Christian challenge is to constantly examine the words we utter to ensure they are designed to achieve a godly objective. With this examination we may discover that sometimes we speak in retaliation, intending the hearer to feel the hurt we are experiencing. This frequently happens in our closest relationships as between spouses or other family members. We may feel vindicated in communicating pain, but God will judge us for causing the injury.

Think of the many times our words were designed to hinder

fellow-believers from pursuing their God-given purpose, because we wanted to keep them from being more successful than ourselves. When we commit ourselves to developing mouth control, we will seek to use our mouths as instruments that will help and heal, to praise and bless. With such speech God will be glorified. Today, let us ensure we design our words with pure and beneficial motives before opening our mouths.

Father, we have read in scripture that You will judge us for the words that we utter. Please help us to examine our hearts before we speak so that the words we deliver will always be designed for Your approval and glory, for Jesus' sake.

June 4

MANNA SERIES: DEVELOPING MOUTH CONTROL
THE POWERFUL LITTLE RULER

Reading Passage: James 3:1-12
Main Text: James 3:5-6 Likewise the tongue is a small part of the body, but it makes great boasts. Consider what a great forest is set on fire by a small spark. The tongue also is a fire, a world of evil among the parts of the body. It corrupts the whole person, sets the whole course of his life on fire, and is itself set on fire by hell. (NIV)

Don't let its size cause you to underestimate its impact. Like the hinge on a large door, the direction of many large objects has been determined by a little, seemingly insignificant item. The passage provides relevant examples. It requires a little bit in a horse's mouth to control the direction of that large powerful animal. A pilot uses a little rudder to determine the direction of a large ship, and a large forest fire can be started by a little spark. These examples all illustrate that the tongue, though a little organ in the body, acts as a powerful ruler.

The tongue, symbolizing our speech, has been used to destroy people's reputation, create dissension, start wars, crush initiative, ruin hope, create anxiety, and steer people away from salvation. Recognizing the power of our speech and the danger it can cause, we have to be diligent in controlling our tongues. But it is nearly impossible to control the outflow of the tongue since it represents the state of the heart. The passage states that no human being can tame the tongue (v.8). It is a powerful ruler that is as destructive as fire.

The solution must lie in the transformation of the heart, which is the source of the tongue's expression. If we have evil thoughts, we may try to 'bite our tongues' to avoid communicating the thoughts of the heart. Eventually the strain on the tongue (or the teeth) will be unbearable. On the other hand, if we take steps to purge ourselves from the evil thoughts as soon as they occur, and replace them with good thoughts, our expressions in speech will be adjusted accordingly. It requires great discipline over our thoughts to ensure they are maintained in a state that leaves our tongues undefiled. This is why James states, "We all stumble in many ways. If anyone is never at fault in what he says, he is a perfect man, able to keep his whole body in check," (v. 2).

Instead of living with regrets over the damage caused by our tongues, we need to take preemptive action and discipline our hearts and minds. Paul instructed us to think only on things that are true, honorable, just, pure, lovely and commendable (Phil 4:8).

Father, we recognize that our speech reveals who we are. We want to be able to be in control of our thoughts so that our speech will demonstrate our complete discipline over our bodies. We need your help, for Jesus' sake.

June 5

MANNA SERIES: DEVELOPING MOUTH CONTROL
INDISCIPLINE RESULTING IN SELF-DECEPTION

Reading Passage: James 1:19-27
Main Text: James 1:26 If anyone considers himself religious and yet does not keep a tight rein on his tongue, he deceives himself and his religion is worthless. (NIV)

The practice of religion requires self-discipline. Religion involves conforming to certain rules of behavior and the practice of certain rituals.

Many of these are contrary to popular social norms and to natural human tendencies. To be successful in the practice of prayer, charity and sexual purity, a practitioner has to be disciplined.

The apostle James, who wrote much on the topic of religion, highlights an area of discipline that is easily overlooked and can cause serious damage if not practiced. His declaration: "Everyone should be quick to listen, slow to speak and slow to become angry" (v. 19), could be puzzling. Being slow to speak is not usually considered a virtue; in fact it is frequently considered a deficiency. For a religious person, the mouth is frequently used as a tool to propagate his religion, and also to boast of one's achievements. The apostle was not urging silence; rather he advocates caution over speech.

There are two good reasons for his position. First, the mouth sometimes expresses anger, and a religious person should demonstrate control over anger. In most instances, through control of speech, we will exhibit control over the expression of anger. Prov. 21:23 NKJV states, "He who guards his mouth and his tongue, guards his soul from troubles," and the Psalmist prays in Psa. 141:3 NKJV "Set a guard, O LORD, over my mouth, keep watch over the door of my lips."

The second reason James stated for caution in speech, is that true religion is expressed in action like "visiting orphans and widows in their distress," and not in talk. There is a great temptation to substitute talk about religion for religious action. While religious talk creates a good impression and causes people to think much of us, it may defeat the value of religion. But even worse, we may begin to convince ourselves that we are making a valuable contribution, when we have done nothing more than mere talk. Such self-deception occurs quite frequently in religious circles. Unfortunately, many observers, especially those who are unbelievers, see beyond the deception and label even genuine practitioners as hypocrites.

Self-deception and a poor reputation in the world can be avoided when we practice discipline with our mouths. Let us strive to be cautious with our speech so that our words are not discolored by our anger. We should also be careful to allow our acts of good works to communicate the depth of our religion before resorting to verbal advertisement.

Father, like the Psalmist, I seek Your help to set a guard over my mouth, and keep a watch over the door of my lips so I will be kept from sin and false religious practice because of my tongue. In the name of Jesus, we seek to practice authentic religion.

June 6

MANNA SERIES: DEVELOPING MOUTH CONTROL
AVOIDING CARELESS WOUNDS

Reading Passage: Prov. 12:13-19
Main Text: Prov. 12:18 Reckless words pierce like a sword,
But the tongue of the wise brings healing. (NIV)

In recent times the phrase "friendly fire" has become popular as we read the reports of the cause of injury and death during the wars in Iraq and Afghanistan. The term is used to describe a situation where a soldier is wounded by a weapon fired by a comrade-soldier rather than by an enemy. We understand from the description that there was a mistake made when the weapon was discharged, and there was no malice intended by the comrade-soldier. Although friendly fire might have been accidental, the resulting injury is just as painful and lethal as if it were intentional.

The reckless use of words is similar in effect to friendly fire. Addressed to a friend or an associate with no malicious intent, the hurt caused by reckless words may be as lethal as wielding a sword. Unfortunately, once the words are out of our mouths they are irretrievable, and like an arrow released by the bow, they will proceed to the target despite the regret of the release.

The wounds caused by "friendly-fire words" have been carried by children into adulthood, stunting their ability to become fully developed, and to achieve their God-given potential. The wounds have discouraged many students from making the effort to be successful. Instead they settle for the labels placed on them by teachers. Some beautiful women have been so demeaned and diminished by words spoken by a boyfriend or husband that they have accepted an ugly self-image, which can only be corrected by divine intervention. In many cases, the person pulling the verbal trigger had no sense of the long-term effect of the words that might have been uttered in a brief moment of anger. But such is the danger of reckless words.

With this awareness of consequences, we ought to be very diligent in developing mouth control. We must consider words before speaking. We should consider how the hearer may receive them, or how they might be misunderstood. Our desire to be wise in our speech will cause us to be "slow to speak" and to avoid times of frivolity when we are under the influence of anything that may cause us to be careless in our speech. In addition, we must be alert to hurts we may have caused, and be quick to apologize and seek forgiveness.

Father, we want to avoid causing friendly fire. We need Your help as we seek to develop a wise tongue that will bring healing. May we be diligent to respond to Your promptings, for Jesus' sake.

June 7

MANNA SERIES: DEVELOPING MOUTH CONTROL
BRAKES ON A RUNAWAY MOUTH

Reading Passage: Prov. 10:1-32
Main Text: Prov. 10:13-14 Wisdom is found on the lips of the discerning,
But a rod is for the back of him who lacks judgment.
Wise men store up knowledge,
But the mouth of a fool invites ruin. (NIV)

Everyone in the group is voicing his or her opinion, so whether I think my opinion is valuable or not, I must say something. It seems as if the one who has more to say, will be the more greatly admired, so I must keep talking. Soon my mouth is out of control and I am enjoying the wild ride, while those around are wondering how to put brakes on the mouth of a fool. I act as if I am an authority on subjects about which I have little knowledge, I am combative with anyone who disagrees with me, and I am surprised when people seem to be politely avoiding me. This is the portrait of the "babbling fool" described in Proverbs 10.

In contrast, the wise person is described as one whose mouth is a fountain of life, and who is so restrained in speech that his words are as precious as "choice silver". A wise man "stores up knowledge," listening and learning, accumulating, sifting information and gaining understanding until the appropriate time when he passes on this knowledge. The purpose of speaking is never to show how much he knows or to prevent "dead moments" in the conversation; rather it is always to communicate "life" to the hearer. Consequently, "the lips of the righteous nourish many" (v. 21).

The challenge posed by this passage is for us to examine whether we seek to increase the volume of our words to dominate conversations, or whether we ensure our contribution is measured, restricted, discreet and life-giving. Remember, "When words are many, sin is not absent, but he who holds his tongue is wise" (v. 19). It is what comes out of our mouths that will allow people (including ourselves) to assess whether we are wise or foolish.

Father, we once more pray that You help us to put brakes on our mouths to keep it from running out of control and ruining our testimony for Jesus. We easily sin by exaggerations, and deceptive speech when we multiply words. Please help us to be restrained and wise in our speech, for Jesus' sake, Amen.

June 8

MANNA SERIES: DEVELOPING MOUTH CONTROL
LIFE'S TRIPLETS: THINKING-SPEAKING-DOING

Reading Passage: Josh. 1:1-9
Main Text: Josh. 1:8 Do not let this Book of the Law depart from your mouth; meditate on it day and night, so that you may be careful to do everything written in it. Then you will be prosperous and successful. (NIV)

How do we know what people are thinking unless they express their thoughts in words? Of course, the visual arts provide another medium for expressing thoughts, but no communication is as precise and clear as words whether written or spoken. How do we know someone's decisions or commitments, except by his or her actions? Our lives reflect the combination of this trifold process - thoughts, words, and action, each aspect reflecting the others.

We understand God's thoughts regarding creation by what he spoke into existence. We also know His thoughts on how mankind should live and prosper in His created world by the law or instructions He gave. Man's lifestyle would not reflect God's instructions until he allowed these instructions to be embedded in his thoughts. It is by the process of meditation that the instructions saturate our thoughts. To initiate the process, we read or listen to God's Word, but if we do not spend time thinking about what we ingested, it will soon be lost to our minds and lives.

The most effective way of ensuring that the instructions will become a part of our lives is by speaking and acting on them. When we speak, we usually reexamine our thoughts until they are better understood. Speaking assists our memory to retain what is spoken, and it helps us to be determined to act on what we speak. It is interesting to note that God told Joshua that the Book of the Law must be in his mouth. He knew that when Joshua began to speak the instructions, it would indicate that the instructions had become embedded, and it would not be difficult for the related actions to be taken. In addition, what was in his mouth could be clearly communicated to others, and he could be held accountable for what was spoken. Finally, we must follow through with action on our convictions, otherwise our thoughts and speech will be fleeting and useless.

This command to Joshua challenges us to ask, "How much of God's Word do we speak on a daily basis?" If we are not speaking God's Word, this may indicate we are not ingesting sufficient amounts of it, or we are not meditating on it. If we fail to have His Word in our thoughts or do not act on it, our prosperity and success will be affected.

Father, we want your Word to abide in our hearts in a rich way, with all wisdom, so it will affect our speech and keep us from sinful and foolish talk. We commit ourselves to ingesting and meditating on Your Word, for Jesus' sake.

June 9

MANNA SERIES: DEVELOPING MOUTH CONTROL
A NEW DEFAULT EXPRESSION

Reading Passage: Psa. 34:1-22
Main Text: Psa. 34:1-4 I will extol the LORD at all times;
His praise will always be on my lips. My soul will boast in the LORD;
Let the afflicted hear and rejoice. Glorify the LORD with me;
Let us exalt his name together.

I sought the LORD, and he answered me;
He delivered me from all my fears. (NIV)

The term "default" has always had a negative connotation, implying failure to take action or meet specific obligations. With the advent of computers, the term now also describes an assumed status before action is taken, and to which the system will return when action is completed. This is illustrated by an elastic band that returns to its original (default) position after it has been stretched.

Before the Holy Spirit regenerated us the default position of our hearts was a bent to sin, rebellion and evil. Our inclination also determined the expressions of our mouths, since verbal expressions are the outflow of the heart. After our conversion, we have to admit that we still struggle with remnants of the old nature, and we still hurt and harm people with our mouths. It takes hard work and discipline under the guidance of the Holy Spirit, to change our default expressions because the tongue is a powerful, deadly instrument that is nearly impossible to tame.

In our text, David gives us his method for changing his default expressions. He made a commitment to "extol the Lord at ALL TIMES," and let "his praise ... ALWAYS BE" on his lips (my emphasis). The background to this Psalm was that David, in running away from King Saul, found himself in enemy territory. He was feeling vulnerable in front of a Philistine king. In desperation, he cried out for help and the Lord heard him, protected him with the help of angels, and delivered him (vv. 6-7). Our battle to practice the commitment, as expressed by David, involves fighting against complaining about our adverse circumstances, or criticizing those who are not meeting our expectations. We must also avoid condemning those who oppose us. When we have experienced God's supernatural interventions in our lives, everything else becomes insignificant and we will be motivated to extol the Lord. It doesn't matter who doesn't like us, or who is working against us when we know from experience that God is for us and will take care of us.

What is inexcusable is to have experienced God's deliverances, not only in salvation from the power of the devil, but in providing healing to our bodies, opening closed doors, and overcoming traps set by our enemies and still our default expressions remain complaining, criticizing and condemning. It is time to adopt a new default expression of praising the Lord, so His praise will always be on our lips.

Father, keep reminding me of the great things You have done, so my speech will not be influenced by my current difficulties. I want my default expression to be praise to Your glorious name.

June 10

MANNA SERIES: DEVELOPING MOUTH CONTROL
BECOMING GOD'S MOUTHPIECE

Reading Passage: Isa. 50:4-10
Main Text: Isa. 50:4 The Sovereign LORD has given me an instructed tongue,

> To know the word that sustains the weary.
> He wakens me morning by morning, wakens my ear
> To listen like one being taught. (NIV)

God wants to use my mouth? What an awesome thought!

When we are presented with this proposition our first reaction is to reject it because we are aware of our battle to keep our mouths from harming and hindering others. We are not alone in this reaction. In the Old Testament when God called men to be His spokesmen, many of these prophets complained of their inadequacy to perform this task (e.g. Moses, Jeremiah, Isaiah). God never accepted any excuse or obstacle in His quest to have His words communicated (e.g. Jonah). This is why the followers of the Lord are required to be disciples.

A disciple is primarily a learner. He listens and learns from his master in order to be able to speak on his master's behalf, as an oracle. The reason God needs our mouths is that there are people with needs, which can only be met by a word from the Lord, delivered by His disciples. In His relentless pursuit of this goal, the Lord disturbs the sleep of His disciples so He can speak to them. The word will usually be scripture brought to our minds. These scriptures may be received without a particular context, but when we meet people during the day, we suddenly realize the relevance of the words received, for the situation described by those with needs. Our words to others become the transforming Word of God that will be able to strengthen them in their weariness, enabling them to accomplish their God-given goals.

It is amazing how God takes a blaspheming, cursing man, converts him into a disciple, and transforms him into His mouthpiece in this world. The apostle Peter is a great example of this process. He later wrote, "If anyone speaks, he should do it as one speaking the very words of God. If anyone serves, he should do it with the strength God provides, so that in all things God may be praised through Jesus Christ..." 1Pet. 4:11 NIV.

In seeking to develop mouth control, are we willing to become disciples, listening and learning from our Master? Are we sensing the prompting of His word in our spirits in our times of prayer and meditation? Do we go out prepared with words to share with the "weary people" we encounter on our path?

Father, our prayer is that the words of our mouths and the meditation of our hearts will be acceptable in Your sight, O Lord, our strength and Redeemer, (Ps. 19:14).

June 11

MANNA SERIES: DEVELOPING MOUTH CONTROL
SUPPLYING WORDS IN SEASON

Reading Passage: Prov. 25:11-14
Main Text: Prov. 15:23 A man has joy by the answer of his mouth,
And a word spoken in due season, how good it is! (NKJV)
Prov. 25:11 A word fitly spoken is like apples of gold
In settings of silver. (NKJV)

There is something about seasonal fruits that indicates divine wisdom in the timing of fruit production. The watermelon comes to maturity and is harvested in summer when the weather is hot and dry, and we are in need of thirst quenchers. We are amazed that a vine grown in such dry conditions could produce a fruit containing so much water. But we have to appreciate that it is the ideal fruit for that time of the year.

In a similar way there is an appropriate season for certain words to be spoken. A wise person will be able to sense the season in someone's life, and fashion words that are ideally suited for the season. When someone is suffering anguish because of the sudden loss of a loved one, if our goal is to help him or her heal, it is not the season to be reminding them of their failure to care for that person, or to be restating the fact that we all suffer loss. When the appropriate word is spoken it is beautiful to observe, powerful in effect, and brings joy to the speaker.

The writer of the Proverbs illustrates the beauty of appropriate words by referring to the presentation of gold colored apples set in a silver bowl. It is artistically pleasing, well- coordinated, and it indicates that great thought was given to the presentation. Do we take such care to plan our words before speaking to someone in need? Do we ensure our words are helpful to the situation we are addressing? A paraphrase of Prov. 25:13 states that the word of a faithful messenger is like a cool drink in the time of sweltering heat… refreshing!

Our challenge is to have the discernment to know the season people are in, and to have the wisdom to speak the appropriate words for that season. This is the reason that we must become disciples who listen to the voice of the Lord, so he can wake us to give us the word in season to speak to someone who is weary (Isa. 50:4).

Father, we desire to speak words that represent Your wisdom and are helpful to the weary listeners. We need Your help as we dedicate ourselves to listening to Your voice. This is our prayer through Jesus Christ our Savior.

June 12

MANNA SERIES: DEVELOPING MOUTH CONTROL
WORDS PROPERLY SEASONED

Reading Passage: Col. 4:1-6
Main Text: Col. 4:6 Let your conversation be always full of grace, seasoned with salt, so that you may know how to answer everyone. (NIV)

Seasoning on food can enhance its taste or destroy it. With the wrong seasoning, or too much of it, food may become unpalatable. However, food without any seasoning is bland and unappealing.

The Apostle urges us to ensure our words are always seasoned, presented with grace. Grace describes anything given for the benefit of another even if the individual is undeserving of it. Therefore the choice and tone of our words should be made with the intention that the hearers are enhanced. This is difficult to practice when someone has said something that made us angry, or has hurt us. Naturally, we want to respond with words seasoned with hot pepper so they will be burned by our words. Or we may decide to season our words with a heavy dose of garlic so that the heart of our antagonist would be hurt by the pungent effect of our comments. To respond appropriately to the Apostle's admonition, we should refrain from speaking until our hearts are in a state that we desire good for the one who has caused us pain. With the proper attitude, our words will be free from malice and sarcasm.

The seasoning of grace is described as "seasoned with salt." This indicates an ingredient that makes our words palatable or tasty, and pure; not the complexity of allspice, but the simplicity of salt with its penetrating and preserving power. Our goal should be to respond with grace to everyone, especially to those who dislike us. The graciousness of our speech will create opportunities for us to influence others positively and to demonstrate the wisdom of Christ. Take the time to ensure that your words are properly seasoned today.

Lord, we desire to have the heart of Jesus so we will be able to know how to respond as He did. Peter said of Him, "When they hurled their insults at Him, He did not retaliate; when He suffered, He made no threats. Instead, He entrusted Himself to Him who judges justly." (1Pet. 2:23 NIV) For His sake let it be so with us.

June 13

MANNA SERIES: DEVELOPING MOUTH CONTROL
WHEN SILENCE IS GOLDEN

Reading Passage: Prov. 17:7-28
Main Text: Prov. 17:27-28 A man of knowledge uses words with restraint,
And a man of understanding is even-tempered.
Even a fool is thought wise if he keeps silent,
And discerning if he holds his tongue. (NIV)

Oratory is attractive and seductive, but it is no proof of knowledge or wisdom. It is said that many Germans were captured in the web of

Hitler's oratory, which led them to tolerate the evils of the Third Reich. We falsely believe that knowledge creates a wellspring that must be released by speaking, in order to educate the less knowledgeable and to win accolades for the speaker. If knowledge is power, we desire to exercise that power through speech.

The Wisdom Book of the Proverbs counters these commonly held views about knowledge and speech. It states that a man of knowledge is really the man who shows restraint of speech. You may hear some news but refrain from sharing it because it is not the proper time or environment where the information should be divulged. This is even more significant in cases where you have to exercise restraint while listening to erroneous information. It is not that you tolerate the spread of error, but you restrain yourself for professional reasons - not divulging information received in confidence. Or you realize that attempts to counter the error in a certain situation could result in an angry confrontation, or cause you to appear boastful.

This ability to show restraint in speech is an indication of your wisdom, and gives evidence that you are even-tempered, possessing a calm disposition. The proverb further states that even a fool is considered wise, if he is able to keep quiet, and hold his tongue when he was expected to be eloquent or to respond in anger. As one sage said, "If your mouth is closed, it is not possible to put your foot in it." A wise politician, when hounded by the usual posse of reporters waiting to trap him, quipped, "When nothing is said, there is nothing to misquote."

Proverbs 17 provides some additional advice about speech:

- 17:7b - it is inappropriate for rulers to lie - with greater authority comes greater responsibility for truth speaking, even at the risk of personal injury.
- 17:8b - news heard about people should not be shared as it could lead to separation among friends.

We need to be careful with our speech, and if in doubt we should be silent, because there are times when silence is golden.

Father, our desire is to be as wise and controlled as our Lord, who was silent before His accusers, although He had the power to condemn them by His speech. May we be able to trust You to vindicate us when we are silent for the sake of Your glory.

MANNA SERIES: DEVELOPING MOUTH CONTROL
TEACHERS WITH HEALTHY MOUTHS

Reading Passage: Titus 2:3-8
Main Text: Titus 2:7-8 In everything set them an example by doing what is good. In your teaching show integrity, seriousness and soundness of speech that cannot be condemned, so that those who oppose you may be ashamed because they have nothing bad to say about us. (NIV)

With respect to the proper use of the mouth, those who teach are in a uniquely significant position. Because of the authority attached to the role, the student is observing the character of the teacher along with receiving information. Reckless teachers, who may have been accurate in their information but misleading in behavior, have led many people astray. For example, teachers who practice using swear words, or are indiscreet in sexual references, may produce students who consider these practices acceptable, and proceed to replicate the behavior. Not surprisingly, the apostle James cautions us not to be anxious to become teachers because we will be subjected to a greater judgment.

Paul instructs teachers to show integrity, seriousness, and soundness of speech. The term soundness of speech refers to wholesomeness in the use and tone of words. It is unbecoming for a Christian teacher to be using what is regarded in a culture as filthy language. The reason Paul gives for practicing wholesome speech is that we are always under scrutiny by opponents who are looking for some flaw in our character to condemn. We should be diligent in not providing them with any ammunition that could be used against us. If we take the attitude that as humans we are expected to have flaws, or that people should not be judging us, we are settling for a mediocre standard that is unacceptable for Jesus' representatives. They should "have nothing bad to say about us." In Col. 3:8 NIV Paul admonishes, "But now you must rid yourselves of all such things as these: anger, rage, malice, slander, and filthy language from your lips."

We may be tempted to excuse ourselves from these exhortations on the grounds that we do not have the title of "teacher," nor do we attempt to assume these responsibilities in church or school. However, being a teacher is not just a position one assumes, but also a role others place us in, sometimes unbeknown to us. You may be the "teacher" to a younger person in a church group, unsaved co-workers, your children, or just friends who respect you. Therefore, we should always be on guard to ensure we keep a wholesome mouth before our "students."

Father, help us to be always aware of our responsibility as teachers, and of the fact that we are always under scrutiny. By Your Spirit, help us to make a determined effort to maintain a wholesome mouth, through Jesus Christ our Lord.

June 15

MANNA SERIES: DEVELOPING MOUTH CONTROL
WAITING TO JOIN THE CHORUS

Reading Passage: Rev. 19:1-8
Main Text: 1Cor. 1:10 Now I plead with you, brethren, by the name of our Lord Jesus Christ, that you all speak the same thing, and that there be no divisions among you, but that you be perfectly joined together in the same mind and in the same judgment. (NKJV)

We listened with great admiration as the soloist sang the verses of the anthem in the large music hall, but when the 500-voice choir joined in the chorus, hardly anyone could remain seated. The difference in listening to one person singing compared to a chorus of 500, was amazing because of the impact of sound and harmony.

This provides an illustration of the impact when people are united in speech. Having examined various aspects of Developing Mouth Control, it is useful to look at the positive impact that can be made when God achieves His goal of getting the mouths of His people purified and unified. The Bible records in Gen 6, that when the people of the earth were unified in rebellion against God, He intervened. He caused them to have different languages because He knew how dangerous it would be if mankind were united. Having differences in language kept mankind divided and ineffective in their rebellion.

However, the plan of God is for mankind to be once more united in celebration of His glory. The evidence of this unity will be seen when we begin to speak the same things about Jesus, who has been set forth as the source of unity of God's people. At present, the only place where this unity is possible is in the church, the body of Christ. For this reason, our text records Paul pleading with the church at Corinth for them to become so united that ultimately they will speak the same things.

The devil knows the power of the chorus, so he will spare no effort to keep the church divided by what we, the members, say to, and about each other. To overcome this tactic of the enemy, we have to keep the focus on Christ, and avoid the petty differences that can arise. Our goal should be to join the chorus in celebration of our Lord. This is what the apostle John saw at the climax of history as described in Revelation 19:5-6 NIV: Then a voice came from the throne, saying, 'Praise our God, all you His servants and those who fear Him, both small and great!' Then I heard what sounded like a great multitude, like the roar of rushing waters and like loud peals of thunder, shouting: 'Hallelujah! For our Lord God Almighty reigns.'

Our mouths are frequently the cause of most of our disunity and divisions, yet the Lord desires that we will become so unified in Jesus that we will be able to join the chorus to sing His praises. Let us now begin to develop our mouth control to bring about this unity.

Father, we desire Jesus to be so exalted in our lives that He will become the main theme in our speech. We commit ourselves to becoming unified with those who will celebrate His glory at the climax of history, for the glory of Jesus.

June 16

MANNA SERIES: REACHING JESUS ON A MOUNTAINTOP
GAINING A KINGDOM PERSPECTIVE

Reading Passage: Matt. 4:23 - 5:2
Main Text: Matt. 5:1-2 Now when he saw the crowds, he went up on a mountainside and sat down. His disciples came to him, and he began to teach them, saying: (NIV)

Leaving the suffocating, narrow streets of the city, we set off in our car to climb the nearby mountain. First, there was the change in the scenery from concrete and asphalt to open fields, vegetation and flowers. Next, there was the fall in temperature and the freshness of the atmosphere, then there was the change of perspective. We were able to see the full spread of the city to its border, with the sea in one direction and mountains in the other. The layout of the city, with its port and commercial district now made sense from this vantage point. The mountain provided a different perspective to life in the city.

It seems that whenever Jesus wanted to provide the disciples with a clearer insight into His nature, His purpose or His destiny, He took them to a mountain to gain a perspective that was lacking on the plain. In this regard, certain mountains are mentioned in the gospels - the Mounts of Transfiguration, Calvary, or Olivet. In this series, we will focus on the first mention of a mountain in the gospels, the mountain on which Jesus delivered His famous sermon in which He discussed matters concerning the Kingdom of God. It is titled "Reaching Jesus on a Mountaintop," because we want to gain His perspective on the Kingdom from the various lessons given on the mountain. To gain this high perspective, we have to attempt the climb from the plains of the ordinary to reach the altitude of life that Jesus demands of Kingdom citizens.

Matthew's gospel introduces us to the birth of the King in chapter 2. In chapter 4:17 Jesus preaches that the Kingdom of Heaven is near, and in verses 23-24, He goes about preaching the good news of the Kingdom and healing all kinds of sicknesses and diseases. Having thus captured the attention of the crowds He goes to the mountainside to teach about the Kingdom so people would know about its nature and entry requirements.

It is interesting to note that of the large crowds that followed Him, only the disciples came for the lessons. Only true disciples are willing to go beyond the excitement of the miracles and the crowds to gain the perspective of the Kingdom that comes from Jesus' lessons on the mountain.

Are you willing to prove your dedication as a disciple by your interest in learning and applying the lessons Jesus gave concerning the Kingdom of God?

Father, we are challenged to examine ourselves to see if we have the heart of a disciple. Grant us the determination to follow Jesus up the mountain beyond the crowds and learn the hard lessons in order to gain a new perspective of the Kingdom. We make this petition in the name of Jesus.

June 17

MANNA SERIES: REACHING JESUS ON A MOUNTAINTOP
THE UNIQUE NATURE OF THIS KINGDOM

Reading Passage: Matt. 6:9-13
Main Text: Luke 17:20-21 Once, having been asked by the Pharisees when the kingdom of God would come, Jesus replied, "The kingdom of God does not come with your careful observation, nor will people say, 'Here it is,' or 'There it is,' because the kingdom of God is within you." (NIV)

The road sign read "You are entering the Kingdom of Jordan." This gave us the assurance that we were heading to our desired destination, and soon we would experience the sights associated with the country. The King of Jordan ruled the kingdom. It was inhabited mostly by people who identified themselves as Jordanians, who were subjected to the laws of that kingdom. The nature of all human kingdoms is similarly identified with boundaries in a specific geographic location. They have rulers, subjects who identify themselves with these kingdoms, and rules and regulations that must be followed.

The kingdom of heaven has many of the features of a human kingdom, but with one fundamental difference. Because the kingdom from heaven is spiritual, it has no geographic location; instead it resides in the hearts of individuals. However, it has a King who rules, and His laws are written in the hearts of His subjects who have been spiritually reborn, and are governed by the Spirit of the ruler. The manifestation of the kingdom on earth occurs whenever and wherever the heavenly citizens cause the kingdom-life to be evidenced by their presence.

The unique nature of the spiritual kingdom causes it not to be easily perceived or understood by those who do not belong, yet individuals can enter it as a real state of existence. Once they have entered it, the citizens not only become its representatives, they also are the possessors of the rights, powers and privileges of the kingdom. Just as the spirit of a person is superior to his or her physical body, similarly the spiritual kingdom is superior to all human kingdoms. While we live in a physical world and are citizens of a physical kingdom, we have a concurrent existence as citizens of a superior spiritual kingdom, whose King will eventually rule the whole world.

Our challenge as citizens of the spiritual kingdom is being able to live in the natural world yet follow heavenly rules that are so contrary to our human nature. How do we counter our human nature with its natural disposition? The sermon on the mountain provides us with the blueprint of the expected lifestyle of heavenly citizens. But the challenge remains - how will this be achieved? Are we willing to follow the blueprint provided by Our Lord?

Lord, we know you will not demand anything from us that is unachievable. As citizens of a spiritual kingdom, help us to understand the nature and requirements of the kingdom so we will pursue its goals and manifest its influence, for Jesus' sake.

June 18

MANNA SERIES: REACHING JESUS ON A MOUNTAINTOP
IS THE BAR SET TOO HIGH?

Reading Passage: Matt. 5:13-20
Main Text: Matt. 5:20 For I tell you that unless your righteousness surpasses that of the Pharisees and the teachers of the law, you will certainly not enter the kingdom of heaven. (NIV)

The high school high jumper was excited and confident after easily clearing the bar at 6 feet 5 inches. He waited for his coach to adjust the bar to a new target, and was expecting an increase of approximately 2 inches. He was shocked when the coach set the bar at 7 feet 5 inches, which was never previously achieved by any schoolboy. The coach then turned to him and asked, "Is the bar set too high?" When there was no response, he continued, "I have done it, and I will enable you to do it."

The demands Jesus made in the Sermon on the Mount put us in a similar position to that young man, as we watch and listen to our "coach" raising the bar of kingdom citizenry to seemingly unattainable levels. In today's main text Jesus said that our righteousness must surpass that of the Pharisees to qualify for entry into the kingdom. The Pharisees were known in Jesus' day for their emphasis on a separated lifestyle by which they endeavored to keep all the demands of the law, along with numerous additional regulations. They were a minority group, as most people found the demands of their lifestyle too difficult to maintain.

The crowds were shocked at Jesus' attack on the Pharisees because it was generally believed that they were superior in their acts of righteousness. But Jesus knew the Pharisees' outward behavior was not backed by an inner transformation. They were seeking to impress people to gain admiration, instead of sincerely seeking to be declared righteous by God. This explains why Jesus accused them of hypocrisy. Their bar was set too low for kingdom citizenship. In Matt. 5:48 NIV, Jesus made another demand, "Be perfect, therefore, as your heavenly Father is perfect." That bar is definitely much too high for us.

Because of the defects in our human nature, we are incapable of achieving the high standard of righteousness required by God. Our deficiencies in light of His demands highlight our dependency on Jesus to enable us to enter the kingdom. Because Jesus took our sin and died in our place, He can provide us with His righteousness, which makes us acceptable to God. Jesus told a Pharisee named Nicodemus in John 3:3, that unless a person is born again, spiritually, he or she cannot even recognize the kingdom of God. Do you know with assurance you have been spiritually reborn?

Lord, your bar for righteousness and entry into your kingdom has been set very high. We thank you for the assurance from Jesus that just as he met the standards of the high bar, He will enable us to do the same.

June 19

MANNA SERIES: REACHING JESUS ON A MOUNTAINTOP
AN UNUSUAL KIND OF BLESSING

Reading Passage: Matt. 5:2-12
Main Text: Matt. 5:3 "Blessed are the poor in spirit,
For theirs is the kingdom of heaven." (NIV)

There is little doubt that most people instinctively have a strong desire to be blessed and to live continuously in such a state. This desire may be traced to the status of the first man Adam at the time of his creation. God first created a paradise, then He made man to inhabit this paradise forever. Blessings are generally understood to represent the absence of sicknesses and adversities, and the possession of adequate supplies of all that is required for the enjoyment of life.

Jesus introduces His sermon on the mount with the Beatitudes, which outlines the basis of true blessing. In the Beatitudes, blessings are not the material things a person may possess or the adversities a person may avoid. Instead, blessings are derived from the attitudes that a person has developed to respond to the various situations of life. This concept is contrary to our usual understanding of the blessed life.

In the first Beatitude Jesus said, "Blessed are the poor in spirit." This is a startling declaration that provides the foundation for our understanding of the kingdom of God, and its relationship to the blessed life. When we appreciate that God's demands of righteousness in His kingdom are much higher than what we are able to achieve by ourselves, we recognize our own poverty. Rather than this poverty of spirit being a liability, it becomes an asset when it drives us to become dependent on the Lord to impart to us His righteousness.

Until we come to the place of acknowledgment of our poverty, either we will struggle to be good in ourselves and continue to be disappointed in our failures, or we will be showy in our performance of religious exercises seeking to earn the applause of God and man. We fight to keep up the appearance of being holy and righteous while internally we battle against the demands of our sinful nature. While having these struggles, we miss out on the blessed life of peace and joy.

What Jesus highlighted was the blessing a person experiences when he ceases the struggle and trusts only in what Jesus has done for him. The poverty of spirit is rewarded by the riches of his grace, and immediately Jesus begins His reign in that person's life thus establishing His kingdom rule within. What a state of blessedness!

My hope is built on nothing less than Jesus' blood and righteousness; I dare not trust the sweetest frame but wholly lean on Jesus' name. On Christ the solid rock I stand.

June 20

MANNA SERIES: REACHING JESUS ON A MOUNTAINTOP
A MOURNERS' OPPORTUNITY

Reading Passage: Matt. 5:2-12
Main Text: Matt. 5:4 Blessed are those who mourn,
For they will be comforted. (NIV)

The dictionary states that to mourn is to feel or express sorrow or grief over misfortune, loss, or anything regretted. There is a gloom associated with being a mourner. Such a gloom may be caused by the sense of irreversible loss at the death of a loved one, especially at the time we place the body in a grave. Or, consider the gloom experienced by King David after he recognized his sin against God. He committed adultery with Bathsheba and murdered her husband. Although he was the king, he was powerless to undo the act of adultery and murder. Moreover, he had broken his covenant with Jehovah and could not avert the consequence. As detailed in Psalms 32 and 51, he became a mourner because of his sin.

There is nothing attractive or desirable about being in mourning, as it highlights our powerlessness to reverse past painful events, and a sense of helplessness in finding an alternative to the associated gloom. How then could Jesus declare that someone entering a state of mourning is blessed? In our state of mourning, we will be willing to seek the true source of comfort, and in our state of gloom the offer of hope will be readily accepted. A person who has not experienced the sorrowful pain caused by death may never question the inevitability of death and seek to place his faith in death's conqueror. If we have never known the anguish caused by our sin, we would have no need of seeking a Savior who can forgive sin and break its power over us. It is only after we recognize that injustices and inequalities are unavoidable in all earthly kingdoms, that we begin to yearn for a heavenly kingdom to be manifested on earth.

This seeking and yearning becomes a source of blessing because God rewards those who seek Him. He provides the assurance to the mourner that there will be comfort in God, which is the main characteristic of the Holy Spirit. The manifestation of God in flesh was for the purpose of bearing our sorrows and providing healing or comfort from our anguish. Through His death Jesus provided salvation from sin, and by His resurrection He reversed the effects of death. When our sin or life's circumstances cause us to mourn, we are blessed that they can bring us to Jesus, and whet our appetites for a heavenly kingdom.

We will sing with the Psalmist "You turned my wailing into dancing; You removed my sackcloth and clothed me with joy, that my heart may sing to You and not be silent. O LORD my God, I will give You thanks forever." Psa. 30:11-12 NIV.

June 21

MANNA SERIES: REACHING JESUS ON A MOUNTAINTOP
PROPERLY DIRECTED STRENGTH

Reading Passage: Matt. 5:2-12
Main Text: Matt. 5:5 Blessed are the meek,
For they will inherit the earth. (NIV)

Webster's dictionary defines the word "meek" as mild of temper; not easily provoked or irritated; patient under injuries; not vain, or haughty, or resentful; forbearing; submissive. The qualities described in this definition are certainly not those we expect to see in people who are seeking to possess the earth. We are much more familiar with the phrase, "to the strong belong the spoils." Contrary to common thought, meekness is not weakness; rather it is strength under control. It is the ability to apply our strength to control our emotions and impulses, so we won't be under the control of circumstances or people. Otherwise, people will be able to "press our buttons" and remotely control us.

Why would we desire to be mild, gentle and patient, instead of allowing others to experience the power of our anger or arrogance? A person who is secure in his power can afford to be gentle, as his power is not enhanced by arrogance. An angry person is not in control and is at risk of making emotional instead of rational decisions. As stated in Prov. 25:28 NIV "Like a city whose walls are broken down is a man who lacks self-control."

Because of our ego, meekness is not a natural or easy virtue for us.

However, if we choose to be meek while pursuing our goals we have to trust God to vindicate us, and to provide the resources necessary to achieve these goals. In such a position we are indeed blessed. Jesus described Himself as "gentle and humble in heart" Matt. 11:29, showing the confidence He had in the relationship with His Father.

As stated in the Beatitude, the reason the meek are blessed is that they will inherit the benefits that the earth can provide. People fight or strive to conquer or earn the benefits of the earth. There is no such struggle for the meek who is trusting God; he simply inherits them. Since the earth and all its treasures are owned by our Father, when we trust Him, He passes us benefits as He deems appropriate. In choosing to be meek we may wish to adopt the following recommendations provided by pastor/author Rick Warren as New Year's resolutions for leaders in his church:

1. When someone serves you, be understanding not demanding.
2. When somebody disappoints you, be gentle and not judgmental.
3. When someone disagrees with you, be tender without surrender.
4. When someone corrects you, be teachable rather than unreachable.
5. When somebody hurts you, be an actor not a reactor.

Father, we desire to be like Jesus with strength under control. Help us to humble ourselves and trust You to exalt us in Your own time, and in Your own way. We trust Your love, through Jesus Christ our Lord.

June 22

MANNA SERIES: REACHING JESUS ON A MOUNTAINTOP
HOPE IN THE FACE OF INJUSTICE

Reading Passage: Matt. 5:2-12
Main Text: Matt. 5:6 Blessed are those who hunger and thirst for righteousness,
For they will be filled. (NIV)

How do we respond to injustice? We may have different responses depending on whether the injustice is carried out against us or those connected to us, or whether the injustice affects us directly or indirectly.

When we suffer because of false accusations, or have been discriminated against because of our color, class or beliefs, we seek redress or revenge. But when the injustice is systemic or practiced by forces too powerful for us, such as governmental authorities supported by unjust laws, or a corrupt legal system, we end up frustrated. Consider being a slave in the pre-emancipation days when victims had no legal rights and no recourse against the authorities. In such circumstances we develop a hunger and thirst for righteousness, justice and equity. This passionate response fueled by self-interest, is natural and expected.

But what about the cases where we are not directly affected, when injustice is practiced against people who are not of our social or racial grouping, or those of other political persuasions, countries or religions? Can we become as passionate for justice in these cases? Many become indifferent to the abuses suffered by these "others" and we do nothing to seek to "proclaim liberty to the captives, the recovery of sight to the blind, to set at liberty those who are oppressed." As Elie Wiesel, Jewish author and holocaust survivor stated, "There may be times when we are powerless to prevent injustice, but there must never be a time when we fail to protest." What Jesus taught in this beatitude is that His disciples should develop a passionate hunger to see injustice corrected, wherever and against whomever it is practiced.

Having this attitude makes us blessed in several ways. We are blessed because we would be sharing in the passion of our Lord who came from heaven on this very mission (Luke 4:17-21). We are also blessed because this hunger will give us a purpose in life with a cause beyond ourselves. Some of the most fulfilled people in life are those pursuing the cause of social justice that makes their lives worth living, and gives them something worth dying for. William Wilberforce and Martin Luther King Jr. are examples. But the greatest blessing is the consolation that justice will eventually be established on earth when Jesus, the King of Righteousness sets up His earthly kingdom. Until then, those hungering and thirsting for righteousness will constantly pray, "your kingdom come ..." Are you missing a blessing because you are ignoring a righteous cause?

Father, save us from frustration, selfishness or indifference on this matter of social justice. May we care about the oppressed and abused, and may this passion drive us to long for the fulfillment of your kingdom on earth.

June 23

CREATING A MERCY LIFELINE

Reading Passage: Matt. 5:2-12
Main Text: Matt. 5:7 Blessed are the merciful,
      For they will be shown mercy. (NIV)

Mercy allows someone, such as a guilty sinner or a conquered enemy, who has failed or is unqualified, to be forgiven, accepted unconditionally, or set free. It cannot be demanded, nor is it deserved, for it is totally based on the benevolence of the mercy-giver. This places the mercy-giver in a position of power over the person needing mercy, like a judge with a guilty prisoner, or a forgiving wife with a cheating husband. The blessed person is not the one who exercises his power over another. Rather, the blessed person is the one who in mercy, willingly accepts the injury or pays the penalty of another because he sees himself in that person's place. He recognizes his own failures and faults, and knows that eventually, he will also be in need of mercy. He is not just a powerful mercy-giver; he has become humbly merciful because of the way he sees himself.

A person who refuses to be merciful fails to see himself in a situation where he may need mercy. If we are judgmental and unforgiving in response to the failures of others, we will have no basis on which to plead for our own mercy. We are blessed when our attitude of mercy has created for us a lifeline through which we can also receive mercy. Our challenge is to be able to remember our weaknesses and our constant need for mercy, when we are faced with the failures of others.

When Jesus gave a parable in Matt. 18:23-33 to illustrate the importance of showing mercy, he told of a servant whose master forgave him a debt of several million dollars after he pleaded for mercy. Subsequently, the servant went out and threw his fellow servant in prison when he failed to pay a debt of a couple thousand dollars, despite his pleas for mercy. The master said to the unmerciful servant, "Shouldn't you have had mercy on your fellow servant just as I had on you?" (Matt. 18:33 NIV). This was a parable describing the kingdom of heaven. Jesus was indicating that in His kingdom we have all received mercy, since we entered as guilty sinners and received forgiveness; therefore we are obligated in turn to offer mercy to anyone requiring it from us.

How willing are you to offer mercy to those needing it? Do you recognize your obligation to offer mercy since you received mercy on entering the kingdom? Remember that the lifeline of mercy we may need tomorrow, may be the one we offer to someone today.

Father, we are so grateful for the mercies we have received, and the opportunity we have to offer mercy in return. We want to keep this blessing flowing to and from us, so help us to always remain humbly merciful, in Jesus' name.

June 24

MANNA SERIES: REACHING JESUS ON A MOUNTAINTOP
VISION CORRECTION FROM INTERNAL CLEANSING

Reading Passage: Matt. 5:2-12
Main Text: Matt. 5:8 Blessed are the pure in heart,
For they will see God. (NIV)

The old man was complaining that the television picture needed adjustment and suggested that his son call the repairman. The son, accustomed to his father's outbursts about the inferior products we have to buy these days, approached his father, removed his eyeglasses and cleaned the lenses. After putting on the glasses, the old man asked his son what he had done to correct the television picture while hiding his glasses.

This story provides a humorous illustration of the relationship between purity and sight. What we see and our perception of things are affected by the state of our hearts and minds. If we are anxious, we tend to see things that justify our fears; if we are thirsty in a desert we see mirages; if we love art and beauty, we tend to see it everywhere. When we are suspicious and judgmental of people, we will always see negative actions that validate our suspicions.

To be pure in heart does not denote innocence in understanding, as in the case of children. Rather it indicates the practice of keeping our hearts free from attitudes or actions that disrupt or discolor our relationship with other people and with God. We seek to be honest and fair, gentle and kind to others, without prejudice or suspicion of evil motives, giving them the benefit of doubts. In the Old Testament this attitude is referred to as "clean hands and pure hearts." Our desire for pure hearts will cause us to desire to be morally pure before God, with our thought-lives being free from sexual, covetous and deceptive contaminants.

When we practice being in such a state of purity, the lens of our hearts will be clean, enabling us to see God. We will see Him active in the lives of people around us, as He gives them the ability to cope with life's challenges. Our pure hearts will allow us to look beneath the surface of their lives, and whereas we used to misjudge them, we now see God taking them on a journey that will challenge and transform them. We will see God granting us grace to endure situations that would normally put a strain on our relationship with difficult people. Our hearts, free from contaminants, will become a welcoming dwelling- place for God where we meet with Him continually.

Father, we pray with the Psalmist, search us and know our hearts, try us and know our thoughts, see if there is any offensive way in us. We want the blessing of seeing You always. This is our desire and prayer in Jesus' wonderful name.

June 25

MANNA SERIES: REACHING JESUS ON A MOUNTAINTOP
THE BLESSED RECOGNITION

Reading Passage: Matt. 5:2-12
Main Text: Matt. 5:9 Blessed are the peacemakers,
For they will be called sons of God. (NIV)

We are made sons of God by our faith in Jesus Christ (Gal. 3:26). Although "made sons," we are not so recognized in the world until we demonstrate the attributes of a son of God. In this beatitude Jesus presents one of the identifying marks of a son of God: it is being a peacemaker.

We understand that a peacemaker is someone who enters a situation with warring factions, and works to bring the parties together in order to cause an end to the conflict. This picture supported by scripture, is perfectly illustrated in the life of Jesus, the Son of God. First, He made peace between man and God, by sacrificing Himself to pay the penalty for the sin that caused the enmity between man and God (Rom. 5:1). He also made peace between Jews, the people of privilege, and Gentiles, the people with no access, rights or privilege. He did this by removing the wall of separation between the two, by His death on the cross (Eph. 2:15-16). Because He came on a mission of peace, and He embodies peace, it is appropriate that He was recognized as a peacemaker by one of His names, "Prince of Peace." When He was leaving the earth, He passed the role of peacemaking to His disciples, stating in John 14:27 NIV, "Peace I leave with you; my peace I give you. I do not give to you as the world gives."

As His assigned peacemakers, we should be the initiators of peace in every situation in our world. The very aura of our lives should be that of peace. Unfortunately, we are too often the instigators of conflict over rights, church practices or politics. Instead of being peacemakers, or peace brokers, we become peace breakers. What this beatitude makes clear is that we will not be identified as sons of God by our doctrines, or our righteous indignation against evil, as valuable as that may be. It is when we act in the role of peacemaker, which is contrary to a world with battling egos, that we are recognized as sons of God. Like Jesus, we must be willing to pay the price of self-sacrifice in order to create peace.

How are we identified in our family, community or workplace? Peacemaking is worth the sacrifice if it leads to our being recognized as sons of God.

Father, we will heed Paul's command to pursue the things that make for peace (Rom. 14:19) so that we may fully represent the kingdom of peace, for Jesus' sake.

June 26

MANNA SERIES: REACHING JESUS ON A MOUNTAINTOP
A BLESSING IN PERSECUTION?

Reading Passage: Matt. 5:2-12
Main Text: Matt. 5:10 Blessed are those who are persecuted because of righteousness,

For theirs is the kingdom of heaven. (NIV)

No normal person chooses to be persecuted or to suffer. Why then did Jesus state that we are blessed when we are persecuted? This is not persecution for misbehavior, for political reasons, or for being a member of any minority group. The persecution comes as a response to the stand we take for righteousness. We may not choose persecution, but 2 Tim. 3:12 states "In fact, everyone who wants to live a godly life in Christ Jesus will be persecuted." The form of persecution will vary in intensity, from ridicule and being ostracized, to being physically assaulted, imprisoned or even murdered. What causes believers to maintain their stand for righteousness in the face of persecution is the awareness that this marks their identity with their Lord, and the confidence in the glory this provides.

Jesus explained that suffering led to His glorification. When He approached the "hour" of His suffering on the cross, He declared in John 17:1 NIV "Father, the time has come; glorify Your Son, that Your Son may glorify You." He also taught His disciples that they would not escape persecution; He said, "A time is coming when anyone who kills you will think he is offering a service to God" (John 16:2 NIV). The early disciples experienced this persecution, but because of Jesus' warning they rejoiced that they were counted worthy to suffer for His name.

Have you been persecuted recently? Is this persecution arising because of your stand for Christ and the standards He proclaimed? Don't give up the fight, don't lower the standards, don't be overcome with self-pity. Instead, consider yourself blessed to be identified with Jesus and to be assured of His glory. Note the following exhortation from the apostle Peter:

> Dear friends, do not be surprised at the painful trial you are suffering, as though something strange were happening to you. But rejoice that you participate in the sufferings of Christ, so that you may be overjoyed when His glory is revealed. If you are insulted because of the name of Christ, you are blessed, for the Spirit of glory and of God rests on you. If you suffer, it should not be as a murderer or thief or any other kind of criminal, or even as a meddler. However, if you suffer as a Christian, do not be ashamed, but praise God that you bear that name. 1 Pet. 4:12-16 NIV.

Father, we confess that persecution and the related suffering is something we would love to avoid. Grant us the grace to value our identity with Christ so that we will not shrink from suffering for His sake.

June 27

MANNA SERIES: REACHING JESUS ON A MOUNTAINTOP
HEAVENLY KINGDOM INFLUENCE

Reading Passage: Matt. 5:13-16
Main Text: Matt. 5:13 "You are the salt of the earth. But if the salt loses its saltiness, how can it be made salty again? It is no longer good for anything, except to be thrown out and trampled by men." (NIV)

If it were possible for salt to lose its flavor, or cease being salty, would it still be regarded as salt? For salt to cease being salty, there would have to be a change in its chemical properties, giving it a different identity. The nature and purpose of salt is to be salty and to influence anything it is brought into contact with, by giving flavor or by causing its preservation.

Jesus began His sermon on the mountainside by stating in nine Beatitudes the attitudes that should be possessed by those belonging to the new kingdom He was establishing. These attitudes that brought blessings were so contrary to the prevailing attitudes of the citizens of worldly kingdoms that they could be considered revolutionary. Why were these revolutionary attitudes required for citizens of the heavenly kingdom that was ruled by Christ? Jesus was establishing a kingdom in the midst of worldly kingdoms, and the task of this kingdom would not be immediate conquest, but to influence while attracting new citizens. In our text He described the characteristics of His kingdom citizens in relationship to the world, and how they would accomplish their task. He described them as salt and light.

As salt we remain in the world, mostly inconspicuous, powerful in flavorful influence, yet undiluted and unaffected by the surrounding world. The world would be tasteless and morally unpalatable without our presence, which makes us desirable without being domineering. Although the ungodly may hate us since our presence reminds them of their sin, yet deep down they should admire us for our standards of righteousness and our commitment to eternal values. Our call to be salt, although most effective in the communal context of the church, begins in the lifestyle of the individual believer.

Do we maintain an association with the people of the world so we can have an impact? We cannot have an impact unless we are in touch. Do we maintain a distinction in our associations, so we can influence without being ourselves influenced? If we are not performing our role as salt in the earth, Jesus said we are worthless, good for nothing, except to be thrown away, no longer to be regarded as salt.

Father, You have called us into Your kingdom to be Your means of influence in the earth as salt and light. Keep us aware of our responsibilities and help us to be effective daily in our function, so the kingdom of our Lord may be manifested. This is our desire for the glory of our King, the Lord Jesus Christ.

June 28

MANNA SERIES: REACHING JESUS ON A MOUNTAINTOP
A HIDDEN LAMP IS USELESS

Reading Passage: Matt. 5:13-16
Main Text: Matt. 5:16 In the same way, let your light shine before men, that they may see your good deeds and praise your Father in heaven. (NIV)

It was an eerie feeling approaching the city by air at night and seeing the continuation of the same darkness we experienced while crossing the ocean. The pilot provided the explanation; there was a power outage over the city. A city in darkness is a scary place. There are hidden dangers and it is easy to get lost. A world in darkness needs light.

Jesus, knowing the dark state of the worldly kingdoms because of the sinful state of the human heart, established the kingdom of heaven to provide light to the world. Addressing His disciples Jesus told them, "You are the light of the world. A city on a hill cannot be hidden" (Matt. 5:14). As light, our role is to provide illumination and direction. Our lifestyles of righteousness, purity and peace should expose the dangerous lifestyles of the world, allowing people to avoid them. Another way to shine our light is by our remarkable deeds, which others would immediately recognize as being reflective of our Father's character. When we bless those who curse and persecute us, the world knows that this is the behavior of sons imitating the Heavenly Father, and thus they glorify Him.

With such a responsibility, the worst thing a lamp bearer can do is to deliberately hide his or her light, leaving the surrounding darkness unchanged. The whole purpose of a lamp is to provide light, so if our light is not affecting our world it begs the question, whether we really are disciples, or whether we are aware of our responsibilities. A hidden lamp is useless. A dark world needs light, and our Heavenly Father is depending on us to get Him glory.

If we find ourselves in dark surroundings where there is a strong presence of evil, we may have been placed there on special assignment by the Father to provide light. If our deeds lead people to glorify us, our deeds are still too ordinary and not sufficiently reflective of the Father's love and mercy. We must never forget that we represent a heavenly kingdom that is in conflict with the worldly kingdoms. Our role is to influence and illuminate people of the other kingdoms, as salt and light, so they will be attracted to our King and His rule.

When the unpleasant state of the world causes us to despair and curse the darkness, let us examine our lives to see whether we are fulfilling our responsibilities to shine our lights.

Father, the challenge of being aware that we have been placed in this world to influence and illuminate our surroundings, sometimes appears daunting. We don't want to fail at this task so help us to take a stand and shine, for Jesus' sake.

June 29

MANNA SERIES: REACHING JESUS ON A MOUNTAINTOP
WHEN IS OUR RIGHTEOUSNESS SUFFICIENT?

Reading Passage: Matt. 5:17-20
Main Text: Matt. 5:20 For I tell you that unless your righteousness surpasses that of the Pharisees and the teachers of the law, you will certainly not enter the kingdom of heaven.. (NIV)

Bartholomew, the devout Pharisee, arrived at the gate of the kingdom of God. The gatekeeper said to him, "Can you meet the standard of righteousness required for entry?" Bartholomew responded, "Surely you are aware of my good deeds and my diligence in keeping the law and the traditions, I must qualify quite easily." The gatekeeper closed the gate as he solemnly said, "This is God's kingdom and the entry standards are based on His perfect righteousness. Sorry, you have fallen short of the requirements; you cannot enter." Bartholomew walked away muttering, "How is it possible for anyone to have sufficient righteousness to qualify?"

The dilemma faced by Bartholomew in this fictitious story, is the one we all face. We live in human kingdoms where outstanding citizenship is represented by the highest standards of human nature. But the kingdom of God is based on heavenly rules that are contrary to our human nature. God's requirements are stated in His commandments and the words He gave the prophets. However, what He desires is obedience from the heart as proof of our love for Him. Many Jews, as exemplified by the Pharisees, responded in a way that suited their human nature. The righteousness was regimented, self-celebrated, external and frequently insincere. They obeyed, not because there was an inward desire to please the Lord in love, but because it was a burdensome demand that would gain the admiration of men for their accomplishment. The scribes and interpreters of the law developed traditions in addition to the law, providing further burdensome requirements to be met in the quest for righteousness.

In His sermon, Jesus explained that He came from heaven, not to abolish or amend the law, but to completely fulfill it. As God, He was the source of the law and was the only one qualified to properly interpret and practice it. He makes his righteousness available to us when we put our faith in Him. All our other attempts at righteousness, such as following the traditions of our church, the moral customs of our culture, are all insufficient to make us qualified.

The message of the gospel is that God accepts us as righteous based on our faith in Christ. Listen to the testimony of a converted Pharisee named Paul in Phil. 3:9 NIV, "...and be found in him, not having a righteousness of my own that comes from the law, but that which is through faith in Christ—the righteousness that comes from God and is by faith." The only righteousness that is acceptable is Christ's righteousness that is imputed to us by faith. Are you trusting Jesus for your righteousness?

Father, I thank you for Jesus who has provided my righteousness and made me qualified to enter the kingdom.

June 30

MANNA SERIES: REACHING JESUS ON A MOUNTAINTOP
RIGHTEOUSNESS IN HORIZONTAL RELATIONSHIPS

Reading Passage: Matt. 5:21-26
Main Text: Matt. 5:23-24 Therefore, if you are offering your gift at the altar and there remember that your brother has something against you, leave your gift there in front of the altar. First go and be reconciled to your brother; then come and offer your gift. (NIV)

The Holy Spirit brings some surprising and uncomfortable thoughts to our minds when we are engaged in prayer and worship. Our usual response is to try to praise and worship over the "distraction" or seek to quickly end our prayer, not appreciating that He is seeking to condition our hearts for kingdom righteousness.

After Jesus denounced the standard of righteousness practiced by the Pharisees and explained that He came to properly fulfill the law, He provided examples using the formula, "You have heard it said .... but I say to you." In so doing, Jesus corrected the teaching of the Pharisees and provided the divinely intended meaning of the law. On the topic of murder, He said that kingdom righteousness makes the judgment of murder long before the act is committed. We are judged guilty of murder when we become angry with, or insult our brother, like calling him a fool. Because of this possibility of being guilty of murder without any external evidence, the Holy Spirit intervenes by speaking to our hearts when we come to worship.

Notice how He interrupts our piety when we think all is well between God and us. He is more interested in the state of our hearts in relation to our brothers and sisters, than in our offerings of praise, prayer, worship or even our tangible gifts. So at those awkward times, He reminds us about those with whom our relationship is not as it should be. Usually we try to justify ourselves by reasoning, "I have nothing against that person, she seems to have something against me, and so I will just wait until she sorts out her problem or eventually gets over it." Sounds reasonable, but it is totally unacceptable for a kingdom citizen. Until we "go and be reconciled" to those who have a problem with us, all our praise, prayer and worship is just noise and "hot air" before God. The work of the Holy Spirit is to keep us from committing murder, and to ensure we exhibit kingdom righteousness.

How sensitive are we to the small voice of the Holy Spirit when He reminds us of things that are not right in our horizontal relationships? Are we willing to interrupt our worship and take the initiative to correct relationships with our brothers and sisters? We will be kept in a spiritual prison until we get it done (Matt. 5:26).

Lord, we are grateful that You keep disturbing us to ensure we are conditioned to the righteousness that is representative of Your kingdom. Keep us always sensitive to the voice of the Spirit, in the name of Jesus.

July 1

MANNA SERIES: REACHING JESUS ON A MOUNTAINTOP
RADICAL SURGERY FOR WRONG DESIRES

Reading Passage: Matt. 5:27-32
Main Text: Matt. 5:28-29 But I tell you that anyone who looks at a woman lustfully has already committed adultery with her in his heart. If your right eye causes you to sin, gouge it out and throw it away. It is better for you to lose one part of your body than for your whole body to be thrown into hell. (NIV)

There is a saying, "You don't have to use a sledgehammer to kill an ant." The idea is that the solution should be proportional to the problem. But Jesus taught this exaggerated response in addressing the matter of sexual sins. His teaching was very different from that of the Pharisees.

The Pharisees' teaching on the seventh commandment emphasized external compliance. For them, adultery was the act of sexual union between persons who were not married to each other, and once this did not occur they could boast that they kept this commandment. Jesus explained the intent of the commandment beginning with His usual introduction, "...but I say to you," and continued by stating that the act of adultery begins with looking with sexual, lustful intentions at a person who is not your spouse.

We easily judge, criticize, and condemn those whom we discover to have broken the commandment by external action, yet we may be guilty before God of the same sin. On one occasion, the Pharisees brought to Jesus a woman caught in the act of adultery. Before addressing the woman, Jesus dared those who were without sin to cast the first stone. When they heard the challenge they all quietly left the scene (John 8:3-11). While we naturally judge outward appearances and performance, God judges the heart. Therefore He expects His kingdom citizens to fulfill the commandments from the heart by not even looking lustfully at someone to whom we are not married.

How do we comply with this command? Jesus knows that in practice we will be tempted, but He teaches us to deal with these temptations with an exaggerated response. To gouge out our eye or to cut off our hand is to permanently remove the source of attraction or opportunity for temptation, in order that the temptation would not be repeated. Just as we would never be able to see again from the torn out eye, we should permanently cut off any relationship, discontinue any practice, including deleting internet access to sites, that would cause us to lust and commit adultery in our hearts. Radical surgery is required to disable wrong desires.

Lord, we know your high standard has been designed to keep us in a place where we will please You with a clear conscience. Help us to be willing to make any sacrifice You demand to maintain Your standards of righteousness, for Jesus' sake.

July 2

MANNA SERIES: REACHING JESUS ON A MOUNTAINTOP
A TIT WITHOUT A TAT

Reading Passage: Matt. 5:38-42
Main Text: Matt. 5:38-39 "You have heard that it was said, 'Eye for eye, and tooth for tooth.' But I tell you, do not resist an evil person. If someone strikes you on the right cheek, turn to him the other also." (NIV)

Growing up as children we instinctively had a sense of retaliatory justice. If a child hit us we were not satisfied until we returned the blow. The danger with the human instinct is the risk of disproportionate retaliation, which could lead to a continuous cycle of retaliation. The Old Testament law of "eye for eye ... " was designed to prevent this. People generally acknowledge the righteousness of appropriate punishment, which forms the basis of the justice system of most countries.

In His sermon, Jesus raises the bar much higher for kingdom citizens, declaring, "Do not resist an evil person." Instead, He instructed them to offer the other cheek. How could Jesus make such an unnatural policy? What could be gained by leaving kingdom citizens open to such abuse in this world? The point is, the righteousness expected in the heavenly kingdom must be clearly seen to have a supernatural characteristic, proving to observers that we are born from above. In confronting someone intending to hurt us, we do not insist on our rights or seek to retaliate, but we turn him over to the Lord as we turn the other cheek.

By suffering the risk of being humiliated and abused, we create the opportunity for the Lord to be glorified when He intervenes on our behalf. This is such a difficult challenge because it is so contrary to our natural instinct and requires great trust in God to protect us. No wonder we rarely see this practiced even among the people of God. The apostle Paul captured the essence of Jesus' teaching when he wrote in Rom. 12:19-20 NIV:

Do not take revenge, my friends, but leave room for God's wrath, for it is written: 'It is mine to avenge; I will repay,' says the Lord. On the contrary: 'If your enemy is hungry, feed him; if he is thirsty, give him something to drink. In doing this, you will heap burning coals on his head.'

Are we displaying this principle of kingdom righteousness? Are you feeling aggrieved because someone has taken advantage of you? Do you find you are fighting to ensure that your rights are not violated? Are you looking for an opportunity to get even with someone who hurt you? The critical question is: Have you turned these situations over to the Lord, and trusted Him to get glory for Himself?

Lord, we surrender our rights to You so You can produce Your righteousness through our circumstances and be glorified.

July 3

MANNA SERIES: REACHING JESUS ON A MOUNTAINTOP
PROVIDING A GRACEFUL SURPRISE

Reading Passage: Matt. 5:38-42
Main Text: Matt. 5:40-42. And if someone wants to sue you and take your tunic, let him have your cloak as well. If someone forces you to go one mile, go with him two miles. Give to the one who asks you, and do not turn away from the one who wants to borrow from you. (NIV)

Jesus used the phrase of "turning the other cheek" to illustrate how we should respond to abuse. While many find the idea of being physically harmed twice without retaliation disturbing, He expanded the illustration of abuse to various areas of life. In each case, our response should be to go beyond what is expected of us, so that our antagonist would be totally surprised. The only explanation for such a response is the demonstration of supernatural grace.

When someone takes action to demand something that is legitimately ours, like a suit, rather than "resisting the abuse" and incurring legal costs, surprise him by also supplying the accessories to the item, like the matching shirt. Just imagine his reaction. If a woman demands that we go out of the way to take her somewhere, rather than complaining or stating how much she already owes us, we also offer to buy her lunch on the journey. "Going the second mile" will baffle most people. When someone has not repaid what was borrowed from us, and he comes for another loan, he expects to be reminded of the outstanding debt and be denied. Jesus said that we should surprise him by giving again.

To the world, and to our human nature these responses appear foolish. But Jesus is requiring us to live at a higher level where His character is manifested, and His grace is demonstrated. Think of how much we receive daily that we do not deserve from Him, yet He "turns the other cheek," gives more than we demand, or goes the extra mile for us. As His children, He wants us to extend the same grace to others, so when they are surprised and ask why, we can point them to the Father. This is the reason the righteousness of the heavenly kingdom has to be based on a new birth that produces a new nature with new values. We can't fake these supernatural responses for very long.

Father, we admit that of ourselves we can never comply with the behavior required for Your kingdom. We expect to be tested in these areas of our relationships in the coming days. Our prayer is that You live in and through us, in Jesus' name.

July 4

MANNA SERIES: REACHING JESUS ON A MOUNTAINTOP
BEING SONS OF A HEAVENLY FATHER

Reading Passage: Matt. 5:43-48
Main Text: Matt. 5:44-45 But I tell you: Love your enemies and pray for those who persecute you, that you may be sons of your Father in heaven. He causes his sun to rise on the evil and the good, and sends rain on the righteous and the unrighteous. (NIV)

Many of us struggle to be our fathers' sons. This struggle is not regarding biological identity; instead we often find it difficult to represent our earthly fathers by behavioral identity. Some fathers who are mechanically minded and love to tinker with car engines produce sons who hate anything mechanical, preferring instead, to pursue the arts. The desire of most fathers is that their sons would be "a chip off the old block" so that people will have no doubt who their fathers are when they see them in action.

In establishing the kingdom of heaven on earth, God has one identity for its citizens: they must be His children. He provides the pattern in Jesus the King, as the perfect Son of God. And as stated in John 1:12-13 NIV: "Yet to all who received Him.... He gave the right to become children of God— children born not of natural descent, nor of human decision or a husband's will, but born of God."

How should the children behave in order to represent the Heavenly Father? We must love our enemies, and pray for those who persecute us. Sometimes, we would much prefer being the son of a powerful, wrathful God who takes vengeance on His enemies. Although the Son of God will one day be revealed in power and wrath, in this period of establishing the kingdom, He wants to be manifested as the Son of the Father of mercy and grace. Our behavior to our enemies will indicate which father we represent. As children of earthly sinful fathers, we have a tendency to love only those who love us, and to be kind and friendly to only those whom we like.

But our Heavenly Father gives rain and sunshine equally to those who are evil and good, equally to the nice and the nasty. To be sons of our Heavenly Father, we have to do the same. When we are confronted with people who are evil or unkind to us, we have to decide which father we will represent in our response.

Father, you have called us to be as perfect as You are in our treatment of the unlovely. May the stamp of Your identity in us by the Holy Spirit be so overwhelming that it will fully replace our identities with our earthly fathers. This we pray in Jesus' name.

July 5

MANNA SERIES: REACHING JESUS ON A MOUNTAINTOP
IF YOU SHOW IT, YOU LOSE IT

Reading Passage: Matt. 6:1-18
Main Text: Matt. 6:1 "Be careful not to do your 'acts of righteousness' before men, to be seen by them. If you do, you will have no reward from your Father in heaven." (NIV)

Some things are so delicate in design that any attempt to force their display immediately causes their ruin. Forcing the display of a budding rose or releasing a butterfly from its pupa are striking examples. The righteousness of the kingdom of God is so uniquely "other worldly" that any attempt to manipulate it for self-promoting, prideful purposes immediately causes it to be debased. It then becomes useless for God's glory, and for gaining rewards from the Heavenly Father.

Jesus used strong words to warn His disciples to avoid the Pharisees' practice of righteousness, which was intended for show in order to gain people's admiration and applause. He highlighted areas where we are often tempted to be pharisaic in practice: giving, praying and fasting. For these practices to be genuinely righteous acts, and rewarded by the Father, they must be done in secret, hidden from people but observed by God. For our giving to be done in secret, even our left hand should not know what our right hand has done. It is hidden to those closest to us. For our praying to be done in secret, it should be done behind "closed doors," without surplus words and empty clichés; in fact, it should be private communication between·Father and child. Fasting should not be an occasion for public display and pious behavior; it should be done just for the audience of the Father who sees in secret.

There is so much in our practice of religion that is external and showy for the purpose of impressing people. We dress to conform to the rules, when we should be dressing to please the Lord. We use "sanctified speech" around the Christian community instead of ensuring our hearts are sanctified, so we can speak naturally. After spending some time around the church, we acquire prayer and worship practices and even facial expressions that will gain the admiration of members and leaders.

Let us never forget that man looks on the outward appearance, but God looks on the heart. As soon as we become conscious of the show, we lose the authenticity of heavenly righteousness.

Father, open the eyes of our hearts so we may see You observing our behavior and grading our sincerity. We want to keep our righteous acts a secret between us, and for Your delight. We seek Your grace to achieve this, in Jesus' name.

July 6

MANNA SERIES: REACHING JESUS ON A MOUNTAINTOP
THE INFLUENCE OF
INVESTMENT LOCATION

Reading Passage: Matt. 6:19-24
Main Text: Matt. 6:20-21 But store up for yourselves treasures in heaven, where moth and rust do not destroy, and where thieves do not break in and steal. For where your treasure is, there your heart will be also. (NIV)

One of the key concerns of investment advisors is how well an investor's portfolio is balanced to minimize risk. Investments should be spread across various instruments, industries and geographic locations. The importance of location balancing is to ensure that an economic downturn in one country will not have too great an effect on the overall portfolio.

In this section of His sermon, Jesus provided investment advice for kingdom citizens, knowing that investments which are valuable to us, become our treasures. But contrary to earthly business advisors, He instructed that all our treasures should be placed in one location, in heaven. None should be placed on earth where it would be subject to loss because of natural disasters, financial misfortune, or theft by even the investment advisors. Treasures in heaven are secure. How does one make investments in heaven? The consistent teaching of scripture is that giving to the poor or helping those in need results in adding to heavenly investments (Matt. 19:21; Luke 12-18-22; 1Tim.6:17-19). What we do with our investments will indicate where we are accumulating our treasure.

Jesus' other statement was, "Where your treasure is, there your heart will be also." When we have our treasure in the stock markets, we keep checking the movements of the market daily, or sometimes, hourly. If our treasure is in a certain country, we keep abreast of the political and financial activities of that country. The location of our treasure determines the center of our interest and passion. Because of this natural link, Jesus' warning of not laying up treasures on earth is not only intended to keep us from inevitable disappointment, but also to ensure that our minds and affection would be heavenly rather than earthly.

The reason we end up in conflicts over material things and lose our peace is that these are valuable to us. But when our treasures are in heaven, it matters little if we lose earthly valuables by an illegitimate capture, a natural disaster, or even when we have to face death. As heavenly citizens, we leave this earth to go to our real treasures. How is your heavenly portfolio looking? Have you made any deposits lately? If your mind is stressed by threats to earthly assets, this may indicate the wrong location of your treasure?

Father, we thank You for giving us the opportunity for an out-of-this-world investment in the unsearchable riches of Christ. Help us to daily seek to add to the heavenly treasure by the way we use our money. This we ask for Jesus' sake.

July 7

MANNA SERIES: REACHING JESUS ON A MOUNTAINTOP
WHY SEEK FOR WHAT GOD WANTS TO ADD?

Reading Passage: Matt. 6:25-34
Main Text: Matt. 6:32-33 For the pagans run after all these things, and your heavenly Father knows that you need them. But seek first his kingdom and his righteousness, and all these things will be given to you as well. (NIV)

The most basic requirements for life include food, drink and clothing, and it is natural that we pursue these things for our survival. After fulfilling the needs of today, humans begin the pursuit of tomorrow's needs. This desire to ensure we are secure for tomorrow results in anxiety and stress. The needs of tomorrow are so undefined and uncertain that we are never sure when we have sufficient. Yet the increased worry over the unknown tomorrow ruins the enjoyment of today, and fails to solve tomorrow's cares.

Jesus identifies two problems that are the source of our worry. First, we have the incorrect understanding of the essence of life. He asked, "Is not life more important than food, and the body more important than clothing?" Food may keep us alive, but it doesn't help us to really live because there is a life that is far more significant than the physical: the life that is associated with God, the creator of life. The other problem is the uncertainty of supply for physical needs. This is solved when we are aware that our Father can supply all our needs and He is aware of them before we ask Him. When we have this source, we can be as carefree as the birds of the air and the lilies in the field. Despite their lack of anxiety over the future, their provisions are supplied and they look impressive.

Therefore, Jesus' command to His kingdom citizens is, "Don't worry, and stop seeking material things". Instead, we should seek our Father's interest, which is the Lord's reign in people's lives, and the demonstration of His righteousness. When we shift our pursuit from the material to the spiritual, we discover that God just adds the material blessing to our lives. Those who don't know God as Father, cannot be expected to shift their desires from the basic requirements, but those who belong to the kingdom will experience the joy of having the Lord add material blessings while they are seeking His glory.

The clear message of Jesus' teaching is for us to quit seeking after what leads to worry, and start seeking what leads to the Father's glory and receive His additions to our lives.

Father, keep us from reverting to the lifestyle of the ungodly, seeking and worrying over material things. Give us the desire to prioritize the kingdom and righteousness of God, for Jesus' glory.

July 8

MANNA SERIES: REACHING JESUS ON A MOUNTAINTOP
AVOIDING BLIND JUDGMENTS

Reading Passage: Matt. 7:1-6
Main Text: Matt. 7:5 You hypocrite, first take the plank out of your own eye, and then you will see clearly to remove the speck from your brother's eye. (NIV)

"Those are awful parents, who fail to control their children." "Look how he wastes his money on luxuries instead of saving for the future." "She dresses for attention without regard for modesty." "He is so smug and snobbish, with a superiority complex." These are observations made of others, whether expressed or not, that reflect our judgment of them.

The fact is, we interact with people on the basis of our judgment of them. Frequently our judgment is incorrect because it is made without knowing all the facts, which indicates we have blind spots. Jesus' command at the beginning of the passage: "Judge not, or you too will be judged," is properly understood as a warning that we should heed before rushing to judgment about anyone or anything. The standards we apply in making judgment of others will be applied to us, by both God and man.

We must always acknowledge that our observations are incomplete because of our blind spots. The beam of wood preventing us from making a proper observation are usually our biases based on our experiences, or our lack of experience in the circumstances of the person we are judging. We tend to think we would behave more admirably than others, given their circumstances. But this element of pride will backfire, because we also will face the judgment of our circumstances. When the beam is removed from our eyes, we develop empathy for others, based on the pain of beam removal. Our judgments will be tempered with mercy.

The other command by Jesus on this topic is: "Don't throw your pearls before pigs." Not only should we be cautious before making a judgment, but we should also be discriminating in offering our advice. Our valuable advice is wasted on people who can never appreciate its value. While they are "grunting" and ignoring what we said, we are left fuming at the waste of our valuable advice. Our wisdom is shown by knowing when and to whom we offer our advice. Think of how much of our parents' advice we ignored before we matured beyond our "pig-like" state.

Our challenge is never to judge before admitting the limitation of our observations. We should first submit ourselves to our own standard of judgment so we can be empathetic with those we are judging, and assess whether the timing of our judgment is appropriate. We must avoid making blind judgments.

Lord, we are humbled by Your teaching. Sometimes our proud hearts cause us to think You have given us the right to sit on Your throne of judgment. May we learn to be merciful so we may obtain mercy. This we pray through Jesus Christ.

July 9

MANNA SERIES: REACHING JESUS ON A MOUNTAINTOP
IT'S ALL ABOUT THE RELATIONSHIP

Reading Passage: Matt. 7:7-11
Main Text: Matt. 7:11 If you, then, though you are evil, know how to give good gifts to your children, how much more will your Father in heaven give good gifts to those who ask him! (NIV)

I remember getting a ride with my friend and his Dad. They stopped at the store on the journey home. When my friend asked for some candy and a comic book, his Dad replied, "Sure, son." I could only observe with envy because I had no basis on which to make any such request.

We easily forget that in the Sermon on the Mount, Jesus was not only stating the superior behavior required of the heavenly kingdom citizens, but was introducing them to the superior level of relationships in this kingdom. His Jewish audience was familiar with earthly kingdoms where the relationship was between a king and his subjects, but the Heavenly King wanted the relationship to be much more intimate, as between a father and his son.

This makes a tremendous difference to our attitude in prayer. Whereas a king responds to his subjects on the basis of the best interest of the king and the kingdom, a father responds in the best interest of the child. He seeks the good of the child even if the response has to be the denial of the desire. Although a citizen resides in the kingdom and contributes to its welfare, he never has a sense of ownership and will be reluctant to make requests of the king. The good news of the heavenly kingdom is that we belong to, and are inheritors of the kingdom. When we approach our Father, we do so on the basis of our rights as sons, and a relationship of love, so we can be bold in making our requests.

Therefore, Jesus told us, His kingdom sons, to ask, seek and knock, because our Heavenly Father is willing to give us good things, and He knows better than we do what is good for us. The process of petitioning is not as much designed to get us good things as it is to enhance our relationship with Him. By asking, we admit our lack, recognize the One who can provide, and acknowledge we couldn't obtain it on our own. By seeking, we admit we would not be able to find anything without His guidance, and by knocking we appreciate that He is the only One who can open the door to our opportunities. It is all about Him, and our relationship with Him.

May we begin to appreciate the value of prayer in developing our relationship with our Heavenly Father.

God, we are grateful we are related to the King of the Heavenly Kingdom and we can call him, "Father." Forgive us for our delinquency in prayer when all You desire is to improve Your relationship with us, and provide good things for us.

July 10

MANNA SERIES: REACHING JESUS ON A MOUNTAINTOP
LET ME SCRATCH YOUR BACK

Reading Passage: Matt. 7:7-12
Main Text: Matt. 7:12 So in everything, do to others what you would have them do to you, for this sums up the Law and the Prophets. (NIV)

Jesus' statement in the text is often referred to as the "golden rule" because it provides in simple terms a life principle that will lead to peaceful and successful interpersonal relationships. Regardless of our religious practices and theological knowledge, our righteousness must be demonstrated by the practice of this principle. As Jesus stated, it represents the teaching of all the Law and the Prophets.

We all love to be treated with love and respect, kindness and hospitality. But how do we treat others? Do we consider how we wish to be treated before offering service or responding to others? Sometimes our acts of kindness are motivated by our selfish desire to obtain favors in return, or they are delayed and only given in proportion to what we have received. This behavior is based on the philosophy, "you scratch my back and I will scratch yours." However, the golden rule does not countenance this reciprocal behavior; instead Jesus made this the concluding statement of all his prior teaching in the sermon. We are kingdom citizens with the attitude of the blessed, who go the extra mile and love even our enemies. Our treasures are secured in heaven, with a Heavenly Father who provides good things for us, therefore we should treat people in a manner that we wish to be treated. Even if they don't scratch our backs we should still scratch theirs.

Our world would be a different place if we all could practice this principle. Before making demands, providing service, hosting guests, or judging people, we should ensure the way we treat them will be just how we wish to be treated. Jesus said this principle applies "in everything." As we apply this principle today and make this behavior standard for our lives, it will affect our roles as parents or children, employers or employees, leaders in church or members of the fellowship, customer at a store or the clerk providing service, a husband or a wife. With this lifestyle we will represent the righteousness demanded of citizens of the Heavenly Kingdom.

Father, we want our righteousness to go beyond religious performance and become practical, normal behavior in our relationships. Help us to conform to the model of Jesus and be willing to grab the towel and be the first to wash the feet of others. This we pray, in the name of our Lord and Savior.

July 11

MANNA SERIES: REACHING JESUS ON A MOUNTAINTOP
THE CHOICE OF DIFFICULTY

Reading Passage: Matt. 7:13-23
Main Text: Matt. 7:13-14 "Enter through the narrow gate. For wide is the gate and broad is the road that leads to destruction, and many enter through it. But small is the gate and narrow the road that leads to life, and only a few find it." (NIV)

Ease is always attractive, but triumph without difficulty doesn't bring glory. It takes effort to climb to the mountaintop but when we get there, the view, the atmosphere and the presence of the Lord, are more than rewarding.

Jesus described the lifestyle of children of the Heavenly Kingdom as being superior to that of the Pharisees, and not easily attained. Why would anyone select this difficult option? The answer is found in the destiny of the different options. Jesus described the options as two gates, one narrow and the other wide that lead to different destinations. The wide gate is the easy path that is popular, fitting our natural tendencies, which results in many people going through it. But the path from that gate leads to destruction. What we observe in popular culture, as the majority rush through the gates to pleasure, wealth and godlessness, is evidence of humanity taking a self-destructive path.

The other option is a narrow gate, which is difficult to locate and a struggle to enter. Not surprisingly, few find it and even fewer proceed to try it. To enter this gate is to attract ridicule and ostracism, as people consider us weird and abnormal. But this is the path that was established for disciples of Jesus, and regardless of how unpopular it seems, we are assured of His presence for the journey. This path leads to the quality of life that the Creator intended.

Daily we face the choice in various areas of our lives, such as the friends we choose, the places we desire to go, and the lifestyle we seek to enjoy. Our choices of gates will indicate whether we have followed the crowd to the path that leads to destruction, or followed the despised disciples to a path that leads to life. Jesus implores us, "Enter through the narrow gate."

May we be willing to choose the path of difficulty in response to Jesus' call.

Father, we recognize that our natural tendency is to go with the flow of the crowd. Yet Jesus has made clear the danger of not choosing the difficult path. Please help us to be discerning in knowing the gates we face, and to make the right choices.

July 12

MANNA SERIES: REACHING JESUS ON A MOUNTAINTOP
UNDISPUTED FRUIT IDENTIFICATION

Reading Passage: Matt. 7:15-23
Main Text: Matt. 7:16-17 By their fruit you will recognize them. Do people pick grapes from thorn bushes, or figs from thistles? Likewise, every good tree bears good fruit, but a bad tree bears bad fruit. (NIV)

"I am sure this is an orange tree," said Colin confidently. "No," retorted Patrick, "you must be a city boy not to know it is a lemon tree." As the argument between the two became more strident, Angela calmly interrupted, "Why don't we just wait until the fruit season so we can be absolutely sure who is correct?"

Trees of the same species can appear so similar in structure and leaf type that they are indistinguishable to the casual observer. But there is a huge difference in taste between an orange and a lemon. There is a similar problem in the realm of those who claim to be followers of Jesus and true representatives of His kingdom. False prophets can easily be mistaken for the genuine, using speech and external appearance as the basis of the assessment. Pious words can be learned and spiritual gifts can be imitated. In closing His sermon, Jesus warned us to be vigilant because there are many deceivers around who prey on innocent believers. They may have great oratory, and with their charisma provide an enticing spiritual performance. But they are motivated by self- interest, and the church is a means by which they achieve their goals.

The problem for us is how to identify these hucksters. Jesus' advice is to wait until we observe the fruit of their lives. He said, "...by their fruit you will recognize them." Fruit, which is the natural and unconscious product of a life, cannot be fabricated for a sustained period of time. After a while the mask will begin to slip and we will begin to see attitudes that are contrary to those of kingdom citizens as described in the beatitudes. Instead of the humility of the poor in spirit, there will be arrogance and pride; instead of being peacemakers they will continuously stir up contention.

The false representatives of the kingdom do not only deceive onlookers but also deceive themselves. They are convinced their activities of prophesying, working miracles, and casting out demons automatically qualifies them as children of the kingdom. So they confidently approach the King with their password, "Lord, Lord," only to be denied entrance to the kingdom of heaven (v. 21). The King replies that He does not know them, because they were operating without His authorization.

These warnings challenge us not just to carefully examine the "performers" around us, but to ensure we are genuine in our profession as children of the kingdom. What is our fruit saying about us?

Father, since You are looking for fruit to prove the sincerity of our commitment, we yield to the Holy Spirit for Him to produce His fruit in us. With our trust in Christ we know this will be accomplished.

July 13

MANNA SERIES: REACHING JESUS ON A MOUNTAINTOP
BUILDING LIKE A FOOL

Reading Passage: Matt. 7:24-27
Main Text: Matt. 7:26 But everyone who hears these words of mine and does not put them into practice is like a foolish man who built his house on sand. (NIV)

When observing the destruction caused by a hurricane, I am often amazed at some losses that appear to have been avoidable if people were wiser in building their houses. Houses are sometimes built in flood prone areas or close to the banks of rivers. Very expensive houses are often located on the beachfront in places known to be in regular hurricane paths, like Miami Beach. Although no insurance coverage may be available for some of these houses, both poor and rich people are willing to take the risk thinking they will survive a hurricane without much damage. How foolish!

In closing His Sermon on the Mount, Jesus provided His hearers with clear choices. There are two gates that lead to two different destinations; two types of followers: the false and genuine, as identified by bad or good fruit; and in our text, two types of builders: wise and foolish, as indicated by whether they build on rock or on sand. How we build depends on how we respond to what we hear, and this will provide evidence of whether we are wise or foolish.

Having delivered a sermon recorded in over 100 verses of scripture, Jesus is challenging us to hear and heed in order to demonstrate that we are wise. We all experience periods of storms with destructive rain and wind, that have the potential to destroy us. What makes the difference is how we construct our lives, whether on a solid foundation or sinking sand. The principles taught by Jesus provide us with a solid rock-like foundation that will enable us to withstand any storm. But we must practice what we have heard, otherwise we will be no different from foolish people who build their houses in places where there is a high risk of destruction.

How well are we practicing loving our enemies and blessing those who curse us? Are we willing to interrupt our worship to ensure we are reconciled with our fellow Christians? Do we avoid practicing our righteousness for show, or endeavor not to recklessly judge others? Because we have heard these words, we are accountable, and subject to divine discipline for not practicing the principles.

Would our Lord regard us as wise or foolish based on the way we respond to the teachings we have received from Him?

Lord, we don't want to foolishly reject the opportunity of building our lives on the solid principles of Your word. We need the Spirit's help to remember and apply these principles consistently, until our lives become structured on a divine foundation. This we pray in the name of Jesus Christ.

July 14

MANNA SERIES: WHY THE OUTPOURING?
HE DESERVES THE HONOR

Reading Passage: Gen. 35:9-15
Main Text: Gen. 35:14 Jacob set up a stone pillar at the place where God had talked with him, and he poured out a drink offering on it; he also poured oil on it. (NIV)

The claim from a popular song in the 1970's "Love Makes You Do Crazy Things" could also be made about sincere worshippers. There may be no rational explanation for certain actions by some worshippers other than their desire to give tangible expression to their sense of obligation to the One whom they honor.

One example of this type of worshipful expression was the pouring out of a drink offering. This practice by pagan worshippers was also done by the Hebrews in the Old Testament. The first Old Testament record was that of Jacob when he came to Bethel. After consecrating a stone pillar as a sacred altar to the Lord, he poured a drink offering on it. The drink offering may have been wine, as later stipulated for tabernacle rituals (Lev. 23:13, Num. 15), but Jacob did not consume any of it.

Surely, he had made some effort to obtain the drink, probably preserving the best wine from his vineyard; so why pour it on the ground? To non-worshippers this seems such a waste, but to Jacob this was worship. Jacob had just received another visit from God at Bethel where he first met Him. God introduced Himself as El Shaddai (God Almighty), changed Jacob's name to Israel, and confirmed promises previously given to him. Jacob recognized he needed to honor his God, and he could do this by sacrificing to Him the best of what he would desire for himself. The difference between what appears to be an absurd waste and a worshipful sacrifice is the motivation behind the outpouring.

When we have experienced God and recognize His greatness and the grace He provides for us, we can't help but give tangible expression to our sense of obligation and honor to Him. Does our giving reflect the sense of honor due to our Lord? Once we begin to rationalize about the value of our gifts or think of our possible enjoyment of the elements of the sacrifice, we begin to lose appreciation for the glory of our God and the reverence due to Him. Our outpouring for our God indicates the glory we believe He deserves.

> Psa. 29:1-2 Ascribe to the LORD, O mighty ones,
> Ascribe to the LORD glory and strength.
> Ascribe to the LORD the glory due his name;
> Worship the LORD in the splendor of his holiness.
> (NIV)

Lord, when we think of who You are and what You have done for us, we will not hold back. Instead we pour out all our offerings of gratitude to You for You deserve all the honor and glory.

July 15

MANNA SERIES: WHY THE OUTPOURING?
TO ILLUSTRATE THE DIVINE FLOW

Reading Passage: Ex. 29:1-9
Main Text: Ex. 29:7 Take the anointing oil and anoint him by pouring it on his head. (NIV)

The priesthood in the Old Testament was established to perform services associated with the tabernacle. This allowed the Hebrews to offer sacrifices and offerings to Yahweh. God ordered the selection of a high priest, in the lineage of Aaron, who would have special access to Him, and represent Him to the people.

In the Hebrew culture, God used various symbolisms to communicate the message of His holiness, and the gulf between Himself and sinful mankind. For the high priest to represent Yahweh, he had to be identified as separate from his fellow Hebrews. Special priestly garments, and a turban with a crown illustrated this. The consecration ceremony for the high priest included the special sacrifice of animals, to show that atonement must be made for a sinful priest before he could be allowed to represent God. He also had to be washed, to illustrate his cleansing before he was dressed in the special priestly attire. But how would the flow of the unction, the Spirit of God to the high priest, be symbolized? God instructed that a special "holy anointing oil" be poured on his head. This was not just a few drops, but, as implied by the term "pour out," it describes a great outpouring on his head, flowing and saturating his robes, running down to its border. Note the description in Ps. 133:2.

The high priest might be washed and dressed, the sacrifices might be offered, yet he is not fully consecrated and qualified to represent God until he is anointed with oil that saturates him. The holy anointing oil was blended by a perfumer, and included sweet smelling spices (Ex. 30:23-25), which gave it a unique scent. After the priest was saturated with the oil, there was no mistaking when the priest was around because of the aroma from him.

This presents a picture and a message to Christians today who are God's priests on the earth. Are we attempting to represent God without being anointed with His Spirit? Outer garments and sacrificial symbols are inadequate to show our consecration to God. Has the Spirit of God so saturated our lives that we naturally exude a distinct aroma of the divine presence?

Father, we need a fresh outpouring of your Spirit on our lives so we may truly represent You to people needing to get in touch with You. Pour it on Lord; we desire to be fully saturated with Your presence.

July 16

MANNA SERIES: WHY THE OUTPOURING?
SACRIFICE IS NOT FOR SELF-CONSUMPTION

Reading Passage: 1Chr. 11:18-19
Main Text: 1Chr. 11:18-19 So the Three broke through the Philistine lines, drew water from the well near the gate of Bethlehem and carried it back to David. But he refused to drink it; instead, he poured it out before the LORD. "God forbid that I should do this!" he said. "Should I drink the blood of these men who went at the risk of their lives?" Because they risked their lives to bring it back, David would not drink it. Such were the exploits of the three mighty men. (NIV)

The evil of slavery lies not only in the abuse of humans by fellow humans, but also in the fact that the suffering of slaves was not for any noble purpose. The slavery on the plantations of the West Indies was primarily established in order to provide sugar and rum for the lavish consumption of the Europeans. Yet from that atrocious waste of human lives, emerged stories of sacrifice by rebellion leaders who inspired movements that led to the deliverance of many from the cruel system. Recognition of sacrifice by others should motivate us to reproduce our own, instead of using their sacrifice for our consumption.

Unfortunately, many who benefitted from the sacrifice of parents who provided a comfortable life and an educational foundation, have proceeded to waste that sacrifice in selfish consumption instead of paving the way for succeeding generations. Missionaries have suffered great deprivation and sometimes loss of their lives so we could get the Good News of the gospel of Jesus. But instead of that sacrifice being reproduced for the benefit of many others who have not yet heard about Jesus, we have become complacent in our churches and organizations and have made little effort to ensure the spread of the gospel. As a result, missionary giving and sending are declining.

Our text describes an interesting incident in David's life before he became king, while he was a fugitive living in the wilderness of Judah. On one occasion while surrounded by some of his loyal, hardened fighters, he expressed his longing for a drink of water from a spring near the gate of Bethlehem. This appeared to be wishful thinking since the Philistine army was controlling that area. But these fighters risked their lives and fought through the enemy lines just to obtain the water for their master. When David got the water, to him it represented the blood and sacrifice of his men. He couldn't drink it; instead he poured it out as his sacrifice to God. He refused to enjoy for his own consumption what represented the sacrifice of others.

What sacrifice of others are we consuming instead of reproducing? Are we so focused on our pleasures that we disregard the sacrificial foundation provided by others? In response to Jesus' sacrifice for our salvation, are we content to selfishly enjoy the benefits, or are we willing to show our appreciation by our giving for missions and our work in ministry?

Lord, deliver us from an indulgent life of consumption of blessings that should be an outpouring for the benefit of others and for your glory.

MANNA SERIES: WHY THE OUTPOURING?
MY BLESSING IS LIMITED BY MY FAITH

Reading Passage: 2Kings 4:1-7
Main Text: 2Kings 4:4-5 "Then go inside and shut the door behind you and your sons. Pour oil into all the jars, and as each is filled, put it to one side." She left him and afterward shut the door behind her and her sons. They brought the jars to her and she kept pouring. (NIV)

We are blessed by God based on our belief and obedience to His word. Our faith creates the capacity for receiving the blessing. The Bible speaks of those to whom the gospel was of no benefit because the word they heard was not combined with faith (Heb. 4:2). If we wait to see the evidence, or to make sense of what we hear before acting on what God says, we destroy the faith basis by which God blesses us. On the other hand, when by faith we begin to act on God's word without seeing the source or knowing how much resource is available, we expand our capacity to receive from God.

The story in our text tells of a widow who was destitute and told the prophet that all she had in her house was a little oil. The word of God through the prophet was that she should get as many vessels as possible and begin to pour out the little she had. If she focused on the amount of oil in her possession instead of the word from God she would get no additional oil. But the more she poured, the more the oil continued to flow, and it did not cease until she stopped providing vessels in which to pour more oil. Because what she was doing defied reason and could make her the subject of ridicule, the prophet instructed her to shut the door before she began to pour the oil.

Like this widow we are frequently challenged by the word of God. When we feel destitute, we are challenged to give money to the needs of others. But we often refuse after looking at the little we have. By not responding to the challenge, we lose the opportunity for God to provide us with new sources of funds or with novel alternatives to meet our needs. Because of past hurts, we often find ourselves feeling destitute of love. Yet at those very times God presents us with others who are hurting and in need of love and compassion. Shall we look at our lack and fail to embrace an opportunity to prove God?

When we give, more will be given to us. God cannot put anything into hands that are clasped, but as we open ourselves we expand our capacity to receive from God. May we trust God and keep pouring.

Father, I realize that my failure to trust You results in my deprivation of the blessing that You desire for me. Please remind me that my blessing is according to my faith. We make this request in Jesus' name.

July 18

MANNA SERIES: WHY THE OUTPOURING?
MAXIMIZING THE OPPORTUNITIES FOR WORSHIP

Reading Passage: Matt. 26:6-13
Main Text: Matt. 26:7-8 A woman came to him with an alabaster jar of very expensive perfume, which she poured on his head as he was reclining at the table. When the disciples saw this, they were indignant. "Why this waste?" they asked. (NIV)

What causes us to be reserved, restrained and economical in our worship and acts of service to God? We may be waiting for a special demonstration of the presence of Jesus, or for others who are eager to offer sacrificial service to take the lead. Sometimes we withhold our worship awaiting "ideal conditions" when we are in good health or have the resources of money and time to give lavishly.

The story of the woman who broke with protocol to anoint Jesus as He reclined while having a meal at the house of Simon the leper, provides a demonstration of sincere worship that brings delight to Jesus. It was done at an unlikely moment when everyone was enjoying the meal. It was lavish, with the outpouring of an expensive perfume that was worth more than one year's wage. The onlookers were cynical and unappreciative of her actions. But Jesus, the object of her devotion declared, "She has done a beautiful thing to me." Our chosen method of worship to God might cause some to think it is a waste. They may even suggest we consider other noble projects for our devotions. But all that really matters is what Jesus thinks about our actions. What those present that day did not know was that it would be the last opportunity they would have to show their devotion to Jesus. He said the anointing was preparing Him for His burial. If the disciples knew this, I imagine they might have been just as generous and uninhibited as this woman was in their expression of devotion.

Sincere devotion born out of great appreciation for what Jesus has done for us will result in expressions of worship that will disregard the conditions and the skeptics. We will be seeking to maximize any opportunity to show our devotion, regardless of the personal cost. We will not want to be guilty of being reserved or restrained in our praise or acts of service, nor will we be lacking in zeal; rather we will be fervent in spirit, serving the Lord (Rom. 12:11).

Can Jesus describe our worship or service as doing a "beautiful thing for Him?" Do we find ourselves waiting for the ideal conditions for expressing our devotions, instead of grasping whatever opportunities are available to us? Do we allow the voices of the skeptics to distract us from our desire to make our Lord find delight in us?

Lord, when we think of the blessing of Your great salvation we don't want anyone or anything to hinder us from being lavish in our expressions of devotion to You. May You be glorified in our acts of worship.

July 19

MANNA SERIES: WHY THE OUTPOURING?
FORGIVENESS REQUIRED BLOOD SACRIFICE

Reading Passage: Matt. 26:26-29
Main Text: Matt. 26:28 This is my blood of the covenant, which is poured out for many for the forgiveness of sins. (NIV)

Sin is a condition suffered by all humans that cause them to act in rebellion against God, and fall short of the standard required for fellowship with Him. This condition is manifested in our many unrighteous thoughts and actions against others. However, ultimately, our sins are committed against a Holy God. Sin puts humanity under God's judgment and deserving of His wrath. Because of sin we live in a state of guilt, and fear of facing a God of wrath.

In an attempt to deal with our basic sinful nature and the burden of guilt, people have devised various ways to cope. Religion with its rituals is practiced with the hope that a supreme being, who will provide us with relief, accepts our sacrifices. This requires continuous repetition as we continue to sin, suffer guilt and need to appease the gods. Modern man hopes that by psychotherapy, meditation and behavior- modification, we will counteract the inward impulses, clear our consciences and achieve a state of peace. When these fail, relief is sometimes sought in mind-altering drugs, but the effect is only temporary.

Since man's problem is with his Creator, the only solution is to be found in what God stipulated. He stated that sin can only be dealt with by forgiveness on His terms, which is the death of the sinner or an acceptable substitute. In the Old Testament (old covenant), He accepted the blood of an undefiled animal as a substitute and provided forgiveness (Heb. 9:22). This was inadequate since an animal is an imperfect substitute. It provided only a temporary token to God; consequently the ritual needed to be constantly repeated. Therefore, God provided a new covenant for us. He sent His only son Jesus, in the form of man, as the perfect substitutionary sacrifice for us.

Jesus came to die for our sins, and provided His blood as evidence of the new covenant. He poured out His blood for the forgiveness of sins for all humanity. He willingly offered Himself as our sin offering, without holding back any part of His life. What an outpouring! and what an effect! By Jesus' blood all our sins are forgiven (past, present and future), we can be free from all guilt, and we have no fear of the judgment because God the Father has accepted His sacrifice as full and final payment.

However, only those who by faith drink His blood, an act which represents the personal acceptance of the sacrifice, can obtain these benefits. Have you had the "faith drink" of the out-poured blood?

Father, thank you for providing the new covenant that offers a permanent cleansing from sin through the blood of Jesus. By faith I drink and keep drinking from His sacrifice that restores my relationship with You.

MANNA SERIES: WHY THE OUTPOURING?
GETTING INTO THE SPIRIT'S FLOW

Reading Passage: Acts 2:17-33
Main Text: Acts 2:32-33 This Jesus God raised up, and of that we all are witnesses. Being therefore exalted at the right hand of God, and having received from the Father the promise of the Holy Spirit, he has poured out this that you yourselves are seeing and hearing. (NIV)

A river flowing down from the mountains after a heavy downpour transforms the landscape, moving obstacles out of its path, making new channels, and providing sources of nourishment for plants, animals and even humans.

The coming of the Holy Spirit is described in scripture as analogous to water being outpoured. This metaphor is most appropriate when we consider the effect of the coming of the Spirit to the world and in our lives. Just as water provides the opportunity for life, the Spirit is the basis for new life in a believer. Our sins are forgiven by faith in the blood of Jesus that was poured out for our sins, and this requires our entering into his death. However, salvation was not designed to leave us in the state of death, but to resurrect us to new life by the power of the Spirit (Rom. 6:3-4).

The unique properties of water as a liquid enables it to occupy all areas of any container into which it is poured, and to accumulate until the container is filled, unless the container is moved away from the flow. Regarding the Spirit, the Bible commands us to be filled with the Spirit, meaning to stay under the flow until He fills every area of our lives, saturating and transforming us. In natural life, the source of water is rain coming down from "above". Similarly, our resurrected Lord sent the Spirit from His exalted position at the right hand of the Father, when He was initially poured out on the day of Pentecost.

In addition to receiving a new transformed life by the outpouring of the Spirit, God desires that we be filled until we also begin to overflow, benefitting those around us. In reference to the Spirit, Jesus stated in John 7 that whoever believes in Him, rivers of living water will flow out from them. Whatever flows into us of the life of God, such as His love, peace and joy, must naturally flow out from us as long as we remain in the flow. How do we get in the flow of the Spirit? By believing in Jesus, and asking the Spirit to flow in and fill us. Once the Spirit was outpoured He has never ceased flowing. If we are not being filled, and not overflowing, the questions are: "Have we believed?" "Have we asked for the Spirit?" or "Have we moved from the flow?"

Spirit of the living God fall afresh on us. Make us, mold us, use us, fill us, so Jesus may be magnified in us.

July 21

MANNA SERIES: WHY THE OUTPOURING?
LOVE, THE IDEAL FOUNDATION FOR OUR HOPE

Reading Passage: Rom. 5:1-8
Main Text: Rom. 5:5 And hope does not disappoint us, because God has poured out his love into our hearts by the Holy Spirit, whom he has given us. (NIV)

We wondered why Justin seemed unexcited about his father's promise to take him to the ball game the following day. His mother explained that Justin's father, from whom she had been divorced, always made promises to his son, raised his hopes then failed to perform. As a result, Justin no longer trusted him, and had become unimpressed with his promises. Hope needs a foundation on which to build.

We are sometimes challenged to explain why we believe the promises in the Bible concerning our salvation, the rewards for sacrificing everything to be Christ's disciple, or our expected glory after death. This challenge comes not only from our critics, but we sometime encounter doubts within ourselves and we question the basis of our faith. Paul states in the text that our hope in Christ will not lead to disappointment because the Holy Spirit has poured the love of God into our hearts. This causes us to trust God. The work of the Spirit in the outpouring of the love of Christ is essential for us to remain hopeful when we are enduring trials, suffering and disappointment.

Unlike Justin, we know every promise God has given to us is assured, because He has proven His love for us in the past. He proved it by sending Jesus to die for us while we were sinners in rebellion against Him. He did not wait for us to change our ways, to become reformed and begin to love Him. No, He looked past our sinful condition, chose to love us in spite of it, and gave up His life as proof. We can never appreciate this sacrifice and act of love by human reasoning, as it defies logic. But the Holy Spirit enters our hearts when we believe, and pours the knowledge of this love in our hearts so we experience it in our souls. This revelation causes us to have hope in Christ and confidence in His promises. His promises are supported by His love for us.

Are you going through some difficult experiences that cause you to question whether God is real or cares about you? Are you being challenged by the arguments of the rationalists and secular thinkers of our day who state that religion, including Christianity is just a myth? It is time to revisit the cross and be reminded of Christ's love and sacrifice, so that our hope may be restored.

Holy Spirit, keep pouring the love of God in our hearts so we will remember the evidence of God's love to us, and continue to hope in His promises, in the name of our Lord Jesus.

July 22

MANNA SERIES: WHY THE OUTPOURING?
IT'S NOW OUR TURN TO BE POURED OUT

Reading Passage: 2Tim. 4:1-8
Main Text: 2Tim. 4:6-7 For I am already being poured out like a drink offering, and the time has come for my departure. I have fought the good fight, I have finished the race, I have kept the faith. (NIV)

We sometimes ask ourselves questions with respect to our Christian life such as, why do I allow people to take advantage of me? Why should I suffer disrespect without making demands? Why must I continue to give to others when I am receiving nothing in return? Why must I forgive the wrongs of others against me, yet they keep repeating their behavior? There are many other similar questions.

We begin to find answers to these questions when we recognize the purpose for which we live the Christian life. It is done for Christ's sake, not for our glory or self-esteem. Paul explained that for Christ's sake he was willing to be poured out as a drink offering. Such offerings were not for anyone's consumption; it was just poured on the ground as an indication that it was being offered to God. In reviewing my life, with the legacy passed to me through ancestry, my investment of academic and technical knowledge, with all the wisdom I think I may possess, there is nothing attractive in just having it poured out as a sacrifice for God.

All lives eventually end in death, back to dust, regardless of the heights they might have attained, or the wealth they might have amassed. But when life is lived with purpose, there is no longer mere existence until our inevitable death; rather our lives are poured into a cause greater and more enduring than ourselves. That makes the sacrifice of our lives worthwhile.

When we pour out our lives for Christ, it doesn't matter how we are treated or the lack of reward, once He is pleased with the sacrifice. Furthermore, the only reason we are motivated to make an outpouring of our lives in ministry or for the cause of Christ, including martyrdom, is that He poured out His life to redeem us.

In the passage, Paul also indicates that there will be a reward after death for his sacrifice. A crown of righteousness will be given to those who are faithful. Don't be discouraged at the sacrifices you are making; remember we are a drink offering for Him. Also remember that our rewards are not on earth in this life, but Christ Himself is waiting to reward our sacrifices after our death.

Lord, help us to be faithful and to keep fighting against all difficulties. We want to finish the race while maintaining our faith, so we can look forward to our reward from You. We seek to do this for Your sake and for Your glory.

MANNA SERIES: WHY THE OUTPOURING?
AN OUTPOURING WE MUST AVOID

Reading Passage: Rev. 16:1-21
Main Text: Rev. 16:1 Then I heard a loud voice from the temple saying to the seven angels, "Go, pour out the seven bowls of God's wrath on the earth." (NIV)

The wrath of God is a topic we don't like to think about. Many even consider it to be inconsistent with their perception of who God should be. He is acceptable as a God of love, compassion and mercy, but it is incongruous with our concept of His character that He should be a God of wrath. Of course, we entertain these thoughts until we have to consider the problem of evil in the world.

We are confronted with the problem of evil when we read of a man entering a house, killing a couple, then taking their 12 year old daughter as his sex slave; or when a leader of a country releases deadly chemicals on those fighting against him in a civil war, resulting in the death of hundreds of innocent victims including little children. History provides the example of the Nazis who captured the Jews in various countries, incarcerated, tortured and then exterminated them just because of their ethnicity. Something in us cries out for justice when we are confronted with evil, and when we feel the penalties on earth are inadequate. We desire divine retribution. The wrath of God is essential to His character of being a God of justice.

God's judgment is not restricted to those occurrences of blatant abuse as in the previous examples. His judgment is against all evil, which comes from rebellion against His rule. Rebellion is the root of all evil. It was initiated by Satan and is manifested by our sins. Once humanity fell into sin, we came under the judgment of God and deserved His wrath. To avoid this outcome, God sent Jesus to pour out His life to redeem us, and sent the Holy Spirit to empower us to live for God's glory. However, if we ignore His offer of salvation through His sacrifice, we will be subject to the outpouring of his wrath.

The Book of Revelation describes the time of the judgment and wrath of God. The descriptions, using symbolic language, are terrifying. In one of the final acts detailed in our text, angels are commanded to pour out seven bowls of the wrath of God. Each of these bowls contains horrible attacks against people's bodies and on nature, which would cause humans to desire death. This is an outpouring we should be desperate to avoid. We can avoid God's outpoured wrath by ensuring that the outpoured blood of Jesus, covers us.

Father, we are thankful that You are a God of justice so we can be assured that evil will be punished. We are also grateful that You have provided Jesus' sacrifice so we don't have suffer Your wrath.

July 24

MANNA SERIES: PROVIDENTIAL DESIGNS BEHIND THE RUTH STORY
OTHER FAILURES PRODUCED BY UNBELIEF

Reading Passage: Ruth 1:1-7
Main Text: Ruth 1:5-6 ... both Mahlon and Kilion also died, and Naomi was left without her two sons and her husband. When she heard in Moab that the LORD had come to the aid of his people by providing food for them, Naomi and her daughters-in-law prepared to return home from there. (NIV)

How does a man of Bethlehem find himself wandering in the land of Moab? Bethlehem means "house of bread" and was a significant Israelite city, where Rachel the mother of the nation was buried. Moab was a heathen country, the enemy of Israel, a nation that God's people were warned to avoid. However, the house of bread was experiencing a famine. It was easy to assume that in such an emergency when there was the risk of starvation, God would understand people suspending compliance with His rules.

Interestingly, the name of the man was Elimelech, which means God is King. As King, He must be obeyed, and we should trust His care of His subjects despite the famine. Sometimes our faith seems ridiculous in view of circumstances that demand commonsense solutions. Faith requires patience, which seems an unrealistic virtue in emergencies.

Elimelech's sojourn in Moab was full of commonsense behavior but equally loaded with unbelief in God as King. This resulted in disaster. He settled in Moab and ended up dying there. Without him being around to provide guidance, his two sons broke God's rules and married heathen Moabite women, since these were the only ones available in their adopted country. Later these boys both died, leaving their mother Naomi, with heathen daughters-in-law in Moab. While Naomi was mourning the loss of her husband and sons, and rueing the disaster caused by her husband's faithlessness, she learned God had provided bread in Bethlehem. If only they had waited; if only Elimelech had trusted God as King.

Which instructions from God are we disregarding because of our "emergencies?" What regrets have been caused by our impatience when we trusted our commonsense over God's word? Unfortunately, the disaster caused by faithlessness does not only affects us, but creates a mess that affects those around us. Even after we are dead, the negative legacy continues in our families. If God allows famine, He is able to sustain us during the famine until He is ready to "come to the aid of His people with food."

Father, we make such a mess of our lives when we take matters into our hands without waiting on You. Please help us to learn the lesson of faith and failure so we do not fail the next test. This we pray in the name of Jesus, Amen.

July 25

MANNA SERIES: PROVIDENTIAL DESIGNS BEHIND THE RUTH STORY
CHOOSING THE HOME FOR OUR RETURN

Reading Passage: Ruth 1:8-15
Main Text: Ruth 1:8 And Naomi said to her two daughters-in-law, "Go, return each to her mother's house. The LORD deal kindly with you, as you have dealt with the dead and with me." Ruth 1:10 And they said to her, "Surely we will return with you to your people." (NKJV)

Homelessness often leads to a state of despair. What makes homelessness particularly difficult to deal with is that we naturally desire to belong somewhere, a place we can call home. It is a place that represents our comfort and rest, a place of values we identify with, to which we can return regardless of how far we have wandered. Spiritually speaking, returning home does not mean going back to where we began, but going to the place of our dreams and our aspirations. But then, we have to choose the home that we wish to identify with, even if we have to forsake all our previously held values and embrace a new faith that gives us hope.

After the death of their husbands, Naomi's daughters-in-law, Orpah and Ruth, chose to return home with her to Judah, which meant embracing her culture, religion and God. Suddenly, Naomi realized these Moabite girls could not be expected to forsake the heathen home of their birth, so she implored them to remain there. She lamented that her misfortunes indicated that her God had abandoned her.

What Naomi did not realize was that the lifestyle of her family, even while living in a heathen culture, convinced her daughters-in-law of the superiority of Israel's religion and God. They wanted more than her sons as husbands; they wanted to choose a new spiritual home. This was a powerful testimony to the integrity of Naomi and her household. Although the young widows had observed adversity they might have attributed to Naomi's God, they recognized that He was still superior to any other god. Eventually, Orpah decided to remain at her "old home," but Ruth's choice of a new spiritual home was fixed.

This story challenges us to think about our witness to those who observe our lives. Is our portrayal of God so powerful and persuasive that others can be attracted to the rest, comfort and hope of our faith? We live around people that are "homeless" and confused about life. They are aware of powerful forces of evil in the world, conscious of their sinfulness and guilt, and puzzled at the futility of life because of death. They need someone to believe in, and a faith to give them hope. Can we help them to find a spiritual home?

Father, we thank You for the reality of the life of Jesus that gives us an understanding of God. We can trust in Him regardless of the misfortunes in our lives, and our souls have found a home in Him.

Help us to live so that we may provide a powerful testimony of the blessedness of trusting in Christ.

July 26

MANNA SERIES: PROVIDENTIAL DESIGNS BEHIND THE RUTH STORY
DEFYING REJECTION WITH DETERMINATION

Reading Passage: Ruth 1:12-18

Main Text: Ruth 1:16-17 But Ruth replied, "Don't urge me to leave you or to turn back from you. Where you go I will go, and where you stay I will stay. Your people will be my people and your God my God. Where you die I will die, and there I will be buried. May the LORD deal with me, be it ever so severely, if anything but death separates you and me." (NIV)

Rejection is very difficult to accept. It is an attack on our self-esteem and our pride. Why should we allow ourselves to be demeaned by someone's decision that indicates we don't belong, or can't measure up to the standards of a club or organization?

We face rejection in relationships, academic institutions, social circles, even in church groups. Sometimes our reaction to rejection is to strike out in anger, or to undermine and condemn the rejecters. Another reaction is to go into withdrawal, and by suffering psychological hurt we become self-condemning. But if we value our aspirations, our reaction will be to defy the rejection with determination. In fact, the rejection will fuel our intensity to pursue the goal, not only to achieve the prize but also to prove our rejecters wrong.

Naomi told Ruth and her sister-in-law Orpah not to accompany her to Judea, but to return to their own homes. They likely felt rejected because they strongly desired to be with her. Orpah tearfully accepted the rejection and returned home, but Ruth determinedly clung to Naomi. In the famous quotation of our text, she stated she was determined to adopt Naomi's people and her God, and only death would be able to cause a separation. With such a determination, Naomi was persuaded to allow her daughter-in-law, a Moabite heathen, to accompany her home to Judea. She knew she would face ridicule and the burden of another person to care for, but she couldn't overcome Ruth's determination.

Another example of someone defying rejection is the story of Abraham Lincoln. He was rejected many times in various elections, but by persistence became one of the outstanding presidents of the United States of America. Are you feeling rejected by someone you love, a group you desired to identify with, or by the denial of your application for a job or promotion? Don't let it affect your self-esteem. Place great value on your dreams. Consider your value to yourself, your family and to God. He chose you. Defy rejection with determination.

Father I thank You that my worth is not determined by the decision of men but by You. I trust You because You are able to cause 'stones rejected by the builders' to become the most significant stones in the building. I am grateful that through Jesus You have confirmed my value to You.

July 27

MANNA SERIES: PROVIDENTIAL DESIGNS BEHIND THE RUTH
DON'T LET CIRCUMSTANCES CHANGE YOUR NAME

Reading Passage: Ruth 1:19-22
Main Text: Ruth 1:20-21 "Don't call me Naomi,'" she told them. "Call me Mara, because the Almighty has made my life very bitter. I went away full, but the LORD has brought me back empty. Why call me Naomi? The LORD has afflicted me; the Almighty has brought misfortune upon me." (NIV)

Misfortune may challenge, strengthen, or educate me, but it doesn't have to change my personality or name. We are frequently not in control of our circumstances. We can never anticipate a car accident that takes the life of a loved one, which in turn alters the course of our lives. Many dangerous illnesses occur suddenly, affecting our outlook for a healthy life and impairing our finances. Sometimes devastating changes suddenly occur in the work environment causing us to lose confidence in future job opportunities and financial security.

If we cannot control these unforeseen changes to our lives, who is in control? Whom can we blame? To whom should we appeal for help and strength to enable us to cope? Humans have always been on a quest to control eventualities or at least to minimize their impact. However, life has taught us that we will never be in control of most factors of life. This is where our faith becomes significant. We will be able to cope when we can trust that circumstances are all under the providence of a personal supreme being; not fate or an impersonal force. That person is someone we believe knows us individually and is working out circumstances for our ultimate good, even if we don't understand the process.

Naomi demonstrated her faith when she declared that the sudden loss of her husband and two sons was ultimately under the control of her God. She declared that He had afflicted her and brought misfortune on her. Where she was mistaken was in thinking nothing good could come out of it, therefore her name should be changed. Her name Naomi meant, my joy, but she wanted to be called Mara, meaning bitter, indicating what she had become because of the circumstances. While she was thinking God had abandoned her, she was overlooking a significant feature in the plot. She was arriving in Bethlehem at the beginning of the barley harvest. She bemoaned the fact that she went out full and came back empty, but she ignored the fact that her family left because of the famine. Yet at the time of her return, God was preparing to bestow abundance.

Our adverse circumstances don't have to embitter us when we can trust that God is in charge, and He can suddenly change misfortunes to blessings for our good.

Father, we complain so frequently when we focus on our circumstances and not on the fact that You are in control. Forgive us, and provide us with the faith to trust You in all the changes of life, and the strength to endure so we don't have to change our names. Hear our prayer for Jesus' sake.

MANNA SERIES: PROVIDENTIAL DESIGNS
BEHIND THE RUTH STORY
THE DESIGNS BEHIND THE HAPPENINGS

Reading Passage: Ruth 2:1-7
Main Text: Ruth 2:3 Then she left, and went and gleaned in the field after the reapers. And she happened to come to the part of the field belonging to Boaz, who was of the family of Elimelech. (NKJV)

Life sometimes seems to be a haphazard journey of encountering different people and experiencing various chance events. We find ourselves wondering why certain things happen to us and how these things contribute to our lives. Are we just victims of fate, the products of time and chance? Or, are our lives fashioned by a wise, benevolent, divine Designer? Although we don't always get the answers to the question "why," there are times we can review our lives and see the development of a storyline that gives purpose to seemingly chance occurrences.

We know the outcome of Ruth's story, but the narrator allows us to view various scenes from her perspective with her limited knowledge of the path she was traveling. Having joined her mother-in-law in her home in Bethlehem, Ruth's next concern was how they were going to exist with no father or husband to provide for them. She took the initiative and decided to go into fields where men were reaping grain, intending to collect the "left overs" for food. Naomi had thought that having the responsibility for Ruth would be a burden, but now it became the source of her survival.

Ruth "happened" into the field of Boaz. The term used to describe this event was "by chance," an unplanned, fortuitous act. She had no idea that the field in which she happened to glean, was owned by a wealthy man who was a relative of her dead husband's father. There was a providence behind Ruth's decision to leave her Moabite homeland, arrive in Bethlehem with her mother-in-law just at the time of the beginning of harvest, and then for her to end up gleaning in the field of a relative of her late husband. These events appeared to be random, chance occurrences but, as we later learn, they were beautifully orchestrated to climax in a success story.

Are you in a place where you are questioning the various "chance" occurrences in your life? You may be wondering why you are in a certain location, interacting with certain people, and why you had certain experiences. If you are a child of God, your life is not in the capricious hands of fate, but in the faithful hands of your loving Father who is mapping your path and will cause all things to work out for your good. Trust Him.

Father, we are thankful that You know us by name and You have a plan for our lives. May we face each day with trust in Your designs and a willingness to cooperate with You in accomplishing Your purposes in us, for the glory of our Lord and Savior.

July 29

MANNA SERIES: PROVIDENTIAL DESIGNS BEHIND THE RUTH STORY
THE REWARD OF A REFUGE

Reading Passage: Ruth 2:5-12
Main Text: Ruth 2:12 "May the LORD repay you for what you have done. May you be richly rewarded by the LORD, the God of Israel, under whose wings you have come to take refuge. " (NIV)

When we are tossed and thrown about by the harsh winds of adversity and sudden changes in our circumstances, we need a refuge that provides rest and peace. After being pursued by Satanic forces, and enduring relentless waves of temptation, our souls seek a place of protection where the enemy is powerless and temptations are made ineffective. When we have journeyed through the wilderness of leanness and thirst, we look forward to the oasis where we can be nourished and refreshed with plenty. The reward of a refuge depends on our choice of a place of refuge. Many who yearn for such a place have selected places where instead of rest and protection they end up disappointed and in a state of turmoil.

Ruth made the choice to forsake the culture and gods of Moab, and cast her lot with the people of Israel. Interestingly, when Naomi urged her daughters-in-law to remain in Moab, she expressed her desire that they find rest in the home of another husband (1:9). Ruth desired more than what could be provided by a husband and home, and sensed that what she desired was available only in the God of Israel. After she met Boaz in his field, he offered a prayer, which became a prophetic statement, "May you be richly rewarded by the LORD, the God of Israel, under whose wings you have come to take refuge." Because she chose to take refuge under the protective care of the Lord, Ruth would experience safety, forgiveness, rest and refreshment.

Many religious and secular institutions fail to fulfill their promise of being a refuge. People offer their financial and other sacrifices and practice their strict rules, yet they never find forgiveness of sins or hope of heaven. Boaz knew that Israel's God gave His people access to Himself and the promise of His protection, so he would agree with the Psalmist, "Taste and see that the LORD is good, blessed is the man who takes refuge in Him" (Psa. 34:8). When we know that our souls need a refuge, we can listen to the invitation given by Jesus Himself, "Come to me, all you who are weary and burdened, and I will give you rest. Take my yoke upon you and learn from me, for I am gentle and humble in heart, and you will find rest for your souls" (Matt. 11:28-29 NIV).

Have you chosen the Lord as your refuge? If not, you will be deprived of the rest and prosperity your soul desires.

Father, we are thankful that in Jesus we have a place where our weary, restless souls can find rest. Because You are our choice for a refuge we have been richly rewarded.

July 30

MANNA SERIES: PROVIDENTIAL DESIGNS BEHIND THE RUTH STORY
RECOGNIZING PROVIDENTIAL ACTS OF GRACE

Reading Passage: Ruth 2:12-18
Main Text: Ruth 2:13 "May I continue to find favor in your eyes, my lord," she said. "You have given me comfort and have spoken kindly to your servant—though I do not have the standing of one of your servant girls." (NIV)

It is one thing to be aware of the providential acts of God in caring for us, but when we take them for granted that is an act of ingratitude. It is much better to recognize how undeserving we are of these acts of grace, for then we become grateful and express our thanksgiving. How easily we take for granted that God provides seasonal rain and daily sunshine to nourish the crops so we can have food. It is not until we become ill that we begin to appreciate the blessing of God in keeping us healthy for long periods, despite living constantly in an environment with viruses and bacteria. We do not recognize the grace extended to us in the blessings received, and instead of giving thanks we complain and grumble at the smallest inconvenience or mishap in our lives.

Ruth could have had much to complain about. She was a young widow living in an alien culture, and now she was scrounging for food in the field of an unknown man, being vulnerable to the advances and abuses of his workers. But Boaz, the owner of the field, took a personal interest in her, and immediately Ruth recognized the grace bestowed on her. She remarked that he gave comfort and spoke kindly to her, even though she was less than his servant girls. She felt completely unqualified and undeserving of the favor she was shown. In response to her words of gratitude, Boaz elevated her status and expanded his benevolence. He invited her to sit and eat with his reapers, which placed her above the level of the servant girls. He instructed that she be allowed to gather wheat from among the sheaves rather than wait for what was left behind, and that the reapers would leave behind some extra bundles of grain for her, giving her abundance without much effort. When we recognize grace and express our gratitude for it, more grace will be bestowed on us.

What blessings are we taking for granted? living in a land of freedom? having income to afford food, shelter and clothing? being in health physically and mentally? having a family that loves us? If we find ourselves inclined to always see the negatives in our lives, or to easily murmur and complain, we need to begin recognizing the grace bestowed on us and resolve to be more thankful.

Father, forgive us for our ingratitude and our complaints. We have been blessed above many, even though we don't deserve it. Thank You Lord.

MANNA SERIES: PROVIDENTIAL DESIGNS
BEHIND THE RUTH STORY
FINDING MORE THAN WE ARE SEEKING

Reading Passage: Ruth 2:17-23

Main Text: Ruth 2:19-20 "Where did you glean today? Where did you work? Blessed be the man who took notice of you!" Then Ruth told her mother-in-law about the one at whose place she had been working. "The name of the man I worked with today is Boaz," she said. "The LORD bless him!" Naomi said to her daughter-in-law. "He has not stopped showing his kindness to the living and the dead." She added, "That man is our close relative; he is one of our kinsman-redeemers." (NIV)

Ruth's desire to find work in the field was solely driven by the need for food to sustain her mother-in-law and herself. It was while pursuing her self-interest she found herself in the field of her kinsman redeemer. He not only met her need for food but also permanently changed her status from that of a servant, to having an inheritance. Moving from poverty to riches, she found far more than what she was seeking.

Many of us have similar stories in our encounter with the Lord. We were not seeking the Lord; we were focused on our need and hoped that this need could be met in "His field." Indeed, in many cases we did not know the owner of the field and did not care to know. Some people were sick and the prognosis was grim so they were seeking some source of healing. Some felt helpless against evil thoughts that harassed their minds and were seeking assurance that the forces of evil would not succeed. Many times the only reason people call out to God is because of imminent danger, such as our airplane being in danger of crashing, or our children being in a crisis situation. Yet in pursuit of divine help for a solely selfish purpose, God in His grace and mercy meets our request, and in addition provides spiritual salvation that meets our truly fundamental, although perhaps unrecognized, need.

In the gospels, ten lepers came for healing of their leprosy, but after one returned to express gratitude; he discovered that Jesus could make him completely whole. There is nothing wrong in seeking to have our needs met, but when we find ourselves at the correct source, in the Lord's field, we will gain far more than what we are seeking. While we may not be seeking Him, we will discover He has been seeking us so that He may bless us.

Father, we are grateful that You can use our fears and our desires as a means of getting our attention and providing the salvation that our souls really need. Thank You for the grace that makes You available to us even when we are not seeking You, for the glory of Your name.

August 1

MANNA SERIES: PROVIDENTIAL DESIGNS BEHIND THE RUTH STORY
STEERING A MOVING VEHICLE

Reading Passage: Ruth 3:1-6
Main Text: Ruth 3:3 Wash and perfume yourself, and put on your best clothes. Then go down to the threshing floor, but don't let him know you are there until he has finished eating and drinking. (NIV)

God arranges the circumstances of our lives through providential acts in order to accomplish his purposes. However, God's plans require our involvement to create the conditions in which He can work. The challenge is knowing the difference between impulsive action on our part, and acting in faith believing that our initiatives are God- directed. Some may argue that we should wait on a sign or confirmation from the Lord before we take any action. But this could lead to a life of excuse-filled inactivity. On the other hand, the child of God in fellowship with Him, should be aware of directions from the Lord in our desires and decisions. Oftentimes, directions will not be provided until we are ready to take a course of action, because it is difficult to steer a stationary vehicle. Frequently, it is not until we begin moving "in the way" that Lord begins to direct us (Gen 24:48).

Naomi wanted to provide an inheritance for Ruth, a place of rest and satisfaction. She decided to implement a plan to achieve this goal. She instructed Ruth to visit the threshing floor where Boaz would be having his harvest celebration. She should watch until he lies down to sleep and then go and lie at his feet. This would force Boaz to respond by making a marriage proposal or by rejecting her. This was a daring, even presumptive act, and one may question whether God supported such action. We know Naomi was not acting selfishly; in fact she was looking after Ruth's best interest, so she may have concluded the idea came from God. In Scripture, one of the ways we can be sure an idea was the will of the Lord is to see how God directed the outcome. She was providing a moving car for God to steer.

What ideas have come to our minds that we are debating whether or not they are in the will of God? The first test is to examine our motives to see whether we are seeking to fulfill our lusts, and to be sure our desires are not contrary to scripture. Then we must commit our plans to God asking Him to direct our paths (Prov. 3:5-6). If after taking these steps we feel a sense of peace to proceed, stop delaying and give God a moving vehicle to steer.

Father, we believe that You want to accomplish Your purposes through us, therefore You have placed in us desires and ideas for us to implement. Help us to sense Your voice and act in faith, trusting You to direct our path. This we ask in the name of our Sovereign Lord Jesus.

August 2

MANNA SERIES: PROVIDENTIAL DESIGNS BEHIND THE RUTH STORY
OBSTACLES THAT PROVE PROVIDENCE

Reading Passage: Ruth 3:7-13
Main Text: Ruth 3:11-12 And now, my daughter, don't be afraid. I will do for you all you ask. All my fellow townsmen know that you are a woman of noble character. Although it is true that I am near of kin, there is a kinsman-redeemer nearer than I. (NIV)

It is erroneous to believe that when we are in the will of God, and being providentially guided, we will have a smooth journey to our destination. Whenever we encounter obstacles, sometimes we not only question our convictions regarding our plans but also doubt whether our path is being guided by God..

Any new ventures in life, or even decisions to maintain our old paths, are acts of faith. No one knows completely the outcome of his or her plans, or whether they have selected the proper goals for life. For persons who put their trust in God, the ultimate objective is not to achieve their life goals, but to deepen their relationship with our Father. Therefore, God places obstacles in our path to challenge our faith through which we develop greater reliance and confidence in Him.

Ruth followed her mother-in-law's instructions to initiate a closer relationship with Boaz to determine whether he, as a kinsman-redeemer, would marry her. Boaz responded that he was willing, but.... there was a problem. After the excitement of hearing the "yes" of approval, and basking in the approval God gives to our plans, we have to face the obstacle that follows - the "but". In Ruth's case, Boaz explained there was another relative closer than he was to her who could claim her kinsman/redeemer status.

How do we respond to the detours on our path, the obstacles that may impede our progress? Our "but" could be that our funding proposal was denied, our job application was rejected, or we failed the exam. At these times we need to be able to trust that God who gave us the assurance of His presence will empower us to conquer the obstacle, or guide us in a path to circumvent it. The obstacle provides an opportunity to prove His ability to lead us to victory over any difficulty, and to strengthen our faith in Him. When the Lord led Israel out of Egypt, He did not bring them immediately to the Promised Land. Instead, He led them to the Red Sea and through the wilderness so they could get to know Him better, and learn to trust Him.

May we view our obstacles as opportunities to increase our knowledge of God.

Father, we won't be dismayed or defeated by the obstacles that are in our way, because we know that "if there wasn't a problem we wouldn't know that You could solve them, we wouldn't know what faith in Your word could do." Through Jesus, may the tests of our faith provide the basis for Your triumph in us.

August 3

MANNA SERIES: PROVIDENTIAL DESIGNS
BEHIND THE RUTH STORY
RESTFUL PURSUIT OF MY DESTINY

Reading Passage: Ruth 3:13-18
Main Text: Ruth 3:18 Then Naomi said, "Wait, my daughter, until you find out what happens. For the man will not rest until the matter is settled today." (NIV)

There are limits to how much we can do in achieving our destiny since there are many factors beyond our control. After we have done all we can, we have to trust that God is doing His part on our behalf. Our anxiety arises from not being certain God is actively working to accomplish our destiny. We are unsure because much of what God is doing takes place where we cannot see it happening, and the areas that we see are sometimes not in accordance with our expectations.

God's main plan is for our complete salvation and the provision of an inheritance with those He has justified. As our kinsman redeemer, He is relentless in pursuing this goal for us, even when we are unaware of His activity. The story of Ruth provides a good illustration of this divine activity. Boaz explained that he wanted to redeem her, but there was an obstacle in the way. He told Ruth, "Go lie down and in the morning I will take care of the matter." Having done as much as she could, the only thing left for Ruth to do was to rest. The reason she could afford to rest was that her kinsman redeemer would "not rest until *he* settled the matter." There is no need for our restlessness while God is busy working on our behalf.

The Bible explains that faith brings us into a state of rest, because the person who truly believes God "ceases from his own work" and trusts the work of God (cf. Heb. 4:10-11). What are you anxious about today? Do you doubt that your salvation is secure; that an inheritance is guaranteed for you after death; that you will be preserved blameless before the Lord at His coming, or that God will take care of you in this life?

Let us trust the work of Jesus our kinsman redeemer, and His promise to accomplish all that is necessary to redeem and preserve us. When we believe, we can rest.

Father, You have made a powerful promise for us in Jesus Christ, causing us to know that our salvation is secure because we placed our trust in You. Keep us from the anxiety that comes from our attempts to work it out for ourselves. We thank You for the rest we have in Jesus. Amen.

August 4

MANNA SERIES: PROVIDENTIAL DESIGNS BEHIND THE RUTH STORY
INCIDENTS THAT ARE NOT ACCIDENTS

Reading Passage: Ruth 4:1-5
Main Text: Ruth 4:1 Meanwhile Boaz went up to the town gate and sat there. When the kinsman-redeemer he had mentioned came along, Boaz said, "Come over here, my friend, and sit down." So he went over and sat down. (NIV)

One of the greatest indications of the hand of providence in our lives is the occurrence of events with such precise timing that they cause us to be amazed. You just happened to be sitting next to someone on an airplane, and the person eventually becomes your spouse. Just after you are laid off from your job, you are asked to fill a temporary position at a company while searching for a new job. The temporary position becomes permanent, which eventually leads to your owning the company. A visit to the doctor for an annoying itch caused by an insect bite, leads to the discovery of cancer cells that would become life threatening if the discovery was delayed. Looking back at these incidents we have to admit the timing was not an accident but was divinely ordained.

Boaz promised that within a day he would settle the matter of Ruth's redemption of her inheritance. He went to sit at the gate with the elders who were the judges of the city. Although not stated explicitly, there is the implication he may have alerted them of his challenge to find the person who had the first claim on redeeming Ruth. But the very person he was seeking just happened to pass by at that very moment. This was yet another of the critically timely interventions in the Ruth story, similar to her ending up in Boaz' field. Looking back at the incident, both Boaz and Ruth would be amazed at the divine timing.

What is the lesson from this awareness that God orchestrates events to achieve His purpose in the lives of His children? We should never despair at how dismal our circumstances may appear, because we may just be on the threshold of a spectacular new dawn that is determined by Him who rules the times and seasons. Also, we always have reason to hope since our lives are in His loving hand. The opportunities for change in our lives may arise from the most obscure and surprising incidents. Therefore, we should keep our eyes open and our faith strong in the Lord who directs our steps.

Father, we rest in the assurance that You ordain our steps, and even if they appear to be missteps, You can cause them to work out for our good. We thank You Lord.

August 5

MANNA SERIES: PROVIDENTIAL DESIGNS BEHIND THE RUTH STORY
REJECTION THAT BECOMES A CELEBRATION

Reading Passage: Ruth 4:1-8
Main Text: Ruth 4:5-6 Then Boaz said, "On the day you buy the land from Naomi and from Ruth the Moabitess, you acquire the dead man's widow, in order to maintain the name of the dead with his property." At this, the kinsman-redeemer said, "Then I cannot redeem it because I might endanger my own estate. You redeem it yourself. I cannot do it." (NIV)

The term rejection has a negative connotation. We think that something we desire has been denied, and this implies failure to meet the standards of acceptance as determined by a person or organization. Rejection can affect our self-esteem and our relationship with people. But when we are made aware of how it can lead us to the destiny God planned for us, rejection can become the point of our celebration. Unfortunately, we don't know the outcome at the time, but when we trust the Lord to direct our path, we can be confident that the rejection will turn out for good.

Boaz approached the man who had the first claim to be the kinsman redeemer for Ruth. When he presented Ruth's case, the priority claimant agreed to assert his right and redeem the land that Naomi and Ruth would have to dispose of. Boaz further explained that on the day he redeemed the land, the redeemer would also have to acquire the responsibility for Ruth and raise up a family by her. When he heard about this additional responsibility, the priority claimant declined the offer of redemption because he rejected the prospect of caring for Ruth. Rather than this decision being a cause for disappointment and dejection, it became a reason for celebration because it meant that Boaz would become the kinsman redeemer. He was the person that Ruth and Naomi desired as the redeemer, and Boaz was hoping he would get this opportunity. There was a blessing in this rejection.

Joseph, the son of Jacob, was rejected by his brothers, which resulted in his being sold into slavery. Yet years later when the family was desperate for food because of a famine, Joseph, who had become the ruler in Egypt, was able to secure food for them. They all celebrated the outcome of his rejection.

Do you feel dejected because of a rejection? If the Lord guides your life, one day you will be able to look back and celebrate the rejection that enabled you to fulfill God's purpose in your life.

Lord, we are grateful that with You as our guide we are never defeated by the circumstances of our lives. You are able to turn whatever was meant for evil into things that work out for our good. Through Jesus we look forward to the celebration that will result from the incidents of our rejection.

August 6

MANNA SERIES: PROVIDENTIAL DESIGNS BEHIND THE RUTH STORY
THE OUTSIDER BECOMES THE HOUSE-BUILDER

Reading Passage: Ruth 4:9-12
Main Text: Ruth 4:11 Then the elders and all those at the gate said, "We are witnesses. May the LORD make the woman who is coming into your home like Rachel and Leah, who together built up the house of Israel. May you have standing in Ephrathah and be famous in Bethlehem." (NIV)

In our modern world, countries go to great lengths to prevent foreigners from becoming permanent residents. They establish strict visa policies to control those entering, and maintain procedures to ensure visitors do not violate their temporary status. Many national barriers are developed from racial and tribal barriers. The objective is to keep outsiders from becoming part of the group and affecting the purity of the race. The fear may be that inheritances will have to be shared with foreigners, or that the race, nation or tribe will be weakened or diluted by intermarriage or intermingling with foreigners.

The Hebrew people were strongly warned by God against intermarriage with foreigners because of the risks of adopting their gods and idolatrous lifestyles. But God's ultimate plan was to bring all nations together under His rule, creating one family of all mankind. The story of Ruth describes how God went across all racial and cultural divides, and against national barriers to incorporate someone who chose to seek refuge "under His wings." She was not just incorporated; she was made a builder of the house of Israel, like the mothers of the nation, Rachel and Leah. The outsider became a house builder. Many scholars have argued that the reason this story was included in the Bible was to show that God's chosen king for Israel, David, was a descendent of an outsider. This proves that God's kingdom will include people of all nations who come under His rule. We all have the opportunity to participate in building God's kingdom.

When Boaz took the risk of bringing the outsider into his home, he never realized he was strengthening his own house, extending his fame, and fulfilling God's plan to expand his house to all nations. What fears do we have in including "outsiders" in our lives, or in our homes? We could be denying the strengthening of our own house and the fulfillment of God's plan through us. Let us be open to the opportunities God provides us to extend our borders and incorporate outsiders who are willing to come under His rule.

Father, we can be so blind to the opportunities You provide for us because of our prejudices, narrow-mindedness and selfishness. Help us to be open to welcoming those outsiders You want to incorporate in Your household through us.

MANNA SERIES: PROVIDENTIAL DESIGNS
BEHIND THE RUTH STORY
BURDENS THAT BECOME BLESSINGS

Reading Passage: Ruth 4:13-17
Main Text: Ruth 4:14-15 The women said to Naomi: "Praise be to the LORD, who this day has not left you without a kinsman-redeemer. May he become famous throughout Israel! He will renew your life and sustain you in your old age. For your daughter-in-law, who loves you and who is better to you than seven sons, has given him birth." (NIV)

The Special Olympics offers people everywhere with intellectual and physical disabilities "the chance to play, the chance to compete and the chance to grow." Eunice Kennedy Shriver, a member of the famous Kennedy family of the USA, is the founder of the Special Olympics. In addition to establishing the Special Olympics, she headed the Kennedy Foundation, which works for the prevention of intellectual disability by identifying its causes, and aims to improve the means by which society deals with disabled citizens. Her motivation for working tirelessly on these causes that have been a blessing to millions, was due to the fact that her sister, Rosemarie, was mentally challenged. What could have been a burden became a blessing. There are many examples of similar scenarios in life. Alexander Graham Bell who invented the telephone was greatly influenced to develop this useful item by the fact that his mother was deaf.

No one normally chooses a burden for his or her life, and most times we cannot prevent their occurrence. Naomi returned home to Bethlehem with the "burden" of Ruth, a Moabite daughter-in-law, who was a widow. She tried unsuccessfully to relieve herself of this "burden" which she thought added to her distress after losing her husband and two sons. But God so directed the story of Ruth that after her marriage to the wealthy Boaz, she had a son. Through the birth of Obed, God restored joy to Naomi, and caused her girlfriends to celebrate with her. They described the newborn as her kinsman redeemer, who would restore her inheritance, renew her life, and sustain her in her old age. Ruth, who was her burden became a tremendous blessing, more valuable to her than if she had seven sons.

What burdens are you bemoaning today? Although you may not be able to see it now, God can use the cause of our present distress to become the source of our rejoicing in the future. It could be the burden of a negligent, unambitious spouse, an unwanted pregnancy, a wayward child, even a 'thorn in the flesh' that keeps disrupting our health. Cast your burdens on the Lord and trust Him to transform them.

Father, we mourn because of our limitations, not being able to see the blessings that can come from our burdens. But in the darkness of our distress, we commit our burdens to You and seek Your sustaining grace to help us to endure until we see their transformation into blessings. This we pray for the glory of Your great name.

August 8

MANNA SERIES: PROVIDENTIAL DESIGNS BEHIND THE RUTH STORY
AN INTRIGUING GENEALOGY OF GRACE

Reading Passage: Ruth 4:16-22
Main Text: Ruth 4:17-18 The women living there said, "Naomi has a son." And they named him Obed. He was the father of Jesse, the father of David. This, then, is the family line of Perez: Perez was the father of Hezron, (NIV)

When people research their genealogy, they are usually looking for individuals who have achieved great fame or wealth that provide grounds for boasting of their family heritage. It is true that to a great extent we are products of our families, but the fact is that our heritage includes the good, the bad and the ugly. We discover the grace of God when we recognize that despite the bad and the ugly in our heritage, he has produced a good outcome in us.

The Israelites were very meticulous about maintaining genealogical records. Their history involved many invasions and periods of exile, and the records helped them to maintain the identity of those who belonged. Furthermore, the tribal identity would determine the location of their land inheritance, and indicate who belonged to priestly families (this was a big issue when the exiles returned from Babylonian captivity). However, it was from these very records that God could indicate to the nation that their ethnicity was not as pure as they liked to boast about. They would discover that He graciously intervened in their history to engraft "outsiders" into the family of His people.

Interestingly, the genealogical record in the book of Ruth begins with Perez. He was the son of Tamar, a Canaanite woman who pretended to be a prostitute in order to have a child by her father-in-law, Judah. She performed this incestuous act because Judah failed to keep his promise to give her another of his sons as a husband when her husband, Judah's son, died (Gen 38). This was the genealogical heritage of Boaz. So when he took the Moabitess Ruth as his wife, it was indeed another case of an outsider with a "past" being engrafted by grace into the lineage of the great king David. What is additionally significant is that this genealogical line eventually "produced" Jesus from a human perspective, but who was in fact the Son of God.

If God chose such a flawed genealogical line for Jesus, this indicates that there is no embarrassment in our heritage. Furthermore, there are no family flaws that cannot be conquered by the grace of God. Jesus adopted our humanity with all its flaws in order to produce His heavenly heritage in us. Regardless of our background, we can become children of God, and that is something to boast about.

Is there something in your family background that causes you embarrassment? Because of Jesus, these flaws can become evidence of His redemption, and a testimony of His grace in our lives.

Father, we thank You for the grace of regeneration that allows sinners with an ugly history to be born anew into the family of God. May Jesus be magnified through us.

August 9

MANNA SERIES: THE CHURCH, JESUS' REPRESENTATIVE BODY ON EARTH
THE REVELATION THAT MAKES US BLESSED

Reading Passage: Matt. 16:13-20
Main Text: Matt. 16:17-18 Jesus replied, "Blessed are you, Simon son of Jonah, for this was not revealed to you by man, but by my Father in heaven.

And I tell you that you are Peter, and on this rock I will build my church, and the gates of Hades will not overcome it." (NIV)

Knowledge is gained by exposure and learning. This knowledge makes us educated and provides the basis by which we are able to make wise decisions. In contrast, revelation is knowledge that is not gained from study or from human reason, but by divine disclosure. The education provided by earthly knowledge may elevate us to a privileged place in the earthly realm, but revelation provides spiritual knowledge that qualifies us for God's use.

At an important juncture in His ministry, Jesus wanted His disciples to disclose their opinion of Him, since they had been with Him for over 3 years. When, in response, Peter declared, "You are the Christ the Son of the living God," Jesus told him that this was a revelation, and it qualified him to be prime material for building the Church of Jesus Christ. The Church would be God's building in the earth to represent Jesus after His departure. Jesus was seeking to identify and call out people whom He could use in constructing this building. Since the church had to be solidly built to withstand all Satanic attacks including hell and death, it needed rock-like material. Peter, whose Greek name means rock, demonstrated that he was blessed with the rock-like knowledge necessary for the foundation of the church. That foundational knowledge is that the man, Christ Jesus, is more than a mere human. He is God in flesh, and the promised anointed ruler of the kingdom of God on the earth.

Significantly, Jesus said this most important knowledge couldn't be obtained by human means such as intuition, reason or study. It can only be obtained by revelation. Those who are part of the Church are all blessed with this revelation. Our membership, association with, or baptism in a local congregation will not qualify us for Jesus' Church, His mystical body. This explains why our confession that Jesus is God in human form, is critical for our salvation experience (Rom 10:9). Without this revelation God cannot use us in building the church of Jesus.

Have you received this revelation? Do you know for sure that you are a member of Jesus' church? If not, pray that you will receive this blessing today.

Father, we thank You for the privilege of the knowledge of who Jesus is, and the blessing of being a part of His representation on the earth.

MANNA SERIES: THE CHURCH, JESUS' REPRESENTATIVE BODY ON EARTH
THE PRINCIPLE OF LIFE THROUGH DEATH

Reading Passage: Matt. 16:17-25
Main Text: John 12:24 I tell you the truth, unless a kernel of wheat falls to the ground and dies, it remains only a single seed. But if it dies, it produces many seeds. (NIV)

The salmon travels around 2,000 miles, sometimes swimming upstream, to return to the place where it was spawned. After laying and fertilizing eggs, the salmon dies. In dying, it produces life. In the main text, Jesus used a kernel of wheat as an illustration of this principle. Unless it dies it will remain only a single seed, but if it dies it produces many seeds. He was referring to Himself.

In the record in Matthew, immediately after declaring His plan to build a church, Jesus began to tell His disciples of His plan to die. Positioning the two plans simultaneously seemed ludicrous. Surely the life of the builder was necessary for the construction of the Church. No wonder Peter, the man with the revelation, rebuked Jesus for this talk about death. But Jesus knew that the birth of the Church required His death. By His death, He would pay the penalty for sin, purchase redemption for mankind, and produce many sons of God. New life would come through death. The Church stands on the foundation of the death of its founder and builder. And central to the message of the Church is the fact that the cross of Jesus, where sin was atoned, represents the basis for our existence.

This principle of life through death must be demonstrated in the functions of the members of the Church. Just like our master and builder, we must be prepared to die in order to produce new life, both in ourselves and in others. We die to self, our natural desires, pleasures and preferences, so that the life of Jesus might be manifested in our bodies. We die to our agenda, our goals and dreams, so that Christ may use us to provide opportunities for life in others. Jesus said that those who would follow Him as His disciples must first deny themselves, take up the cross and follow Him. For whoever loves his life will lose it, but whoever loses his life for Christ's sake will find it (Matt 16:24-26).

Are we holding on to our lives, trying to avoid the painful sacrifice of self while depriving others of life? Jesus demands that His Church follow His example of life through death.

Lord, this is a sobering and challenging thought because we hate to even think of our death. But we thank You for also showing us that the reward of our death to self will be Your abundant life in us and the giving of life to many. By Your grace we will make the sacrifice and join Your Church.

August 11

MANNA SERIES: THE CHURCH, JESUS' REPRESENTATIVE BODY ON EARTH
THE BIRTH OF THE CHURCH

Reading Passage: Acts 2:1-21
Main Text: Acts 2:1-4 When the day of Pentecost came, they were all together in one place. Suddenly a sound like the blowing of a violent wind came from heaven and filled the whole house where they were sitting. They saw what seemed to be tongues of fire that separated and came to rest on each of them. All of them were filled with the Holy Spirit and began to speak in other tongues as the Spirit enabled them. (NIV)

The period of gestation is over, labor has become exhausting, the midwife is in attendance, and all is set waiting the moment. After the last push of anguish, comes the cry of a baby. The announcement is made: "It's a boy." New life has started, a new journey has begun with expectations and challenges on the path to fulfillment of purpose. The key factor in the birth is the timing. The baby comes when he is ready to be born.

In a similar manner, timing was key in the birth of the Church. Jesus, the founder and builder, had ascended to the right hand of the Father. The Holy Spirit was poised, ready to descend to inhabit and give life to the Church. In obedience, the disciples were gathered in one place in Jerusalem. The day of Pentecost arrived 50 days after Passover. This was the time of the celebration of the first-fruits, when Jews and religious Gentiles from all over the world came to Jerusalem for the harvest festival. The Holy Spirit entered the room of the assembled disciples sounding like a mighty rushing wind. The noise attracted the festive crowd to the room where the disciples were gathered. They arrived to see a phenomenon of the appearance of fire in the form of a tongue over each disciple and heard them speaking in a language that was not native to them.

It was clear the observers were witnessing a very unusual and miraculous event. It was the birth of the Church. What was the significance of the timing? It provided the opportunity for people of various ethnic and national backgrounds to hear in their own language the message of the mighty works of God (v. 11). The curiosity of the observers provided the opportunity for Peter to deliver the central message of the Church. They heard that Jesus, the Son of God, died, was buried and rose again, and all who believed this message would be saved and added to the Church.

The lesson from this Pentecostal event is that the Church has been established in the world, and its main mission is to proclaim the message of Jesus so that the Spirit may supernaturally add new members to the Church.

Let us be faithful to the mission and message of the Church in the world.

Lord, we are grateful that You have made supernatural provision to add members from diverse backgrounds to the Church. Help us never to lose the central mission and message of the Church, so that Your kingdom may be expanded, for the glory of Jesus.

August 12

MANNA SERIES: THE CHURCH, JESUS' REPRESENTATIVE BODY ON EARTH
GOD'S PATTERN FOR COMMUNITY

Reading Passage: Acts 2:41-47
Main Text: Acts 2:46-47 Every day they continued to meet together in the temple courts. They broke bread in their homes and ate together with glad and sincere hearts, praising God and enjoying the favor of all the

people. And the Lord added to their number daily those who were being saved. (NIV)

The most heartfelt desires of humanity include having a sense of belonging, being respected by others, and having sufficiency for life. In the pursuit of fulfilling these desires, people have formed themselves into various social groupings such as, clubs, associations, lodges or political parties. Yet they have been left unfulfilled because many of these organizations lack a unifying spiritual core. For a proper sense of community, the total needs of a person have to be met: the social, emotional, intellectual and spiritual.

Jesus, who knows the nature of humans, established the Church as His pattern for community in the earth. His goal for the church, both locally and universally, is that it should represent the unity and community that is portrayed by a human body. Just as each member of a physical body is valuable, interdependent and nurtured, so it should be for each member of a local church.

Just after the birth of the Church, we see the emerging pattern of the practices and culture of the new community. The first indicator was what they devoted themselves to. They continually met together to study the apostles' teachings, to fellowship and to celebrate the communion meal (v. 42). The meeting together for these practices is fundamental in maintaining the pattern of community established for the church.

These days, people are claiming to be Christians; yet they avoid the gathering together, stating that one can serve the Lord as an isolated individual. But the practice of isolation by believers fragments the Church and fails to provide the pattern of community Jesus wants to present to the world. We also see where members of this early Church shared their possessions so none of its members would suffer any lack. They worshipped together with such joy and excitement that the surrounding society was impressed, leading many to be added to the Church.

Having seen this pattern, we are challenged to consider how we individually have contributed to the profile of the Church in our community. Do we ensure we are joined to a local church, and are we contributing to the ministries that meet needs and enhance fellowship? Do observers see us participating in joyful worship that is attractive?

Lord, although You called us to salvation individually, You have designed us to be part of a community that we may present You uniquely to the world. This is a great opportunity for our fulfillment and for Your glory. Help us to fight against any spirit of isolationism that would diminish the profile of Your Church. This we pray in the name of Jesus.

August 13

MANNA SERIES: THE CHURCH, JESUS' REPRESENTATIVE BODY ON EARTH
BELONGING TO A PRAYING CHURCH

Reading Passage: Acts 4:18-34
Main Text: Acts 4:31 When they had prayed, the place where they were assembled together was shaken, and they were all filled with the Holy Spirit and began to speak the word of God courageously. (NIV)

The journey of life usually takes us through difficult situations where we need help to deal with the mental, physical, financial and spiritual pressures we encounter. Sometimes the help of family and friends is inadequate. Despite their love and good intentions, we need God to intervene. Prayer is the means by which we seek God's help, and this is most effectively done through the cooperative effort of His representative on earth, the Church.

The apostles, Peter and John, were being persecuted and threatened for preaching in the name of Jesus. On being released by the authorities, "they went back to their own people," who listened to their report and began to pray (v. 23). Surely these apostles could have prayed about the situation by themselves, but they recognized there was a certain power with God when the whole Church unites in prayer. The literal translation of the Greek text states, "they went to their own," which referred to the Church. The apostles knew they were identified with and belonged to a local body of believers, which they could call their own.

Prayer by this Church was not being made for unfamiliar people or just names on a prayer list, but for people whom they knew personally and cared about. They could petition God with empathy for their beloved brothers. The passage states, "when they heard this they raised their voices together in prayer to God" (v. 24). There is nothing on earth that compares with the power of a petition to God made by the Church on behalf of one of their own, in the name of Jesus, the head of the Church. No wonder after the prayer was finished, God demonstrated His approval physically - the place was shaken, and spiritually - the believers were refilled with the Holy Spirit.

How pitiful for people to find themselves in trouble and have no church they can call their own to help them bear the burden and to take it to the Lord in prayer. But how blessed are those who know that their cries to God in their distress are being reinforced by people who know them, and to whom they belong. Just as when Jesus, in agony in the garden, desired the support of His disciples in prayer, and years later, when the apostle Paul pleaded with his beloved congregations to support him in prayer, we need to belong to a church that will help us in praying.

Do you belong to a praying church you can call "your own?"

Father, thank You for providing the Church as the means of support for us as we face the challenges of life, and thank You for recognizing the collective petitions of Your people.

August 14

MANNA SERIES: THE CHURCH, JESUS' REPRESENTATIVE BODY ON EARTH
TESTING THE CHURCH'S SECURITY SYSTEMS

Reading Passage: Acts 4:36-5:11
Main Text: Acts 5:9-10 Peter said to her, "How could you agree to test the Spirit of the Lord? Look! The feet of the men who buried your husband are at the door, and they will carry you out also." At that moment she fell down at his feet and died. Then the young men came in and, finding her dead, carried her out and buried her beside her husband. (NIV)

In establishing the Church, Jesus declared that the gates of Hades would not overcome her. Although Satan will make every attempt to destroy her, the Church will resist all his efforts and be victorious over him.

Knowing the tendency of the enemy to undermine her by deception, how can the Church detect, disrupt and destroy these schemes of the enemy?

Satan primarily uses people, and frequently members of the Church, to perform his devious tasks against her. When Jesus announced his plan to establish the Church, Satan used Peter to challenge Jesus' plan to suffer and die in order to produce members for the Church. In our text, Satan tried to undermine the purity of the young Church by using two of her members, Ananias and his wife Sapphira, to promote a deceptive scheme.

Some members were demonstrating sacrificial giving by selling their properties and giving the full proceeds to the Church. This couple wanted the esteem without making the sacrifice. Satan convinced them that they could sell their property, donate some of the proceeds to the Church, keep the rest for themselves, but give the impression they gave all. If the Church innocently celebrated this deception, this small germ of sin could grow and contaminate the whole body.

What Satan overlooked was that the Holy Spirit, the administrator of the Church, supplies the security system that detects and destroys anything that would undermine her. The couple thought they were deceiving human apostles, but Peter explained that they were lying to the Holy Spirit (5:3) and testing the Spirit of God (5:9). To provide an example for anyone who disregards or underestimates the effectiveness and efficacy of the Church's security system, Ananias and Sapphira were struck dead immediately. Fear gripped the whole Church.

Thank God, He doesn't always execute judgment in the same manner for infringements against the Church, or else the number of the living members would be severely depleted. But the warning is clear: Don't ever let us consider Jesus' Church as a mere human organization. She is a spiritual body divinely protected by God's security system, which is always alert to detect and destroy every scheme and devious act Satan would tempt us to practice within her.

Let us cooperate with the Holy Spirit to protect the purity of the Church.

Lord, we want to take the warning of this devotional very seriously so we may constantly guard our hearts against any acts of deception in the Church.

August 15

MANNA SERIES: THE CHURCH, JESUS' REPRESENTATIVE BODY ON EARTH
DISAGREEMENTS THAT CAN DERAIL PROGRESS

Reading Passage: Acts 6:1-7

Main Text: Acts 6:1-2 In those days when the number of disciples was increasing, the Grecian Jews among them complained against the Hebraic Jews because their widows were being overlooked in the daily distribution of food. So the Twelve gathered all the disciples together and said, "It would not be right for us to neglect the ministry of the word of God in order to wait on tables." (NIV)

The distinguishing characteristics of the early Church were the effectiveness of her witness and her unity. The historical account in the Book of Acts, described the miraculous signs that were performed, the multiplication of the membership, and the fact that they had things in common because they were of one heart and soul (Acts 2:42-44; 4:32-35). A disruption of the unity could derail the powerful progress of the Church.

There are two basic manifestations of the Church on the planet. There is the universal Church comprised of all saved people of every nation, forming a spiritual body. And there is the local gathering of professing Christians, some of whom may not be genuine, who form a human organization. Even the genuine believers in the local Church are actually redeemed sinners who are in the process of sanctification, but not yet perfected. There will always be differences between members in the local Church, but we have to be careful to ensure these differences do not become disagreements that will affect the progress of the Church. The first such instance in the life of the early Church provides a pattern of how to respond to these differences.

The Church in Jerusalem was involved in a social program of supplying food daily to widows in the membership. The Grecian Jews, who were mostly proselytes that came from non-Judean cities, complained that they were being discriminated against, as they were overlooked in the daily distribution of food. They were accustomed to this discrimination in the general society, but were surprised to find it in the local Church also. These differences could not be ignored or glossed over, as they would disrupt the unity of the Church and provide the devil with ammunition to undermine its mission. The apostles intervened and explained that other leaders must be selected by the congregation to address the problem; in effect, they didn't want to be distracted from their priority of teaching the word, and prayer. But also, they wouldn't disregard this matter that was critical to harmony among the members of the church.

We must never let our prejudices based on race, social class, education, nationality or political affiliation disrupt the fellowship of the Church, and whenever these surface, they must be addressed. When unity is disrupted, effectiveness is diminished.

Lord, please cleanse us from the sins of the flesh that cause us not to love our fellow members with sincere brotherly and unconditional love. May Jesus' prayer for the unity of the believers be answered, for the glory of His name.

August 16

MANNA SERIES: THE CHURCH, JESUS' REPRESENTATIVE BODY ON EARTH
JOLTING A COMPLACENT CHURCH

Reading Passage: Acts 7:55-8:8
Main Text: Acts 8:1 And Saul was there, giving approval to his death. On that day a great persecution broke out against the Church at Jerusalem, and all except the apostles were scattered throughout Judea and Samaria. (NIV)

Complacency is a disease that can affect all of us. It tends to infect individuals, businesses, churches and even marriages, when we become satisfied with our successes and lose sight of our mission. Sometimes people awake from their stupor of complacency after self-examination, or by listening to a sermon or a motivational speech. However, the most common and effective motivator is usually adversity or potential threats.

The early Church suffered frequent and harsh persecution by the religious authorities. The leaders were often imprisoned and physically assaulted, yet the Church multiplied quickly despite the persecutions. It appears that the successful growth of the early Church led to complacency, because it did not expand beyond the borders of Jerusalem. Jesus gave the Church a clear mandate, both in Matt. 28:19 and Acts 1:8. Her mission was to make disciples and give witness to Jesus throughout the whole world. Nothing should cause the missionary movement to cease. When the Church becomes part of the establishment, and success causes her to be powerful in the society, there is the risk she will lose her missionary vision, and cease giving witness to the rejected Christ.

Persecution was intensified against the early Church and this resulted in the martyrdom of Stephen, one of her prominent leaders. After his death, the persecution, led by a man named Saul, was so great that all the Church, except the apostles were scattered throughout Judea and Samaria. Although the persecution was harsh and unpleasant, it finally jolted the Church in Jerusalem out of her complacency and caused her to recover her missionary mandate. She began to spread herself to the surrounding countries as instructed by the Lord.

Have we again been lulled into a state of complacency? The Church in the West has become rich, sophisticated and prominent in the society, but have we been fulfilling the commission of spreading the gospel beyond our borders, and making disciples of people of all nations? When we become complacent, our passion is about superficial things, such as the size and beauty of our buildings, the esteem given to us by the ungodly society, competition with other local Churches, and our monthly income. When we have recovered our missionary mandate, our primary passion will be the salvation of souls, and the discipling of new believers.

Lord, help us to avoid the state of complacency like the Church at Laodicea in Rev 3:14-18 that you condemned. We want to avoid Your having to use Your harsh instruments of adversity to jolt us into pursuing the mission You have given us. Keep reminding us of the priority of Your mission, this we ask in Jesus' name.

August 17

MANNA SERIES: THE CHURCH, JESUS' REPRESENTATIVE BODY ON EARTH
WHEN OUR PURPOSE OVERTAKES OUR PURSUITS

Reading Passage: Acts 9:1-18
Main Text: Acts 9:15-16 But the Lord said to Ananias, "Go! This man is my chosen instrument to carry my name before the Gentiles and their kings and before the people of Israel. I will show him how much he must suffer for my name." (NIV)

Many people are passionately engaged in activities that are not in accordance with their divinely ordained purpose. Some of these activities may be unrelated to the Christian faith, and in some cases they may be directly opposing the mission of the Church. As humans with limited knowledge, we pursue goals and dreams that we find suitable to our dispositions and abilities, and hope that in so doing we will discover our purpose in life, the goal for which we were born. However, we must acknowledge that our omniscient Creator knows the purpose for which we were created. He simply waits for that time in our lives when His designed purpose will overtake our "wild" pursuits.

The life of the apostle Paul, previously known as Saul, is an appropriate illustration of this fact. As Saul, he was strongly and violently opposed to the existence of the Church and her preaching of salvation through Jesus Christ. With great zeal he spearheaded the persecution of members of the Church, seeking to have them imprisoned and tortured. He was so passionate and successful in his pursuit that the Church regarded him as their main enemy. Yet God knew that He designed Saul to be His choice instrument to lead the mission of the Church to the Gentiles. This reveals the huge gap between what God knows, what we conclude about others, and what we know about ourselves. Ultimately, only the designer knows our purpose with certainty.

What Saul discovered was that fighting against the Church amounted to fighting against Jesus (v. 5). If our pursuits are against the Church, they will be futile because Jesus takes such opposition personally. If God has chosen us for His purpose (which we have to discover for ourselves), all our other pursuits will be wasted time until we submit to His will. Saul's story also teaches us to be careful how we judge those who oppose our mission and us. We need to treat all people, even our enemies, with love, and pray for them because we might just be condemning one of God's chosen instruments that He plans to reveal in the future.

Have you discovered God's purpose for your life? Are you demonstrating patience with others while God works to bring their lives in accordance with His purposes?

Lord, we acknowledge that we all have a past of sin and failure. So we are all in need of your grace. May we be patient with each other while You work out Your purposes in our lives, for the glory of Jesus.

August 18

MANNA SERIES: THE CHURCH, JESUS' REPRESENTATIVE BODY ON EARTH
CALLING PEOPLE AS GOD CALLS THEM

Reading Passage: Acts 10:1-38
Main Text: Acts 10:28 He said to them: "You are well aware that it is against our law for a Jew to associate with a Gentile or visit him. But God has shown me that I should not call any man impure or unclean." (NIV)

In order to "manage" social relationships we usually place people into various categories and label these groups for easy identification. The danger of this practice is that we generalize and stereotype people for this purpose without making the effort to know them. What we call them reflect our prejudices toward these categories. Consider the connotation behind some names we call people – ghetto dwellers, outsiders, ignoramus. At the time of the establishment of the Church, the naming of categories of people was prevalent. Calling someone Greek or Hellenist implied that he was cultured, in contrast to identifying him as a Barbarian, which meant uncultured. Jews were recognized as people with a great religious and moral heritage, who were chosen as God's special people, while Gentiles were those who had no relationship with the Jewish God.

One purpose of the Church is to present to the world, a group of people who have overcome all the previous categorizations and differences to become one body united in the person of Jesus Christ. Since the birth of the Church, the Holy Spirit has been working to unite the body of Christ. When the Spirit wanted to move the Church from being a Jewish organization, He had to convince Peter, the key leader in the Church, of the new status of non-Jews. To get Peter to visit the house of the gentile Cornelius, He gave Peter a vision in which he was commanded to kill and eat all types of animals regarded by Jews as unclean. Peter was instructed not to call any man impure or unclean.

The lesson for the Church, is to call people the way God calls them. Because He has cleansed them, whether or not they appear clean to us, we are never to call them unclean. After a woman who was hemorrhaging for 12 years, and regarded by the Jews as unclean, touched Jesus' garment, He called her "daughter." While the prodigal was away in a far country, his father never called him a rebel; he was called, "my son." Paul, writing to the problem-ridden Church at Corinth, called them saints.

What we call people determine how we treat them. In the Church we are required to call them our brothers and sisters despite their behavior, their failings, our personal dislike of them, or the fact they are different from us. How will we respond to this command of our Lord today?

Lord, we admit the difficulty of seeing some people except through the lens of our prejudices. We ask for Your grace and help to truly represent You in our relationships with our fellow members in the Church.

August 19

MANNA SERIES: THE CHURCH, JESUS' REPRESENTATIVE BODY ON EARTH
BEHAVIOR THAT MODELS THE MASTER

Reading Passage: Acts 11:22-30
Main Text: Acts 11:25-26 Then Barnabas went to Tarsus to look for Saul, and when he found him, he brought him to Antioch. So for a whole year Barnabas and Saul met with the Church and taught great numbers of people. The disciples were called Christians first at Antioch. (NIV)

The term Christian is applied to so many different groups and individuals that oftentimes we are uncertain of its meaning. Many Jews regard any westerner who is non-Jewish as Christian. For Muslims, if someone is not Muslim or Jewish, it is assumed he or she is Christian. Being brought up in a church or being baptized, even as an infant, can earn you the description of Christian. What qualifies a person to be called a Christian?

In reviewing the first Biblical use of the term as described in our passage, we note it was not applied in reference to ethnicity, nationality or membership in a religious organization. The suffix "ian" means "belonging to the party of," which indicates that Christians belonged to the party of Christ. In Jerusalem, the believers were referred to as "people of the Way," which described Jews who believed Jesus was the promised Jewish messiah. With the gospel producing so many believers in non-Jewish territories such as Antioch, they were recognized as those who followed Jesus: the Christ party. Although this term appeared to be used derisively, it indicated they saw something in the behavior of this group of people that was similar to that of their master, Christ.

Immediately after the name was first used, we read that the Church in Antioch heard a prophecy about an expected famine in Judea. They quickly decided to make a collection for the believers in this region. The fact that Jerusalem was the established headquarters of the Church with the senior leaders, and Antioch was the new majority Gentile Church, though not yet respected, did not affect the decision. They heard of a need and responded immediately. They didn't just sympathize, or offer to pray for them. They offered practical solutions to meet the need. This behavior was so similar to their master that it justified their identity as Christians.

Whereas we are now well known as Christians, attending Christian churches, with a Christian theology and seeking to establish Christian countries, can people justifiably apply the term to us because our behavior imitates our Master? Do we love and care for people unconditionally as He did? Are we able to overlook the things that could divide us in order to focus on the One who unites us? If not, we do not deserve to be called Christian.

Father, we are thankful that You did not send us a philosophy or a set of rules, You sent us Your Son as a human so we would know how to live. May we allow Him to live through us so we can be identified as His followers.

MANNA SERIES: THE CHURCH, JESUS' REPRESENTATIVE BODY ON EARTH
BEING IN AGREEMENT WITH THE HOLY SPIRIT.

Reading Passage: Acts 15:5-25
Main Text: Acts 15:28 It seemed good to the Holy Spirit and to us not to burden you with anything beyond the following requirements: (NIV)

The uniqueness of the Church lies in the fact that although it is comprised of humans, it is divinely ruled. Like any other human organization, it functions with leadership structure, but that leadership is accountable to, and directed by the Holy Spirit, who also resides in all of the membership. Therefore, decisions made by the Church should find agreement with the whole membership. This presents a challenge and a check on leaders who may think that because of their position they can operate autocratically, imposing their decisions on the body of Christ.

In Acts 15, the Church was facing a major dispute over the basis on which to accept Gentiles into the local assembly. A group of the Jewish believers was insisting that the new Gentile believers must adopt the Jewish practice of circumcision, identifying them as Jews, before they could be accepted into the Church. This idea was strongly opposed by Paul and Barnabas, the main evangelists to the Gentiles, and also Peter, who first brought the gospel to the Gentiles. Because of the seriousness of the dispute, and its potential to divide the Church, the apostles convened the first Council at Jerusalem, under the chairmanship of James, to consider the matter.

After the Council listened to the various submissions, James announced his decision. Since it was evident that God had accepted the Gentiles as saved without the precondition of circumcision, this burden should not be imposed on them. However, to maintain harmony in the Church, the Gentiles should avoid practices that Jews found abhorrent, as it relates to dietary practices and sexual immorality (15:19-21). This decision found agreement with "the apostles, elders and the whole Church" (15:22). Because of this agreement, the letter from the Council to the Gentiles stated that the decision seemed good "to the Holy Spirit and to us." The unanimity of the membership confirmed the direction of the Holy Spirit.

Until the Spirit in other members confirms the voice of the Spirit in one member, whether in leadership or general membership, we cannot be certain the Spirit is leading. Beware of decisions made unilaterally. Be wary of churches that are organized with an autocratic leadership style. Be open to the Spirit as He speaks through the supernatural consensus in the Church.

Lord, we want to be certain we are following your leadership in Your Church. Convert us from being man-centered to being Spirit focused, appreciating that You have provided the fellowship of Believers as the means of confirming Your presence.

August 21

MANNA SERIES: THE CHURCH, JESUS' REPRESENTATIVE BODY ON EARTH
RESPONDING TO THE THREATS AGAINST THE CHURCH

Reading Passage: Acts 20:22-35
Main Text: Acts 20:28-30 Keep watch over yourselves and all the flock of which the Holy Spirit has made you overseers. Be shepherds of the church of God, which he bought with his own blood. I know that after I leave, savage wolves will come in among you and will not spare the flock. Even from your own number men will arise and distort the truth in order to draw away disciples after them. (NIV)

Jesus left His church in a hostile world with the challenge of representing His character, while providing a demonstration of the kingdom of God. The assurance that she would be triumphant against the gates of hell does not minimize the threats the Church constantly faces.

Paul highlighted these threats in his farewell address to the elders of the Church at Ephesus, a church he established and loved but knew he would not see again. He disclosed the source and nature of the threats, and gave instructions on how to counter them. The Church was located in a pluralistic culture that was hostile to the claims of Christianity. It was a culture that officially sanctioned immorality and debauchery. We recognize that threats against the Church were expected from the Roman authorities and from the anti-Christian population, which persecuted Paul and his associates when they began preaching. But Paul also mentioned that individuals would arise from among the membership who would ravage the flock with their false teaching. This latter threat would not be external, physical or political, yet it would be devastating.

Paul's admonition to the leaders was for them to guard against external and internal enemy attacks, first against themselves, and also against those for whom they were responsible. These attacks should be countered by proper teaching by the elders (feeding the flock), and caring for the needs of the members.

The threats against the church today are the same as in Paul's day. Unfortunately, some church leaders become absorbed with fighting battles in the wider society while neglecting their primary responsibility for the Church "over which the Holy Spirit made them overseers." They become distracted from their task of guarding against the infiltration of false teachings, and countering these with proper teaching and caring for the Church.

Let us pray for our leaders that they may be diligent to respond to the real threats and not be deceived and distracted into wasting their energies on the wrong enemies.

Father, we thank you for the experience of Paul that provides an exhortation which is so beneficial to the life of the Church today. Help us to take the warning seriously and make the necessary adjustments in our care of the Church, for Jesus' sake.

August 22

MANNA SERIES: THE CHURCH, JESUS' REPRESENTATIVE BODY ON EARTH
AVOIDING UNNECESSARY CHURCH FIGHTS

Reading Passage: Acts 21:17-26
Main Text: Acts 21:24 Take these men, join in their purification rites and pay their expenses, so that they can have their heads shaved. Then everybody will know there is no truth in these reports about you, but that you yourself are living in obedience to the law. (NIV)

The Church, which is Jesus' representative on earth, is often portrayed as an organization with constant war among its many different factions and members. The frequency of the public disputes and fights has led to many modern believers declaring their commitment to Jesus, while avoiding any association with the church. (Although it is doubtful whether genuine believers can avoid the responsibility of representing their Lord as a part of His Church in the world). Because the Church is comprised of redeemed sinners in the process of sanctification, it is inevitable there will be disagreements and dissensions. However, the goal of each Christian should be to grow in love and avoid unnecessary fights, so that we can work together towards the unity in the body that Jesus prayed for.

The example of Paul's return to Jerusalem at the end of his third missionary journey is instructive. On his journeys he had been preaching about the grace of God that allowed Gentiles to become part of the Church without the requirements of Jewish law, and the necessity of faith in Jesus for salvation for both Jews and Gentiles. However, the Jewish believers in Jesus found it difficult to accept that their laws, traditions and cultural practices were redundant for salvation. So Paul was falsely accused of teaching that Jews should denounce or discontinue their cultural practices that provided them their ethnic identity. James, the leader of the Jerusalem church, requested that Paul join four Jewish men in a purification ceremony, even paying their expenses, to prove to the great number of Jewish converts that rumors about his teachings were false.

Several Bible teachers have stated Paul was wrong to accede to this request since it seemed contrary to his teaching that these practices were meaningless with respect to salvation. But Paul was looking at the bigger picture of unity, so he chose to avoid an unnecessary fight. Since he knew his involvement did not affect his core message and it would help the Jewish believers to be more comfortable with him, he wanted to avoid a fight to try to justify his doctrine or satisfy his ego.

Do we find ourselves engaging in fights over issues that do not affect our core beliefs on salvation through faith in Jesus? Are these fights necessary, or just an effort for self-justification? Let us strive to keep the unity of the church in peace, and to grow in our love.

Father, we desire to have the attitude of Paul who stated, "to the weak I became weak, to win the weak. I have become all things to all

*men so that by all possible means I might save some." (1Cor 9:22 NIV).
We need your help to grow in love, for Jesus' sake.*

August 23

MANNA SERIES: THE CHURCH, JESUS' REPRESENTATIVE BODY ON EARTH
A BODY WITH AN AWESOME HEAD

Reading Passage: Eph.1:15-23
Main Text: Eph.1:22-23 And God placed all things under his feet and appointed him to be head over everything for the church, which is his body, the fullness of him who fills everything in every way. (NIV)

Paul used the analogy of the human body to describe the Church and her relationship with her leader, the Lord Jesus Christ. He is called the head and the Church is His body.

In humans and animals, the head contains the critical organ for the functioning of the body, making the body fully dependent on the head. In fact, without the head the body is dead, just as without Christ, the Church is non-existent, without any means of functioning. Beyond the physical analogy, the head represents the center of the intellect, mind, thought and emotions of a person. It is that which provides the body with purpose of being. The will and desires of the head is manifested in the activities of the body. Similarly, Jesus is "head over all things for the benefit of the Church" and He fills every part of the Church with Himself so that she represents His presence everywhere, and in everything she does.

Paul saw this indivisible relationship between Christ and the Church as a consequence of God's work in producing her by the work of Christ. He said God "...chose us in Christ before the foundation of the world" (v. 4), "...we were predestined to adoption as sons through Jesus Christ" (v. 5), we obtained "...redemption through His (Christ's) blood" (v. 7), and in Christ "...we have been claimed as God's own possession" (v. 11). The Church is not the invention of man, nor does she exist for the purpose of man. She was designed, developed and now functions for the purpose of God as determined by her head, Jesus Christ.

Paul also explained that God has planned that at the end of this age, all things in earth and in heaven, including political systems, scientific enterprises, business organizations, and academic institutions, will be brought together and made subject to one head, Jesus Christ (v. 10). He who is the head of the Church will become the head of all things. The Church has an awesome head, and a triumphant future. When we become a part of the Church, we are submitting to the authority of this awesome head, we are positioning ourselves as God's special possession, and we are joining God's eternal program to make Christ the exalted head of the universe. Surely you would not want to miss out on this glorious opportunity?

Father, it is amazing that Your plans for ruling the world through Christ should include wretched sinners like us. We thank You for the amazing grace that redeems us and gives us the privilege of being the body of Christ.

August 24

MANNA SERIES: THE CHURCH, JESUS' REPRESENTATIVE BODY ON EARTH
YOU ARE MORE THAN AN APPENDIX

Reading Passage: Eph. 4:1-16
Main Text: Eph. 4:15-16 Instead, speaking the truth in love, we will in all things grow up into him who is the Head, that is, Christ. From him the whole body, joined and held together by every supporting ligament, grows and builds itself up in love, as each part does its work. (NIV)

The appendix is a worm-like tissue at the end of the large intestines. It has been generally accepted that the appendix has no function in the human body, although recent research is challenging this claim. The reason for this conclusion is that there has been no noticeable effect on the body after the removal of the appendix. It is viewed as unnecessary tissue.

Paul used the analogy of the human body to describe the church in relationship to Christ as her head. He also used the analogy of the body to describe the significance of each member of the Church and how each contributes to her development. As with the human body, each member is essential and performs an important function for the body of Christ. No matter how insignificant a member of the Church may appear, like the toenails or eyelashes in the body, we are placed there for a purpose and are provided with gifts and abilities to fulfill our role. No member is a mere appendix that can be excised from the body and not affect the proper functioning of the whole Church.

The purpose of the body is growth and reproduction. The qualitative growth goal of the church is to become like her head: Christ. As we become developed in our understanding of God, mature in our decision making, and pure in our character, we become Christ-like fully representing Him. For this to happen, every member has to be active in contributing to the development of one another, by speaking the truth in love concerning each person's faults and weaknesses. There may be no improvement in our lives if no one makes us aware of our flaws.

We must be very protective of our unity, holding one another closely while being accountable, like the joints and muscles in the body. The Church will grow both in character and numerically when each member "does its work." If you don't do your work, I am deprived and the growth of the body is affected, because you are more than an appendix.

Are you fully identified with the Church? Do you know your role in the body? Are you functioning in that role so the whole body benefits?

Lord, we have been blessed by Your salvation, which has placed us in Your body, and provided us with a role to play. Help us to always appreciate the significance of the responsibility You have given to us for the proper functioning and development of the Church for Your glory.

August 25

MANNA SERIES: THE CHURCH, JESUS' REPRESENTATIVE BODY ON EARTH
GIVE GOD SOMEWHERE TO LIVE

Reading Passage: Eph. 2:11-22
Main Text: Eph. 2:21-22 In him the whole building is joined together and rises to become a holy temple in the Lord. And in him you too are being built together to become a dwelling in which God lives by his Spirit. (NIV)

Most religions put great significance on the buildings where their deities can be accessed, so sacrifices can be made and worship conducted. The devotees build temples, like the Pantheon in Rome, and other sacred places to represent the home of their gods.

When Yahweh introduced Himself to the Hebrews as the "formless" God, they had the problem of attempting to prepare a home for a God that was invisible. After King Solomon built a temple for Yahweh, he wondered if God could dwell among men when not even the heavens could contain Him (2 Chron. 6:18). The eventual destruction of the Hebrew temples indicated that these were inadequate as dwelling places for the eternal God.

Jesus came to earth representing God and dwelt among humanity. He soon returned to heaven and sent the Holy Spirit to "construct" a new dwelling place for God on the earth. Using the analogy of a building, Paul describes how God brings together various people of different nationalities, ethnicities and backgrounds and fits them together, block upon block to construct this dwelling place. The first thing the Spirit does is to make peace between these naturally warring parties. This peace is engineered by the blood of Jesus through His death on the cross that destroys any basis for hostility. The foundation on which the building is constructed is the teachings of the apostles and prophets; concerning Jesus who is the chief stone holding it together.

Each member of the Church becomes God's individual project as He shapes us, chipping off our selfish ways and hateful attitudes, until we can be fitted with the other building blocks on which He is working. When we are thus put together, the building begins to expand into a structure that God is pleased to inhabit; one that we call "the Church." It is the place where fitted blocks show the unity, which cannot be achieved by any man-made organization. It is the place to which the world has to turn when they need to find God. It is the place where there should always be the worship of God and the evidence of His presence.

Quite possibly, the challenges we sometimes face in relating to our brothers and sisters in the local fellowship may be God's way of shaping our personality so we can be fitted together with the other blocks in His building. We need to be mindful that we cannot properly represent God to the world until we do it corporately as a member of His Church.

Lord, we know the Spirit is working on us individually in order that He may dwell among us corporately. Help us to be open to the work of the Spirit.

August 26

MANNA SERIES: THE CHURCH, JESUS' REPRESENTATIVE BODY ON EARTH
A DIVINE ROMANCE

Reading Passage: Eph. 5:22-33, Rev. 21:9-14
Main Text: Eph. 5:25-27 Husbands, love your wives, just as Christ loved the church and gave himself up for her to make her holy, cleansing her by the washing with water through the word, and to present her to himself as a radiant church, without stain or wrinkle or any other blemish, but holy and blameless. (NIV)

The plot is fairly similar to the usual romantic script. Boy sees girl, loves her, and pursues her through many difficulties and personal sacrifices, until he wins her heart and hand in marriage. But this story has significant differences. The pursuer is the God of the universe, the pursued is humanity, who is God's own creation but who has become corrupted by sin and is totally unworthy of His love.

In order to accomplish the amazing plan of a divine romance with humanity, God had to reveal the different personalities within the godhead. We are introduced to God the Son, who would Himself become human and be identified with fallen humanity so He could redeem her. This required the greatest sacrifice possible in the cause of love - divinity becoming humanity, purity bearing sin, a throne being exchanged for a cross, and the justice of God the Father being satisfied by the sacrifice of God the Son. The redeemed humanity is called the Church, and Paul declared that husbands should love their wives as Christ loved the Church and sacrificed Himself for her. The response of the Church to this sacrificial love is to sanctify herself. She must separate herself from any sin, or competing interest to the love of her Lord, so she can be a holy and pure bride.

The culmination of scripture is a wedding celebration. In Revelation 19, in the scenes from the wedding supper of the Lamb, the angel declared, "The Bride has made herself ready." She is now fully sanctified and ready for presentation to the Lord, her husband. The angel identified the Bride in Rev. 21:9-14, and showed John a city representing the Church. The statement of the Church as the Body of Christ describes her function. As the Building of God, she manifests His presence in the world, and as the Bride of Christ, she is the demonstration of His love, His choice possession for eternity.

When human beings know they are loved, it causes them to feel significant, valued and self-assured. One of our most powerful weapons against the devil's negative assault against us is to declare our position as the beloved Bride of Christ. Let us use that declaration today.

Father, we are amazed at the extent to which You went to demonstrate Your love to us. In response, we dedicate ourselves to live sanctified lives to show our love to You, and to prepare for our wedding to the Lamb.

August 27

MANNA SERIES: THE CHURCH, JESUS' REPRESENTATIVE BODY ON EARTH
THE BODY'S SELF-SUSTAINING DESIGN

Reading Passage: Rom. 12:4-8, Eph. 4:8-13, 1Cor. 12:4-11
Main Text: Eph. 4:11-12 It was he who gave some to be apostles, some to be prophets, some to be evangelists, and some to be pastors and teachers, to prepare God's people for works of service, so that the body of Christ may be built up. (NIV)

The human body consists of trillions of cells, each with a limited lifespan. When these cells die, new cells replace them. This has caused some people to theorize that certain parts of the body are renewed every 7-10 years. Scientists have discovered that stem cells have the ability to regenerate themselves and develop into various tissues. From this we understand that the body was designed to be a self-sustaining, self-repairing and self-renewing machine.

The record of the gifts given to the Church by the Spirit indicates that this spiritual body was also designed to be self-sustaining and self-renewing. It is important to note that Paul always gave the lists of gifts (see reading passages) in the context of the collective membership of the church. This indicates that the spiritual gifts were never given for the benefit of the unbelieving world, and never intended for personal use or self- aggrandizement. Paul clearly stated that the sole purpose of the gifts was for the edifying or building up of the body of Christ. Different gifts are provided to different members in the body with no one person having all the gifts. This means we need all the members using their gifts collectively so that the Church can be built up. Without the contribution of some gifted members, the body will begin to deteriorate and cease to be effective.

Every believer has been provided with a gift, and "to each one the manifestation of the Spirit is given for the common good" (1Cor. 12:7 NIV). Therefore, churches must be so structured that all the members recognize their spiritual gifts, and opportunity is provided for them to exercise these gifts. Any supposed demonstration of a gift that is not edifying by contributing to the building up of the body should be prohibited. The ministries of the Church should be varied and inclusive so all members become contributors to the life of the Church. All members must be ministers and all must be actively involved.

Have you recognized your gift(s)? Have you been using your gift(s) so the Church can be built up? The Giver of the gift will hold us accountable for the non-use of our gifts.

Lord, we don't want to be like the servant you described as wicked and lazy because he hid the gift You gave him. Help us to appreciate the divine allocation of Your gifts, and the divine purpose for them. We desire to contribute to the edification of the Church for Jesus' sake.

August 28

MANNA SERIES: THE CHURCH, JESUS' REPRESENTATIVE BODY ON EARTH
ADJUSTING TO A COLLECTIVE CULTURE

Reading Passage: Eph. 4:8-13,
Main Text: Eph. 4:31-32 Get rid of all bitterness, rage and anger, brawling and slander, along with every form of malice. Be kind and compassionate to one another, forgiving each other, just as in Christ God forgave you. (NIV)

Individuality is natural to us. We were born as individuals, with our own minds and wills, and we will die as individuals. When we were babies, we only had interest in satisfying our needs, without any consideration of the resources or desires of our parents and siblings. Later, we were socialized to accommodate the needs of others for the common good. This was first done in families and then in school groupings, yet we struggled against our basic selfish desires. Western culture and economies emphasize superiority through competition, by which each person seeks to outperform all others in the quest to be the winner and accepted as number one.

Jesus established the Church where the emphasis is on our collective identity, not our individualism. Although we were saved as individuals, we were baptized into the Church and became members of an interdependent body, and building blocks in Christ's building. We have to reprogram our minds and adjust our behavior to a collective culture. Because the adjustment is a work in progress, the Church still has many examples of the old individualistic, competitive nature among her membership. People jostle for the high seats of position and power to gain recognition. Rather than cooperating, local churches and denominations compete for the greater membership numbers and jockey to have influence in the public square.

The very meaning of the term 'church' implies a group and not an individual. Therefore, Paul frequently used the Greek pronoun translated "one another" to describe the relationship that should be practiced in the Church. We are members of one another (Rom. 12:5); we should live in harmony with one another (Rom. 12:16); we bear one another's burden (Gal. 6:2); we bear with one another in love (Eph. 4:2); we must be kind to one another (Eph. 4:32); we encourage one another, and build one another up (1Thes. 5:11).

This change in our orientation must begin with a heart of love for the members of the Church, and an appreciation that we have a common salvation and a common destiny. We must be prepared to live together as one in Christ Jesus. Paul expressed this determination when he said to the Corinthian church, "... I have said before that you have such a place in our hearts that we would live or die with you" (2Cor. 7:3b). Are we allowing the Spirit of God to transform our minds from the worldly orientation of individualism to the collective culture of the Church?

Father, we understand that we cannot truly belong to You unless we also belong to Your Church. Help us to esteem others better than we do ourselves, because we are members of Your body.

MANNA SERIES: THE CHURCH, JESUS' REPRESENTATIVE BODY ON EARTH
IMPORTANCE OF ORDERLY HOUSEHOLD

Reading Passage:, 1Tim. 3:1-16
Main Text: 1Tim. 3:14-15 Although I hope to come to you soon, I am writing you these instructions so that, if I am delayed, you will know how people ought to conduct themselves in God's household, which is the church of the living God, the pillar and foundation of the truth. (NIV)

Every family has its own style of operating its household. The rules that the members follow and the way they organize the house represent the thoughts of the house leadership on matters of respect, acceptable behavior and priorities. These are communicated non-verbally to outside observers.

Paul describes the Church as the household of God. He instructed Timothy, the pastor of the Church at Ephesus, about various arrangements that should be put in place for the proper functioning of the Church. These included the various offices and the roles each should play. The offices and their functions were not evangelical or missional, as much as they were pastoral and organizational. They allowed the Church to have good order and provide a good impression of God's household to observers.

The reason a good impression is important is that the Church represents the place where God's truth is safeguarded and exhibited. Because the Church is God's household, His Spirit resides in her, the Word of God is accepted and taught, and the truth of the Word is evidenced in the lives of her membership. If there is disorder and a lack of decorum in the Church, it may cause outsiders to question the truth in the Church's message. Nobody expects to see Crown Jewels in a junkyard. Behavior must reflect belief. Therefore, we should be careful of the type of people that are selected for leadership, and the membership must respond to the leadership with respect.

The Christian faith may be mysterious, but the Church should be able to make the mystery understandable and relevant by the way she lives out the truth before the world. We must do our part to ensure the Church has a good reputation in the public square. The world is looking for a place that represents truth, and first impressions are lasting.

Lord, as members of Your household we want Your truth to be evident in our behavior and in our response to leadership. We don't want to take lightly our responsibility for communicating Your truth by proper order in Your household.

August 30

MANNA SERIES: THE CHURCH, JESUS' REPRESENTATIVE BODY ON EARTH
WHAT MAKES A CHURCH ATTRACTIVE?

Reading Passage:, Gal. 5:13-26
Main Text: Phil. 4:16-17 "For even in Thessalonica ye sent once and again unto my necessity. Not because I desire a gift: but I desire fruit that may abound to your account." (KJV)

Churches are promoted by highlighting features that are considered attractive to the public. Sometimes it is the architectural beauty of the building, or the relaxed feeling of modern theatre-like seats. It may be the style of music, the professional presentation by choirs and orchestra, or it may be the great sermons delivered by the preacher. These are all very attractive features of a local church but they don't capture the essence of what makes the Body of Christ at the local level, uniquely attractive, whether it consists of a small, poor, uneducated, congregation, or a large, wealthy, sophisticated membership. The Church is made attractive by the fruit produced by her members; those virtues and characteristics placed in them by the Holy Spirit.

The fruit serves three primary purposes for a plant; identification, attraction, and reproduction. The features are related. A tree is identified as an apple tree because it produces apples. People and animals are attracted to the tree, not because of its design, but primarily because of its fruit. The fruit contains a seed that provides for the reproduction of numerous similar plants.

In a similar way, the Holy Spirit infuses the believer with the power to produce fruit that is identified with the nature of Christ. This fruit, as detailed in the list in Galatians 5:22-23 to include love, joy, peace, etc. makes the believer attractive to a world hungry for these expressions in their lives and communities. After seeing the genuine display of the fruit, and knowing it comes from a supernatural source, an observer is moved beyond curiosity to desire and experience the transformation produced by Christ.

Spiritual gifts serve to build up the Church so she will become spiritually fruitful. But gifts without the fruit result in exhibitionism, division and confusion, which is detrimental to the Church and unattractive to the world. For this reason, Paul inserted 1Cor. 13 in the center of his discussion of the exercise of spiritual gifts in the Church. In another context, Paul told the Church at Philippi that while he appreciated the gifts they sent him, he was more desirous that the gifts represented fruit they had developed in their lives. It is the fruit behind the gifts that would accrue to their account.

Are we placing the emphasis on the production of fruit in our lives so that our fruit bearing will identify our church? It is not our gifts, but our fruit that will make us attractive, and consequently reproductive for Christ's sake.

Lord, we are aware that you are desirous and insistent that we become fruitful Christians, so we can be reproductive. Transform our priorities and desires that they conform to Your will, so that we will please You.

August 31

MANNA SERIES: NOTABLE PRAYERS IN THE BIBLE
PRAYING FOR SPECIFIC GUIDANCE

Reading Passage:, Gen. 24:1-28
Main Text: Gen. 24:14 "May it be that when I say to a girl, 'Please let down your jar that I may have a drink,' and she says, 'Drink, and I'll water your camels too'—let her be the one you have chosen for your servant Isaac. By this I will know that you have shown kindness to my master." (NIV)

The myriad circumstances and requests surrounding various prayers presented in Scripture provide us with the assurance that God is ready and able to respond to all situations in our lives. We can never become dogmatic about the format of prayers or the type of situations that God responds to. Prayer is best understood as described by Jesus: we come as children before our Heavenly Father and we ask for anything we need.

Sometimes we wonder if it is acceptable to make our requests so specific that we seem to restrict God to the type of answer we have predetermined. In today's passage we note how God responded to a very specific request by Abraham's servant.

Abraham was living in the land of Canaan among the heathen. He wanted to get a wife for his son Isaac, who would be the inheritor of the promises he received from God. He did not want Isaac to marry any of the Canaanite women, so he instructed his faithful servant to go to his homeland in Nahor to get a bride for Isaac from among his own family. This was an awesome task for the servant. He knew how to find the city but had no idea how to locate Abraham's family. Even more problematic was to be able to identify an unmarried girl that would be a suitable bride for Isaac. Faced with the difficulty of finding the proverbial "needle in a haystack", the servant prayed to the God of his master. He asked God for very specific directions as shown in the text. The chosen girl should be willing, not only to show him hospitality as a stranger, but also offer to provide water for his camels.

Amazingly, before he finished the prayer a young lady named Rebekah arrived and did all that the servant requested in his prayer. He discovered that she was the daughter of Abraham's nephew. The servant was so moved by this answer to prayer, he worshipped the Lord and celebrated how precisely God had led him to fulfill his master's desire.

You may be confronting a situation that seems so puzzling that you feel you are facing an impossible maze. This story of Abraham's servant indicates that you can seek God for precise direction and trust His guidance into His purpose for your life. We can be assured that God answers prayers when in humility we acknowledge our need and our dependency on Him. He is willing to lead us when we put our trust completely in Him.

Lord, we thank You for the accounts in the Bible that show us examples of Your willingness to provide us guidance for the dark and puzzling situations of our lives. We acknowledge our inability to find our own way, so we place our trust in You today, in Jesus' name.

MANNA SERIES: NOTABLE PRAYERS IN THE BIBLE
INTERCESSION FOR THE REBELLIOUS

Reading Passage: Deut. 9:7-19, 25-29
Main Text: Deut. 9:26 I prayed to the LORD and said, "O Sovereign LORD, do not destroy your people, your own inheritance that you redeemed by your great power and brought out of Egypt with a mighty hand." (NIV)

The role of an intercessor is difficult. To intercede is to stand between two persons and intervene by pleading to one on behalf of the other. This is not a position one would easily assume, but it is often necessary in order to provide assistance to those in need or to seek to avert judgment against the rebellious.

What makes the task so challenging is that oftentimes the intercessor has to ignore his own state of comfort and take on the burden of those who are injured or at risk, in order to properly represent them. Although the avenue of prayer is available to everyone, many do not seek God's help in prayer, perhaps because they are ignorant of the resources available in God. Some people don't pray because they are unaware of the extent of their need, or the dangers they are facing. But there are others who are in such a state of rebellion against God that they adamantly refuse to seek His help. In all these cases there is a great need for an intercessor to represent these people before the Lord of justice.

In the reading passage, Moses was recalling the history of Israel's rebellion against the Lord. He reminded the people that when they were at Mount Horeb, while he went to meet with the Lord and to receive the tablets of the covenant, they prevailed upon Aaron to construct the image of a golden calf. The Israelites then began to worship the idol. The Lord was so angry with their idolatry that he was ready to destroy the nation because of their rebellion. But Moses interceded for them, prostrating himself before the Lord for 40 days and nights. He begged the Lord not to destroy them, and based his appeal on the Lord's promise to His people and His honor before the heathen. The Lord listened to Moses' appeal (Deut. 9:19).

The power of intercession is shown in its effectiveness in getting God to respond and defer judgment against the rebellious. As Christ's representatives on earth, we are required to act as priests before the Lord on behalf of the needy, the ignorant and the rebellious. Are we prepared to take on the role of an intercessor so God can have mercy on someone, just as He had mercy on us while we were in rebellion against Him? God is still looking for people to "stand in the breech" as intercessors before Him (Ezek, 22:30).

Lord, we thank You for Your willingness to respond to our pleas for mercy on behalf of others. Forgive us for our negligence to act in the role of an intercessor for those You desire to help. Open our eyes to the need, for Your name's sake.

September 2

MANNA SERIES: NOTABLE PRAYERS IN THE BIBLE
BEING AUDACIOUS IN PETITIONING

Reading Passage: 1Chr. 4:9-10
Main Text: 1Chr. 4:10 Jabez cried out to the God of Israel, "Oh, that you would bless me and enlarge my territory! Let your hand be with me, and keep me from harm so that I will be free from pain." And God granted his request. (NIV)

We are sometimes bashful or reluctant when making petitions for personal blessing. We try to make these petitions in a manner that gives the appearance that we are not too selfish or demanding. Some bible teachers make the valid point that Jesus, in the model prayer taught to His disciples, indicated that petitions should be made from a collective perspective, "Give us this day, our daily bread." However, this doesn't mean that petitioning for personal blessings are unacceptable or should be avoided.

We cannot overlook the fact that Jesus also taught us to pray as children approaching their Heavenly Father. With this relationship we are free to ask our Father for anything. Furthermore, our Father knows our needs before we ask and He knows our hearts. In fact, we show our trust in our Father when we come to Him honestly and boldly, expressing our needs, believing that He will answer appropriately by approval, denial or correction.

The well-known prayer of Jabez describes a sincere petition that appears surprisingly audacious. The story tells of a man who was given a name meaning pain or grief because of the pain his mother suffered while birthing him. Jabez was concerned about living with the stigma of this name, so he boldly petitioned God to make a drastic change in his situation. He asked that God would bless and prosper him by enlarging his sphere of influence. He also asked the Lord to assure him of His presence and protect him. The goal of this request was that Jabez would avoid the pain predicted by his birth, or conferred by his identity. While some may consider this a selfish demanding request, Jabez was honest about the personal challenge he was facing. He trusted that God cared about him and would be willing and able to change his predicament from pain to prosperity. He was bold in his petitioning and God granted his request.

This prayer inspires us to recognize that God cares about our personal predicament whether caused by unfortunate circumstances over which we had no control, like the type of family or the economic status to which we were born or whether there are people who are determined to cause us to have a painful life. Let us not be shy or reluctant to petition our Lord to change our situation from pain to prosperity. He cares for us.

Lord, we thank You for the assurance that You care about us and the needs of our lives. We believe You are able to transform our situation, regardless of how painful, into a state of great influence and prosperity. So we boldly ask You to bless us today and make us a blessing, in Jesus' name.

September 3

MANNA SERIES: NOTABLE PRAYERS IN THE BIBLE
SEEKING INSTRUCTIONS FOR RAISING CHILDREN

Reading Passage: Judg. 13:8
Main Text: Judg. 13:8 Then Manoah prayed to the LORD: "O Lord, I beg you, let the man of God you sent to us come again to teach us how to bring up the boy who is to be born."
Judg. 13:12 So Manoah asked him, "When your words are fulfilled, what is to be the rule for the boy's life and work?" (NIV)

It is natural for mature humans to seek to fulfill the desire to reproduce and have children. We appreciate the fact that primarily, children are born to be our replacement on the earth. However, they come with their own disposition and destiny, which are unknown to us at the time of their birth. As parents we have the awesome task of caring for and nurturing them so that they will achieve the purpose for which they were born. Most parents will admit that raising children is one of the most challenging tasks ever faced. Although it can be a joyous experience, it is often interspersed with missteps, misunderstandings and frustrations. We wish babies came with an instruction manual to provide us with guidance. Yet many of us fail to pray to the Lord our Maker, for the specific instructions for each child.

The angel of the Lord appeared to Manoah and his wife who was barren, and told her she would bear a son. After the news sank in, Manoah entreated the Lord to send the angel again in order to provide instructions on how to bring up his son. Perhaps he made the request because of the unique circumstances surrounding the birth of Samson; nevertheless, his actions indicate the admission of helplessness in rearing his son and his need of help from the Lord. The questions posed by Manoah when the angel returned reflect the main concern that any parent should have when given the task of raising children. He asked:" ...what is to be the rule for the boy's life and work?" (v. 12).

If only we could be divinely instructed on the disposition of our children and how we should handle them, instead of having to discover this by trial and error. Equally important is to know the life-purpose for the child God has given us, so we can focus on ensuring we contribute to the fulfillment of that purpose. Prayer is essential if we are to put in effect Paul's admonition to fathers: "Do not exasperate your children; instead, bring them up in the training and instruction of the Lord." (Eph. 6:4 NIV).

Father, thank You for showing in the story of Manoah that You are available to provide guidance for the challenging task of training our children. We admit our inadequacy for the task and our need for Your help. We look to You since You know their manner and the mission that must be accomplished in their lives. We offer this prayer in the name of Jesus.

September 4

MANNA SERIES: NOTABLE PRAYERS IN THE BIBLE
BECOMING SELFLESS IN PRAYER

Reading Passage: 1Sam. 1:1-28
Main Text: 1Sam. 1:11 And she made a vow, saying, "O LORD Almighty, if you will only look upon your servant's misery and remember me, and not forget your servant but give her a son, then I will give him to the LORD for all the days of his life, and no razor will ever be used on his head." (NIV)

Prayer is more than our merely making entreaties to God. Rather it should be communication with our Father in which we remain sensitive to His voice speaking to our spirit. Because of our basic selfish nature, we are inclined to make petitions that are contrary to God's will for our lives. God has to decline these requests. The Apostle James explains the cause for this denial: "When you ask, you do not receive, because you ask with wrong motives, that you may spend what you get on your pleasures" (James 4:3 NIV). When we become sensitive to God in prayer, we will become aware of Him, working on our hearts, adjusting our petitioning so our desires will be in tune with His desire for us. We then begin to pray according to the will of God.

The story of Hannah in our text is a good example of the operation of this process in prayer. Hannah was the favored wife of her husband, but she was barren, while the other wife, Peninnah, had children. Peninnah aggravated the situation by taunting Hannah, thus creating conflict and causing her grief. When Hannah sought the Lord, she prayed out of deep distress because of her need. She wanted to lose the shame of barrenness, to be fulfilled as a mother, and to counter the teasing of her adversary. But God had shut her womb so her prayers were in vain (vv. 5-6). Eventually, she altered her prayer by promising the Lord that if He blessed her with a son, she would dedicate him to the Lord for the rest of his life. Her previous desires for self-fulfillment and vindication were now replaced by the desire to give glory to God. The Lord answered her prayer and she bore a son named Samuel. After nursing him until he was weaned, Hannah fulfilled her vow and presented Samuel to the Lord. The son she wanted for her pleasure was given to the priest to remain in the temple for service to God.

Ultimately, all we desire and seek after must have the goal that God is glorified through us. If our prayers are focused on our need without the pursuit of the glory of God, we will discover through the denials of our requests, that He is pressing us to re-examine our motives. He wants our prayers to be less self-focused and more God glorifying.

Father, help us to become so selfless in prayer that we can pray like Jesus, "Not my will, but thy will be done." We want to find delight in the transformation of our motives to the things that please You, for the glory of Jesus.

September 5

MANNA SERIES: NOTABLE PRAYERS IN THE BIBLE
PRAYING BASED ON THE CHARACTER OF GOD

Reading Passage: 2 Chr. 6:13-42
Main Text: 2 Chr. 6:19-21. Yet give attention to your servant's prayer and his plea for mercy, O LORD my God. Hear the cry and the prayer that your servant is praying in your presence. May your eyes be open toward this temple day and night, this place of which you said you would put your Name there. May you hear the prayer your servant prays toward this place. Hear the supplications of your servant and of your people Israel when they pray toward this place. Hear from heaven, your dwelling place; and when you hear, forgive. (NIV)

Prayer is not a vain, powerless exercise based on mere ritual or wishful thinking. There must be some basis for our faith. We are approaching a personal God with our requests and we must believe that He is willing and able to respond to us. On what basis can we confidently offer prayers to God? It must be because of our knowledge of the character of our God, expressed by His promises to us. If we don't believe that He exists and that He is committed to rewarding those who seek Him (Heb. 11:6), prayer is futile.

The prayer offered by Solomon at the dedication of the temple in Jerusalem is one of the classic prayers in the Bible. At the beginning of the prayer, Solomon acknowledged the unique characteristic of the Lord, "O LORD, God of Israel, there is no God like You in heaven or on earth—You who keep your covenant of love with Your servants" (v. 14). This uniqueness made Solomon realize that although he built a temple to represent the Lord's dwelling on earth, God could not be restricted or localized; not even the heavens can contain Him (v. 18). However, his request was that whenever prayers were made toward the temple, God would hear from heaven and respond in forgiveness, deliverance or vindication. The basis for Solomon's confidence that God would hear and respond was that God is good, and His mercies or covenant love endures forever (2 Chr. 5:13). This is the character of our God.

As New Testament believers, we are able to place our faith in this God because we know Him through Jesus Christ. In Christ He demonstrates that He is good and merciful; so He is willing and able to forgive, deliver and vindicate us. We don't need a physical temple because in Jesus we have full access at any time to the true temple of God. Whether we have sinned, are being harassed or held captive by the Devil, or facing enemies that cause us to fear, we can pray in the name of Jesus and be assured that we will be heard by our Heavenly Father. This is our confidence in prayer.

Father, we are so thankful that in Jesus we have access to the throne room of heaven, where You are delighted to receive our requests. Help us not to be neglectful of this privilege to pray to You at any time for anything in Jesus' name.

September 6

MANNA SERIES: NOTABLE PRAYERS IN THE BIBLE
PRAYING FOR GOD TO VINDICATE HIMSELF

Reading Passage: 1Kings 18:20-40
Main Text: 1Kings 18:36-37 At the time of sacrifice, the prophet Elijah stepped forward and prayed: "O LORD, God of Abraham, Isaac and Israel, let it be known today that you are God in Israel and that I am your servant and have done all these things at your command. Answer me, O LORD, answer me, so these people will know that you, O LORD, are God, and that you are turning their hearts back again." (NIV)

God is protective of His own glory and honor. From the time sin entered the world, mankind has sought to replace the glory due to God and substitute idols, whether of self or of others. This quest to replace God intensifies with our scientific discoveries and the desire to predict and control the events of life. These pursuits usually result in times of confrontation between those who worship the Lord and those who seek to replace Him. We can be sure that the Lord will respond to the challenge to vindicate Himself. He is just waiting for the man or woman who is willing to stand for Him against His enemies.

At the time when Elijah the prophet appeared on the scene, God's chosen people Israel had gone astray into the worship of Baal, led by King Ahab and his wife Jezebel. Elijah was distressed when he observed that the people who had the revelation of the true God were substituting Him with a man-made idol that was powerless and useless. He challenged the people to a showdown on Mount Carmel to prove who was the true God. He told the prophets of Baal to prepare an altar with the sacrifice but with no fire. They should call on their god Baal, and he would call on the Lord. The God who answered by providing the fire for the sacrifice should be accepted as the true God. After accepting this challenge, the prophets of Baal cried from morning until noon pleading with Baal to answer, but there was no answer. Then Elijah prayed asking the Lord to prove to the people that He was the true God. The Lord immediately sent fire that consumed the sacrifice and the altar. When the people saw it they worshipped saying, "The Lord, He is God."

We may not be faced with a similar dramatic challenge as to the authenticity of our God, but we will have encounters with people who will question whether our God is real. We can be assured that the Lord is still willing to vindicate Himself when we take a stand for Him. We can challenge our opponents to pray to their god in their difficulties, and we will pray to our God who will vindicate Himself. Let us not be afraid to let the world know that we serve a God who answers our prayers and who will prove that He alone is the One who should be worshipped.

Father, it is good to know that You are prepared to vindicate Your glory against Your enemies. Help us to boldly stand for You and trust Your faithfulness in answering our prayers in Jesus' name.

September 7

MANNA SERIES: NOTABLE PRAYERS IN THE BIBLE
PRAYING WHEN FRUSTRATED

Reading Passage: 1Kings 19:1-8
Main Text: 1Kings 19:4 While he himself went a day's journey into the desert. He came to a broom tree, sat down under it and prayed that he might die. "I have had enough, LORD," he said. "Take my life; I am no better than my ancestors." (NIV)

When we pray, we humans are approaching the One who is divine, but we are doing so through our Mediator who is both human and divine. Because of His humanity, He understands the frustration we have to endure, so He is not surprised when this is reflected in our prayers. The author of the letter to the Hebrews states, "For we do not have a high priest who is unable to sympathize with our weaknesses, but we have one who has been tempted in every way, just as we are—yet was without sin" (Heb. 4:15 NIV). This knowledge allows us to be honest with our weaknesses when we pray.

Elijah had just won an amazing victory for God against the Baal worshipers on Mount Carmel. After this victory, Elijah arranged for the slaughter of 450 prophets of Baal. Later, following the prayer by Elijah, the three-year drought over the land of Israel was broken with heavy rainfall. When Queen Jezebel heard that Elijah had killed the prophets of Baal, she sent him a message threatening to kill him just as he had killed the prophets of Baal. This message so scared Elijah that he ran for his life to the desert of Beersheba and prayed asking God to take his life. The powerful prophet was now filled with human frustration because of the threat of an evil woman. He cried, "It is enough." The Lord did not condemn Elijah for his weakness; instead He sent His angel to meet his need. The angel realized the frustration was intensified by exhaustion so he brought food and drink and encouraged Elijah to refresh himself and rest.

The lesson from Elijah's meltdown is that regardless of how much we have been used by God to do great exploits and attain the heights of our spiritual achievements, we are still human beings with human weaknesses. We also learn that the Lord understands us when we pray in the midst of our frustrations. He hears our prayers, ignores the foolishness we state because of our emotional weakness, and lovingly meets our needs. We don't know how to pray as we should but the Holy Spirit is our helper so that the deep needs of our lives are met.

Like Elijah and a number of the notable prophets of the Bible, let us be honest with our feelings before the Lord and trust His mercy.

Lord, our challenges sometimes cause us to despair and we feel as if no one can make our lives meaningful. Please forgive us for our lack of trust. Help us to remember that You understand our humanity and that You can restore our soul. We thank You, in Jesus' name.

September 8

MANNA SERIES: NOTABLE PRAYERS IN THE BIBLE
USING PRAYER FOR SIGHT CONTROL

Reading Passage: 2 Kings 6:8-20
Main Text: 2 Kings 6:17-18. And Elisha prayed, "O LORD, open his eyes so he may see." Then the LORD opened the servant's eyes, and he looked and saw the hills full of horses and chariots of fire all around Elisha. As the enemy came down toward him, Elisha prayed to the LORD, "Strike these people with blindness." So he struck them with blindness, as Elisha had asked (NIV)

In the Bible, physical sight is frequently presented as an illustration of spiritual revelation. Without the revelation of the light of the gospel of Jesus Christ, we are in the darkness of sin, groping around in uncertainty and danger like a blind man. The need for spiritual sight is also necessary for believers to see the resources that are available to them in Christ Jesus. How can someone gain sight? How can our eyes be opened so that the revelation of truth can be received? This can be achieved through prayer.

When the King of Syria wanted to capture the prophet Elisha because he was providing information to the King of Israel that exposed the plans of the Syrian army, he sent his army with chariots and horses to surround the city where the prophet resided. Elisha's servant got up early in the morning and when he saw the heavily equipped army surrounding the city he panicked, and went in fear to report the situation to his master. Elisha calmly assured him that there was a greater army protecting them. He then prayed, "Lord open his eyes that he may see." When the servant's eyes were opened, he saw the hills full of horses and chariots of fire surrounding Elisha. Before the servant's eyes were opened, all he could see were enemies and danger, but when his eyes were opened, he could see what Elisha had been seeing: the protection God had placed around his children.

Interestingly, in order to conquer the Syrian army, Elisha prayed, but this time asking the Lord to strike the enemy with blindness. The control of sight, whether opening for revelation, or closing for conquest was done through prayer.

The story of Saul who became the Apostle Paul in Acts 9, demonstrated the importance of sight in his conversion. When he was opposing the gospel and persecuting the disciples, the Lord struck him with blindness in order to conquer his rebellion. When he submitted to the Lord, he was instructed to go to the house of Ananias so he could regain his sight and receive the Holy Spirit.

Let us diligently apply the power of prayer so the scales may be removed from the eyes of those who are resistant to the preaching of the gospel. We also need to pray that the eyes of believers will be enlightened so they will begin to appreciate the riches that are available to them in Christ. Let us also use prayer as a weapon to blind with confusion the forces of evil that are opposing the truth of Christ.

Lord, help us to appreciate the power of sight control available to us in prayer, so we may use it for the advancement of Your kingdom, in the name of Jesus.

September 9

MANNA SERIES: NOTABLE PRAYERS IN THE BIBLE
THE SUPERNATURAL COOPERATION IN PRAYER

Reading Passage: 2Kings 19:9-28
Main Text: 2Kings 19:15-16 And Hezekiah prayed to the LORD: "O LORD, God of Israel, enthroned between the cherubim, you alone are God over all the kingdoms of the earth. You have made heaven and earth. Give ear, O LORD, and hear; open your eyes, O LORD, and see; listen to the words Sennacherib has sent to insult the living God." (NIV)

Prayer requires the participation of, and the cooperation between, people on earth and God in heaven. This does not mean that God does not act on behalf of mankind without prayer, He is constantly maintaining the universe without prayer and sustaining even those who don't acknowledge His existence. God's plan when He created the earth was that mankind would be His delegated authority on earth, and that we would work in fellowship with Him to fill the earth with His glory. To accomplish the coordination between heaven and earth, it requires communication in prayer, so the will of God would be done on earth as it is done in heaven.

Because all the power and wisdom in this relationship resides in God, our duty is to be alert to happenings in the world that dishonor God, and to bring these concerns before our Heavenly Father. It is not that our all-knowing God would be unaware of these concerns unless we informed Him. Rather, He desires that we become involved in His activity in the earth so we may participate in glorifying Him for His answers to prayer.

Sennacherib, the King of Assyria, had laid siege on Jerusalem and was demanding that Hezekiah, King of Judah, surrender. He sent a message to Hezekiah stating that the God of Judah could not prevent the capture of Jerusalem, for no god of any nation could withstand the power of Assyria and its army. The demand was written in a letter and sent to Hezekiah. When he received the letter, Hezekiah was distressed so he went to the house of the Lord and spread it before the Lord and prayed. He said, "Lord, hear the threats, open Your eyes and see the insulting words spoken against the Lord".

Certainly, the Lord knew what was happening, but it was important for Hezekiah to be involved in bringing the situation to the Lord in prayer so he could participate in the process of having the Lord provide the answer. The Lord informed Hezekiah that He took the blasphemy as a personal insult and would defend the city. That night He sent an angel who killed 185,000 of the Assyrian army, and this caused Sennacherib to retreat to his country.

Are there situations, which are dishonoring to God that we are failing to pray about? The Lord may be waiting for us to become concerned and burdened so He can intervene in response to our prayers, and thereby receive glory.

Lord, help us to remain sensitive to the needs and the burdens in our world that You want to address. We want to play our part through prayer so Your will may be done on earth as it is in heaven.

September 10

MANNA SERIES: NOTABLE PRAYERS IN THE BIBLE
CHALLENGING A DIVINE DECREE

Reading Passage: 2 Kings 20:1-11
Main Text: 2 Kings 20:2-3 Hezekiah turned his face to the wall and prayed to the LORD, "Remember, O LORD, how I have walked before you faithfully and with wholehearted devotion and have done what is good in your eyes." And Hezekiah wept bitterly.
2 Kings 20:5 "Go back and tell Hezekiah, the leader of my people, 'This is what the LORD, the God of your father David, says: I have heard your prayer and seen your tears; I will heal you.'" (NIV)

Are there certain topics that are off-limits for prayer? Some people argue that we should not pray about anything since our Sovereign God has already determined the outcome of everything. This conclusion does not reflect the relationship that we share with our Lord. God called us into a Father/child relationship through Jesus, who instructed us to ask the Father for anything in His name.

But what about cases where it seems God has already decreed the outcome? This raises problematic theological issues. God doesn't change His mind because He is immutable. On the other hand, a decree could be given with the intention of causing us to come to Him in penitence and perseverance so He can respond in mercy, which is consistent with His character. As finite humans we cannot fathom the mind of God who knows in advance what our responses will be to His decrees. We should have the confidence to pray fervently until God speaks to us. Sometimes the Spirit will guide us to cease praying because God will not give us what we are asking.

In the case of King Hezekiah, the Lord told him through the prophet Isaiah to put his house in order, because he would die and not recover from his sickness (2 Kings 20:1). In response to this decree, Hezekiah went before the Lord with bitter weeping, begging for healing and a longer life. God answered positively and instructed Isaiah to tell the king that his life would be extended by fifteen years. Hezekiah challenged God's pronouncement and the decree was altered in his favor.

This is a difficult idea for us to understand concerning the acts of God and their consistency with His character. There was also the case of Jonah where God decreed destruction on the Ninevites. But when they repented, God withheld the punishment. These cases suggest to us, not to cease praying over any condition regardless of indications of the certainty of adverse results. God could be presenting these circumstances as a test of our faith to see whether we will be persistent in prayer.

Lord, we give up praying so easily, when You desire us to be as persistent as the widow with the unjust judge, since our Heavenly Father is merciful. We desire to demonstrate our faith by willingness to overcome all obstacles in pursuing You.

September 11

MANNA SERIES: NOTABLE PRAYERS IN THE BIBLE
GRACE TRIUMPHS OVER RULES

Reading Passage: 2 Chr. 30:13-22
Main Text: 2 Chr. 30:18 Although most of the many people who came from Ephraim, Manasseh, Issachar and Zebulun had not purified themselves, yet they ate the Passover, contrary to what was written. But Hezekiah prayed for them, saying, "May the LORD, who is good, pardon everyone who sets his heart on seeking God—the LORD, the God of his fathers—even if he is not clean according to the rules of the sanctuary." And the LORD heard Hezekiah and healed the people. (NIV)

The basis of our prayers is the grace of God, by which God hears us, not because we deserve His attention but because of HIs mercy and goodness. Without this grace we would have to offer sacrifice to atone for our sins and unfaithfulness before we could ever consider coming to the Lord to ask anything from Him.

The relationship between the Lord and Israel under the Old Covenant was based on rules and regulations and not grace. When rules were broken the people would have to suffer the consequences of their transgression until they could find a priest and bring a sacrifice and hope this was acceptable to reconcile them to God. There was no provision for praying directly to the

Lord, as God was unapproachable by sinful man. Yet during the practice of that Old Testament system, there were occasions where we saw glimpses of the grace of God that would later be fully revealed by the coming of Jesus Christ.

King Hezekiah brought reformation in Judah after a period of rebellion and idolatry. After he cleansed the temple, he was preparing for the celebration of the Feast of Unleavened Bread. The rules required that the people were consecrated before they could eat the Passover lamb. Because of the schedule, there was no time for them to go through the consecration ritual, yet following their repentance, they were sincerely desirous of worshipping the Lord in the Passover meal. This caused a dilemma. Should the people be rejected so the rules could be maintained or should the priests and Levites risk the judgment of the Lord for allowing unconsecrated people to participate? Hezekiah decided to seek the Lord in prayer on the basis of grace and trust in His forgiveness. Consequently, the Lord heard and healed the people.

Some people emphasize the rules and overlook the relationship. When we have broken the rules and people would seek to condemn us for our failures, we must remember that our relationship with God is not based on rules but on the grace provided through Jesus Christ. We can come confidently to His throne of grace and be assured of mercy and forgiveness because grace overcomes broken rules.

Father, we are grateful for the grace You have provided through Jesus Christ that allows us to pray to You at any time. Help us to ignore the voices that would condemn us for breaking the rules, and cause us to stand in the liberty and forgiveness provided by the grace of God.

September 12

MANNA SERIES: NOTABLE PRAYERS IN THE BIBLE
YOUR PRAYER-LIFE COULD BE MOTIVATIONAL

Reading Passage: Ezra 9:5-10:1
Main Text: Ezra 9:15 "O LORD, God of Israel, you are righteous! We are left this day as a remnant. Here we are before you in our guilt, though because of it not one of us can stand in your presence."

Ezra 10:1 While Ezra was praying and confessing, weeping and throwing himself down before the house of God, a large crowd of Israelites—men, women and children—gathered around him. They too wept bitterly. (NIV)

We are aware that our prayers reflect our relationship between the Lord, and us. But we rarely give thought to the impact our prayers can have on others around us. It is not that we make an attempt to be admired or observed as we bare our souls before the Lord in prayer. It is just that we cannot always avoid being heard by people when we are engaged in the personal exercise of prayer. The observers could be members of our household, friends and neighbors, or others of the church fellowship. The way we approach the time of prayer, the intensity of our focus and the depth of our supplication, all have an impact on others.

The Bible includes several references to the attitude of people in prayer. There is the prayer of Daniel that irritated his fellow officials in the royal palace, the prayer of the Pharisee in the temple which was in striking contrast to the prayer of the Publican, and the prayer-life of Jesus that prompted the disciples to ask Him to teach them to pray. Our attitude in prayer informs observers of the priority we place on prayer, our sense of burden when we present our petitions, and whether we pray with a conviction that God is hearing us. Those observing us may be convicted by our prayer-life and could be motivated to make their prayers more fervent, or they could be turned off from praying.

Ezra was burdened because the Jewish exiles that returned to Jerusalem from Babylon, including the leaders, were inter-marrying with the non-Jewish people of the surrounding nations. He was concerned that by breaking the law in this way, the Jews would provoke God to anger and would risk being exiled again. In his distress, Ezra tore his clothes, prostrated himself and cried out to the Lord with weeping and supplication. When a large crowd of the Jews observed Ezra's attitude in prayer, they gathered around him, and they were motivated to begin weeping in repentance.

Have you considered the impact your prayers are having on those who observe you? Will they be motivated to increase their sincerity and supplication in prayer? Will the unbeliever begin to think there is a reality in prayer? Let us make our praying motivational.

Father, we confess that sometimes we pray out of routine, mouthing words without ensuring they reflect our recognition that You are listening to us. We desire to pray with such sincerity that observers will be motivated to engage in a relationship with You. Help us Lord.

September 13

MANNA SERIES: NOTABLE PRAYERS IN THE BIBLE
ARE WE PREPARED TO PRAY FOR THE NATION?

Reading Passage: Neh. 1:1-11
Main Text: Neh. 1:4-6 When I heard these things, I sat down and wept. For some days I mourned and fasted and prayed before the God of heaven. Then I said: "O LORD, God of heaven, the great and awesome God, who keeps his covenant of love with those who love him and obey his commands, let your ear be attentive and your eyes open to hear the prayer your servant is praying before you day and night for your servants, the people of Israel. I confess the sins we Israelites, including myself and my father's house, have committed against you." (NIV)

There are times when conditions in our countries deteriorate to the extent that we realize that there are no human remedies to the problems. The conditions might include rampant violence, corruption, and immorality. The forces of evil may be so pervasive that the righteous constantly feels under threat. At these times, we know that believers must seek divine intervention through prayer. However, as we engage in prayer, we should consider whether we are fully prepared to pray for the nation.

In the Bible the record of prayers offered for the Jewish nation contain certain patterns that may be helpful for us to consider in our preparation for praying. One such example was the prayer offered by Nehemiah while he was working in the palace at Susa serving King Artaxerxes of Persia. He received news that the Jews who returned to Babylon were in distress because Jerusalem's wall was broken down, its gates burned, and the city was left defenseless against her enemies. On hearing this news Nehemiah was burdened and distressed, so along with his mourning and weeping he fasted and prayed.

Nehemiah began his prayer by acknowledging the greatness of God and His faithfulness to His covenant. He confessed that the people had broken the covenant, and more importantly, he included himself with those who had sinned against the Lord, thus he requested restoration based on the promises of God. He was committed to doing something to help in the restoration of Jerusalem, therefore he asked the Lord to grant him favor as he approached the king for permission to go and help.

When we consider the problems of our nation we must first be convinced that God is powerful enough to change conditions and people for the sake of His glory. We need to become so burdened with the situation that we are willing to make strong supplication to God. We cannot intercede for the nation unless we also identify ourselves with the sin of the nation so we can be motivated to participate in whatever may be necessary to bring about solutions. Let us be willing to adopt the prayer pattern of Nehemiah as we prepare to pray for our country.

Father, we sometimes find it easier to complain and assign blame instead of becoming burdened for the sin of the country. Help us to be willing to pray for our country with the passion of people like Nehemiah, who identified himself with the problems of his country.

September 14

MANNA SERIES: NOTABLE PRAYERS IN THE BIBLE
THE CRY FOR PROTECTION AND PRESERVATION

Reading Passage: Psa. 17:1-15
Main Text: Psa. 17:6-8 I call on you, O God, for you will answer me;
Give ear to me and hear my prayer.
Show the wonder of your great love,
You who save by your right hand
Those who take refuge in you from their foes.
Keep me as the apple of your eye;
Hide me in the shadow of your wings (NIV)

Many of David's prayers in the Psalms follow a particular pattern.

He is surrounded by enemies who are trying to harm him physically, or socially by destroying his reputation. He calls on the Lord for deliverance and protection, and points to his record of righteous behavior as the reason that God should vindicate him. What vary in these prayers are the analogies David uses to describe the type of protection he is asking the Lord to provide.

In Psalm 17:8, David asks the Lord to keep him as the apple of his eye and hide him in the shadow of his wings. Some commentators believe the "apple of the eye" refers to the pupil, which allows light to enter the eye and form images on the retina. We may not be sure as to the exact reference being made, but it is reasonable to assume the reference is to the delicate inner eye that controls sight. The psalmist is asking God to guard and protect him in the manner someone would protect his eyes, because they are fragile and valuable. The next request is similar, with the picture being that of a mother bird who ensures that her young chicks do not stray beyond where she can quickly hide them under the protection of her wings.

David was saying to God that he realized his fragility, and how vulnerable he was to the attacks of his enemies. He was pleading that the Lord regards him as being so precious that He would guard and protect him from harm. He wanted to be kept close, never beyond the shadow of the wings of His protection.

There are times when the misfortunes we face and the criticisms that are hurled at us cause us to believe we are of no value to anyone. It is at these times we can cry to our Heavenly Father asking Him to regard us as being precious, so He will guard us as He would the apple of His eye, and protect us like a mother bird protects her chicks. We do not make these requests because we are deserving, but because of His great love (v. 7). Regardless of the hostility of the enemies that surround us, and the negative feelings we may have because of the pressures we face, when we pray we can feel the affirmation of our Heavenly Father, so we can be strengthened to face the world.

Lord, we are grateful that through prayer we have the opportunity to hear Your voice and be assured of Your protection and provision. We now learn that You regard us as precious, despite our fragility. We thank You in Jesus' name.

MANNA SERIES: NOTABLE PRAYERS IN THE BIBLE
GAINING AN ELEVATED REFUGE THROUGH PRAYER

Reading Passage: Psa. 61:1-8
Main Text: Psa. 61:1-2 Hear my cry, O God;
> Listen to my prayer.
> From the ends of the earth I call to you,
> I call as my heart grows faint;
> Lead me to the rock that is higher than I. (NIV)

Sometimes, what we need in prayer is more than God's response to our prayer requests for others. What we seek is personal relief from the stress and pressures of life in order to obtain temporary relief for our souls.

In our life's journey we face the daily challenges of earning sufficient to live, providing for those depending on us, and putting aside funds to take care of us in the future. There are always uncertainties regarding the sources of income, the stability of the economy or the state of our health, and these contribute to the stress in life. Frequently we also face stress caused by the demands of relatives, or from children who need help to sort out their problems. Pressure intensifies when we have to interact with people who dislike us for various reasons and are determined to attack us at every opportunity. Because of these pressures, there are times we feel like the Psalmist when he cried in frustration, "Oh that I had wings like a dove, I would fly away and be at rest" (Ps. 55:6 NIV).

In Psalm 61, King David seemed to be suffering from the pressures that come with leadership, so he prays for relief. He felt so distant and alone that he described his posture in prayer as a cry from the ends of the earth. His plea was that despite the distance he felt from the presence of God, the Lord would hear and listen to his cry. He described his condition as one where his heart was getting feeble and weak, growing faint because of his anguish. At that time, he wanted the Lord to lead him to the rock that was beyond his ability to reach. A rock is an Old Testament symbol of a place of safety and security. David was seeking the type of refuge that would provide relief from the stresses that caused him anguish, and he believed this could be found through prayer. He could not achieve this refuge by his own efforts or by the status of his office as king; instead he pleaded that the Lord would take him there.

When the pressures of life get you down and your soul becomes burdened and distressed, have you sought a refuge through prayer? Ask God to lift you from the doldrums and take you to a higher place where you can rest in the power and peace of His presence.

Lord, we thank You for the opportunity of prayer in seasons of distress and grief when our souls need relief. We desire Your presence that will enable us to face the pressures of life with the assurance of Your power and peace.

September 16

MANNA SERIES: NOTABLE PRAYERS IN THE BIBLE
DON'T DELAY SEEKING FORGIVENESS OF SINS

Reading Passage: Psa. 51:1-19
Main Text: Psa. 51:1 Have mercy on me, O God,
According to your unfailing love;
According to your great compassion
Blot out my transgressions.
Wash away all my iniquity
And cleanse me from my sin. (NIV)

Prayer provides the opportunity for one of the greatest blessings we can ever experience, which is the opportunity to repent and obtain forgiveness of sins from our Heavenly Father. Our sins cause us suffering, which will be unrelieved until they are forgiven, so why do we delay seeking forgiveness from our merciful Father?

Psalm 51 is the famous prayer offered by King David after the prophet Nathan went to him to disclose that the Lord was displeased with his sin of adultery with Bathsheba. David not only slept with Uriah's wife but also arranged for him to be killed in an attempt to cover up his sin. David lived with the unconfessed sin for about one year, believing that he had succeeded with his deceitful plan. After he was exposed, David admitted in his prayer that during that time, his sin was "always before him" (v. 3), he was missing joy and gladness because he felt as if his bones were broken (v. 8), he was separated from the presence of the Lord and he was missing the joy of salvation (vv. 11-12).

This type of suffering arises because sin is never only against people, like Bathsheba or Uriah. Ultimately sin is always against God (v. 4), and we will never be at peace until we are reconciled to God. However, our pride keeps us from acknowledging the grievous nature of our sin, and from sincerely asking for forgiveness. Because of our wretched state of being born in sin (v. 5), we have no basis on which to ask for forgiveness except for our plea for mercy. We are deserving of the judgment of God for our sins and He would be just if He condemns us. But because of His faithful love, He is willing to have mercy on us when we repent.

Like David, we can ask God to blot out our transgressions so that there will be no trace on our record, to wash the stain of sin out of our lives so we will be whiter than snow, and to cleanse us by declaring us purged from defilement and free to enjoy the fellowship of His presence. In this regard, there is no sacrifice or offering that will be acceptable to God, except a broken and contrite heart. Although, like David, we may have to suffer some natural consequence for our sins, we will have the blessing of forgiveness and the joy of a restored relationship with God. It is foolish to delay obtaining this blessing.

Lord, please help us never to allow pride to cause us to delay coming to You in repentance when we sin. Thank You for being merciful and willing to forgive us and to restore us to fellowship with You, because of the grace that is in Christ Jesus.

September 17

MANNA SERIES: NOTABLE PRAYERS IN THE BIBLE
PRAYING WHEN THE SITUATION SEEMS IMPOSSIBLE

Reading Passage: Jer. 32:1-44
Main Text: Jer. 32:16-17 After I had given the deed of purchase to Baruch son of Neriah, I prayed to the LORD: "Ah, Sovereign LORD, you have made the heavens and the earth by your great power and outstretched arm. Nothing is too hard for you." (NIV)

What do we do when faced with situations that seem impossible to change? Having concluded that the situation is impossible, we may even consider prayer a waste of time. Too frequently we become influenced by a humanistic perspective and project our limitations on the Almighty. We have to remember that we are not divine, and God's thoughts and power are far beyond our imagination and abilities. What seems impossible to us is possible with God.

The prophet Jeremiah was facing a situation he considered an impossibility. The Babylonian army had laid siege against the city of Jerusalem and was preparing for the invasion. The Lord had already warned Jeremiah that the city would be captured, the inhabitants including the king would be taken captive, and the city destroyed by means of the sword, famine and pestilence. Yet the Lord also told Jeremiah to purchase a plot of land in the city because it would be a good investment for the future when the land would be restored and re-inhabited. The prophet could not imagine the possibility of the recovery of the city from destruction, so he had great doubts about making this investment. He decided to obey the Lord, but he prayed about his doubts.

Jeremiah began his prayer by acknowledging the power and sovereignty of the Lord, and confessed that nothing is too hard for Him. He recalled the awesome works that the Lord performed in the past when He delivered the Israelites out of Egypt and gave them a promised land. By recalling these past wonders performed by the Lord, the prophet began adjusting his attitude to one of believing that what he thought was impossible was indeed possible with God.

One of the great benefits of prayer is that when we are in communion with the Lord, we begin to have a change of perspective, allowing us to see God as all-powerful and our situations as being insignificant in comparison to Him. Faith begins to grow when we have the proper perspective of God and our problems. For this reason, it is important that we begin our prayers with worship in which we contemplate the greatness and power of our God. After stirring our faith in our awesome God, we too will declare that nothing is impossible with Him. Then we can offer our petitions.

Lord, we come to You in prayer so that our hearts will be in communion with You and we will gain new perspectives of Your power and love. We confess that nothing is impossible with You so we believe You can accomplish the impossible for us. Thank You Lord.

September 18

MANNA SERIES: NOTABLE PRAYERS IN THE BIBLE
PRAYING, BUT NOT DEMANDING

Reading Passage: Dan. 9:2-23
Main Text: Dan. 9:16-18 O Lord, in keeping with all your righteous acts, turn away your anger and your wrath from Jerusalem, your city, your holy hill. Our sins and the iniquities of our fathers have made Jerusalem and your people an object of scorn to all those around us. "Now, our God, hear the prayers and petitions of your servant. For your sake, O Lord, look with favor on your desolate sanctuary. Give ear, O God, and hear; open your eyes and see the desolation of the city that bears your Name. We do not make requests of you because we are righteous, but because of your great mercy." (NIV)

In prayer we must always remember that we are addressing our Lord and Master who is above us, and superior to us in all respects. Although this statement seems self-evident, making the emphasis unnecessary, we have an inclination to elevate ourselves while diminishing our Lord. One manifestation of this inclination is the tendency to make demands of God rather than humbly petitioning Him. Sometimes our prayers sound like directives being given, rather than requests being made to God. One reason for this practice could be that God has given us promises and we desire the fulfillment of these promises. However, we must remember the Promisor is the Sovereign Lord who has the right to decide the timing for the fulfillment of His Word.

Daniel was one of the Jewish exiles in Babylon. By research, he determined that based on God's promises, the end of the captivity of the Jews was near. He went to God in fasting and prayer, confessing the sins of the nation, pleading with Him to fulfill His promise to restore the city of Jerusalem and the temple, and asking Him to forgive the sins of the people. Although Daniel had God's promise for the restoration after 70 years, and this time was about completed, he did not demand the fulfillment of the promise. Instead he recognized the righteousness of God in judgment, the sinfulness and unworthiness of the people, and he begged for mercy. He stated that the basis for making his request was not the righteousness of the people, but the mercy of God (v. 18). Because of this act of penitence, the Lord dispatched an angel to explain to Daniel God's plans concerning the future of Jerusalem, the nation of Israel, and the world.

We need to maintain a humble attitude before God in prayer, recognizing that we have no basis to demand anything from Him. We can only appeal to Him on the basis of mercy that we have received through Jesus Christ, who represents the confirmation of all the promises of God. That's why we pray to the Father in the name of Jesus and for His glory, not ours.

Father, we cannot demand anything from You since we are already richly blessed in Christ Jesus. When we pray we trust Your grace to give us far more than we ever can deserve, for the glory of Your name.

September 19

MANNA SERIES: NOTABLE PRAYERS IN THE BIBLE
JONAH'S PRAYER FROM INSIDE A FISH

Reading Passage: Jonah 2:1-10
Main Text: Jonah 2:1-2 From inside the fish Jonah prayed to the LORD his God.

He said: "In my distress I called to the LORD,
And he answered me.

From the depths of the grave I called for help,
And you listened to my cry.
Jonah 2:7 "When my life was ebbing away,
I remembered you, LORD,
And my prayer rose to you,
To your holy temple.
Jonah 2:8 "Those who cling to worthless idols
Forfeit the grace that could be theirs." (NIV)

One of the more remarkable prayers in the Bible is the one offered by Jonah. It is unusual for its setting, surprising as to the opportunities available for prayer, and it provides a symbolic presentation of the amazing distance covered by prayer.

The well-known story of Jonah tells of God recruiting a prophet to go to Nineveh to deliver a message warning of the destruction of the city after 40 days. Because he disliked them, Jonah was unwilling to provide any warning to the Ninevites, so he took a boat that was heading to a country in the opposite direction of Nineveh. While on the journey, God sent a violent storm that almost destroyed the boat. Eventually, in order to calm the storm, the sailors cast Jonah into the sea. God then sent a large fish to swallow Jonah. While undergoing the turmoil of being in the fish's belly, the rebellious prophet decided to pray to the Lord his God. Jonah previously disregarded the command of the Lord, but God arranged the circumstances of his life so that he would have to make an altar of prayer in a most distressing setting. Regardless of our previous rebellion and the difficulties we are currently facing, God is always available to hear our prayers from any location and at any time.

Jonah didn't remember to pray until his life was ebbing away. It may seem that he was using God as a last resort having waited until he was near the end of his life to pray. Yet God was willing to listen to his unfaithful servant because the desperate prayer was made in faith. Our previous unfaithfulness does not disqualify us from praying. Some people only feel constrained to pray in the desperate moments just before dying. This may seem ineffective or useless to us, but not to our merciful Father who will respond to sincere faith. Jonah's prayer rose from inside a fish in the depths of the sea, and ascended to the throne of God in the heavens. Prayer is so powerful that barriers of distance, time or even demonic interference do not affect it. God is so delighted in our prayers that He will send angels to ensure that hindrances to our prayers are conquered.

Nothing should keep us from praying to our merciful God who is so ready to accept us despite our past failures, faithlessness or our distance from Him.

Lord, we thank You for Your grace that allows you to look beyond our faults and respond to our needs when we pray. Help us never to neglect the opportunity of approaching Your throne in prayer.

September 20

MANNA SERIES: NOTABLE PRAYERS IN THE BIBLE
A PRAYER REFLECTING HABAKKUK'S DILEMMA

Reading Passage: Hab. 3:1-19
Main Text: Hab. 3:1-2. A prayer of Habakkuk the prophet. On shigionoth.
LORD, I have heard of your fame;
I stand in awe of your deeds, O LORD. Renew them in our day,
In our time make them known;
In wrath remember mercy. (NIV)

We are often ambivalent about how we want God to deal with problems that we face, because we ourselves are not sure how they should be resolved. We are upset at the level of evil existing in our country and we desire some divine judgment so people can be alerted to their sinfulness. But when we consider the impact of the calamity on the righteous residents and on the innocent children, we desire a partial or selective level of judgment, just sufficient to affect the unrighteous and spare the righteous. Similarly, when we have children who are living in rebellion, we want the Lord to intervene just enough to scare them to repentance. However, at the same time, we would plead with God to protect them from any serious harm when punishing them. These situations illustrate how difficult it is for us to undertake the role of an all-wise God.

The book of Habakkuk shows the prophet in a similar dilemma. He begins in chapter 1 complaining that God is turning a blind eye to the violence and injustice in his country of Judah. After listening to his rant, God informs the prophet that He is planning to raise up the Babylonians to sweep across the world. This nation would also punish the nation of Judah. Habakkuk was shocked and perplexed to hear this news. He questioned how a Righteous God could use such an evil, violent and ruthless nation to punish His own special people. In response to the prophet, God explained that He planned the eventual destruction of Babylon because of her pride, wickedness and idolatry. With such conflicting circumstances requiring such perplexing solutions, God advised Habakkuk to live by faith in God, trusting His judgments (2:4).

In his final prayer, Habakkuk admitted that he was in awe of what God planned to do. Then he begged the Lord to execute the plan as soon as possible, but in the wrath of His judgment He should remember mercy. He wanted the punishment of his people in Judah but he desired that this punishment be tempered with mercy.

Although we know that we should trust the Lord to provide the correct balance between judgment and mercy that is needed for each situation, we still feel the need to express this concern in prayer. God does not reprove us for such expressions; He instead reminds us of past occasions when He demonstrated His power and we ended up rejoicing in the outcome. His message is that we can trust Him to know what is best in all situations.

Lord, we acknowledge our limitations and inability to solve the problems of our world. But in our confusion and ambivalence, we trust You as the only wise God, and we will live by faith, in Jesus' name.

September 21

MANNA SERIES: NOTABLE PRAYERS IN THE BIBLE
A PATTERN FOR PRIORITY IN PRAYER

Reading Passage: Matt. 6:5-15
Main Text: Matt. 6:9-13 This, then, is how you should pray:
'Our Father in heaven, hallowed be your name,
Your kingdom come, your will be done
On earth as it is in heaven. Give us today our daily bread.

Forgive us our debts, as we also have forgiven our debtors. And lead us not into temptation, but deliver us from the evil one.' (NIV)

Jesus was teaching His disciples about prayer and introduced the subject by indicating the flaws in the common practice of prayers by the religious people of that day. After explaining how prayers should not be conducted, Jesus proceeded to provide them with a prayer that is mistakenly called "The Lord's Prayer", but which is really a model prayer for disciples. It is interesting to note the elements that are prioritized in this prayer.

The prayer begins with the claim of a relationship that provides the basis for making any petition later on, "Our Father in heaven." We proceed to offer worship declaring, "hallowed be your name," indicating His name is honored and set apart above any other name. The next priority highlighted by our Lord has nothing to do with our needs but everything to do with what should be our primary concern, which is our desire to see the kingdom of God established in the earth. With such a declaration, we are also making a commitment to work with God for ensuring the kingdom will come in the areas where we have influence. Only after we have acknowledged and worshipped our Heavenly Father, and recognized His purpose for the kingdom of God on earth, that we address our personal needs in prayer, "give us today our daily bread." By including this request, Jesus is indicating that the Father is concerned about our daily needs and these must be brought to Him in prayer. But He previously explained in vv. 7-8, that we should not pray with excessive words or try to use fancy techniques, because our Heavenly Father knows what we need before we ask. We should pray conscious of this fact.

Along with petitioning for our needs we should include a request for forgiveness of our debts, meaning our sins before God and our offenses against others. However, our request for forgiveness is predicated on our willingness to forgive anyone who has offended us. In including this statement in the model prayer, Jesus wants us to declare our commitment to forgive others before asking God for forgiveness for ourselves. This requires us to perform an examination of our relationship with others, even while praying concerning our relationship with our Father.

Do our prayers conform to the pattern of the model prayer presented by Jesus? Do our priorities in prayer match His, so that personal petitions come after worship and concerns for His kingdom?

Lord, we don't want our prayers to be just a ritualistic or legalistic exercise. We want to sincerely express Your heart's desire back to You in prayer. So help us to prioritize what You consider a priority in prayer, in Jesus' name.

September 22

MANNA SERIES: NOTABLE PRAYERS IN THE BIBLE
WE WERE INCLUDED IN HIS PRAYER

Reading Passage: John 17:1-26
Main Text: John 17:20-22 "My prayer is not for them alone. I pray also for those who will believe in me through their message, that all of them may be one, Father, just as you are in me and I am in you. May they also be in us so that the world may believe that you have sent me. I have given them the glory that you gave me, that they may be one as we are one:" (NIV)

As Christians who believe in the power of prayer, and we get a feeling of comfort and assurance whenever we hear someone calling our names in prayer, especially if the petition was unrequested and unexpected. There is the sense that the Holy Spirit is aware of our situation and has prompted somebody to bring it before the Lord, because He is interested in acting in our interest. Even if we never hear someone praying for us, the Bible provides a good basis for us to have this sense that God is thinking about us, because Jesus included us in His prayer to the Father.

John 17 records what can accurately be called the Lord's Prayer, which Jesus offered on the night when He was betrayed. This prayer is significant, not only because it contains the most words of any prayer made by Jesus, but also because it highlights matters that were of greatest concern to Him at the time of His agony, before His death. He did not mention His expected suffering on the cross, except to reference the fact that He had completed the work He was sent to do, and was preparing to return to His former glory with the Father. Instead, He was filled with concern for the disciples He was preparing to leave in the world, and prayed that they would be preserved and protected from the evil that is in the world. He also prayed for the unity of these believers, both with God and with each other, "that all of them may be one." Jesus said this prayer was made, not only for the disciples present with Him at that time, but also for all who would believe in Him in the future. This includes us.

Having heard Jesus' prayer for us, we can be confident that God is working to ensure our preservation and protection from the evil forces in this world, and that we will be sanctified until we are able to join Him in glory. We are also made aware of the divine agenda, that God is working on all of us to bring us into unity with each other so we can become the testimony of the incarnation of Jesus, "that the world may believe you sent me." What are we doing to ensure we remain in unity with God and with our fellow believers? Let us play our part for the answer to Jesus' prayer.

Lord, thank You for the evidence of Your concern for us, as we battle the evil around us. We ask for Your help as we seek to remove the hindrances to unity with our fellow believers. Make us one with You, so You may work through us to fulfill Your agenda, for Jesus' sake.

September 23

MANNA SERIES: NOTABLE PRAYERS IN THE BIBLE
PRAYING WHILE SUBMITTING

Reading Passage: Matt. 26:36-46
Main Text: Matt. 26:38-39 Then he said to them, "My soul is overwhelmed with sorrow to the point of death. Stay here and keep watch with me." Going a little farther, he fell with his face to the ground and prayed, "My Father, if it is possible, may this cup be taken from me. Yet not as I will, but as you will." (NIV)

Gethsemane was a garden of olive trees at the foot of the Mount of Olives. The name meant oil press because at this location the olives were crushed to produce oil. Jesus entered this garden the night before He was crucified, because He wanted to spend time in prayer. He was feeling the crushing burden of being the sin-bearer for the world, and this put His soul in great agony. He knew He would find relief and strength only through prayer.

The words of His prayer reveal some of the agony He was enduring. It is difficult to fully understand what He meant by asking the Father to take away the cup from Him. The cup could refer to the burden of bearing the sins of the whole world, or the agony of the Son of God being separated from the Heavenly Father. The cup could also be a reference to imminent death in the garden before facing the cross. Nevertheless, Jesus' submission to the Father's will seems far more significant than gaining an understanding of the cup in this context. The cup symbolized something that He encountered that was contrary to what He desired to do. Yet He was in total submission to His Father even if He did not get to fulfill His own will.

This provides us with a great example in prayer. What is the "cup" that we are facing today? Regardless of the worth of the cause, the scriptural support for the petition, or our sincerity in asking, ultimately what really matters is that the will of God is done. This constrains us to be in humble submission to the Father, and to be always open for His will to override ours. Charlotte Elliot beautifully expresses this in the following verse of a hymn.

> Renew my will from day to day,
> Blend it with Thine and take away,
> All that now makes it hard to say,
> Thy will be done.

Father, we find ourselves so determined to get our own way and so resistant when Your will is different from ours. Help us to follow the example of Jesus and be willing to submit all our desires to You, so Your will may be done. We yield to You, in Jesus' name.

September 24

MANNA SERIES: NOTABLE PRAYERS IN THE BIBLE
PRAYING WITHOUT CONDEMNING

Reading Passage: Acts 4:13-31
Main Text: Acts 4:23-24 On their release, Peter and John went back to their own people and reported all that the chief priests and elders had said to them. When they heard this, they raised their voices together in prayer to God. "Sovereign Lord," they said, "You made the heaven and the earth and the sea, and everything in them.

Acts 4:29-30 Now, Lord, consider their threats and enable your servants to speak your word with great boldness. Stretch out your hand to heal and perform miraculous signs and wonders through the name of your holy servant Jesus." (NIV)

Prayer connects us to the supernatural source of power - God Himself. When we have been persecuted, abused, or treated unjustly, we are easily tempted to pray seeking revenge and punishment against our oppressors. In the Psalms, there are many examples of these kinds of prayers, known as imprecatory psalms. However, this is not the way we were instructed to pray by Jesus, who told us to love our enemies and pray for those who persecute us (Matt. 5:44). In following Jesus' instructions, our prayers become positive and merciful, not negative and condemning.

Acts 4 recorded the events following the healing of the crippled man by Peter and John, and the overwhelming response of the crowd to Peter's sermon. The high priest and the rulers were incensed because Peter preached about the resurrection of Jesus Christ, and his declaration was that salvation was available only in His name. They imprisoned the apostles, and later released them after threatening them with further punishment if they continued to preach in the name of Jesus. Peter and John bluntly told the authorities they would not obey, and they were willing to risk the punishment.

When they told the congregation about the threats, they all began to pray. In the prayer they first celebrated the Lord as being sovereign over creation and the activity of men. Then they asked the Lord to observe the threats, and enable His followers to keep preaching and to support the message with miraculous signs. There was no condemnation of the actions of the authorities and no demand for judgment against them. The believers rested in the assurance that God was in charge of everything, so their petitions were for their own empowerment and the exaltation of Jesus. This was a positive prayer.

If we succumb to the negative emotions of condemnation and judgment, we can easily miss the purpose of our assignment and the greater goal of God being glorified in all things. Let us trust that the Lord is in charge, even of our enemies, and that He doesn't need our help to deal with them.

Lord, we confess that when we suffer, we easily become so self-consumed that we forget that You are aware of what is happening. Help us to focus on Your glory and the tasks You assigned us, and leave the judgment to You. May Jesus always be glorified in our prayers.

September 25

MANNA SERIES: NOTABLE PRAYERS IN THE BIBLE
GOD UNDERSTANDS OUR PROTESTATIONS

Reading Passage: Acts 9:1-19
Main Text: Acts 9:13-14 "Lord," Ananias answered, "I have heard many reports about this man and all the harm he has done to your saints in Jerusalem. And he has come here with authority from the chief priests to arrest all who call on your name." (NIV)

In accepting that our God is Lord and we are His servants, we must also accept that we must be in submission to Him. In this relationship of submission, we often wonder if we are not permitted to have a viewpoint that may be different from that of our Lord. Are we mere robots without the capacity to reason, or are we compelled not to mention to God our disagreements? The fact is that God created us with the ability to reason, and He is aware that from a human perspective, many of His acts are puzzling to us. Prayer offers us the opportunity to bring to God our concerns, misunderstandings, misgivings, and even our dissent with what He seems to be doing. The biblical record of God's dealings with His servants reveals that He understands our protestations.

The example in Acts 9 shows the problem Ananias had with the instructions the Lord gave him in a vision. Saul was terrorizing the followers of Christ. While on his way to Damascus to arrest any disciples he could find, the Lord interrupted his journey, knocking him off his horse and blinding him. Because of this dramatic encounter, Saul acknowledged Jesus as Lord, and was instructed to enter the city for direction regarding his next steps. When the Lord told Ananias to meet with Saul, Ananias responded in fear, pointing out the evil Saul was doing against the believers, and how dangerous he was. The Lord listened to these protestations, but insisted on obedience by providing an explanation for His decision.

God may not always cause us to understand His ways, but He allows us to make our case before Him. When Job felt God unfairly punished him, his strongest desire was to be able to reason with the Almighty and present his case (Job 13:3). God's response to this human desire was not to provide an explanation to Job, but to provide evidence as to why Job should be able to trust God even when he didn't understand Him.

You may be facing some situations today that cause you to question what God is doing. Quoting the prophet Isaiah, the Lord says, "Present your case, set forth your arguments" (Is. 41:21 NIV). If He does not allow us to understand His ways now, He will provide the faith to know that we will understand them better in the future.

Lord, like Job, we are sometimes puzzled at what You are doing. We thank You that we have the opportunity to bring our concerns to You in prayer. We are confident that You understand us, and that You will work things out for our good and Your glory. We trust Your love, in Jesus' name.

September 26

MANNA SERIES: NOTABLE PRAYERS IN THE BIBLE
A VALUABLE PRAYER FOR BLESSED PEOPLE

Reading Passage: Eph. 1:11-23
Main Text: Eph. 1:16-18 I have not stopped giving thanks for you, remembering you in my prayers. I keep asking that the God of our Lord Jesus Christ, the glorious Father, may give you the Spirit of wisdom and revelation, so that you may know him better. I pray also that the eyes of your heart may be enlightened in order that you may know the hope to which he has called you, the riches of his glorious inheritance in the saints, (NIV)

What petitions do we make for people who are in Christ, who are already blessed with every spiritual blessing (Eph. 1:3)? Paul, in his letter to the Ephesian believers, began by describing the blessings they had because God chose them and placed them in Jesus Christ. They received redemption, forgiveness, an inheritance, and they were sealed by the Holy Spirit.

As the person who established those congregations, and because of his pastoral heart, Paul continuously prayed for them. Since they were already so blessed, it is interesting to observe that he did not pray for their protection, health or earthly prosperity. Perhaps he considered these to be so mundane compared with the heavenly riches they already possessed. Instead, Paul prayed that God would give them a spirit of wisdom and revelation to know God better. It is possible for us to receive blessings yet fail to increase in our knowledge of the Blesser. This might cause us to take the blessings for granted, or even attribute the blessings to the wrong source, like our own goodness or wisdom. We constantly need the spirit of wisdom and revelation so our knowledge of God will be increased through the blessings He provides.

Secondly, Paul prayed that the eyes of their hearts would be enlightened so they might understand the extent of the riches they possessed. We have heard a number of stories of people living in abject poverty while there are large inheritances that they are unaware of, left to them by relatives. Similarly, sometimes we live lives of spiritual poverty because we are unaware of the riches we possess in Christ. May God open our spiritual eyes to make us always aware of how rich we are in Christ, so we will begin to live in accordance with our status and possessions.

Finally, he prayed that they would be made aware of the power available to them because of their position in Christ. There is no need for us to live weak, powerless lives when we can be energized by the resurrection power of Christ.

Paul's petitions for the Ephesians are appropriate for us, and should also be our petitions for all our fellow believers.

Father, we thank You for the abundant blessing we have in Christ Jesus. We desire that the petitions Paul offered for the Ephesian believers will also become our reality, so we will begin to appreciate our riches and the power available to us in Christ.

September 27

MANNA SERIES: NOTABLE PRAYERS IN THE BIBLE
PRAYER FOR A SPECIAL SUPPLY OF STRENGTH

Reading Passage: Eph. 3:1-21
Main Text: Eph. 3:14-18. For this reason I kneel before the Father, from whom his whole family in heaven and on earth derives its name. I pray that

out of his glorious riches he may strengthen you with power through his Spirit in your inner being, so that Christ may dwell in your hearts through faith. And I pray that you, being rooted and established in love, may have power, together with all the saints, to grasp how wide and long and high and deep is the love of Christ. (NIV)

We all need strength from the Lord to meet the various challenges of life. Sometimes the strength is needed because sudden changes such as the death of a relative, the deterioration in our health, or financial misfortunes are beyond our ability to cope. At other times we may have new ventures or assignments for which we need strength from the Lord so we may confidently meet these challenges. While these requests may be important to us as individuals, there are other areas where the need for strength may be more significant to believers collectively classified as the Church.

Paul's prayer for the Ephesian believers was that they would be strengthened by the Spirit's power so Christ would make His home in their hearts, and that they would be rooted and established in love. Paul explained how God saved us by grace because He loved us, and how He planned to unite both Jews and Gentiles together into the Church, breaking down all divisions. The Church would become the showpiece of God's wisdom to the rulers and authorities in the heavenly places (3:10). When he considered the responsible role the Church has to play in the plans of God, Paul knew that love would be the factor to hold the Church together; therefore it was critical that the believers would be filled with love for each other.

When Christ's love is established in our hearts, we will have the power and ability to understand the incredible dimensions of God's love for humanity. Our understanding of God's love leads us to being filled with that love so we can express it to others. It all begins with the Spirit giving us a special supply of His strength. When we find ourselves disliking people who annoy us, or discriminating against those who don't fit in with our group, we need to remember Paul's prayer for us and ask the Lord for a special supply of strength so we might be filled with the love of God.

This is the type of strength the Church needs now more than ever, so we can properly represent our triune God to an unbelieving world.

Lord, we desire Your strength and power to be able to love as we ought. Without Your help we struggle to respond properly to people whom we find difficult to love. Come and dwell in our hearts and manifest Your love through us, in Jesus' name.

September 28

MANNA SERIES: NOTABLE PRAYERS IN THE BIBLE
PRAYING FOR A FILLING WITH A PURPOSE

Reading Passage: Col. 1:1-14
Main Text: Col. 1:9-10. For this reason, since the day we heard about you, we have not stopped praying for you and asking God to fill you with the knowledge of his will through all spiritual wisdom and understanding. And we pray this in order that you may live a life worthy of the Lord and may please him in every way: bearing fruit in every good work, growing in the knowledge of God. (NIV)

Most believers desire that their lives would be morally, ethically, and productively in accordance with the standards set by the Lord. Our goal is that our conduct pleases the Lord in every way, even if it does not meet the approval of other people. This can be a struggle, as there are those who will try to impose their personal convictions or religious traditions on us, even when these preferences have no basis in the standards set by the Lord. How can we be certain of the proper conduct we should adopt, and avoid suffering from a spiritual inferiority complex?

Paul was excited at the news about the new church at Colosse. He was anxious for the members to become properly grounded in the doctrine of Christ, so he prayed unceasingly that they would be filled with the knowledge of the will of God in spiritual wisdom and understanding. He recognized that faith for salvation should lead a believer to seek to be filled with knowledge of the will of God. This is not a one-off event, but a continuous process by which we ask Him to give us the fullness of His will and desires, and request that these would replace ours. With this knowledge of His will, we will gain spiritual wisdom to know in a practical way what God desires. We will have a clear understanding of situations from God's perspective so we can make decisions in accordance with God's will. Consequently, our lives will be conducted in a way that pleases the Lord, and we will be productive in good works for His glory.

This prayer for a filling of the knowledge of the will of God should be the daily prayer of a believer for himself and also for his fellow believers. The answer to this prayer will produce spiritual growth so we may all become mature Christians, confident in everything God wants us to do (4:12).

Do your prayers include a request to be filled with knowledge of the will of God for your life?

Lord, we don't want to remain immature, uncertain believers because we have not grown in the knowledge of Your will. Please fill us completely with Your presence so we will have spiritual wisdom and discerning. We want to live lives that please You, that we may be productive for the glory of Jesus'.

September 29

MANNA SERIES: NOTABLE PRAYERS IN THE BIBLE
AVOIDING THE SCRAPHEAP OF GOOD IDEAS

Reading Passage: 2Th. 1:4-12
Main Text: 2Th. 1:11-12. With this in mind, we constantly pray for you, that our God may count you worthy of his calling, and that by his power he may fulfill every good purpose of yours and every act prompted by your faith. We pray this so that the name of our Lord Jesus may be glorified in you, and you in him, according to the grace of our God and the Lord Jesus Christ. (NIV)

How many good ideas have you thought of but failed to execute? Our failure to execute may be caused by laziness and procrastination, a lack of knowledge regarding how to develop ideas beyond the conception stage, or sometimes a fear of dealing with the challenges that our ideas could generate. The ideas may have been brilliant and God-glorifying, but the failure to follow through with a course of action often causes them to end up on a scrapheap where they can only be a memory to be reflected on, accompanied by the regret of unfulfilled possibilities. These are not necessarily major or extraordinary ideas. It could be a simple act like making contact with some lonely housebound individual, or a gesture of kindness to a needy child. How can we avoid the scrapheap for our good ideas?

Paul was writing to the believers in Thessalonica who were suffering from great persecution, yet remained steadfast in their faith and expression of love to one another. He reminded them that God would one day take vengeance against their enemies, and reward with glory those who remain faithful. Paul therefore prayed that they would live lives in keeping with the rewards planned for them, and also that God would provide them with power to fulfill all their ideas for good that had been prompted by their faith. He wanted them to avoid seeing their ideas that were really sourced from God by faith, end up on the scrapheap of non-fulfillment. So he prayed that God would supply the energy and power to support their ideas.

This should also be our prayer for our fellow believers and ourselves. We need God's energy and power to overcome our lethargy or our fears, and to provide us with guidance on how we may be able to execute the good ideas He gives us. It is God who works in us both to have the ideas and the desire to perform the things that will provide Him with joy and glory (Phil. 2:13). Let us avoid the scrapheap through prayer, and work to execute ideas.

Lord, we know that some of the ideas that we sometimes produce could only come from You, yet we often allow these ideas to remain unfulfilled because of failure to execute. Please forgive us and grant us Your power and energy so we will be active in producing good works that glorify You. This we pray in the name of Jesus.

September 30

MANNA SERIES: NOTABLE PRAYERS IN THE BIBLE
THE GREAT IMPORTANCE OF PRAYER FOR BELIEVERS

Reading Passage: James 5:7-20
Main Text: James 5:13-15. Is any one of you in trouble? He should pray. Is anyone happy? Let him sing songs of praise. Is any one of you sick? He should call the elders of the church to pray over him and anoint him with

oil in the name of the Lord. And the prayer offered in faith will make the sick person well; the Lord will raise him up. If he has sinned, he will be forgiven. (NIV)

Billy Graham is quoted as saying that prayer is the rope that pulls God and man together. It doesn't pull God down to us, rather it pulls us up to Him. This relationship allows believers to expose ourselves to the heart of God and learn His will for us. In addition, prayer is our admission that we have needs we are incapable of meeting, but we believe in a God who is able to do what we cannot accomplish.

The Apostle James ends his epistle by explaining why prayer is so important for the believer. He asks, "Is any one of you in trouble?" He instructed that that person should pray. The term translated "trouble" in the text means weak, or deficient in strength. James knew that all believers suffer from weakness at some time in their lives. His solution was prayer so that in our weakness we would find help from God's strength. James further asked, "Is any one of you sick?" He recommended that he should call the elders of the church for them to pray over him. Whether the sickness is physical or spiritual, prayer would be the means of recovery to health, because in answer to prayer the Lord would raise him up. If the sickness was caused by sin, he would be forgiven.

James was confident that prayer could meet the needs of the believers because he knew that prayers by righteous people provided access to a powerful God. These prayers have powerful effects. As an example of the power of prayer, James reminds us that the prophet Elijah, who suffered from human frailties like us, caused the cessation and resumption of rain in the land, through prayer. With such power at our disposal, the question is: Why should we suffer trouble and sickness and not seek relief through prayer?

The Apostle encourages us to pray for one another so we can be healed. Are you suffering or praying? Indeed, someone may be in need of your prayers today.

Lord, we are thankful for the privilege we have of accessing Your power through prayer. Yet we are guilty of neglecting this privilege while suffering from physical and spiritual weaknesses. Help us, Lord, to develop a consistent and fervent prayer life for the benefit of our fellow believers and ourselves. This we ask in the name of our Savior, Jesus Christ.

October 1

MANNA SERIES: ANCIENT HEROES AS FAITH MODELS
SACRIFICE INDICATES FAITH

Reading Passage: Gen. 4:1-7
Main Text: Heb. 11:4. By faith Abel offered God a better sacrifice than Cain did. By faith he was commended as a righteous man, when God spoke well of his offerings. And by faith he still speaks, even though he is dead. (NIV)

Faith moves us beyond the use of our natural senses. It causes us to be fully assured that what we hope for will be realized, and it enables us to accept as real, things that have not yet become a reality. It is a challenge to conduct our lives on the basis of faith when it is contrary to our instincts, dispositions and the standards of our society. We need models of the faith-life to inspire us; we need examples we can emulate.

The writer of the Epistle to the Hebrews wanted to encourage and inspire the believers who were abandoning their faith because they were under severe persecution. He highlighted significant people in their history whose lives demonstrated the exercise of faith under difficult circumstances.

The first example was Abel, who was the second child of the first family in history. As recorded in the Book of Genesis, both Abel and his brother Cain brought sacrifices to God. Cain who was a land farmer, brought a sacrifice from his crops, while Abel who was a shepherd, brought "the best of the firstborn of his flock." The sacrifices appear to be the natural output from their occupations, but God accepted Abel's gift while rejecting Cain's. The Genesis story does not provide any explanation for God's action, but the Hebrew Epistle states the difference was the faith behind the gift. Abel offered what he considered to be his best, to a God whom he could not see, based on his expectation of God's acceptance and approval.

Why bother to make the effort to sacrifice things that we can enjoy now, for spiritual intangibles that appear uncertain and unrealizable? Because faith makes those intangibles "real" and those uncertainties "sure." Once they become real and valuable, we know our present sacrifices are worthwhile. How much is God's approval, His love, and

His promise of future reward real and valuable to us? Like Cain, we often only consider immediate benefits. We will sacrifice for God in order to get an immediate recompense of health, happiness and wealth. But we resist sacrificing if it requires faith for rewards that are more abstract, such as the Lord's presence, or afterlife rewards. These rewards are similar to God's commendation of Abel after his death. Despite our faith-talk, our sacrifice for God is the true indication of our faith in him.

Father, we have to admit that our eyes are frequently so focused on the visible, tangible and temporal benefits, we fail to make the sacrifice for invisible eternal rewards. Help us to trust You completely so that what You have promised will become valuable to us.

October 2

MANNA SERIES: ANCIENT HEROES AS FAITH MODELS
LIVING WITH DIVINE COMPANIONSHIP

Reading Passage: Gen. 5:22-24; Jude 11-16
Main Text: Heb. 11:5. By faith Enoch was taken from this life, so that he did not experience death; he could not be found, because God had taken him away. For before he was taken, he was commended as one who pleased God. (NIV)

Blind American author, Helen Keller, stated: "Walking with a friend in the dark is better than walking alone in the light." Her statement reflects the reality that the journey of life is very treacherous, and because of our human limitations, we need the help of a friend for a successful journey.

God has made Himself available to guide and empower us for life's journey, but it requires faith in order to have Him as our companion. He is not visible and His directions are contrary to our natural inclinations. The reward for walking with God is His commendation; not material compensation or social recognition. Regardless of what might be achieved during this life, nothing is as important as having God's commendation at the end of life. But it is possible to live now with the assurance of the ultimate divine commendation when we live with divine companionship. The life of Enoch illustrates this lifestyle.

Enoch was a part of the seventh generation from Adam that had become wicked and ungodly. God's judgment against unrighteousness, which seemed fictional to the people of that generation, was real to Enoch. Rather than following the herd of evil doers of his generation, he walked with God and preached against their wicked lifestyles. God was so pleased with Enoch that He took him away so he would not experience death. After death was pronounced on Adam, Enoch became the first person to avoid the effect and experience of death. This was the result of God's commendation.

We may not avoid the experience of death at the end of our lives, but we learn from the life of Enoch that we can avoid the destructive effect of death if we have God's commendation before death. And to obtain this commendation we must, by faith, live with the companionship of God. "Enoch walked with God" (Gen. 5:22 NIV). How different would be our lifestyles if we lived in companionship with God? We would never be alone or be without guidance. His power would always be available to us. But this lifestyle requires faith to believe God is available to us, and will respond when we seek Him (Heb. 11:6).

When we continually practice having His presence, we have His promise: "I am with you always, even to the end of the age." (Matt 28:20 NIV)

Lord, we are guilty of ignoring Your companionship and seeking earthly help. We depend on our own understanding, which frequently causes us to be consumed with the lifestyles of the surrounding generation. Please increase our faith to value the reward of Your companionship and Your commendation. We make this request in the name of Jesus.

October 3

MANNA SERIES: ANCIENT HEROES AS FAITH MODELS
BUILDING DESPITE RIDICULE

Reading Passage:, Gen. 6:11-22
Main Text: Heb. 11:7. By faith Noah, when warned about things not yet seen, in holy fear built an ark to save his family. By his faith he condemned the world and became heir of the righteousness that comes by faith. (NIV)

It is easy to claim we have faith, but genuine faith demands action that validates it. Such action may appear risky to observers who do not have the faith that makes them convinced that things not yet realized are real. Perseverance to bring a dream to reality despite ridicule is proof of faith.

This was the story of the Wright brothers who had a dream of manned airplane flight. Despite the ridicule of many skeptics, they persevered through disappointments and lack of support to bring the dream into existence. In December 1903, in Kitty Hawk, North Carolina, they successfully flew an airplane 852 feet in a flight that lasted 59 seconds. Even after news of this first flight was reported, most people still disbelieved. But the brothers were vindicated because they continued to act on their faith despite the ridicule and opposition.

When God told Noah to build an ark because He planned to destroy the earth with a flood, no rain had previously fallen on the earth. Yet Noah believed the warning from God and began to build the ark. He preached for 120 years while building the ark, and no one other than his immediate family believed his message. But he kept on building and preaching. The ridicule of those who thought he was crazy did not stop him. The doubts that arose because the disaster stated in his warning never previously occurred didn't deter him. He believed the word of God and acted on his faith. Eventually he completed the ark. The floods came and destroyed the earth and all the inhabitants; only those in the ark survived. His faith was vindicated.

We are currently in the period between receiving the message from God, and the fulfillment of the judgment of God. It is the period in which we must be sure we have a conviction, and we must prove our faith by our actions. Those who declare that God is a myth, that the scriptures are just fascinating literature, and the idea of heaven and future judgment, a fantasy, will ridicule us. Our response must be like Noah's; keep building our "ark of deliverance" despite the ridicule.

Do your actions reflect your faith in the word of God and the message of salvation? Keep building your spiritual lives. Keep warning others of God's judgment on those who rejects His salvation.

Father, we thank You for the revelation of truth that allows us to prepare for Your deliverance despite the scoffers and unbelievers. May our faith remain strong in Your word until the time of its fulfillment. We rely on Your help, in the name of Jesus.

October 4

MANNA SERIES: ANCIENT HEROES AS FAITH MODELS
FAITH'S ONLY CERTAINTY

Reading Passage:, Gen. 12:1-9
Main Text: Heb. 11:8 By faith Abraham, when called to go to a place he would later receive as his inheritance, obeyed and went, even though he did not know where he was going. (NIV)

Uncertainty makes us very uncomfortable. Yet with human limitations in knowledge and power, there is very little in life that we have control over and can be certain about. For the believer, our faith makes real and substantive the things that have not yet materialized, and makes certain what is yet unseen. Faith removes the uncertainties that make us uncomfortable.

When God told Abraham to leave the certainty of his homeland, relatives and possessions, and journey to a place where he would be established as a new nation, he obeyed. How could Abraham obey this command when he did not know the location of the destination, did not have directions to it, and he did not yet have any offspring? He responded in faith. It is awesome that he could have such trust in the word of a God he was meeting for the first time. Yet he responded without reservation. No wonder God declared that this faith qualified Abraham as a righteous man, even without any moral achievements. If he could trust God as indicated by his obedience, God would provide the means for his moral qualification and his salvation.

We find it very disconcerting to attempt to obey when we have not been provided with the certainty of process and outcome. We don't want to give unless we are assured we will receive a return greater than what we gave. We don't want to be exposed to danger unless we are guaranteed protection from harm. Along with our salvation, we want guarantees of health, prosperity and happiness. The life of faith provides no guarantees. As it was for Abraham, faith's only certainty is the integrity of the One who gives the command. We trust Him to lead the way, to help us overcome the obstacles on the journey and to take us to whatever destination He desires.

When we have guarantees before obeying, we don't have to rely on

God's presence or power. Why pray when we know we cannot be harmed, or we are certain of the outcome? But when we don't know the outcome or what God wants to do in the circumstance, we shift our focus to Him and build our relationship by prayer and dependence. Like Paul we will be able to declare: " For I am convinced that neither death nor life, neither angels nor demons, neither the present nor the future, nor any powers, neither height nor depth, nor anything else in all creation, will be able to separate us from the love of God that is in Christ Jesus our Lord," (Rom. 8:38-39 NIV).

Lord, our faith is in You, not in the circumstances or in our preferences, but in the knowledge that You know what is best for us, and we can be certain of Your love. We give all praise and honor to our Lord Jesus.

October 5

MANNA SERIES: ANCIENT HEROES AS FAITH MODELS
A PILGRIM LIFESTYLE

Reading Passage:, Psa. 105:8-24
Main Text: Heb. 11:9-10 By faith he made his home in the promised land like a stranger in a foreign country; he lived in tents, as did Isaac and Jacob, who were heirs with him of the same promise. For he was looking forward to the city with foundations, whose architect and builder is God. (NIV)

We are all pilgrims on a journey that will take us to our final destination. We have a natural inclination to resist our pilgrim status, and many exert great energy in the futile attempt to make this life permanent. Because the future beyond this life is a mysterious unknown, we have no desire to exchange the known present for it, as miserable as the present might be. But if we are convinced by faith that the future is more glorious, we will eagerly accept a pilgrim lifestyle, with our eyes fixed on the future. With this lifestyle, we accept that nothing here is permanent; there will be no attempt to build monuments, or accumulate wealth, and we will always acknowledge that we are dispensable.

This was the lifestyle of the Hebrew patriarchs. Even after they entered the land promised to them as an inheritance, rather than building permanent dwellings to demonstrate ownership, they lived in moveable tents. They acted as foreigners in the place provided for them as home. Why this unusual behavior? They realized they needed more than a promised land; they were awaiting the eternal city that had to be built by God. This city would be based on divine principles with a divine ruler, and they would have a secure place in it. They were convinced this city was in their future, so they kept looking forward to it as they lived.

The Bible teaches that the followers of Christ will be a part of a glorious future kingdom on earth where the Lord will reign as king in righteousness. Rebellious humans, corrupted by their lust for power, have always tried to construct their own cities, hoping to make permanent what God designated as temporary (Gen. 11). The people of faith are able to live on the earth, the place of future inheritance, and not attempt to make it permanent until God builds his kingdom on earth. So we live the pilgrim lifestyle while we look forward to the future.

Do you struggle with a desire to hold on to possessions, positions and people in this life? Learn to live with confidence in God's future provision, so you can wear this world loosely.

Father, we thank You that in Christ we have a hope beyond this life that keeps us from becoming subjected to the vanities of this life. Help us to keep this focus, so death will not be a struggle for us. This we ask in Jesus' great name.

October 6

MANNA SERIES: ANCIENT HEROES AS FAITH MODELS
FAITH TO SACRIFICE THE PROVISION

Reading Passage: Gen. 22:1-14

Main Text: Heb. 11:17-18. By faith Abraham, when God tested him, offered Isaac as a sacrifice. He who had received the promises was about to sacrifice his one and only son, even though God had said to him, "It is through Isaac that your offspring will be reckoned." (NIV)

We desire blessings from God, but there is a risk that blessings can distort our focus. One danger is that we may develop an attitude of entitlement and begin to think God is obligated to bless us since we have done Him the favor of choosing to serve Him. Or we may fail to regard blessings as gifts of grace and begin to accept them as rewards for performance. Another danger is that we may become so attached to the blessing that we place greater emphasis on the provision than on the Provider.

To prevent His children from remaining underdeveloped in their faith and love for Him, the Father will intervene to correct our focus and enhance our maturity. This was the case with Abraham when God tested him by asking him to sacrifice Isaac. This son was his miracle child, born when it was seemingly impossible for Abraham and Sarah to produce offspring. Isaac was the fulfillment of the promise that through him God would make Abraham the father of nations. It made no sense for Isaac to be sacrificed. Was God reneging on His promise? Did Abraham do something that disqualified him from God's favor? Abraham probably wished God had given him a warning that this was just a test, but a test is far more effective if it is unexpected.

There is no record that Abraham questioned God or doubted His motives, although these would be understandable human reactions. Abraham obeyed and was prepared to do the difficult thing and sacrifice God's provision, because his faith was in the Provider. He was convinced that God would find some way of fulfilling His word even if Isaac was to be resurrected. He learned from this experience that God was not just a Promisor but also a Provider, who can use unconventional and supernatural means to prove His faithfulness.

Is our faith dependent on some blessing from God, such as a job, a companion, the salvation of our children, the daily necessities of life? How will we react should God decide to test us and require us to sacrifice any of these? Will we still have faith to believe that He is our Provider and we don't need to see the means or understand His methods in order to trust and obey Him?

Father, our faith is in You not because we have received Your blessings but because You are good. Help us so that when we cannot see blessings from Your hand, we will still trust Your heart. When You test us we want to be able to declare like Job, "… though He slays me, I will trust Him."

October 7

MANNA SERIES: ANCIENT HEROES AS FAITH MODELS
FAITH THAT INFLUENCES THE
NEXT GENERATION

Reading Passage:, Gen. 49:28-33, 50:22-26
Main Text: Heb. 11:21-22. By faith Jacob, when he was dying, blessed each of Joseph's sons, and worshipped as he leaned on the top of his staff. By faith Joseph, when his end was near, spoke about the exodus of the Israelites from Egypt and gave instructions about his bones. (NIV)

Can parents pass on their faith to their children? Although some argue that there is a collective faith that can be transferred from parents to children in a community, this is different from the faith required for salvation or relationship with God. However, it is possible that one person's faith can influence another, and this frequently occurs in family relationships where influence is most effective. Paul referred to this influence when he stated that Timothy exhibited the same faith that he observed in his grandmother Lois, and mother Eunice (2Tim. 1:5).

Our text provides examples of the type of faith that can influence the next generation. Jacob was dying and before him were Joseph's two sons who were born of an Egyptian mother and grew up in the heathen Egyptian culture. Jacob disregarded these foreign influences in their lives and blessed them with the promises Jehovah gave to his ancestors. Then he worshipped God. These boys observed a grandfather demonstrating his conviction that God can overcome the barriers of their social and cultural deficiencies and still bless them. The blessing came with worship, recognizing the greatness of his God. This experience must have been influential.

Although Joseph was a member of the royal class in Egypt, when he was dying he never allowed his esteemed status and privilege in that environment to distract him from his core conviction and the purpose for his life. His focus was on God's promise to give His people their own land away from Egypt. He was so convinced that God would fulfill His promises that he instructed that his bones be taken with them on their exodus from Egypt. After almost 400 years of captivity in Egypt, when the Israelites thought they might never escape, Joseph's declared faith that God would deliver them must have sustained them with hope.

While our lectures and cajoling may seem ineffective in influencing our children, our demonstrations of faith in God and His promises will be difficult for them to ignore. After we die, they may find themselves in "enemy territory." But when difficult times come in their lives, the memory of the strength of their parents' faith in God may provide them with a basis for hope through their hardships.

Are you leaving a faith legacy for the next generation?

Father, we are reminded of our responsibility to provide practical examples of our faith before our children, so they might be influenced to trust in the God of their parents when they face their own challenges in life.

"Faith of our fathers' holy faith, we will be true to thee till death."

October 8

MANNA SERIES: ANCIENT HEROES AS FAITH MODELS
DISCERNING THE COUNTERFEITS

Reading Passage:, Ex. 2:1-15
Main Text: Heb. 11:24-26. By faith Moses, when he had grown up, refused to be known as the son of Pharaoh's daughter. He chose to be mistreated along with the people of God rather than to enjoy the pleasures of sin for a short time. He regarded disgrace for the sake of Christ as of greater value than the treasures of Egypt, because he was looking ahead to his reward. (NIV)

It was the prized exhibit of the art collector who paid a small fortune to obtain the masterpiece at an auction. Later, his world came crashing down when a noted art critic published the results of an investigation, which revealed that the supposed masterpiece was a fake. What the collector thought was worth millions of dollars was now virtually worthless. He failed to discern the counterfeit and suffered loss.

Life is filled with counterfeit attractions, lifestyles, personalities, and goals. Sometimes the revelation of a counterfeit lifestyle comes as shocking sad news, like the suicide of a popular, wealthy entertainer who always seemed to have it together. Most of the time, by around middle age, we have the gradual realization that what was considered valuable and what consumed our energy in our young adult years was actually virtually worthless. How can we do a better job at discerning the counterfeits in life and save ourselves heartaches, wasted time and money?

The life of Moses illustrates how his faith in God allowed him to make the correct choice at a critical moment. He grew up in the palace environment in Egypt with access to the throne, and privileged involvement in the culture and learning of the country. After being exposed to his heritage by fellow Hebrews living in Egypt, he learned that these oppressed people had a special relationship with their God. The Lord promised them their own land and kingdom. Moses chose to discard his privileged life with its pleasures, and attach himself to the oppressed people because of his faith in the promises of their God. He regarded the Egyptian life as a worthless counterfeit in comparison to the great reward that the suffering Hebrews expected to gain because of their relationship with the Lord.

We face the same challenges and choices encountered by Moses. What we see around us seems so enticing and glamorous, and what is portrayed as the Christian life appears so austere, boring and unrewarding. But which is genuinely valuable? Do we have the faith to see that the present, unattractive portraits of Christian discipleship obscure the future glorious rewards? It is faith in the reward of winning races and gold medals that causes the athlete to endure pain and suffering during difficult training exercises. Faith in the reward will help us to make the right choice and disregard counterfeits.

Did Moses make the right choice? Few people remember the name of the Pharaoh he confronted.

Father, grant us the faith to value the rewards You offer as of greater worth than the counterfeits that entice us daily. We trust You to provide us with spiritual discernment, through Jesus Christ.

October 9

MANNA SERIES: ANCIENT HEROES AS FAITH MODELS
FAITH THAT CONQUERS FEAR

Reading Passage:, Ex. 2:1-15
Main Text: Heb. 11:27. By faith he left Egypt, not fearing the king's anger; he persevered because he saw him who is invisible. (NIV)

Fear is the unwelcome companion of anyone who ventures into new areas of life. It is experienced by the young person who leaves the docile environment of high school to choose a course of study in college or university, or by one who leaves the comforts of home to live in a foreign country. It shows up when individuals decide to leave the certainty of a salaried job to pursue their dreams of owning their own business. Although much is said about the excitement of marriage, little mention is made of the real fear experienced by the bride and groom as they make the decision to pledge their lives to each other.

Since fear is crippling yet unavoidable, we must be able to conquer our fears in order to be successful in life. Nelson Mandela stated, "I learned that courage was not the absence of fear, but the triumph over it. The brave man is not he who does not feel afraid, but he who conquers that fear." Many self-help books focus on the development of inner strength and confidence as the means of overcoming fear. The problem is trying to use the weak material of our flawed inner person to build a fortress to withstand real or perceived threats posed by outside forces. We need help beyond ourselves, from someone who we are confident can conquer our foes.

Moses' enemy was the powerful King of Egypt who was angry with him for killing an Egyptian and becoming a fugitive. With these odds against him, Moses left Egypt because his faith was in the help he could get from God. His faith enabled him to see the invisible God who would provide him with guidance and protection. If we can see God in our situations, we will be able to conquer the fear caused by our foes. We may not be able to avoid the reality of our overwhelming circumstances, but when we can look beyond the circumstances and see God who is more powerful, we will be triumphant.

What fearful situation are you facing today? May your faith enable you to see what is invisible to your natural eyes, so you may declare: "The LORD is my light and my salvation, whom shall I fear? The LORD is the stronghold of my life, of whom shall I be afraid?" Psa. 27:1 NIV.

Father, we acknowledge that our problem with fear is caused by what we focus on. We see giants, when we should be seeing You. Give us the faith to know that You are sovereign over all our circumstances and there is nothing that we encounter that You are unaware of. You will provide us with the grace and strength to conquer all our problems. We give You thanks, in the name of Jesus.

October 10

MANNA SERIES: ANCIENT HEROES AS FAITH MODELS
FOR FAITH USERS ONLY

Reading Passage:, Ex. 14:21-31
Main Text: Heb. 11:29 By faith the people passed through the Red Sea as on dry land; but when the Egyptians tried to do so, they were drowned. (NIV)

Faith enables us to know God and to recognize when He is providing us with divine moments. These are times when God acts supernaturally on our behalf to provide amazing miraculous opportunities for us. Without faith, we either can't believe that God is able to do what appears to us to be impossible, or we begin to trust our own abilities and instincts.

After the Israelites left the land of Egypt, the Egyptians regretted that they allowed them to leave. The army pursued them hoping to recover their former slaves. The defenseless Israelites were no match for the powerful Egyptian army chasing them with chariots, while their escape route was blocked by the Red Sea. Naturally, the Israelites panicked. After Moses obeyed God and stretched his hand over the sea, God sent a strong wind that made the seabed dry, and created a passageway with walls of water on each side. It was amazing to observe the miracle, but it took faith for them to enter the pathway believing they would not sink in mud, and that the water would unnaturally remain as a wall. This was a special occurrence that provided an opportunity for only those who could believe that it was God who was doing it for them. The Egyptian army, for whom the passageway was not prepared and who did not have the faith, attempted to cross. But they discovered that the wall dissolved, leading to their death by drowning.

There are times in our lives when we are facing impossible circumstances and we can't see any way out. God may decide to give us a miracle, but it takes faith to see what God is doing and realize that He is providing an opportunity just for our benefit and His glory. Without faith we will not be able to recognize or use the opportunities God is providing. When Jesus told Peter to come out of the boat and join Him walking on the water, Peter recognized the opportunity and began walking. However, he soon turned to doubting and began to sink. Jesus remarked that his faith was too little because he began to doubt. Peter's miracle disappeared in doubt.

Is there a miracle we are missing today because we doubt God is able to do the impossible? Do we limit God to our ability and instincts, or what appears natural? By faith let us open our eyes to appreciate the unlimited power of our God, and look for the moment when He will provide an opportunity for our benefit and His glory.

Father, we believe that nothing in our situation is impossible for You. We declare that You are able to do exceedingly and abundantly above all we can ask or think. May Jesus be glorified through our faith.

October 11

MANNA SERIES: ANCIENT HEROES AS FAITH MODELS
FAITH THAT DEFIES THE ODDS

Reading Passage:, Joshua 2:1-24
Main Text: Heb. 11:31. By faith the harlot Rahab did not perish with those who did not believe, when she had received the spies with peace. (NKJV)

Former USA President, Calvin Coolidge stated that "heroism is not only in the man, but in the occasion." Sometimes it is an unexpected incident that reveals the hero that was obscured and suppressed under layers of misfortune in a person's life. Then seizing the opportunity, he or she is able to exercise faith to defy the obstacles and transform their destiny.

Rahab stands out like a sore thumb in the list of heroes of faith in Israel's history. First, she was not born an Israelite. Furthermore, she was always identified in scripture by her profession, 'Rahab the harlot', which would make her socially despised and spiritually rejected. How did she make the list, and what can we learn from the story of her faith?

She was a resident of the city of Jericho, with a lodging house on the city wall. One day, two men who were spies for the Israelites entered her lodging house. At that time the Israelites were encamped opposite Jericho across the Jordan river. The people of Jericho were aware of the reputation of the Israelite army for conquering nations, and the fact that the Israelite God did miracles to assist them in their battles. The people of Jericho were fearful. The Israelite spies were sent to ascertain the ability of the country to withstand an assault. Rahab was faced with a decision. She could turn the spies over to the Jericho authorities and help her country to prepare for the attack by the Israelites, or she could transfer her allegiance to the 'enemies' and hide the spies. In protecting the spies, she would have to trust that Israel's God was superior to the gods of Jericho, that Israel would be victorious in the battle and the city would be destroyed, and that the spies would keep their word to protect her and her family.

Rehab was not deterred by her reputation nor dismayed at the odds that her faith would be vindicated. She proved her faith by hiding the spies. Eventually she was rewarded by escaping the destruction of her city, and being accepted in the Israelite nation. Despite her past reputation, the only time she was mentioned in the New Testament without being called a harlot was when she was listed in the genealogy of Jesus as being the mother of Boaz, who was the great grandfather of King David.

Regardless of your past reputation or the seemingly impossible odds you are now facing, God can provide you with an opportunity to exercise faith that will transform your future.

Father, we thank You for providing the opportunity for anyone to become a hero by exercising faith in You. Help us not to miss these opportunities to be courageous and to defy the odds. This is our prayer in the name of our Lord Jesus Christ.

October 12

MANNA SERIES: ANCIENT HEROES AS FAITH MODELS
WILLING TO APPEAR RIDICULOUS

Reading Passage:, Josh. 6:1-17
Main Text: Heb. 11:30 By faith the walls of Jericho fell, after the people had marched around them for seven days. (NIV)

For someone seeking to enter a location, a wall can be a barrier, a statement of defiance, or an obstacle, which must be overcome to gain entrance. Our strategies for challenging the walls in our path reveal much about our character, naturally and spiritually.

For some people, a wall provides an easy excuse not to proceed. They retreat from their goals without making much effort, accepting defeat and blaming providence for permitting the wall. Many of these non-achievers have given up on seeking an education, pursuing a career, or have abandoned a challenging marriage and family responsibilities. Others have welcomed the challenge of the wall and will expend all their energy and employ their abilities in conquering it. But in their proud and valiant efforts they never seek God's help, as if this may indicate weakness on their part. They don't want anything to detract from their boast that they are masters of their fate and captains of their souls. In contrast, the people of faith trust the Lord for direction for life and seek his help to deal with the walls they encounter, even if they appear ridiculous in the process.

The Israelites were journeying to Canaan and were about to enter at the location of Jericho, one of the most fortified cities of Canaan with huge reinforced walls. When Joshua, the leader of the Israelites sought God on how he should meet the challenge of these walls, the response seemed utterly ridiculous. They were commanded to march around the walls once a day for six days, and on the seventh day to march around seven times. On the last circle of the walls, they were to give a victorious shout, and those massive walls would fall flat. Who would be prepared to follow these instructions knowing the people of Jericho were observing their antics?

People of faith should be prepared to obey God, even the ridiculous instructions, fully accepting that they can trust Him with the results. They know that the foolishness of God is wiser than men, and God chose what is foolish in this world to shame the wise (1Cor. 1:25,27). This is a challenge to our pride and our esteem in the eyes of the people of the world.

God instructs us not to worry about anything, but to pray about everything. To the unbeliever this is a ridiculous approach to problems. Why pray when we should be doing? The instructions we will get in prayer could not be conceived by us. They may appear foolish to us, but are very effective, because faith as little as a mustard seed can move mountains.

Father, we trust Your wisdom, and we are willing to appear ridiculous in order to obtain Your victory over our obstacles. We want to be people of faith so You may be glorified through us, for the glory of Jesus.

October 13

MANNA SERIES: ANCIENT HEROES AS FAITH MODELS
FAITH, THE BASIS FOR AMAZING EXPLOITS

Reading Passage: Heb. 11:32-38
Main Text: Heb. 11:32-34 And what more shall I say? I do not have time to tell about Gideon, Barak, Samson, Jephthah, David, Samuel and the prophets, who through faith conquered kingdoms, administered justice, and gained what was promised; who shut the mouths of lions, quenched the fury of the flames, and escaped the edge of the sword; whose weakness was turned to strength; and who became powerful in battle and routed foreign armies. (NIV)

God is known, and His glory exalted by the marvelous works He performs in the earth (Psa. 77:14). Some of these works without human involvement are seen in nature. There are also times when God chooses to use humans to perform great deeds on His behalf, but there are potential risks when humans are involved in the performance of amazing exploits that should be attributable to God.

Our sinful nature desires glory, which can place us on a divine level and attract the adulation of fellow humans. The original sin arose from the desire of man to be as God. Unless a person is fully submitted to God and is willing to admit his or her inadequacies and lack of worth before God, the hunger for self-glory will easily be aroused by the slightest involvement in supernatural activity.

In the above text, which gives an account of God using men to perform amazing exploits, we observe in each case the careful process God used in choosing them. In many cases their involvement came only after their strong personalities were broken down by circumstances until they became dependent on God.

Faith places us in a relationship with God. As this relationship is developed into a consistent lifestyle, it transforms our personalities from self-centeredness to God-centeredness. Eventually we reach the stage where God can use us to accomplish His amazing exploits in the earth, and be confident that none of the glory due to Him will be diverted to ourselves.

God still wants to use us to accomplish amazing exploits in the earth. There are still evil nations and systems that hold the people of God in captivity, and God needs some Gideons or Samsons to lead an assault against these enemies. There are still Goliaths around that defy the Almighty, so God is looking for Davids who will be able to use insignificant weapons to defeat them. God's power is available for these exploits, but are we prepared to develop a faith relationship with Him, so He can trust us to use the power and not seek our own glory?

Father, we want to be tools in Your hand so that Your name will be great in the earth through us, but we admit our egos get in the way. Help our faith to be so developed that we will become God-centered and not self-centered.

October 14

MANNA SERIES: ANCIENT HEROES AS FAITH MODELS
FAITH FOR PATIENT ENDURANCE

Reading Passage: Heb. 11:32-38
Main Text: Heb. 11:36-38. Some faced jeers and flogging, while still others were chained and put in prison. They were stoned; they were sawed in two; they were put to death by the sword. They went about in sheepskins and goatskins, destitute, persecuted and mistreated— the

world was not worthy of them. They wandered in deserts and mountains, and in caves and holes in the ground. (NIV)

We tend to have a natural preference for the spectacular and glamorous demonstrations of faith. So when we read about the heroes of faith in Hebrews 11, we focus on the "action heroes" up to verse 35. Like children with fertile imaginations, we long to imitate these heroes and be able to "stop the mouths of lions, quench the power of fire, or cause foreign armies to flee." We overlook the fact that we require the same quality of faith for patient endurance as for performing amazing exploits.

Most of us will never be involved in any spectacular miraculous deeds of faith in our lives, but we all will have to endure some hardship in our Christian journey. "We must go through many hardships to enter the kingdom of God" (Acts 14:22b). Although we don't get excited at this prospect, it does explain our experience after conversion. There are times we face ridicule, misrepresentation, ostracism and even vicious attacks because of our Christian beliefs and values. In addition to the external forces, we also experience inward battles with temptations and doubts that sometimes lead us to wonder whether it is worthwhile continuing on this path.

We learn from the passage that while some performed exploits "through faith," others also through faith suffered great hardship. "They were stoned; they were sawed in two, they were put to death by the sword. They went about in sheepskins and goatskins, destitute, persecuted and mistreated." They had faith in the fact that they were called to bear reproach for Christ. This qualified them to be special in God's eyes, "the world was undeserving of them," and caused them to endure in patient hope of their reward. The faith that endures hardship allows us to be associated with Jesus who endured the cross and gained the crown (Heb. 12:2).

Without faith, we no longer find Jesus attractive, the rewards are not worth pursuing, and we will give up the pursuit of spiritual goals. In contrast, faith enables us to be a strong anvil that will wear out the hammer of any attack against us.

We need to pray the words of the 19th century hymn by William Bathurst:
O, for a faith that will not shrink, Though pressed by every foe, That will not tremble on the brink, Of any earthly woe!

That will not murmur nor complain, Beneath the chastening rod,
But, in the hour of grief or pain, Will lean upon its God.

October 15

MANNA SERIES: PETER'S CALL FOR SPIRITUAL GROWTH
BORN WITH MORE THAN A SILVER SPOON

Reading Passage: 1Pet. 1:1-12
Main Text: 1Pet. 1:3-4. Praise be to the God and Father of our Lord Jesus Christ! In his great mercy he has given us new birth into a living hope through the resurrection of Jesus Christ from the dead, and into an inheritance that can never perish, spoil or fade—kept in heaven for you. (NIV)

In his epistles, the Apostle Peter wrote to believers who were suffering persecution from the Roman authorities, encouraging them with the hope of the gospel, and exhorting them to spiritual growth despite their suffering.

He reminded the believers that God the Father chose them for this salvation by the process of a new birth. As babies, we are unable to appreciate our socio-economic status in the natural world. Similarly, as spiritual babies we can only understand the privilege of our spiritual inheritance as we grow in our understanding of salvation. Some children are born with the proverbial silver spoon in their mouths, because their parents are wealthy with great influence. These privileges are sometimes squandered because these children grow up without a sense of identity or responsibility.

Peter encouraged the believers by explaining that the privilege of their new birth provided them with an inheritance that is imperishable, pure and unfading, and is reserved in heaven for us. While all earthly wealth will suffer decline or lose its attraction and suffer from the effects of corruption, the inheritance of the new birth is secured with respect to its worth, and is held securely for our future possession. This message was important for people who were under persecution, suffering confiscation of their earthly possessions, and some who were even being killed. The new spiritual birth is far more valuable than our earthly physical birth.

This inheritance will be fully realized when we see Jesus physically. However, while waiting for Him, we live by faith. As our faith grows, our understanding of our inheritance increases, our love of Jesus expands, and we begin to rejoice in expectation of our inheritance (vv. 8-9).

Whatever the challenges we are now facing, whether financial burdens, health issues, or heartbreak because of relationships, we can be encouraged by the knowledge that our new birth provides us with a secure future that surpasses anything we can enjoy on earth. We must persevere to grow in our faith so we can be filled with anticipation of the return of our Lord and the realization of our inheritance. With this understanding we will be able to rejoice now in expectancy despite our challenges.

Lord, we thank You for choosing us for the privilege of a new spiritual birth which provides such awesome benefits. As we become more disillusioned with the corruption of our earthly inheritance, may we grow in our understanding and anticipation for our future inheritance, so we can live in joyful expectation of Jesus Christ.

October 16

MANNA SERIES: PETER'S CALL FOR SPIRITUAL GROWTH
GROWING IN AN EXILIC LIFESTYLE

Reading Passage: 1Pet. 1:13-22
Main Text: 1Pet. 1:17. Since you call on a Father who judges each man's work impartially, live your lives as strangers here in reverent fear. (NIV)

To a great extent we spend the days of our earthly existence in conflict, trying to make permanent what is designed to be temporary. We battle to extend what was given to us with an expiry date, and to hold on to a life that is being forced from our grasp as we age. Sometimes it takes the pain of loss or persecution to remind us that this world is not our home. We are exiles on a journey to a permanent destination. There is a sense of peace in our lives when we reconcile our minds to this fact and adjust our lifestyles accordingly.

Peter exhorted the believers who perhaps were becoming discouraged and disillusioned because of the hardship they were enduring, to focus their minds on the hope of the return of Christ and to live their lives with a deep consciousness of God during the time of their exile. With focused minds they would be self-controlled in their lifestyles, and avoid the excesses of wild, passionate and sinful indulgences, that later lead to embarrassment and regrets. Instead, they would seek to conduct their lives in a manner that is pleasing to the Father, who is holy.

We need to grow in our perspective that this period of our earthly sojourn has been provided to us by God, as an opportunity to prepare for eternity with Him. With this development we will become less interested in the perishable, corruptible aspects of our lives, like fulfilling our desires for pleasure, wealth and power, which desires are the result of our natural birth. Instead, we will be more interested in the imperishable virtues of faith, hope and love that accompany the new birth, which was purchased for us by the death of Jesus Christ. Our lifestyles will become more heavenly and less conformed to the place of our exile on earth.

Are we prepared to make that shift in our perspectives, although we may be regarded as weird or "other-worldly"? Although we are saved positionally the moment we believe the gospel, it takes a lifetime of discipline to develop the lifestyle of an exile that is bound for heaven to be with our holy Lord.

Our Holy Father, we admit the challenge of living on earth while trying to adjust our lives for heaven. We thank You for the trials and difficulties that remind us of the temporary nature of our earthly sojourn and help us to adjust our lifestyles for our permanent destination with You. We rely on Your help as we continue on our exilic journey, in Jesus' name.

October 17

MANNA SERIES: PETER'S CALL FOR SPIRITUAL GROWTH
ESSENTIAL DIET FOR GROWING CHRISTIANS

Reading Passage: 1Pet. 1:23 - 2:3
Main Text: 1Pet. 2:2-3. Like newborn babies, crave pure spiritual milk, so that by it you may grow up in your salvation, now that you have tasted that the Lord is good. (NIV)

A book entitled "You Are What You Eat: How To Win And Keep Health With Diet" was published by nutritionist, Victor Lindlahr in the 1940's. Although the title may be regarded as an overstatement of the facts, there is a great deal of truth to the central message that peoples' natural health is directly related to their diet. With respect to our spiritual lives, a proper diet is essential for our spiritual growth.

Peter explained that we began our spiritual journey as spiritual babies, having the full DNA and potential of a fully matured Christian, but needing to grow to realize this potential. This growth is effected as we feed on the diet of the word of God. Peter pointed out that our spiritual birth occurred when the imperishable seed of the word of God was received in our hearts (1:23-25). This living word of God, having generated spiritual life creates a spiritual appetite in us for more of itself. The word of God reveals to us the goodness of God, and this knowledge of God causes us to desire increased knowledge about our good God. This desire is similar to that of a newborn baby who instinctively craves food so he or she may be able to grow physically.

Our spiritual growth is the by-product of the nourishment we obtain from feeding on the word of God. If we claim to be born again Christians and don't have a strong desire for the word of God, we should be concerned about whether we were truly born of the Spirit of God in the first place. If we are not growing spiritually, the cause may be our neglect of our spiritual food. The evidence of stunted or arrested growth is our lack of sincere love for our fellow believers (1:22), and/or our failure to rid ourselves of sinful attitudes such as malice, deceit, hypocrisy and envy (2:1).

Spiritual growth is required for all "living" Christians. We must be diligent to examine our lives consistently to ensure we are maintaining a healthy diet in the word of God, and we are providing all the evidence of spiritual growth. Our Lord expects it and the world is waiting to be inspired by the fruit of our lives.

Dear Lord, we thank You for providing Your Word so we can learn of Your goodness and thereby grow spiritually. Help us to maintain a consistent diet in the Word so we may provide evidence of growth in our love and our Christian attitudes.

MANNA SERIES: PETER'S CALL FOR SPIRITUAL GROWTH
GOOD FRUIT FROM GOOD GROWTH

Reading Passage: 1Pet. 2:4-12
Main Text: 1Pet. 2:12 Live such good lives among the pagans that, though they accuse you of doing wrong, they may see your good deeds and glorify God on the day he visits us. (NIV)

The spiritual trees planted by the Lord are never for decorative purposes; rather the trees are planted for fruit bearing for the benefit of others and the glory of God. The care and nurture that is required for growth is rewarded when our lives become productive, producing good fruit. Our good works represent this fruit.

Peter described the former lives of the believers as being in darkness, ignorant of God's salvation and not receiving the mercies of God (v. 10). In such a state they could not be regarded as people of any repute or value. But God intervened in their lives to redeem them and make them His chosen people, so they could function as a royal priesthood and a holy nation. The purpose of providing this redemption was so they could proclaim the praises of the One who redeemed them. For these believers, the arena where this proclamation should be made was before the unbelievers who were mistreating them and slandering their reputation as Christians.

Their growth as Christians should provide them with the ability to produce good works that would contradict the falsehood being spread by their accusers. In fact, these accusers would be converted into people glorifying God because of the good fruit seen in the lives of the believers.

We often overlook the powerful effect our good conduct can have on skeptics and critics of Christianity. We usually become defensive and offensive when we are under attack by those who are opposed to our Lord and the Christian faith. What we should be doing is letting the light of our good deeds and attitudes become so illustrious that merely observing our good lifestyles will convict these opposers. Having tasted that the Lord is good (v. 3) by appreciating His goodness in redeeming us, we should allow His life to grow in us, so the accusers will conclude that God is being manifested in our lives and give the glory to Him. Jesus said "every good tree bears good fruit, but a bad tree bears bad fruit" (Matt. 7:17 NIV). The Bible also said that every tree that does not bear good fruit is cut down and thrown into the fire (Matt. 3:10).

Does our lifestyle manifest the fruit of God's goodness to our enemies, despite their opposition and accusations? If we are not being productive, we risk being destroyed.

Lord, we ask that You will help us to grow in the grace of Your goodness so we can provide a powerful testimony of Your life in us as a witness against the accusations of our enemies. This we ask in the name of Jesus.

October 19

MANNA SERIES: PETER'S CALL FOR SPIRITUAL GROWTH
GROWTH MANIFESTED BY A SUBMISSIVE ATTITUDE

Reading Passage: 1Pet. 2:13-25
Main Text: 1Pet. 2:13 Submit yourselves for the Lord's sake to every authority instituted among men: whether to the king, as the supreme authority, 1Pet. 2:15 For it is God's will that by doing good you should silence the ignorant talk of foolish men. (NIV)

In our natural lives, we understand growth from childhood to adulthood as indicated by our ability to think independently, assert ourselves and not allow anyone to force us to do anything contrary to our will. This is the reason we find ourselves so antagonistic to the idea of submission to another person.

To submit is to yield to the power or authority of another, not because you like or agree with the other person, but because you accept the authority of the position held by that person. When we are submitted, we have an attitude of respect to the authority. We will be respectful even if we have to disobey an order because it is contrary to our convictions. In these situations, we will be willing to accept the punishment for disobeying without resentment and retaliation, because we accept the power of the authority to establish the rules and also the penalties for their violation.

Peter instructed the believers, who were facing persecution from the civil authorities, in this important principle of submission. He knew that the authorities were unjustly targeting Christians and would demand obedience for actions that were contrary to their Christian principles. Peter was not telling the believers to obey the ungodly demands, but he wanted them to have a submissive spirit. He told them to submit themselves to every human authority, so that by their humble attitude and good behavior they would silence the slanderous talk about Christians being a rebellious cult.

The reason we are to submit is for the "Lord's sake." We are really only submitting to a human authority because of our submission to the Lord, the supreme authority of our lives. We usually think that by submitting to another person we are demeaning ourselves, and we proudly resist any such actions, especially when we consider ourselves equal to or superior to this other person. What Peter is teaching us is that when we grow up spiritually, we also grow in humility, undermining our proud nature. As spiritually mature people we no longer focus on the human authority, rather we should now be able to see our supreme Lord pleading with us, saying, "Do it for My sake."

Peter provided Jesus as a prime example of the type of humility we should emulate. When He faced the evil authorities, they hurled their insults at Him, but He did not retaliate; when He suffered, He made no threats. Instead, "He entrusted Himself to Him who judges justly" (v. 23). Are we growing up to be like our Lord?

Lord, we confess that we find it very difficult to be submissive to human authorities. We desire to become so developed spiritually that we will be willing to sacrifice our pride for the Lord's sake. We seek Your help and grace.

October 20

MANNA SERIES: PETER'S CALL FOR SPIRITUAL GROWTH
SPIRITUAL MATURITY IMPACTS HOME LIFE

Reading Passage: 1Pet. 3:1-9
Main Text: 1Pet. 3:1 Wives, in the same way be submissive to your husbands so that, if any of them do not believe the word, they may be won over without words by the behavior of their wives,

1Pet. 3:6 ...like Sarah, who obeyed Abraham and called him her master. You are her daughters if you do what is right and do not give way to fear. 1Pet. 3:7 Husbands, in the same way be considerate as you live with your wives, and treat them with respect as the weaker partner and as heirs with you of the gracious gift of life, so that nothing will hinder your prayers. (NIV)

In 1Peter 2 we are reminded that as we grow spiritually we are able to shift our focus from human authority to focusing on our Lord, the supreme authority. This change in focus also allows us to adjust the way we look at our spouses in the home, which can lead to a God-honoring home with an atmosphere of peace.

In today's passage, Peter exhorted the believers that in the same manner in which we should submit ourselves to human authorities for the Lord's sake, wives should submit themselves to their husbands. Women often resent this demand because they consider this another act of disregard to the value of women in a male dominated society. But the apostle highlighted two outcomes when the wife decides to adorn herself with a gentle and quiet spirit. She will be able to influence and win over even an unchristian husband by her behavior, and she makes herself of great worth in God's sight (v. 4). Wives are usually reluctant to make this sacrifice, as in most cases they fear their husbands may use the opportunity of their submission to abuse them. But Peter gave the example of Sarah who was able to submit to her husband Abraham without fear, because she was interested in making herself beautiful to God.

Peter also implored the husband to alter the way he viewed his wife. He should see her as a delicate, fragile treasure needing special care and attention, yet at the same time he should accept her as his equal before God regarding the blessing of salvation. Failure to honor our wives in this way affects our relationship with the Lord and our ability to pray successfully. In order for the husband to live with his wife while holding this perspective of her, he needs to understand her by diligently studying her moods, strengths and desires.

Wives and husbands are unable to develop this perspective of each other when they are still spiritual babies, sensitive to offenses by the other party and protective of their egos. With spiritual growth, comes sensitivity to how God sees us, and His approval of our behavior. Consequently, God will be pleased with us and our homes will be blessed.

Lord, although we know what You require of us, we find it very difficult to make these adjustments in our attitudes to our spouses. Help us to grow spiritually so we can become more responsive to Your demands on our lives.

October 21

MANNA SERIES: PETER'S CALL FOR SPIRITUAL GROWTH
SUFFERING-ASSISTED GROWTH

Reading Passage: 1Pet. 4:1-6, 12-19
Main Text: 1Pet. 4:1-2. Therefore, since Christ suffered in his body, arm yourselves also with the same attitude, because he who has suffered in his body is done with sin. As a result, he does not live the rest of his earthly life for evil human desires, but rather for the will of God. (NIV)

No normal individual likes to suffer. Therefore, it is not easy to convince anyone that there are hidden blessings in suffering, or that suffering can assist in their spiritual growth. But this was the message Peter gave to the recipients of his letters - Christians who were beginning to face great persecution from the civil authorities.

He told them not to be surprised at the fiery trials that will come to test them, as if it is something strange that is happening to them (v. 12). Why should they welcome these testing circumstances that cause suffering? The first benefit of suffering indicated by Peter is the cathartic effect, because those who have suffered in the body lose the desire for a sinful lifestyle. Pain has a way of focusing our minds on what is truly valuable in life, and the uselessness of our sinful passions.

Peter also pointed out that when we suffer we can be identified with Christ in His suffering. This is cause for rejoicing because it means we will also share in His glory in the future (v. 13). Furthermore, when we suffer because of our identification with Christ, we are blessed because God will provide the Spirit of glory to refresh our souls (v. 14). Finally, our suffering may indicate God's judgment on us to correct us and refine our character. Such correction is the discipline that God imposes on His children in order to enable them to grow up as He desires.

With these benefits of suffering: purifying us from sin, identifying us with our Lord, and disciplining us for proper development, we should not see suffering as an enemy but an aid provided for our spiritual growth. As proposed by Peter we should arm ourselves, like a soldier putting on protective gear, with the attitude to suffer. This was Christ's way of thinking.

What circumstances are you facing that seem designed to cause you to suffer - physical illness, financial loss, painful problems in relationships? If you are not suffering for unrighteous conduct, then adopt the proper attitude to the suffering and see it as a growth opportunity. With this attitude you can rejoice in your suffering and consider yourself blessed, looking forward to the rewards of being identified with Christ.

Lord, we can appreciate that You have called us to join in Your suffering so we can share in Your glory. We confess that it is difficult to accept suffering, but we know You will help us to develop the attitude that will cause us to rejoice in our trials. This we ask in Jesus' precious name.

October 22

MANNA SERIES: PETER'S CALL FOR SPIRITUAL GROWTH
GROW BY USING OUR GIFTS

Reading Passage: 1Pet. 4:7-11
Main Text: 1Pet. 4:10 Each one should use whatever gift he has received to serve others, faithfully administering God's grace in its various forms. (NIV)

The various talents we have are properly described in Scripture as gifts, since we have received them not because we have earned or deserved them, but because of God's grace. These gifts were not received to show how special we are, or for self-advertisement. The purpose of the gifts is that we may use them in service to others in such a way that God may be glorified.

Scripture clearly teaches that every believer has received at least one gift from the Lord. Our task is to discover these gifts and deploy them for the maximum benefit. When Peter was exhorting the believers on spiritual growth while enduring suffering, he surprisingly included comments about the use of their spiritual gifts. One explanation for the insertion of these comments at this point could be that there are many opportunities for the use of our gifts for the benefit of those who are suffering. Another explanation is that the use of gifts actually strengthens and matures the users, while blessing others. While helping others, we are often surprised at how much our own problems seem to diminish, and how fulfilled we feel afterwards.

Peter mentions a number of gifts, such as showing hospitality, speaking the words of God, and serving others. While using these gifts we will discover that our ministry will be empowered by God, which will prove that we are not functioning out of our natural abilities, but by the enablement of the Spirit of God. The more we exercise our gifts, the more we become empowered, and grow in the ability to exercise these gifts.

Jesus' parable of the talents (Matt. 25:14-30) provides certain lessons: (a) the Lord provides the talents, but it is up to us to exercise them; (b) there is an appointed time when we will be required to give an account of our stewardship of the talents we received; (c) when we exercise the talents, they grow, so we have more to present to the Lord; (d) it is very dangerous to have talents and neglect using them, as we will be chastised by the Lord who is looking for growth.

Have you recognized the gifts the Lord has given you? A simple way to identify these is by identifying the things you love to do that can be a blessing to others. Have you been using these gifts for the glory of God? Are you growing in the use of these gifts? Remember there is going to be the day of accounting of our stewardship.

Lord, we thank You for the gifts we have received for service to others and growth in our lives. Please forgive us for the times of neglect, and help us to be diligent to use these gifts so You can be glorified through our lives.

October 23

MANNA SERIES: PETER'S CALL FOR SPIRITUAL GROWTH
BUILDING RESISTANCE TO
THE DEVIL'S ATTACKS

Reading Passage: 1Pet. 5:1-14
Main Text: 1Pet. 5:8-9. Be self-controlled and alert. Your enemy the devil prowls around like a roaring lion looking for someone to devour. Resist him, standing firm in the faith, because you know that your brothers throughout the world are undergoing the same kind of sufferings. (NIV)

The Apostle Peter has taught us the importance of spiritual growth for the development of flourishing Christian lives. We have learned that physical suffering which could be a hindrance must be used to assist in our growth. In today's text, Peter informs us that we have an adversary who will use our physical discomfort to attack our minds with thoughts and suggestions to cause us mental anguish. This adversary is called the devil, who is an evil accuser and slanderer. For the believers undergoing persecution from the civil authorities, the devil might keep telling them that God has forsaken them, or that faith in God is useless against the power of secular forces.

Peter portrays the devil as a roaring lion that is prowling around looking for vulnerable prey to overwhelm and destroy. The most effective weapon of this lion is his roar, which is intended to frighten and weaken his intended victims. Accepting false information, like the devil's accusations, can mentally and spiritually defeat us. Peter admonishes us to resist the devil. To be able to resist him we must be alert and vigilant, always watching for the devil's attacks, being aware of his methods, and always having our defenses prepared.

Our strongest defense is our faith in the redemption purchased by Jesus, which assures us of our salvation and confirms the defeat of the devil. The devil primarily seeks to attack our faith, but the attacks are necessary in order to prove that our faith is genuine (v. 7). In resisting the devil, we are also encouraged by the fact that we are not alone in our suffering. Other believers are undergoing the same physical attacks as we are, and facing the same devilish assaults of doubts and fears. As we are in the same battles, we should unite in a counterattack against our common enemy. We must never forsake assembling with fellow sufferers.

Most importantly, we can be encouraged by the promise that the God of grace, after we have suffered a while, will Himself (note His personal involvement) restore us, support and strengthen us, and place us on a firm foundation (cf. 1Pet. 5:10 NLT). Don't let the devil cause us to believe that God is not able to deliver us from temptation, keep us saved and preserved from evil, or enable us to fulfill our purpose before we die. Resist the devil and he will flee.

Lord, it is a glorious thought that we can overcome the devil by our faith in Jesus Christ. Thank You for providing the encouragement of fellow believers, and the promise of Your strength and restoration at the end. We will not be afraid of the devil's roar; we will remain confident in Your power and assistance.

October 24

MANNA SERIES: PETER'S CALL FOR SPIRITUAL GROWTH
ADDITION THAT LEADS TO MULTIPLICATION

Reading Passage: 2Pet. 1:1-11
Main Text: 2Pet. 1:5-8 For this very reason, make every effort to add to your faith goodness; and to goodness, knowledge; and to knowledge, self-control; and to self-control, perseverance; and to perseverance, godliness; and to godliness, brotherly kindness; and to brotherly kindness, love. For if you possess these qualities in increasing measure, they will keep you from being ineffective and unproductive in your knowledge of our Lord Jesus Christ. (NIV)

We understand that a cell goes through a process of division called a cell cycle, whereby it splits in two and each of the two "baby" cells begins its own development. The result is a continuous process of replication, which leads to the exponential growth of the cell population. Growth is the natural evidence that a cell is alive.

We begin our spiritual life by faith in Jesus, and this provides us with grace, peace and power as we come to know Jesus our Lord (vv. 2-3). The knowledge of Jesus grants us the privilege to be partakers of His divine nature, which motivates us to add virtues to our faith. Virtues are our actions that give evidence of the faith we claim to possess. We make every effort to continuously add virtues to our faith as evidence that we are spiritually alive. Peter portrayed the process of addition as a ladder of virtues, with virtues being added to other virtues. Goodness added to faith, and self-control added to goodness, etc., culminating with the addition of love.

If we are spiritually alive, people should be able to see these qualities displayed in our lives, and these will manifest the life of Jesus in us. There will be no doubt that we share in His divine nature. When we practice the addition, these virtues will become multiplied in their effectiveness and productivity as we grow in our knowledge of the Lord Jesus Christ (v. 8). This lifestyle of growth will not only increase our knowledge and representation of Jesus, but also will provide us with an assurance of our salvation so we will have no fear of death. We will know that a rich welcome awaits our arrival in the eternal kingdom of our Lord (v. 11).

Although we receive salvation and the initial knowledge of Jesus only by grace, we have the responsibility to do the diligent work of adding the virtues. Have you been making the effort to add the virtues, such as self-control or brotherly kindness to your faith? Can people see the demonstration of the divine love in your life?

Lord, we desire not only to know You by faith, but to allow Your divine nature to be evident by the qualities we display. By living out Your life, we believe our knowledge of You will grow exponentially, and this is the goal of our lives. We need Your help as we pursue this goal, for Jesus' sake.

October 25

MANNA SERIES: PETER'S CALL FOR SPIRITUAL GROWTH
KEY INCENTIVE FOR GROWTH

Reading Passage: 2Pet. 1:12-21, 3:1-13
Main Text: 2Pet. 1:16 We did not follow cleverly invented stories when we told you about the power and coming of our Lord Jesus Christ, but we were eyewitnesses of his majesty.

2Pet. 3:10 But the day of the Lord will come like a thief. The heavens will disappear with a roar; the elements will be destroyed by fire, and the earth and everything in it will be laid bare. (NIV)

When we are provoked by people who despise us and seek to destroy us, we know we should exercise self-control in the pursuit of spiritual growth. But after a while it is easy for us to become weary. Why shouldn't we yield to our passion and retaliate, even though this would cause our fleshy nature to grow at the expense of our spiritual nature? The incentive to keep attending to our spiritual growth is the expectation of the return of our Lord Jesus. He will come back to judge those who oppose and oppress us, and to reward us for our efforts at becoming spiritually mature.

Since the return of our Lord is such a key incentive for our spiritual growth, it is not surprising that the enemies of Christianity have targeted this doctrine for attack. Peter's letter showed his concern about both the risk of growth fatigue, and the attempts by our adversaries to undermine our belief in the return of the Lord. He told the believers that he always wanted to remind them to pursue spiritual growth (v. 12) so that after he died they would not forget his teachings (v. 15). In 3:1-2. He told them that his purpose in writing was to remind them of the prophetic predictions concerning the return of the Lord. The longer the Lord delays His return, the more likely it is that we will begin to question the truth of the prophetic predictions and this will lead to our losing our incentive for spiritual growth. Peter hoped that by providing these reminders we would maintain this incentive.

He was also aware that skeptics and false prophets would arise who would teach heresies that deny the prophecies of scripture regarding the Lord's return. In countering their arguments, Peter assures us that we are not following "cleverly invented stories" or myths when we believe the words of scripture. Although he was an eyewitness of the spectacular event of Jesus' transfiguration, the prophecy of scripture is an even more reliable record than his personal experiences (vv. 19-21). Since scripture states that the Lord Jesus will return, we can be assured that the day of the Lord will come.

With the assurance of scripture and the reminders from Peter, let us not become discouraged and fatigued in our pursuit of spiritual growth. One day the Lord will return to reward our efforts and to condemn the critics.

Lord, we admit that the delay of Your return does cause us to become weary in our pursuit of spiritual growth, especially as we face testing situations and encounter persuasive critics. Help us to always trust the prophecy of scripture and remember the encouragement of the apostles as we look forward to our reward.

October 26

MANNA SERIES: PETER'S CALL FOR SPIRITUAL GROWTH
PURSUING A BALANCED GROWTH

Reading Passage: 2Pet. 3:11-18
Main Text: 2Pet. 3:18. But grow in the grace and knowledge of our Lord and Savior Jesus Christ. To him be glory both now and forever! Amen. (NIV)

The glands in the human body that are part of the endocrine system produce hormones that regulate growth and control various bodily functions. If these are not functioning properly, it can lead to abnormal growth, which is detrimental to the development and survival of the body. While spiritual growth is required for the Christian life, it is important that this growth is properly balanced to avoid over-emphasis in certain areas, which can make us poor representatives of Christ in the world.

Peter wrote his letters to believers who were facing severe persecutions. He encouraged them to be steadfast in their hope of salvation through faith in Jesus, and exhorted them to pursue spiritual growth despite their trials. Their growth would not only provide assurance of their salvation, but would also be a testimony of the excellence of salvation in Christ before their oppressors. He closed the letters by emphasizing that their growth should be balanced, growing both in grace and in knowledge of Jesus Christ. In his first letter, Peter emphasized the grace that God provided in salvation, giving us a new birth with a divine nature, and supplying the imperishable Word to sustain our growth. In the second letter, he emphasized knowledge of our Lord. As we use the grace that God supplies to develop virtues, our knowledge of Jesus increases. Both grace and knowledge work together to produce growth into the character and personality of our Lord.

When we grow in knowledge we will know the principles that represent the Christ-life, but our growth in grace will cause us to demonstrate the practices of the life in a gracious manner. The balance is significant because it is characteristic of God's nature to hold seemingly opposing qualities in perfect harmony: like His justice and mercy, love and power, or His wrath and His kindness. When we emphasize grace without balancing it with knowledge of the principles of the Christ-life, we can end up with loose living, and if we emphasize knowledge of the principles without also focusing on the grace He provides, we will be legalistic.

Our growth in the grace and knowledge of Jesus Christ will mature us into the full model of Jesus, which will be perfected when He returns to reveal the fullness of our salvation. For we know that when He shall appear we shall be like Him, for we shall see Him as He is (cf. 1John 3:2). Let us diligently pursue spiritual growth, but also let us ensure that the growth is balanced.

Father, we thank You for providing instructions through the Apostle Peter on the importance of growth in our Christian life, and the lesson that this growth should be balanced so we might properly represent Jesus in the world. We rely on the help of the Holy Spirit so this may be accomplished in our lives, for Jesus' sake.

October 27

MANNA SERIES: THE CALL TO STEWARDSHIP
THE QUESTION OF OWNERSHIP

Reading Passage: 1Chr. 29:1-18
Main Text: 1Chr. 29:14. "But who am I, and who are my people, that we should be able to give as generously as this? Everything comes from you, and we have given you only what comes from your hand." (NIV)

The term stewardship is used directly or referred to, a number of times in the scriptures. The concept of stewardship underlies the relationship between the Creator God, the earth He created, and His human representatives on the earth. A steward originally referred to a person with the responsibility to service and manage a household with respect to domestic duties. The term has evolved to include anyone who has to manage people, an entity, or an enterprise on behalf of others, from a farm manager to the CEO of a large corporation.

The key factors to recognize in the stewardship function is that (i) the steward is not the owner, and since he manages on behalf of an owner, (ii) he is required to give an accounting of his stewardship. The question of ownership has always been a struggle for us because after managing for a while many of the things God has blessed us with, we easily forget we are not the owners and are merely the stewards. Whether it is the beautiful things of creation, the assets we enjoy such as houses and cars, the families we have been blessed with, or our very lives, we are stewards and God is the owner. In the Genesis account of creation, the Lord made all things and declared that they were good, before He made man to manage and enjoy creation. Man was never made the owner.

In 1Chronicles 29, we read of the time when King David was about to turn over the kingdom of Israel to his son Solomon. He was passing over to Solomon the treasures gained from his conquests and also his personal resources, for the purpose of building a temple for God. Spurred by his actions, the leaders and all the people began giving up their possessions for the temple fund. This led to great celebration by both King and people (vv. 6-9). While blessing the Lord, David declared that God owns everything including the heavens and the earth, riches and honor, power and might (vv. 11-12), therefore whatever they offered to God was only what He already owned.

If we live with the consciousness that we are only stewards of what God has blessed us with, for use as He directs, we will have much less struggle fighting to grasp what we can't own. C. S. Lewis correctly stated: "Every faculty you have, your power of thinking or of moving your limbs from moment to moment, is given you by God. If you devoted every moment of your whole life exclusively to His service, you could not give Him anything that was not in a sense His own already."

Father, we stress ourselves trying to tightly grasp what we cannot own and what we must leave one day. Please help us to live with the awareness that You own all things, and we are just stewards to use what You have provided for the purposes, and in the manner, You have prescribed.

October 28

MANNA SERIES: THE CALL TO STEWARDSHIP
CAN WE BE TRUSTED AS A STEWARD?

Reading Passage:, Luke 12:35-48
Main Text: Luke 12:45-46 But suppose the servant says to himself, 'My master is taking a long time in coming,' and he then begins to beat the menservants and maidservants and to eat and drink and get drunk. The master of that servant will come on a day when he does not expect him and at an hour he is not aware of. He will cut him to pieces and assign him a place with the unbelievers. (NIV)

Jesus, in teaching the disciples about the kingdom, occasionally described Himself as a master who has left the household of the kingdom and has gone away, either on a journey to a far country or to a wedding feast. The servants were left to manage the household in His absence. However, the servants were not advised of the date or time of His return. Could these servants be relied on to be faithful stewards during the absence of the master, diligently fulfilling their tasks and maintaining a state of readiness for his return? Jesus declared that servants who are faithful will be blessed, and the master will expand their responsibilities, placing them over all His possessions (vv. 42-44).

However, when the master's return is delayed, there are certain servants who will begin to abuse the household staff, and become careless in their lifestyles. These servants will be surprised by the master's unexpected return, and they will face a deserved punishment for their unfaithfulness. In the context of this lesson, Jesus was likely referring to the failure of the Jewish leaders to be faithful stewards of the truth of the Divine revelation. But there is a valuable lesson with universal application.

The Lord has left us as stewards to manage His creation. How faithful have we been in taking care of the environment? Some of us have been placed in positions of privilege where we have the opportunity to assist and care for those who are less fortunate. Have we performed these duties as stewards accountable to our Lord, or have we taken advantage of the weak and failed to help those in need, abusing our privilege? Because the return of the Lord seems to be delayed, have we begun to live irresponsible lives of self-indulgence, failing to properly represent our Lord? The sobering point is that the Lord will return at an unexpected moment. Will He find that we were faithful stewards in His absence?

Jesus concluded this teaching with a solemn warning, "That servant who knows His master's will and does not get ready or does not do what His master wants, will be beaten with many blows" (v. 47).

Lord, we are often delinquent regarding the responsibilities assigned to us because we have been lulled into a state of complacency due to the delay of Your return. We want You to be able to trust us as faithful stewards. Keep reminding us of Your chilling words of warning, as we wait for Your return.

October 29

MANNA SERIES: THE CALL TO STEWARDSHIP
INDICATORS OF AN UNFAITHFUL SERVANT

Reading Passage: Luke 16:1-13
Main Text: Luke 16:10-12 "Whoever can be trusted with very little can also be trusted with much, and whoever is dishonest with very little will also be dishonest with much. So if you have not been trustworthy in handling worldly wealth, who will trust you with true riches? And if you have not been trustworthy with someone else's property, who will give you property of your own?" (NIV)

Jesus taught the principle that people's conduct with little things provides an indicator of their character, which will be magnified when they are presented with larger opportunities. This principle, which can be used to identify the type of steward someone will become, will help to avoid entrusting great responsibilities to unfaithful people.

The illustration Jesus provided that concluded with this principle, has been the subject of many controversial interpretations. He told the story of a wealthy man who had a manager that was misusing his master's finances. When the master decided to fire him, the manager planned a ruse. He contacted the clients who were in debt to his master, and offered them huge discounts in settlement of their balances. By making this generous offer, the manager ensured that these debtors would take care of him after he was fired. On discovering what the dishonest manager did, the master commended him for his shrewdness. Jesus indicated that disciples could learn from the manager's shrewdness about how to use money in this world so it can provide benefits after we depart this life, in the world to come. We should manage our money with a view to eternal rewards.

The other valuable lesson was that the manager who was unfaithful with his master's funds on a small scale, graduated into a large embezzler when he was threatened with dismissal. The pressure only magnified his character flaw. If we are careless in looking after a small portfolio, it is unlikely we will become prudent when we have a large portfolio. If we are dishonest in handling our personal finances, can we be trusted to handle the finances of the corporation? If we are unfaithful to prepare ourselves and minister to a few people, can we be trusted to be faithful with the crowds? If we are unfaithful in handling worldly assets, why should we be trusted with true spiritual riches?

The things we easily disregard as insignificant because they are small, obscure or little esteemed, provide important tests of our character. Our response to them can determine how much more responsibility God will entrust to us. Let us be faithful with the "small things" as they provide valuable indicators of trustworthy character, whether in others or ourselves.

Lord, we realize that You seek to prove our character by various means, and You take into account all areas of our lives. We desire to be trustworthy stewards in the little things, so help us to have the humble attitude of Jesus, who was willing to serve faithfully even in washing the feet of His disciples.

October 30

MANNA SERIES: THE CALL TO STEWARDSHIP
THE BASIS OF EVALUATING GOD'S SERVANTS

Reading Passage: 1Cor. 3:18 - 4:5
Main Text: 1Cor. 4:1-2 So then, men ought to regard us as servants of Christ and as those entrusted with the secret things of God. Now it is required that those who have been given a trust must prove faithful. (NIV)

It has become normal in organizations that the performance of employees is periodically evaluated on a consistent basis. This process allows the employees to know how their managers view their work, and to get feedback on their strengths and weakness. They can discuss what steps should be taken for improvement in their performance. The performance evaluation also provides a basis on which compensation can be determined.

While this is a useful tool for employment in an organization, is it appropriate for spiritual service? Perhaps performance evaluations should be applied in all human organizations including those performing spiritual services, but these evaluations should not be considered the true assessment of a servant of God from His perspective. Servants of God are called and deployed by the Master, and only He can make the true evaluation of the service performed. In 1Cor. 4:2, Paul declared that the only requirement of servants of God is that they are found to be faithful. They are not required to be successful by worldly standards, as achieving certain goals, and accomplishing certain tasks or receiving meritorious awards or accolades.

The Lord may direct His servant to minister in a place where He knows there will be no visible results. Only the Master knows the goals He wants His servants to accomplish, so only He can judge the success of the mission. The Lord sent Jeremiah to prophecy to Judah, but told him not to expect anyone to listen to him; instead he should expect to be persecuted. Similarly, God sends his servants to people and places just to plant a seed of truth, the results of which they will never see in their lifetime. Therefore, the only basis on which these servants can be evaluated is whether they have been faithful to perform what God asked them to do.

Paul was criticizing the practice of the Corinthians to use worldly means of evaluating various church leaders, and then to boast about these men. He explained that these leaders should all be regarded as servants of God entrusted with a task. They should only be judged on the basis of their faithfulness. Furthermore, we are unable to truly judge faithfulness, even our own, since we are unable to assess the motive behind each action. Only God will be able to render a judgment on faithfulness with sincere motives, which will be done when He comes to reward His servants (4:3-5).

As servants of God let us strive to be faithful, whether or not it seems we are successful.

Lord, as Your servants help us not to be distracted by worldly

evaluations, but to focus on being faithful and honest before You, regardless of the challenges we face. Grant this in Jesus' name.

October 31

MANNA SERIES: THE CALL TO STEWARDSHIP
CHARACTERISTICS OF GOD'S STEWARDS

Reading Passage: Titus 1:1-16
Main Text: Titus 1:7-9 For a bishop must be blameless, as a steward of God, not self-willed, not quick-tempered, not given to wine, not violent, not greedy for money, but hospitable, a lover of what is good, sober-minded, just, holy, self-controlled, holding fast the faithful word as he has been taught, that he may be able, by sound doctrine, both to exhort and convict those who contradict. (NKJV)

Retired four-star general in the United States Army, and former U.S. Secretary of State, General Colin Powell said that the hopelessness or enthusiasm a leader brings to his or her position can be contagious, and can in fact spread through an entire country like ripples in the proverbial pond. This description of the impact of a leader highlights the reason why leaders should be carefully chosen. More than what they say and do, leaders influence by who they are in their character.

Paul left Titus in Crete, with the assignment of establishing leadership in those churches. Within the churches there were many false teachers and deceivers who were teaching erroneous doctrines and disrupting the faith of the believers (vv. 10-11). In addition, Cretans had a reputation of being "liars, evil beasts, lazy gluttons" (v. 12). Strong leadership was required to counter the influence of these false teachers, protect the genuine believers, and guide the church in her witness against a corrupt culture. Paul said these leaders (referred to interchangeably as elders and bishops) must first be blameless. This does not mean they were perfect, but they should have a lifestyle against which no accusations could be maintained. As God's representative, we must provide a good reflection of the Master's character, especially when leading the church in an environment that is hostile to Christian values. We also represent God's household to the society. The society will identify our failures as representative of the whole church.

Paul explained blamelessness by stating the negative characteristics that should not exist in the steward's life - not self-willed, not quick-tempered, not given to wine, not violent, not greedy for money. He proceeded to list the positive characteristics that should be present - hospitable, lover of good, self-controlled, upright, holy and disciplined. These characteristics are not required for the leaders only; they should also be identified with everyone who has to represent God and the church in the world. We have to live the message we preach, and walk what we talk, so there will be no inconsistencies with who we say we are, and what the world observes.

While it may not matter to us if our physician is an adulterer, our accountant is arrogant, or our lawyer is inhospitable, for the steward of God, it is the character that counts.

Lord, we desire that we possess Your holiness so completely that we will provide a wonderful witness to the world that we represent You, and that we will do no damage to the reputation of the church.

November 1

MANNA SERIES: THE CALL TO STEWARDSHIP
STEWARDS OF GOD'S GRACE

Reading Passage: 1Pet. 4:7-11
Main Text: 1Pet. 4:10 As each one has received a gift, minister it to one another, as good stewards of the manifold grace of God. (NKJV)

Grace is the freely given, unmerited favor and love of God. This favor places us into a relationship with God, by which we are supplied with salvation, strength, opportunities, power, mercy and every good thing. God uses His children as conduits of His grace. Peter describes us as stewards who administer God's grace in its various forms. This is a role to which we rarely pay sufficient attention.

Each of us has received a gift from God by grace. Because it is a gift of grace, we did nothing to earn or deserve it, and although it may cause us to be highly esteemed by others, we should always be careful to give the credit and glory to the Giver of the gift. Peter further explains that the gift was given for use - not to be treasured or showcased. God's gifts always have a utilitarian value so the Body of Christ, and people in general, may benefit. We are not owners of the gifts; we are merely stewards entrusted with them for the purpose of their administration. The manner in which we administer the gifts will indicate whether we are good or bad stewards.

We also know, from the parables of Jesus, that there will be a day when all stewards will have to give an account of their administration of the gifts for which they were responsible. The parable of the talents in Matthew 25 explains that the Lord gives us gifts according to our ability (Matt 25:15), so we have no basis to be envious of any person's gifts since God knows what is appropriate to the individual. Regardless of the type of gift we have been given, the Master intends that we use it so that He will be able to see tangible results. If we fail to use the gifts, we will be depriving people from obtaining some favor that God wants to bestow on their lives, as we are the conduits God desires to use.

The list of gifts in 1Pet. 4:7-11 is not exhaustive (there are other lists provided by Paul in 1Cor. 12 and Eph. 4) but should assist us in identifying the gifts God has given us according to our abilities. He mentioned hospitality, speaking, and serving. Our recognition that we are stewards will determine our attitude in administering the gifts. As good stewards, we will not choose the time, occasions or people to benefit from the gifts; rather, whenever God places people needing help in our path, we must use our gifts to the best of our ability and for the glory of the gift Giver.

Lord, we thank You for the privilege of being conduits of Your grace on the earth. Help us to be faithful in our stewardship so people will get a glimpse of God's grace by the way we administer the gifts, with enthusiasm, love and compassion, and without respect of persons.

November 2

MANNA SERIES: THE CALL TO STEWARDSHIP
FACTORS INFLUENCING COMPENSATION FOR STEWARDSHIP

Reading Passage: 1Cor. 9:4-18
Main Text: 1Cor. 9:16-17. Yet when I preach the gospel, I cannot boast, for I am compelled to preach. Woe to me if I do not preach the gospel!

If I preach voluntarily, I have a reward; if not voluntarily, I am simply discharging the trust committed to me. (NIV)

Should the Christian minister be compensated for his stewardship? How much should he be paid? If someone is 'working for the Lord', should he be demanding a certain compensation, and what if the demands are not met? Shouldn't the preacher be able to enjoy a decent living from his ministry, or should he have to supplement his income by secular employment? These and similar questions have been the subject of strong debate and much disagreement in churches for many years. Paul addressed these issues in 1Cor. 9, and used himself as an interesting case study for ministers, their compensation, and their rewards for stewardship.

At the outset, Paul presents the principle that Christian ministers have certain rights, one of which is to be properly compensated for their work. Reasoning from the common examples in the secular world, he argues that soldiers don't serve their country at their own expense, and farmers are entitled to enjoy the fruits of their labor (v. 7). Therefore, those who minister spiritual seed should reap a harvest of material compensation (v. 11). He further stated that the Lord commanded that those who preach the gospel should receive their living from the gospel (v. 14). However, Paul explained that with respect to the Corinthian church, he never exercised his rights to compensation because of his unique relationship with them. He wanted to be sure they couldn't accuse him of being a peddler of the gospel, as were some persons involved with that church.

He raised the interesting issue: since he didn't receive compensation from them could he refuse to preach? No, he was compelled to preach; he had no choice for God entrusted him with the responsibility of stewardship, and this was a sacred obligation. If he insisted on his rights, he could forfeit the joy of voluntarily becoming the slave of all people so that he could win many more people to Christ (v. 19).

Paul's example serves as an important lesson to all of us desiring to fulfill our roles as stewards. Although we have the right to compensation, the denial of these rights should not affect our obligation to fulfill our responsibilities as God's stewards. The greater reward will be the fruit of our work in the lives of people, as well as the approval of our Lord. Our overriding motivation should be "freely we have received so freely we give." Our guiding consideration when we have served without recognition or appreciation should be that our Master keeps account and will reward us at the end.

Lord, You have promised to reward the faithful servants, so we work looking forward to hearing You say "Well done." Help us not to be weary while doing good since we are assured that one day we will reap if we don't give up.

November 3

MANNA SERIES: REQUIRING A WARDROBE TRANSFORMATION
THE FAILURE OF FIG LEAVES

Reading Passage: Gen. 3:1-21
Main Text: Gen. 3:7. Then the eyes of both of them were opened, and they realized they were naked; so they sewed fig leaves together and made coverings for themselves.
Gen. 3:21 The LORD God made garments of skin for Adam and his wife and clothed them. (NIV)

More than just a name for the cabinet where clothes are stored or hung, the term wardrobe is used to denote a person's entire collection of clothes. When someone changes their status in life, such as moving from a hippie lifestyle to that of a corporate banker, a dramatic transformation is required in his or her wardrobe. In the Bible there were occasions when a wardrobe transformation was required, and this was signified by the provision of new clothes or the exchange of old apparel for new ones.

One of the early occurrences of this transformation is recorded in the Genesis story of the fall of Adam. He went from being the sinless companion of God, to being a sinful man under the rule of Satan. The first couple, Adam and Eve, was created in innocence without a concept of good and evil. In this state of innocence, they were naked without any self-consciousness or fear of exploitation: "the man and his wife were both naked, and they felt no shame" (Gen 2:25 NIV). Satan entered the scene, telling them that if they disobeyed God's command and ate the forbidden fruit, their eyes would be opened, meaning they would be enlightened, and they would be like God, knowing good and evil.

They yielded to the temptation and ate the fruit. Immediately, their eyes were opened as they lost their innocence and they became conscious of their nakedness. To cover their nakedness, they sewed fig leaves to make clothes. Fig leaves consisting of easily perishable vegetable material were clearly inadequate to provide durable material or sufficient yardage for a proper covering. This flimsy attempt to provide external covering also left them exposed in their minds. When God came for His usual daily meeting with them, they hid themselves. God immediately knew that the couple had submitted to Satan and had sinned, losing their innocence. After God pronounced the judgment as a consequence for their sin, He mercifully provided a replacement covering for the sinful couple. He made garments of skin and clothed them.

Fig leaves represent humanity's flimsy, inadequate attempt to deal with the problem of sin. Knowing how unsuccessful we are at making a covering, we try to rename it, excuse it, or maybe numb it with narcotics. God's solution was to provide His own covering, which required that an animal be killed as a substitute, to provide clothes for covering. This was a preview of the Lamb of God who would be killed on a cross for our sins. Sinful man can only be properly covered by accepting the wardrobe transformation provided by God.

Father, we have made such a mess of our lives because of our sins, and have failed in our attempts to provide covering. We are thankful for Your provision for covering our nakedness and our guilty conscience, through Jesus Christ.

November 4

MANNA SERIES: REQUIRING A WARDROBE TRANSFORMATION
DRESSING FOR A DIVINE ENCOUNTER

Reading Passage: Gen. 35:1-7

Main Text: Gen. 35:1-2 Then God said to Jacob, "Go up to Bethel and settle there, and build an altar there to God, who appeared to you when you were fleeing from your brother Esau." So Jacob said to his household and to all who were with him, "Get rid of the foreign gods you have with you, and purify yourselves and change your clothes." (NIV)

In Genesis 35:1, the Lord ordered Jacob to return to Bethel and build an altar there to God. The return to Bethel signified the completion of a journey that began at that place and the fulfillment of God's promise to Jacob, over twenty years earlier. At that time, Jacob was fleeing from his older brother Esau, from whom he had stolen the blessing of the firstborn. On his way to visit his uncle Laban in Haran, he stopped to sleep in a city named Luz. While sleeping he had a dream in which he had an encounter with the Lord. The Lord promised Jacob He would fulfill the Abrahamic covenant with him, and accompany him on his journeys and bring him back to that location. Having left his father's house, Jacob was surprised to discover God there, so he named the city Bethel, meaning house of God. He was so overawed by this event that he made a deal with God. If the Lord kept His promise and brought him back to the land, then the Lord would be his God, the stone on which he slept would be God's sacred house and he would give God a tenth of all he had accumulated during his journey.

Jacob lived in the land of Haran for twenty years, during which time he married two of his uncle's daughters and had many children. His uncle Laban swindled him, yet the Lord caused him to prosper. After a while the relationship became toxic and the Lord instructed Jacob to leave his uncle and return home. Jacob left Haran with his family and his wealth, but his wives stole the idols belonging to their father. On the return journey home, Jacob camped in Shechem. He had a horrible experience there including the rape of his daughter, and war erupted between the men of the city and his sons. In the midst of the turmoil, the Lord appeared to Jacob to remind him of his vow, and ordered him to return to Bethel.

In preparation for this renewal of his relationship with the Lord, and the fulfillment of his vow, Jacob ordered his household to get rid of their idols, purify themselves and change their clothes. Their clothing represented the lifestyle of Haran with its idol worshipping and ungodliness.

In order to meet with the Lord, the old lifestyle must be dispensed with, so we can be acceptable to Him. We know that God is calling us to a renewed relationship, but we try to avoid giving up the habits and lifestyles of our old life. Sometimes it takes heartbreaking incidents in our lives to cause us to remember our vows, make the sacrifices, change our clothes and return to Him.

Father, we so easily forget our commitments to You and become

content with lifestyles that are not pleasing to You. Cause us to hear You calling us to return to Bethel, so we might purify ourselves and prepare to meet with You.

November 5

MANNA SERIES: REQUIRING A WARDROBE TRANSFORMATION
ATTIRE REPRESENTING THE DIVINE PRESENCE

Reading Passage: Ex. 28:1-43
Main Text: Ex. 28:40-41 Make tunics, sashes and headbands for Aaron's sons, to give them dignity and honor. After you put these clothes on your brother Aaron and his sons, anoint and ordain them. Consecrate them so they may serve me as priests. (NIV)

As followers of Jesus, we represent the temple of God in which the Holy Spirit dwells (1Cor. 3:16, 1Cor. 6:19). We also function as priests unto God (1Pet. 2:5, Rev. 1:6). With this status and function, we should have attire that represents our relationship with the divine presence, and one that makes us distinct from those not having this relationship.

The only person in the Jewish religious tradition who was authorized to enter the presence of God was the high priest, and this appearance could only be made once a year. High priests were specifically chosen from the family of Aaron. In establishing the priesthood, God instructed Moses to have special garments made, consisting of a breast-piece, an ephod, a robe, a woven tunic, a turban and a sash (v. 4). After dressing Aaron and his sons in these outfits, they would be anointed and ordained to serve in the office of the high priest. No other person was allowed to wear these garments. They were designed for glory and beauty in order to provide dignity and honor to the priests, and signify their consecration as representatives with access to God.

In the same way, the attire of followers of Jesus should identify them as people with a special relationship with God. But, unlike as it was for Jewish priests, these are not literal garments; rather, this refers to the characteristics we portray which will quickly identify us as representatives of God. When we are clothed with righteousness and humility, people will observe the glory and beauty of our lives and be reminded of the holiness of the Lord. People who are overwhelmed with their struggles against evil and are seeking for some indication of salvation and connection with God, should be able to see us as witnesses of the presence of God.

Psalm 132 was written to celebrate the memorial of the time when King David decided to establish a place where the ark of the presence of God would be permanently located. Having found a resting place for the ark, the Psalmist declared,

> 132:9 NIV. May your priests be clothed with righteousness; may your saints sing for joy,
> 132:16 NIV. I will clothe her priests with salvation, and her saints will ever sing for joy.

As followers of Christ, it is important that we face the world each day properly attired as representatives of the divine presence so that the saints will be able to sing for joy.

Lord, we acknowledge that our attire as representatives of Your glory and honor is significant to the world who needs to seek for You. Help us to ensure that we properly represent Your righteousness and salvation every day.

November 6

MANNA SERIES: REQUIRING A WARDROBE TRANSFORMATION
CLEANSING THE SIN OF A NATION

Reading Passage: Zech. 3:1-10
Main Text: Zech. 3:4-5. The angel said to those who were standing before him, "Take off his filthy clothes." Then he said to Joshua, "See, I have taken away your sin, and I will put rich garments on you." Then I said, "Put a clean turban on his head." So they put a clean turban on his head and clothed him, while the angel of the LORD stood by. (NIV)

In chapter three of Zechariah, the prophet recounts a vision that describes the process the Lord would use to cleanse the sin of the nation of Judah and the city of Jerusalem, and restore them to a place of peace and prosperity. This was one of several visions Zechariah received during the time when the majority of the Jews were still living in Babylon, and a small remnant had returned to Jerusalem to commence the building of the temple.

After seeing the devastation of the homeland, the destruction of the temple and the exile of the people to Babylon, the Jews were still in a state of despair, wondering if there was any hope for the recovery of the nation. The captivity taught them that the Lord had justly punished them for their sins of rebellion and idolatry. But how could they know that God had forgiven them, so they could put their past behind them? In this vision the Lord used the high priest, Joshua, to represent the entire nation before Him. This was an appropriate symbolism, since only the priest was authorized to approach the presence of God, and his role was to present the people to the Lord. The failure of the nation represented the failure of the priesthood.

The vision showed Joshua with filthy garments defiled by sin (v. 3), and beside him stood Satan to accuse him before the presence of God (v. 1). The first action by the Lord was to rebuke Satan (v. 2), thus removing the accusation against the priest and the nation. Then He arranged that the filthy garments of the priest be removed, and be replaced by clean vestments and a clean turban (vv. 4-5). This symbolized the taking away of sin from the priest and the restoration of purity. Afterwards, a new charge was given to Joshua: to rule the temple and the kingdom in accordance with God's instructions (v. 7). This required Joshua to function in a new role as both a priest and king. Knowing Joshua's inability to fulfill this task, the Lord promised to send Messiah who would be a priest-king and upon His coming He would remove the iniquity of the land in a single day (v. 9).

One day Jesus came as our priest-king and by His death on the cross, the sins of the whole world was cleansed. Our filthy, sinful garments were removed and replaced by His righteous garments. Now we are able to invite people to join us in the state of peace and prosperity He has provided, "under His vine and fig tree" (v. 10).

Lord, we are amazed at this wonderful news that our sin and guilt were cleansed in one day, and by accepting the work of the cross, we can be clothed with rich, clean attire and live in Your prosperity. Thank You for the hope provided by our Priest-King.

November 7

MANNA SERIES: REQUIRING A WARDROBE TRANSFORMATION
LOVE THAT TRANSFORMS THE STATUS QUO

Reading Passage: 1Sam. 17:55 - 18:9

Main Text: 1Sam. 18:3-4 And Jonathan made a covenant with David because he loved him as himself. Jonathan took off the robe he was wearing and gave it to David, along with his tunic, and even his sword, his bow and his belt. (NIV)

There are several interesting twists to the story of David and his journey from being a humble shepherd boy to his elevation as the King of Israel. One of the most intriguing is the relationship that developed between Jonathan, the son of King Saul and David.

When he was a just a boy, David was chosen by God as the person who would replace Saul as king. Yet he did not come to prominence until he defeated the Philistine giant named Goliath, with just his slingshot and stones.

With this victory, David gained the attention of King Saul who took him into the palace, unaware of his divine appointment. However, Saul grew increasingly jealous of David's successful exploits and his popularity in the country, and sought to destroy him. But Jonathan loved David "as his own soul," so he covenanted with him, although he was the natural heir to the throne and the one with the most to lose if David became king. To demonstrate his love, Jonathan stripped himself of his princely robe and tunic and gave them to David, along with his sword, bow and belt. The prince covenanted with the pauper; the one with the right to the royal throne covenanted with the shepherd boy from the fields. But by the act of transferring his clothes and equipment, he was conferring on David the right to replace himself. This was done because of love.

Jonathan had nothing to gain; yet he made a covenant to sacrifice everything, thereby transforming the status of David. Jonathan provided an early picture of Jesus who came with all the riches and glory of heaven, and sacrificed everything in order to transform our status as helpless, hopeless sinners. Because of love, for our sakes, He who knew no sin became sin for us, so we could be clothed in His righteousness (2Cor. 5:21).

Are we willing to give sacrificially of our time and resources to someone in need so we might change their status in life? Can we give because of the love of God in us, expecting nothing in return? Let us learn from the examples of Jonathan and Jesus and seek to bestow the clothing of status and honor on others to make a difference in their lives. We may just be bringing to prominence those whom God had previously chosen.

Lord, it is truly amazing to know that our King would die for us in order to transform our lives. What love! Please develop this love in us so we will be willing to sacrifice for others so they can be transformed by the power of our love.

November 8

MANNA SERIES: REQUIRING A WARDROBE TRANSFORMATION
WHEN MESSIAH COMES ...

Reading Passage: Is. 61:1-11
Main Text: Is. 61:3 ... and provide for those who grieve in Zion—
to bestow on them a crown of beauty instead of ashes,
the oil of gladness instead of mourning,
and a garment of praise instead of a spirit of despair.
They will be called oaks of righteousness, a planting of the LORD
for the display of his splendor. (NIV)

For centuries the expectant cry of the Jews has been, "... when Messiah comes." This cry of hope was based on two main factors. First, life was not what it should have been, both in the world and in their personal circumstances. Injustice was rampant, their inheritance was gone, foreigners ruled over them. As a result, they were brokenhearted, and in mourning, living with sadness and despair. The second factor was the promise in the scriptures that messiah would come and correct all wrongs, ushering in a state of righteousness and peace. This hope has sustained the Jews throughout their horrific history, whether it was the Babylonian captivity, Roman domination, Christian crusades or the Nazi holocaust.

Isaiah 61 is one of the messianic texts on which the Jews based their hopes. Messiah would come declaring that He was anointed with the Spirit of the Sovereign Lord and this empowered Him to preach good news to the poor, relieve the burden of the brokenhearted and to bring into effect the reign of the Lord's favor (vv. 1-2). On a personal basis, for those grieving in Zion, He would replace the ashes on their heads that signify mourning, with a crown of beauty. They would receive oil of gladness to replace their mourning. For those having a spirit of despair because of hopelessness, He would clothe them in a garment of praise (v. 3). This transformation would be solely the work of Messiah; it would not be achieved by self-help methods, the power of positive thinking, meditation or finding a new spiritual guru. Therefore, they would display the splendor and beauty of the Lord, like stalwart oak trees planted by God.

One day Messiah came and quoted this specific text, then stated that the scripture was fulfilled on that day (Luke 4:18-19). But the Jews that heard Jesus at that time rejected Him as the Messiah, and eventually demanded His crucifixion. Since then those who accept Jesus, not just as the Jewish Messiah, but also as their personal Savior, can declare that Messiah has come. As the Christmas carol states, "Joy to the world the Lord has come. Let earth receive her king." Although He has not yet begun His messianic reign over all the earth, He should be reigning in the heart of every believer. Because of His reign, we have experienced the transformation, and our attire has been changed. Despite our circumstances, we no longer have to mourn or be in despair since He has caused us to exchange beauty for ashes, gladness for mourning, and a garment of praise for a spirit of heaviness.

What are we portraying to the world? Does our countenance testify to the fact that our Messiah has come and is reigning in our hearts?

Lord, we are grateful that we recognized Your coming and allowed You to exchange our sorrows for joy and our spirit of heaviness for a garment of praise. May we live this truth every day so people will recognize us as the plantings of God through Jesus Christ.

MANNA SERIES: REQUIRING A WARDROBE TRANSFORMATION
THE MAN WHO REFUSED NEW CLOTHES

Reading Passage: Esth. 4:1-17

Main Text: Esth. 4:4-5 When Esther's maids and eunuchs came and told her about Mordecai, she was in great distress. She sent clothes for him to put on instead of his sackcloth, but he would not accept them. Then Esther summoned Hathach, one of the king's eunuchs assigned to attend her, and ordered him to find out what was troubling Mordecai and why. (NIV)

Clothes provide more than just a covering for our bodies. They are also a reflection of our moods. People can read our mood, or the message we want to convey by the type of clothes we are wearing, whether the solemn, dark attire for a funeral, the playful, casual outfit for a party, or the formal clothing for an official ceremony. In Jewish tradition, the times of repentance, mourning and distress were symbolized by the tearing of the clothes and the wearing of sackcloth, which was a thick, coarse cloth made of black goat's hair.

When the Jews were in captivity, under the reign of the Persian king, Xerxes, the prime minister, Haman, devised a plot to destroy all the Jews. His main motivation was anger that a prominent Jew, Mordecai, would not pay homage to him by kneeling. Unknown to him, Mordecai was the guardian of Esther, who, after winning a beauty contest, became one of the king's favorite wives. When Mordecai became aware of Haman's plan against the Jews, he tore his clothes, put on sackcloth and ashes, and lay before the king's gate while weeping loudly. Queen Esther learned of Mordecai's behavior, and was greatly concerned and possibly embarrassed. She immediately arranged for new clothes to be sent to him, but he refused them.

Mordecai's peaceful demonstration was done in order to get the message to Esther of the threat to the lives of her people in the kingdom, and to urge her to petition the king on their behalf. Eventually, she agreed to speak to the king when Mordecai explained that although she was in the palace, she would not be safe when it was discovered that she was Jewish. The story ended with Esther's petition being accepted by the king, Haman being hanged, the Jews being protected and Mordecai promoted. In chapter 9 we read that the Jews exchanged their sackcloth for garments of celebration at the outcome of these events. This deliverance was precipitated by the fact that Mordecai refused to wear regular clothes and be complacent when his people were facing a crisis.

We learn from his attitude that times of crisis demand drastic responses. We cannot be at ease and be indifferent when our people are facing perilous times, our children are being murdered, our moral values are under threat, and our leaders are puzzled as to the solutions. We need people who are prepared to mourn and make the sacrifice in order to get the attention of the King of Kings who alone can provide us with mercy.

Lord, we are facing times of crisis in our land and we need Your intervention and Your mercy. As a demonstration of the sincerity of our supplication, help us to be willing to refuse the garments of ease and indifference so we may gain Your attention.

November 10

MANNA SERIES: REQUIRING A WARDROBE TRANSFORMATION
GETTING DRESSED FOR THE DAY

Reading Passage: Rom. 13:8-14
Main Text: Rom. 13:12-14. The night is nearly over; the day is almost here. So let us put aside the deeds of darkness and put on the armor of light. Let us behave decently, as in the daytime, not in orgies and drunkenness, not in sexual immorality and debauchery, not in dissension and jealousy. Rather, clothe yourselves with the Lord Jesus Christ, and do not think about how to gratify the desires of the sinful nature. (NIV)

One morning while getting ready for work, Robert faced the challenge of dressing in limited light as there was a power cut. He arrived at work just as the sun came up. It was then that he noticed that he had put on two different color socks, and his necktie did not match with his shirt. In response to teasing comments from his co-workers, Robert's standard answer was, "I dressed in the dark."

Whatever we could get away with in the dark, will be revealed by the daylight. Although we may have to dress in the night we must remain aware that we are dressing for the day. In Romans 13, Paul used the figurative language of night and day to exhort the believers to adjust their conduct so they would be properly attired for daytime scrutiny. He said that the day of the coming of the Lord was almost here; therefore we must put away sinful conduct that was tolerated in the night of our old lifestyle, before we were enlightened by God.

It is interesting to note that Paul was giving this exhortation to believers. This means that after our conversion we continue to have struggles with certain attitudes and behavior. Our desire is that these are hidden, as we know it would be embarrassing if they were publicly known. But knowing that the light of Christ's presence will soon examine us, we must get rid of our darkness mentality and deeds. Instead we must put on the protective armor of light that will guard our thought-life from the infiltration of dark thoughts. This will monitor our activities when we are away from people who know us, when we are in our private quarters on our computers, or alone with our thoughts.

Paul's recommendation is that we clothe ourselves with the Lord Jesus Christ. We will then be able to focus on adjusting our behavior to conform to our "clothes," and become sensitive to anything that will soil His image in our lives. We will develop our love for everyone, since that is the chief characteristic of Christ, and it fulfills all the law (v. 8).

The world may be dark and evil, however, we must dress in preparation for the day so others might see the garment of Christ's righteousness and His love in our lives.

Lord, we want to be prepared for the "daytime" scrutiny of Your presence, so by faith we put on the armor of light, and the clothing of Christ, in order to escape the darkness of our sinful nature. We seek the help of the Holy Spirit, in Jesus' name.

November 11

MANNA SERIES: REQUIRING A
WARDROBE TRANSFORMATION
DEMYSTIFYING AND DEFANGING DEATH

Reading Passage: 1Cor. 15:12-55
Main Text: 1Cor. 15:53-55 For the perishable must clothe itself with the imperishable, and the mortal with immortality. When the perishable has been clothed with the imperishable, and the mortal with immortality, then the saying that is written will come true: "Death has been swallowed up in victory." "Where, O death, is your victory? Where, O death, is your sting?" (NIV)

Death is the most fearsome enemy of humanity, and since creation we have lived under the tyranny of its power. One of the main causes of this fear is the mystery as to what happens after death. Does man cease to exist after death? Is there any hope of life after death? Can anyone know for sure what we should expect?

In 1Corinthians 15, Paul provides a perspective on death that helps to remove its mystery, and causes its power over us to be nullified. He indicates that there must be life after death, because if the Christian hope in Christ was only for this life, we should be more pitied than anyone else in the world (v. 19). The fact is that our physical bodies, which are perishable and subject to death, cannot enter the eternal state of existence where there is no more death (v. 50). In order to enter the new state, the old body has to die. As nature teaches us regarding seeds, what is sown does not come to life unless it dies (v. 36).

Once we understand that death is a necessary changing room to allow the Christian to transition from this mortal life to a more glorious future, we can have less fear of the process and a greater anticipation of the outcome. When a man enters the changing room at a clothing store, he has no intention of making this a permanent residence. Rather, he expects to exit the room to display the new clothes he tried on. With respect to the changing room of death, Paul states that what is sown is perishable, what is raised is imperishable; it is sown in dishonor, it is raised in glory; it is sown in weakness, it is raised in power; it is sown a natural body, it is raised a spiritual body (vv. 42-44). When we appreciate that what is perishable and will die, must be clothed with the imperishable, which cannot die; and the mortal must be clothed with immortality; we can celebrate the fact that death will be overwhelmed and destroyed by the victory of life. With this realization, the sting of death is removed.

But how can we be certain of this expectation? By our belief in the resurrection of Jesus Christ. He died, experiencing the changing room for all humanity, and came back from the dead in a glorious new body. As Christians, our faith is in His experience and His promise that if we are in Him by faith, we shall be resurrected like Him.

Father, this is exciting news for all of us who used to live under the fear of death because of its mystery. We thank You for Jesus and the hope we have because of His resurrection. With the expectation of resurrection, we can now live free from the fear of death. Thank You Lord.

November 12

MANNA SERIES: REQUIRING A WARDROBE TRANSFORMATION
DRESS FOR SUCCESS

Reading Passage: Eph. 4:17-32
Main Text: Eph. 4:22-24 You were taught, with regard to your former way of life, to put off your old self, which is being corrupted by its deceitful desires; to be made new in the attitude of your minds; and to put on the new self, created to be like God in true righteousness and holiness. (NIV)

"Dress for success" has become a popular phrase, included in advice given to young people who are preparing for interviews to enter the job market. This has led to the establishment of an international, not-for-profit organization that provides professional attire, a network of support, and career development tools to low income women to help them thrive in work and life. By dressing for success, we are communicating the impression that we know what success should look like, and we are identifying with that success. Sometimes this requires that we overhaul our closet, throwing out old clothes that no longer match our new identity, and stocking up on new clothes to present a fresh image.

This wardrobe transformation must have been what the Apostle Paul had in mind when he wrote to the churches he established in the Gentile territories. Unlike people of a Jewish culture, these believers came from a Gentile culture where sensuality and indecency were the norm. In fact, some of the religious ceremonies in that culture involved sexual acts with temple prostitutes, both male and female. Paul admonished the Ephesian believers, and by extension all Christ followers, that becoming Christians required putting off their old corrupt practices, and dressing in a new lifestyle, which begins with a new attitude that comes from God. This new attitude will be demonstrated by speaking truth, instead of falsehood, being angry without sinning, and working for our sustenance instead of stealing (vv. 25-28). Finally, we must be kind and compassionate, forgiving one another just as Christ has forgiven us (v. 32).

In Colossians 3:5-14, Paul gave a similar exhortation to the church at Colosse. He concluded the admonition by indicating that above all, they should put on love as this binds all the virtues together (Col. 3:14 NIV). By using the analogy of clothing, Paul emphasized that the demonstration of Christian virtues was not automatic with conversion. Rather, it requires deliberate effort involving putting aside certain attitudes and actions to which we were accustomed (our old life), and making the effort to practice new behavior that is consistent with the Christ-life. We must dress to show our new identity and direction. We must also remember that our "appearance" creates an impression on those who need to see a demonstration of what Christianity should be.

Can Christ depend on you to provide this demonstration?

Lord, we recognize that in saving our souls You require that we live to demonstrate a lifestyle that represents Your life in us. Help us as we seek to put off behavior that comes from our "old life" and adjust to the new life that Christ brings to us.

MANNA SERIES: REQUIRING A WARDROBE TRANSFORMATION
WHEN GOD DISLIKES OUR OUTFIT

Reading Passage: 1Pet. 5:5-11
Main Text: 1Pet. 5:5-6. Young men, in the same way be submissive to those who are older. All of you, clothe yourselves with humility toward one another, because, "God opposes the proud but gives grace to the humble." Humble yourselves, therefore, under God's mighty hand, that he may lift you up in due time (NIV)

We desire to have the presence of the Lord continuously with us as we journey through life. Yet we know that there are certain things that interrupt our fellowship with Him, such as unrepented sins or an unforgiving spirit. But since we value His companionship, we usually seek to correct these disruptions quickly, so our fellowship might be restored.

However, there is an attitude that can easily and subtly infiltrate our lives, which God finds repulsive, and which will cause Him to resist fellowship with us. It is the attitude of pride, which causes us to think of ourselves more than we ought, and to look down on others. Pride replaces God in our lives, because it attributes our accomplishments and successes to our innate abilities, and self-effort. We fail to recognize that God provides us with breath to live, gives us the ability to perform, and places us in the ideal circumstances where we can make an impact and achieve success. Therefore, we seek glory for ourselves, instead of giving praise to God.

Pride manifests itself even in our religious activities when we begin to view our spiritual lives as superior achievements when compared with others. We smugly compare our efforts at prayer and fasting, our performance at ministry in preaching, healing and giving, or our ability to keep religious laws. Knowing our tendency for these practices, the Apostle Peter exhorts us to clothe ourselves in humility, so we will ensure that our outward display will always be free from the odor of pride. We sometimes fear that to appear humble will result in people overlooking our achievements, or demeaning and abusing us. Peter tells us that while God opposes the proud, He provides grace to the humble. His grace will allow us to endure the abuse of others until He is ready to exalt us.

In our world of self-promotion and celebrity worship, it is never easy to swallow our pride and trust God for recognition. But when we make the effort to clothe ourselves in humility, we can be assured of His presence and grace, and He will obtain glory through our lives. Jesus provided the perfect example of humbling Himself to death on the cross; therefore God exalted Him by giving Him the most exalted name (Phil. 2:5-11). Also, remember the words of Psalm 138:6 NIV, "Though the LORD is on high, He looks upon the lowly, but the proud He knows from afar."

Lord, Your word has again challenged us to deal with the pride of our hearts, and to make a life of humility our priority. We desire that You will always walk with us and get glory from our lives. We ask this, in the name of our exalted Savior Jesus Christ.

November 14

MANNA SERIES: REQUIRING A WARDROBE TRANSFORMATION
THE CLOTHING OF THE TRIUMPHANT SAINTS

Reading Passage: Rev. 7:9-17
Main Text: Rev. 7:13-14. Then one of the elders asked me, "These in white robes—who are they, and where did they come from?" I answered, "Sir, you know." And he said, "These are they who have come out of the great tribulation; they have washed their robes and made them white in the blood of the Lamb." (NIV)

The Apostle John wrote the Book of Revelation in which he described his vision of various scenes in heaven as they unfolded in history, until the end of time. In chapter seven he described the scene before the throne of God where a great multitude was gathered, giving praise to God, who was seated on the throne, and to the Lamb. Before ascertaining the identity of the multitude, he highlighted their clothing. They were all dressed in white robes (vv. 9, 13).

The multitude consisted of people from every nation, tribes, peoples and languages, who had come out of the great tribulation. The great tribulation describes a time when there will be various calamities, widespread destruction and great loss of life, because of the activity of evil forces in the world. This will result in great suffering for those who are loyal to God. Very likely, the multitude represented the saints who had been martyred and were now in heaven. Their triumph over evil during the tribulation was symbolized by their white robes, which signified their purity.

How did these saints acquire the white robes? They were not given to them, but it appears that their robes of whatever color became white after they washed them. All robes were washed in the same substance; the blood of the Lamb, thus they all became white. Although this is symbolic language it presents a wonderful truth. Becoming a saint requires that we pass through the same process, regardless of our background of nationality, social status, or ethnicity. This is the same process that is required whether we were "vile sinners" such as murderers and rapists, or "good people" of high moral standards. The one criterion for the transformation of the robes of our souls is that we have washed them in the blood of the Lamb. His blood was shed to provide cleansing from all sin. We can be washed by acknowledging the fact that we are sinners and by accepting through faith the cleansing He has provided.

The result of the cleansing of our robes is the assurance that after our suffering on earth, we will be placed around His throne in heaven to serve Him night and day. In addition, the Lamb will forever be our shepherd, so we will never hunger or thirst again, and He will wipe away our tears bringing an end to our sorrows (vv. 16-17).

Lord, we thank You for the provision made for our cleansing through the blood of Jesus. By faith we wash our souls so that our robes will become white and we will be qualified to stand around Your throne in triumph forever. Amen.

November 15

MANNA SERIES: WELCOME TO THE WAR ZONE
WE HAVE A REAL ENEMY

Reading Passage: 1Pet. 5:1-14
Main Text: 1Pet. 5:8-9. Be self-controlled and alert. Your enemy the devil prowls around like a roaring lion looking for someone to devour. Resist him, standing firm in the faith, because you know that your brothers throughout the world are undergoing the same kind of sufferings. (NIV)

The herd of gazelles seemed so contented as they fed on the grass of the savannah. This peaceful scene from the Nature Show was abruptly interrupted when a lion suddenly leaped out of the nearby bush and began chasing the herd. He swiftly caught a young gazelle that was lagging behind, and overpowered her. She became his afternoon meal. As cruel as this may appear, this is life in the jungle. Danger is never far away, and animals like the gazelle know they have to live with predators.

We accept this reality of life in the jungle, but have difficulty accepting that the Christian lives in a spiritual war zone where we have to confront a real enemy. In the spiritual realm, there is a constant war between the light of God and the power of darkness. The prince of darkness called Satan, the adversary, or the Devil, the slanderer, represents the power of darkness. When we gave our lives to Christ, God took us out from the domain of darkness ruled by the devil, and placed us in the kingdom of Jesus (Col. 1:13). Consequently, we became an enemy of the devil.

The Apostle Peter warns us that we are in the war zone where our enemy the devil, is always on the prowl like a lion that is seeking someone to devour. Sometimes he attacks us by slander, seeking to undermine what God wants to establish in our lives. At other times, as Satan, he opposes and hinders anything we attempt to do for the advancement of the kingdom of God. We have become a target for the devil because we represent Christ and His kingdom of light.

Since we have a real enemy, we cannot be indifferent or careless in our Christian lives, as we are always at risk for attack. Peter's advice is to be self-controlled and alert, expecting the attack and knowing how to defend ourselves. We defend ourselves by resisting the devil with our faith in Christ. His attacks are usually attempts to get us to question the reality of Jesus as God in the flesh, with whom we can have a relationship, or to doubt our experience of salvation and the truth of His promises in scripture. When we stand strong in our faith, the devil will flee (Jam. 4:7). Any weakness in our faith will result in his constant harassment.

Are you prepared for life in the war zone with an enemy waiting to attack? Be prepared to resist him today.

Lord, You have placed us in the war zone so please help us to fight against the enemy. We commit ourselves, not to be indifferent or careless, but to be strong in our faith in Christ.

November 16

MANNA SERIES: WELCOME TO THE WAR ZONE
JESUS' ENCOUNTER WITH THE DEVIL

Reading Passage: Matt. 4:1-11
Main Text: Matt. 4:1-4 Then Jesus was led by the Spirit into the desert to be tempted by the devil. After fasting forty days and forty nights, he was hungry. The tempter came to him and said, "If you are the Son of God, tell these stones to become bread." Jesus answered, "It is written: 'Man does not live on bread alone, but on every word that comes from the mouth of God.'" (NIV)

The Bible does not provide any information on the life of Jesus between the age of twelve when He accompanied His parents to the Passover feast in Jerusalem, and when He was around thirty and appeared at the Jordan to be baptized. His baptism marked the beginning of His public ministry. But before embarking on His ministry, the Spirit led Him into the wilderness for an encounter with the devil. This incident points to the fact that no follower of Christ will be exempt from battles with the enemy. However, it helps us to learn the strategy employed by the devil against us, and our most effective defense against his attacks.

The devil's attack on Jesus provides some interesting contrasts with his attack against the first Adam. The first man Adam, as the son of God, was placed in a garden where everything was provided for his comfort and sustenance. The devil appeared and tempted him to question and then disobey the Word of God (Gen. 3:1-5). After Adam succumbed to the devil, God decreed that one day the offspring of the woman would crush the head of the offspring of the satanic forces (Gen. 3:15). Jesus came as the "new" Adam, the seed of the woman and the second man from heaven (1Cor. 15:47).

The devil, knowing that the Son of God would be coming to destroy his activity on earth, (1John 3:8), tried to prevent His appearance by using Herod in an attempt to kill Him as a baby. Now that Jesus was ready for His ministry, He was led into a desert place, which had conditions representing the curse of the ground caused by Adam's sin (Gen. 3:18). The first Adam was tempted with the fruit of one tree, while he was in a setting with abundant supply of food; yet he failed. Jesus, the "second man", was hungry in a desert, and the devil began by tempting Him with food, and Jesus defeated him. The devil was triumphant over the first Adam when he misrepresented what God said. When he tried this tactic with the "second man", Jesus applied His knowledge of the word of God and responded, stating "It is written …" (vv. 4, 7, 10).

We know that the devil will try to tempt us by distorting what God desires for us, and we know we can defeat him as Jesus did, by applying the word of God. As followers of Jesus, the encounter with the enemy is inevitable, but we have the weapons to defeat him.

Lord, we thank You for the victory of Jesus over the devil that assures us of our own victory. With His Spirit in us, and the weapon of the Word of God, we know we will be triumphant over our enemy, in the name of Jesus.

November 17

MANNA SERIES: WELCOME TO THE WAR ZONE
PREPARATION FOR THE BATTLE

Reading Passage: Eph. 6:10-14
Main Text: Eph. 6:11-12 Put on the full armor of God so that you can take your stand against the devil's schemes. For our struggle is not against flesh and blood, but against the rulers, against the authorities, against the

powers of this dark world and against the spiritual forces of evil in the heavenly realms. (NIV)

To prepare for battle effectively, we must have good knowledge of our enemy and his strategies. We must also ensure we have acquired the resources to wage a successful war against him. Without knowledge of the enemy, we may underestimate his power or fall into the trap of focusing our efforts on the wrong adversary. We also need to have a clear objective for the battle, otherwise we will be unsure whether we are succeeding or losing in our efforts.

All these elements were included in Paul's exhortation on our preparation for battle against the devil as stated in Ephesians 6. He explained that we are not fighting against flesh and blood, but against spiritual forces. This does not mean that our enemy may not come in the form of human agents; in fact, attacks in the form of accusations, criticisms and persecutions, are made by humans. But we need to look beyond the persons, who are sometimes our fellow believers, and discern the spirit that is directing them in their actions. When we expend our energy seeking to retaliate or be defensive against humans, we are wasting our resources on the wrong enemy. When we focus on the devilish spirit that motivated the action, we are able to use our weapons effectively. This will allow us to forgive and be sympathetic to the human vessel who was thus exploited. In fact, we may be able to get the human agent to join forces with us in the fight against the evil spirit.

Paul described the spiritual forces as comprising a demonic ruling class of principalities and powers. By ourselves we are no match for this assault force of evil powers. This explains the apostle's urging that we put on the complete armor of God, as this is the only effective defense against the devil's powers. Our human weapons are useless, but with the armor of God, our weapons have divine power to demolish strongholds (2Cor. 10:4). It is important that we put on the full armor of God as listed in vv. 14-18, so the devil will not find any vulnerable spots where we are not protected by God. He is ready to exploit any weaknesses we have.

The objective of our battle is to be able to stand firm against the schemes - the methodical strategies - of the devil (v. 11) and withstand his assault when he brings his full force of evil against us (v. 13). The devil seeks to get us to move from our confidence in God and our belief that Jesus will ultimately, permanently destroy him. As we prepare for battle, let us remain strong in the Lord and in His mighty power so that we will be able to withstand any assault.

Lord, we desire to stand in the victory of Jesus. Therefore, we put on the full armor that He provides as we prepare for the assault by the devil in the evil day. We will not be afraid, but remain confident in the Lord.

November 18

MANNA SERIES: WELCOME TO THE WAR ZONE
DEFENSIVE ARMOR OF TRUTH AND RIGHTEOUSNESS

Reading Passage: Eph. 6:10-18
Main Text: Eph. 6:14 Stand firm then, with the belt of truth buckled around your waist, with the breastplate of righteousness in place, (NIV)

Paul exhorts us to put on the whole armor of God, not for destroying the enemy, but for defending ourselves from the enemy's assault, especially in the "evil day" when he intensifies his attack. The exhortation was followed by the command to stand firm with specific articles of spiritual armor, which corresponded to the armor of a Roman soldier in a defensive stance.

The first two articles, the belt or girdle, and the breastplate, were essential for protection in a battle. The belt of a soldier served two main purposes: (i) to allow him to bind his loose clothing together so that he could move freely without tripping, and (ii) to provide a place to carry weapons like his sword. After buckling his belt around his waist, the soldier would have mobility to avoid the attack, and would be able to defend himself with the weapons in his belt.

Paul stated that the Christian facing a battle with the devil should buckle his belt of truth around his waist. Truth in this context is not just the knowledge of truth, but also the application of truth in a life that makes a person truthful, faithful or sincere in character. We make a confession of certain truths such as the power of Christ to transform us into a new creation with a new lifestyle that has replaced our old one.

If we don't really believe what we declare or fail to live consistent with this confession, we will be easy targets for the devil. He will reveal our inconsistencies and because our belts of truth were not buckled, the enemy will easily trip us, and we will have no weapons to fight back. We must have the belt of truthful living to defend ourselves against this assault.

The breastplate is the most visible article of a soldier's armor. It protects his delicate chest area from the enemy's weapons. The Christian's breastplate is righteousness, or righteous living. What we do is very visible to the world and the devil. When we are involved in any unrighteous behavior, such as cheating time or goods on our jobs, making false declarations for our taxes, cursing out people when provoked, or practicing immoral sexual acts, there will be obvious gaps in our breastplate. The enemy will exploit these gaps and attack us, ridiculing our claims of conversion, and challenging our declarations of faith in God.

Without truthful behavior and a righteous display, the devil will question whether we are any different from others who have no claims of faith. This will lead us to doubt our claims of Christianity, which can result in our defeat. To avoid defeat let us stand firm with our belt and our breastplate firmly in place.

Lord, we don't want to be vulnerable to the devil's attack on our claims of being Christian believers. Guide us to the discipline of properly arming ourselves with truthful and righteous living so we will be prepared for the enemy's attacks. We make this request in the Name of our Great Savior.

November 19

MANNA SERIES: WELCOME TO THE WAR ZONE
PROPER FOOTWEAR FOR THE BATTLE

Reading Passage: Eph. 6:10-18
Main Text: Eph. 6:15 ...and with your feet fitted with the readiness that comes from the gospel of peace. (NIV)

Proper footwear was very important for a Roman soldier. This was needed for protection from injury and for ease of mobility. Without protection the soldier could be injured by stepping on sharp nails. Regardless of the ability of the soldier or the number of weapons available to him, if his feet were injured he would be unable to respond to any attack. When under attack, the soldier must be able to move quickly to evade missiles or to run away. He must have the type of footwear that enables quick movement.

Paul stated that the Christian warrior must stand firm with shoes that were ready to respond to the battles that might arise because of the gospel of peace. There is the paradoxical indication that the gospel of peace may be the cause of a battle. Jesus the Prince of Peace came to earth announcing Himself as the way by which people could have peace with God, from whom we have been alienated by sin (Rom. 5:1). He also preached peace between the Jews and Gentiles, and between all groups that were hostile to each other. This was accomplished by His death, which destroyed the basis of enmity between people (Eph. 2:14-17). The devil hates God's plan of peace and does everything to create hostility.

In response to the devil's attacks, we must be quick to counter with the message of peace to thwart his efforts. With shoes that are fitted with readiness, we will move swiftly with great verbal agility to interrupt disputes, smooth over hurt feelings, and reconcile warring parties. The prophet Isaiah exclaimed, "How beautiful upon the mountains are the feet of him who brings good tidings, who publishes peace.." (Isa. 52:7). When we can be known as people who stand for peace, we have beautiful feet. This is in contrast to those who have feet that are "swift to shed blood" (Rom. 3:15), meaning that they run quickly to situations intending to cause harm, or those who are quick to stir up strife and to spread gossip.

How would people describe the readiness of our feet? The reputation we gain for responding to situations will indicate whether we are standing firm against the devil or whether we are agents who assist the devil.

Lord, we desire to be known as peacemakers, who respond quickly to bring calm and be the bridge over troubled waters. We expect to be opposed in our mission of peace so please help us to stand firm against the devil.

MANNA SERIES: WELCOME TO THE WAR ZONE
THE ADVANTAGE OF THE SHIELD

Reading Passage: Eph. 6:10-18
Main Text: Eph. 6:16 In addition to all this, take up the shield of faith, with which you can extinguish all the flaming arrows of the evil one. (NIV)

There was a time when a fight between ancient warriors involved hand-to-hand combat. Later, combatants discovered they could effectively fight their enemies by firing arrows at them and reduce the risk of personal injury. They further realized that they could intensify the damage on their foes if they dipped the arrow in an inflammable substance and set it ablaze before launching it. This would create a fire that could destroy the enemies and their surroundings. To respond to this threat, fighters carried shields that could be used to intercept incoming arrows. The leather portion of the shield would be soaked in water so that blazing arrows could be extinguished on contact.

After listing various items of armor the Christian needed to put on in order to stand firm against attacks by the devil, Paul stated that in addition to these, and in all circumstances, we must take up the shield of faith. Faith will intercept all the fiery arrows of the enemy and keep the enemy at a distance. There is no type of weapon and no method of attack the devil might use that cannot be successfully defeated by our faith in God. Our faith brings God to our defense, and reminds the devil of his previous defeat by Jesus on the cross. By the exercise of our faith, we are declaring our inability to defend ourselves, but we are fully trusting the Lord's resources for our deliverance: "the battle is not ours but the Lord's."

It would be foolish for us to enter the battle without our shield, as the enemy is prepared to destroy us with fiery arrows. We can never depend on our strength of character, our membership in the church, our ability to keep God's laws or anything that has its source in human effort. Only our faith in God provides the victory that overcomes the world, the flesh and the devil.

Are you prepared to take up the protection provided by faith?

Whenever we are under attack by the devil, who may be questioning our salvation or our failure to be consistently holy, in response to the accusation, we should declare to the devil that we are the workmanship of the Lord (Eph. 2:10), and we trust Him to complete what He started in our lives. The Lord is faithful to defend us.

Lord, we are blessed to have the provision of the shield of faith as our defense against the attacks of the devil. We will not be afraid of His arrows since our trust is in You. Thank You Jesus.

November 21

MANNA SERIES: WELCOME TO THE WAR ZONE
COMBINING THE DEFENSIVE WITH THE OFFENSIVE

Reading Passage: Eph. 6:10-18
Main Text: Eph. 6:17 Take the helmet of salvation and the sword of the Spirit, which is the word of God. (NIV)

The final two items listed by Paul, which must be taken by the Christian into the battle are a helmet and a sword. We notice that the helmet is for protection, while the sword is for attack; in fact the latter is the first offensive item listed by Paul.

The purpose of a helmet is to protect the most vulnerable part of the body, that is the head. When we suffer head injuries, we are immediately incapacitated, not being able to think properly. In any battle an enemy would make great effort to land a blow to our heads as soon as possible, since this would make it easy to defeat us. To stand against this deadly attack, we need to have the protection of the helmet of salvation. Why salvation? Salvation is deliverance and refers both to our experience and our expectation. It is one of the major themes of the Old Testament: God is our salvation. Whether the people of Israel or David the King, they can all recall the time when God intervened in their lives to rescue them from oppressive circumstances and a powerful enemy.

When Christ entered our lives by faith, we experienced salvation, deliverance from sin and Satan. The plan of attack from the devil is to get to our minds and try to convince us that we have not been delivered, and are still under his bondage. To defend ourselves from this attack we must be sure of our salvation, and convinced that nothing the devil does can reverse that fact. When our failures or our feelings cause us to think we are no longer saved, we must ensure that our minds are properly protected, and remind the devil about the finished work of Christ on the cross. In addition to our experience of salvation, we also have the expectation that in the future our salvation will be fully realized, and this is guaranteed by God Himself.

There are times when the best defense is our offense. For that purpose, we are provided with the sword, sharpened and empowered by the Spirit of God. This sword is the Word of God. When Jesus battled the devil, this was the weapon He used to defeat him. We can use the same weapon and remind the devil that he was cast out of heaven, he was defeated on the cross, and his future doom is certain. Jesus is Lord and even the devil must bow to Him.

Paul commanded us to take these items for our armor, which indicates that they are provided for the taking. We note that both items represent the use of the word of God. If we don't know and apply the word, we will be facing the devil without our helmet and our sword.

Lord, we don't want to be negligent and enter the war zone without our helmet of salvation and the sword of the word of God. We want to be prepared for the devil's attacks with the combination of our defensive and offensive armor.

November 22

MANNA SERIES: WELCOME TO THE WAR ZONE
PRAYER IS ESSENTIAL FOR THE BATTLE

Reading Passage: Eph. 6:10-18
Main Text: Eph. 6:18. And pray in the Spirit on all occasions with all kinds of prayers and requests. With this in mind, be alert and always keep on praying for all the saints. (NIV)

An effective war strategy involves one party seeking to disrupt the communication of his opponent, so the troops fighting on the field will not be in touch with their commanders in headquarters. Very early in a battle, the military will destroy the radio transmission towers and radio stations of the opponent, or discreetly intercept communication so they can know their plans. When field troops cannot know or trust the plans of their commanders, they will make wrong moves and be easily defeated in battle.

After describing all the armor required to successfully stand firm against the enemy's attacks, Paul explains how essential prayer is for our battle strategy. Basically, prayer is our means of communicating with God, "our headquarters," to obtain information and direction in our fight against the devil. By this we understand that prayer is more than making our requests to God. It also involves listening to what He has to say about the devil's attacks and his strategies against us.

Paul mentions the following elements in this type of prayer:

1. Prayer must be continuous. His use of the Greek present participle indicates that prayer must be made continuously and for everything, "in all occasions." No time or situation should be excluded from our prayers.
2. Prayer must be directed by the Spirit. We must pray in the Spirit, sensitive to the directives we receive from Him in our prayers.
3. Prayer must be intense. Our prayers should be made with all variety of prayers and supplications. This indicates thoroughness and deep passion in prayer.
4. We must persevere in prayer. He stated that we must keep alert and keep on praying. When we don't receive prompt responses we will be tempted to become less intense or even give up praying. Hence he urged us not to lose our vigilance and not to cease praying.
5. Our prayers should include all believers. We have fellow believers involved in fierce battles against the devil. Some of them could be at the point of giving up, which will cause the devil to gain an advantage over them. But our prayers on their behalf can provide them with strong assistance. We must support each other in prayer so we can be a united force in the battle against our common enemy.

Our enemy, the devil knows how important prayer is in fighting against him so he will do everything to lull us into a state of complacency and a lack of diligence. Once he succeeds in getting us into a state of prayerlessness, he is sure of our defeat in the battle.

With all our armor in readiness against the devil, we must ensure we keep praying and following the instructions from headquarters.

Jesus, we are reminded of Your admonition to Your disciples that they should always pray and not give up (Lk. 18:1). Just as You were always in communication with the Heavenly Father, especially at the time of intense attack from the devil, we want to be prepared in prayer for him. Help us to stand firm in prayer, we ask in Your name, Amen.

November 23

MANNA SERIES: WELCOME TO THE WAR ZONE
DEALING WITH SATAN'S DECEIT

Reading Passage: 2Cor. 2:5-11
Main Text: 2Cor. 2:10-11 If you forgive anyone, I also forgive him. And what I have forgiven—if there was anything to forgive—I have forgiven in the sight of Christ for your sake, in order that Satan might not outwit us. For we are not unaware of his schemes.
2Cor. 11:14 And no wonder, for Satan himself masquerades as an angel of light. (NIV)

The strategies of war involve more than the movement of troops and the use of weapons. Deception and disguise are very important means of tricking the opponent into not knowing when you are planning to attack and the location of the attack. To achieve this objective, military planners have used spies to penetrate enemy ranks to obtain information, or they have employed the tactic of misinformation and propaganda to cause the enemy to focus on the wrong timing or point of attack.

Satan is not just our adversary; he is also the devil, the master deceiver. Our attitudes toward fellow believers often create the setting that the devil can easily exploit, and use to launch an attack against us. Whenever there are disagreements among believers, Satan will use such occasions to foster mistrust that sometimes become major fights. In such situations, the only victor is Satan, as disunity in the body of Christ is manifested and the cause of Christ is discredited.

A brother in the church at Corinth was involved in a public act of immorality. Paul wrote to the church demanding action against him. After he had been punished for a while, Paul wrote to the church asking them to end the brother's punishment, then forgive and restore him to the fellowship. He did not want the punishment to be excessive since this could lead to bitterness. Satan would exploit this situation to mar the testimony of the church. Paul explained that we cannot act as if we are unaware of Satan's schemes against us. Whatever actions we take in our fellowship, we must always be sure we are not creating an opening that Satan can exploit.

In order to lull us into a false sense of security, Satan sometimes uses disguises, which make it difficult to identify his activity. One of the problems that Paul encountered with the Corinthian church was that there were several individuals going around claiming to be apostles, claiming to be miracle workers, yet their objective was personal financial gain. Paul warned the church to be careful and not be deceived, because even Satan sometimes comes in disguise as an angel of light.

To deal with Satan's deception and disguises, we must be alert, prayerful and discerning so we don't get fooled. Let us focus on love for the believers and love for the word of God.

Lord, we realize how difficult it is to fight the enemy because of his various methods of attack. We thank You for Paul's instructions as to what we need to look for to avoid being deceived. Help us to be alert to the tricks and schemes of the enemy.

November 24

MANNA SERIES: WELCOME TO THE WAR ZONE
ULTIMATE VICTORY IS ASSURED

Reading Passage: Rev. 20:1-15
Main Text: Rev. 20:2. He seized the dragon, that ancient serpent, who is the devil, or Satan, and bound him for a thousand years.

Rev. 20:10 And the devil, who deceived them, was thrown into the lake of burning sulfur, where the beast and the false prophet had been thrown. They will be tormented day and night for ever and ever. (NIV)

How does knowledge of the outcome affect one's performance in a matter? Consider a student who has been informed that the results of the exam she is taking were predetermined, so she is guaranteed to receive the top prize. Or, the case of a country entering a war and receiving reports from its intelligence unit that their enemy does not stand a chance of winning against them. The student should have no fear of the challenge presented by the exam or by competing students because of what she already knows. Similarly, the country should enter the war with confidence that victory is assured. On the contrary, in both scenarios, they could doubt the information they received and revert to relying on their own abilities and living with the possibility of failure.

The Bible provides us with the account of the origin of our battle against the devil in the book of Genesis. It also provides the preview of the end of the battle in the book of Revelation. Although Satan may appear fearsome and his attacks powerful, we know that in the end he will be defeated, and thrown in a lake of fire where he will be tormented forever. With this knowledge of the outcome, we should face every battle with the devil, confident of the victory that will be ours at the end. But in fact, we are not usually confident because we sometimes doubt the information we have received in the word of God. These doubts arise because we listen to those who question the common sense interpretation of the book of Revelation, or we find that our experience in the battle does not correspond with the script of the outcome.

The devil has a vested interest in having us doubt the word of God concerning himself and his end, as he knows this will cause us to live in fear of him. Our challenge is not our ability to put up a good fight; rather it is to believe what God says concerning the devil. No matter how difficult the fight may be, and how formidable the strength of the attack of the enemy, we must not lose the confidence that in the end we will win and he will be defeated. The reason he fights us with such fury is that he knows his time is short (Rev. 12:12).

Let us face the devil, confident of victory in God who always leads us in a triumphal procession in Christ (2Cor. 2:14).

Lord, we thank You for the assurance of victory against the devil because this has already been secured by Jesus Christ. We will not fight in fear but in confidence that our enemy is fully aware that he will not be victorious over us.

November 25

MANNA SERIES: GLEANINGS FROM THE PSALMS II
THANKFUL FOR PETITIONS DENIED

Reading Passage: Psalm 106:1-15
Main Text: Psa. 106:15. So he gave them what they asked for,
But sent a wasting disease upon them. (NIV)

We pray expecting that God would answer our prayers by giving us the things for which we petitioned. But we know from experience that a number of our petitions seem to be denied, and this causes us to question whether God is concerned about some of our desires, or we question the value of prayer. Perhaps it was our request for the individual we wanted to marry, a financial investment we wanted to make, or a job we wanted to get. In retrospect, we now appreciate that if He granted our requests, our lives might have been a disaster.

The Psalmist, in reviewing Israel's history, included the time in the wilderness when the people began to crave meat because they were tired of manna. Although they were well fed and healthy with the manna, they accused God of depriving them of the meat and vegetables they enjoyed in Egypt. Their rebellion was so strong that God decided to give them what they asked for. He supplied it in such abundance that they immediately suffered the negative consequence of their request. The meat came with a wasting disease, and many died. The Israelites regretted making this request, and were sorry God answered positively.

From this incident we learn that many of our requests, which appear noble and pure, arise from our selfish and unwise desires, and not from God's plan for our lives. The challenge is to know when our desires are contrary to God's will for us. James 4:3 explains that our petitions are contrary to God's desires when our motive is for something that will only fulfill our pleasure. Jesus taught us to pray to the Father in His name, which means our prayers should be in accordance with His character, ones that He Himself would make to the Father. The Psalmist stated that the reason the Israelites had this sinful craving for meat was "they did not wait for his (God's) counsel" (106:13 NIV). We learn the counsel of God by studying and meditating on His word, and seeking His guidance. Of course, we may not find instruction in scripture for everything we need to pray about, but we can trust His Spirit to guide us (Rom 8:26-27).

Our prayers should always be made subject to His will for our lives. When our petitions are not granted, we can be confident there will come a time when, on reflection, we will be thankful that the request was denied.

Father, we are in need of Your help even for the purpose of praying. We thank You for Your mercy in denying us the things that are contrary to Your will for us. We will continue to trust Your plans for our lives.

November 26

MANNA SERIES: GLEANINGS FROM THE PSALMS II
NOT THE DELIVERANCE WE EXPECTED, BUT …

Reading Passage: Psalm 106:34-46
Main Text: Psa. 106:44-46 But he took note of their distress
When he heard their cry;
For their sake he remembered his covenant
And out of his great love he relented.
He caused them to be pitied
By all who held them captive. (NIV)

They cried, He heard, He acted, but it was not the deliverance they expected. Similarly, we find ourselves in captivity, in an unpleasant relationship, a business deal that has gone bad, or a job that has become intolerable. Seeing no way out, we beg God for deliverance. Our idea of deliverance is, the partner in the relationship is moved out of the way, our bad business deal is reversed, or we find a new job. Our prayers usually are accompanied with our prescriptions for the best solutions, and we are surprised that God has solutions that differ from ours.

Israel's captivity was the result of God's judgment for their idolatry and rebellion. He also intended that captivity would provide the Israelites with lessons about their unfaithfulness and God's mercy. When they cried to Him, instead of providing immediate deliverance for people who had not learned their lesson, God caused them to remain in captivity but to be pitied by their captors. Then they learned the lesson that God's power was demonstrated by causing their captors to grant them favor that they did not deserve. He did not deliver them from the captivity, but gave them victory in the midst of captivity. This follows the pattern of deliverance God gave to Joseph while in captivity in Potiphar's house and in prison. He eventually became the prime minister in the land of his captivity.

What do we prefer, our prescription or God's plan? There is nothing so rewarding as God's favor when He makes the "enemy" to have pity on us and gives us favor. When this happens we will have no doubt that we have seen the hand of God, changing a partner's or boss' bad attitude into a favorable disposition towards us.

We need to learn to trust God and patiently wait until He makes "our enemies become our footstool."

Father, we admit that our prayer is that we avoid adverse circumstances. Yet to be removed from our "captors" may not always be the solution to give You the greatest glory. Our struggle is to be able to believe that Your glory will also be for our good. Grant us the faith to trust both Your character and Your methods.

November 27

MANNA SERIES: GLEANINGS FROM THE PSALMS II
WHY DO WE DELAY CALLING FOR HELP?

Reading Passage: Psalm 107:1-9
Main Text: Psa. 107:6 Then they cried out to the LORD in their trouble,
> And he delivered them from their distress.
> He led them by a straight way
> To a city where they could settle. (NIV)

It is said that male drivers will spend many hours trying to convince themselves that they know where they are going before seeking help with directions. This refusal to admit being lost and seeking help is attributed to the male ego that wants to always appear to be in control. The source of this attitude is pride, which also causes humans to seek to be independent of God. This was the basis of the temptation that led to the sin of the first humans: "You will be like God knowing good and evil" (Gen 3:5 NIV). Once we can be independent of God, we are only accountable to ourselves, and there is no need to worship.

The reality is that we don't know the path to a life of peace and prosperity where we can feel settled. Some of us find ourselves like the Israelites in this psalm, wandering in desert wastelands finding no city where they could settle (v. 4). In our wasteful search, we try following the traditional path of a middle-class life, with a good education, a secure job with a steady income and a home. But after a while we still feel restless, as if something is missing; we are unfulfilled and the search continues. Others try the more adventurous side of life, exploring travel, encountering new people, places, and experiences. It is great for a while, but with time, the excitement diminishes. As they get older they are brought back to the reality that they did not find settlement. Hungry and thirsty, despite having money and friends, the soul is exhausted (v. 5). It is at this point we admit we are in distress and cry to the Lord.

Why do we wait so long before calling to God? Our pride will not allow us to admit we don't know the path to a fulfilling life. In our futile search for our own solution, we are brought to a crisis before we cry to God. In fatherly mercy He watches over us while we flounder, just waiting for our cry. Then He responds. He leads us by a straight or level path to the place that we are searching for, a city where our souls can settle and be fulfilled. It may be a place of ministry or service we tried to avoid, because it has no glamour or glitz, but which offers meaning and purpose. Until we can humbly admit our dependence on God, we will not call. Why are you delaying?

Lord, we admit our dependence on You, and cry to You for direction for our lives. Save us from wasted time and futile effort, pursuing paths that will never bring us satisfaction and peace.

MANNA SERIES: GLEANINGS FROM THE PSALMS II
HE INTERVENES TO INVERT OUR STATUS

Reading Passage: Psalm 113
Main Text: Psa. 113:7 He raises the poor from the dust
And lifts the needy from the ash heap;
Psa. 113:8 he seats them with princes,
With the princes of their people.
Psa. 113:9 He settles the barren woman in her home
As a happy mother of children.
Praise the LORD (NIV)

Many religions worship a god who is so transcendent and isolated, that he is useless to his subjects in their daily challenges of life. In contrast, the God of the Bible is portrayed as supreme ruler of the universe, but He is also intimately involved in the lives of humanity. This causes us to worship Him for His greatness in creation, and also His greatness in our personal experiences. In Psalm 113, the author praised God who is exalted over all the nations and enthroned on high. He also praises Him for stooping from His lofty position to observe and intervene in the affairs of the earth.

He observes that there are people in the earth who are disadvantaged and discriminated against because of injustice by the powerful, or the unfortunate circumstances of their birth. He identifies the former as the poor, and the latter as the barren woman. When God stoops to intervene, he raises the poor from their helpless state of poverty and elevates them to the status and privileges of a prince. He transforms the biological state of the barren woman who suffers ridicule, and enables her to become the mother of children in her own household. His intervention results in the inversion of the lives of His people. Consequently, His people praise Him.

Not surprisingly, this psalm includes words repeated by two women of the Bible who experienced the divine intervention that inverts. Hannah was barren and ridiculed, but after God's intervention to make her the mother of Samuel, she sang a song that has similar lyrics to this psalm. In the New Testament, Mary, who was a poor, obscure girl, was chosen to become the mother of the Messiah. In her song, known as the Magnificat, she praised the Lord, who brings down rulers from their thrones and exalts those who are humble in heart (Luke 1:51-53).

This is the experience of everyone who has made Him their Lord. Our status as hopeless sinners is changed and we are made to sit in heavenly places with Christ. As we face life with its daily challenges, we can have hope that our great and powerful God will intervene on our behalf and raise us above the abuses, ridicule and injustices we suffer, so we will be able to praise His great name.

We thank You Father for deciding to stoop from Your elevated throne to intervene in the affairs of Your poor suffering children. I praise You for transforming my status through Jesus Christ.

November 29

MANNA SERIES: GLEANINGS FROM THE PSALMS II
IDENTIFIED WITH AN INVISIBLE, UNCONTROLLABLE GOD

Reading Passage: Psalm 115
Main Text: Psa. 115:2 Why do the nations say,
"Where is their God?"
Our God is in heaven;
He does whatever pleases him. (NIV)

A significant difference between the Israelites and the heathen nations was the nature of their gods. Heathen nations had gods who were usually associated with their various needs, such as agriculture or war. These gods had identifiable forms and were maintained in specific locations. In contrast, the people of Israel claim that they have only one God who is invisible and is superior to any other god. When Israel was in trouble arising from natural disaster or warfare, the question posed by observers was, "Where is their God?" This could have been a source of embarrassment to Israel, since they could not show anyone the physical form of their god or point to His location. The Psalmist responds to this comment of mockery by explaining the unique nature of Israel's God. He is invisible and lives in heaven, a place inaccessible to humans, and "does whatever pleases Him."

Because Christians recognize Israel's God as the only true God, this statement is very significant to us. Mankind has an instinctive desire to see God in finite terms, in order to be able to define Him. When God can be defined He can be controlled. Even sincere believers love to state what God is expected to do in every situation as if we are in control of God. According to the Psalmist, since God is superior to us and does whatever pleases Him, He has no obligation to please us. So although He didn't heal us when we demanded it, didn't restore our marriage when we requested it, or make our country prosperous when we declared it, remember He is the uncontrollable God.

The heathen are so intent on having a god they can control; they design him to suit their purposes. They oftentimes end up with an idol with human appearances but who is dumb, blind and deaf, under human control, but totally worthless. The Psalmist further explains that we become like any god we identify with (vv. 4-8). Idol worshippers become like their idols, worthless. Our invisible, uncontrollable God is identified not in physical terms but by His character of loyal love and faithfulness. As we worship Him we become more like Him.

When the circumstances of our lives cause people to wonder, "where is their God?" we do not have to be embarrassed or perplexed. Rather, we celebrate that our God is in control of us, and although we may not be able to explain Him, we can trust His love and faithfulness.

Father, we are happy that You are not a god made by us, but You are greater than we are and beyond our control. Yet because we can trust Your character, You are worthy to be praised. You are the Most High God, and there is none like You.

November 30

MANNA SERIES: GLEANINGS FROM THE PSALMS II
A GOD WHO IS UNIVERSALLY ATTRACTIVE

Reading Passage: Psalm 117
Main Text: Psa. 117:1-2 Praise the LORD, all you nations;

Extol him, all you peoples.
For great is his love toward us,
And the faithfulness of the LORD endures forever.
Praise the LORD. (NIV)

Do we have a concept of God that is so attractive that we can invite others, even non-believers, to praise and worship Him? Sometimes we picture only a God of wrath and judgment based on an incomplete reading of Scripture, or unbalanced reports of people's experiences.

We read of God's judgments against Israel, sending her into captivity, but we fail to consider how long the Lord tolerated her rebellion and idolatry before executing punishment. By Israel's own testimony after returning from captivity, they experienced the covenant love and faithfulness of God. He disciplined them not to destroy them but in order that they might be developed into faithful children of God. This was different from how heathen nations related to their gods, and it motivated Israel to advertise their God to these heathen. She invited them to "praise the Lord all you nations, and peoples." The reason they should praise Israel's God (Yahweh, or the Lord) was because His covenant love pursues His people, and the Lord is by His nature, faithful to His promises. Rather than being destined for only judgment and wrath, they are overtaken by His mercy and love.

Despite what others may say about our God, we should be able to testify that He is a God of love and faithfulness. When we perceive only a God who causes us to fear, or a God who is waiting for us to make mistakes so He can quickly respond with punishment, it is because we have failed to remember the goodness and mercies we have already received. Remember Psalm 103:10, He never punishes us as our sins deserve. When we think of how many people have a distorted view of our God, we should be anxious to correct them and advertise Him as universally attractive, because He is a God of love.

If we had any doubts about the extent of His love and mercy, we need to remember how God the Son laid aside His heavenly privileges of divinity so He could visit us in our sin and redeem us. This is such good news concerning the nature of our God, we need to go and tell the world about Him.

Let us become evangelists of our attractive God and invite the world to praise Him.

Father, having experienced the impact of your great love, we want to tell the world living under the fear of divine judgment that You are a God of love. Grant us the courage to be Your ambassadors in Jesus' name.

December 1

MANNA SERIES: GLEANINGS FROM THE PSALMS II
COUNTERACTING FEAR

Reading Passage: Psalm 118:1-16
Main Text: Psa. 118:6 The LORD is with me; I will not be afraid. What can man do to me? (NIV)

We usually become fearful when we feel threatened by people or situations over which we have no control in determining how they will affect our lives. What might be causing us to fear today? It could be the possibility of physical danger such as symptoms of a debilitating disease, or the insecurity of residing in a high crime location. It could be concerns about the future because of a new business venture, an unstable economy or even entering the institution of marriage. Sometimes our fear of people may be due to our inability to control the judgments they will make without having all the facts. Fear will imprison our minds; keep us from the enjoyment of life and from developing genuine relationships. Naturally, we all have a strong desire to be free from fear, to be loosed from people and situations that hold us captive.

The Psalmist found his deliverance in the Lord who is good and whose love endures forever. He is in control of every situation and rules over people. We can declare with the Psalmist that because the Lord is with us as our helper, we need not be afraid. People can do nothing to us without first having to contend with our loving Lord. Therefore, whatever happens must be allowed by the Lord, who is with us to help us to endure and even triumph over them.

How then do we counteract fear? We must trust the word of the Lord that He is with us. He keeps His promise to be our helper and nothing can separate us from His loving care. When we fail to trust, we will begin to fear. Although we desire that He removes situations and people from our lives so we can be free, He may choose not to change the situations so we can learn to trust Him in the situations. It is by trust that our relationship grows and He is glorified.

The Psalmist testified that enemies surrounded him "like bees" but God did not remove the enemies; instead He helped him to cut them off "in the name of the Lord," (vv. 10-12). The lesson he learned from these experiences was that it is better to trust in the Lord than to put confidence in men, even those in authority (vv. 8-9). There may be some situation that God is waiting to help us to defeat today, while we are fearfully seeking an escape. Allow God to be glorified through us.

Father, help us learn how much You desire that we become free by conquest and not just by escape. We want to trust You so that by Your help we will counteract our fear, in the precious and secure name of Jesus.

December 2

MANNA SERIES: GLEANINGS FROM THE PSALMS II
IT DEPENDS ON WHO REJECTED ME

Reading Passage: Psalm 118:17-29
Main Text: Psa. 118:22-24 The stone the builders rejected
Has become the capstone;
The LORD has done this,
And it is marvelous in our eyes.
This is the day the LORD has made;
Let us rejoice and be glad in it. (NIV)

It is difficult to deal with rejection. This normally leads to a questioning of our self- worth, which can result in lack of self-confidence. How can we stand confidently with self-assurance in the presence of the persons who rejected us, and others who were accepted instead of us? It all depends on who rejected us. When we have been rejected by a potential romantic partner who we later discover is of unsavory character, we celebrate rejection. If a school or a business firm rejects us, then we are later accepted by a more esteemed establishment, we can afford to celebrate rejection.

The Psalmist declared that the stone that the builders rejected became the capstone or the headstone of the building. He may have been referring to Israel's experience of being rejected by the nations, then later becoming the chief of the nations, moving from humiliation to honor. When Jesus quoted these verses in the parable of the landowner and tenants in Matt 21:42, it may have been a reference to the Gentiles who were originally excluded from divine promises, but who became the chief beneficiaries of God's blessings. He could also be referring to Himself as the Stone, rejected by Israel, but exalted by God to be the chief stone of the kingdom.

Regardless, the application to our lives is beautiful. Family, friends, institutions or fraternities may have rejected us, but that does not matter when we know we have been accepted by the King of Kings. He made us to become the chief stone. He delights in taking what others reject, then working with the skillfulness of His hands motivated by His grace, He fashions something that becomes the envy of those who previously rejected us. "The Lord has done this, and it is marvelous in our eyes."

Let us not worry over any rejection we may suffer in this life, since we know the Lord has accepted us, and what He accepts He perfects.

Father, with this knowledge, we will use every incident of rejection to remember Your acceptance of us. We will celebrate by declaring: "This is the day the Lord has made, we will rejoice and be glad in it." It is all because of Your grace.

December 3

MANNA SERIES: GLEANINGS FROM THE PSALMS II
AN AGONIZING CRY FROM OUR DEPRAVITY

Reading Passage: Psalm 119:1-8
Main Text: Psa. 119:4-5 You have laid down precepts
That are to be fully obeyed.
Oh, that my ways were steadfast
In obeying your decrees! (NIV)

Sometimes we surprise ourselves with our inner thoughts, some of which would be embarrassing if they were displayed on a billboard. Although we may have been nurtured in a Christian home, we know the values accepted by the society, and have avoided breaking the law, we have not been able to eliminate these errant thoughts from our minds. Someone steals our purse with our valuables, and we relish the thoughts of the punishment we would inflict if we caught the culprit. We hear the malicious statements made about us, and we begin to fantasize about the revenge we would take against the perpetrator if we could get away with it.

If we are honest, we must come to the conclusion that we are by nature. depraved creatures who are striving to live above the negative pull within us. We wish our minds could be so pure we didn't have to battle these negative thoughts. To increase our dilemma, God established laws and precepts so we might know the righteous standards we are expected to achieve, and He provided the measure that will be used to determine our sin. After failing in our efforts to keep his precepts, we cry with the Psalmist. "Oh that I was predisposed to keeping your instructions." Then there would be no battles, no striving against internal negative forces, no yielding to the devil, no falling into sin.

The blessedness of the new birth is that it not only begins with an awareness of the sin nature in our hearts, but it also provides us with another nature that is not subject to sin. We have the option of choosing how we will live, either with the old depraved nature or the new spiritual nature. Our struggle now is in making the choice of the life we will nurture and make predominant. Once we choose the spiritual life, we have the help of the Holy Spirit. This provides us with a heart disposed to God's righteous laws and we will have victory over the depravity of the natural life. This is the way we want to live so we will please the Lord. However, we must remember our old life is not completely dead and will seek to reassert itself; but if we treat it as if it is dead, it will lose its power over us.

Our agonizing cry of depravity can be transformed into a celebration of victory, "Thanks be to God through Jesus Christ our Lord" (Rom 7:25 NIV).

Thank You, Father, for providing an escape from our depraved nature, forgiveness for our sin, and the help of the Holy Spirit. Thank You for placing us in Christ so we can live to please You.

MANNA SERIES: GLEANINGS FROM THE PSALMS II
TREASURING A DETOUR-MINATION

Reading Passage: Psalm 119:9-16
Main Text: Psa. 119:11 I have hidden your word in my heart
That I might not sin against you. (NIV)

Sin is a path that we find enticing and easy to pursue because we are naturally disposed to it. Consequently, to avoid sin we have to fight against our natural impulses. Many times we are unsuccessful in the fight, and we are left with the question: How can we be consistently successful? This is the question posed by the Psalmist in 119:9, How can a young man keep himself pure? The use of the term "young man" in this context represents anyone facing temptation when he or she is in an environment that provides the images and opportunities to fulfill immoral desires. Usually the individual provides his own justification for the action. In these circumstances, purity appears impossible, especially when society regards some of the sinful behavior as acceptable. But if the individual follows the instruction of the Word of God, he can keep himself pure.

The Word of God provides instructions and triggers spiritual impulses that lead to detours from the path of sin. To avoid sin, we have to consider the Word of God as a treasure by valuing it highly, then holding it closely in our hearts. Thus the Word of God would be hidden in the place of our affections and decision-making. In addition to holding it closely, we have to follow it determinedly so that the instructions might become our reality. A tablet prescribed by our doctor will be useless to us until we consider it valuable to heal our condition. This causes us to move from keeping it in our cupboard to putting it in our mouths. Once ingested, the medication has the capability of treating the disease, which is attacking our bodies.

The value we place on the Word of God is evidenced by our practice of memorizing and applying Scripture. By submission to the Word, we will be able to follow its instruction whenever we are faced with temptation. Consequently, we will take the detour and not fall into the path of sin.

Lord, we admit we face a battle in trying to avoid sin. Although we know that Your Word will help us to avoid sin, through laziness and neglect we have failed to treasure and apply the instruction in Your Word. Grant us such a fear of sinning against You that we will begin to seriously treasure the detour from sin with a new determination. We seek the help of the Holy Spirit in this quest, in Jesus name, Amen.

December 5

MANNA SERIES: GLEANINGS FROM THE PSALMS II
I CAN'T STOP LOOKING UP

Reading Passage: Psalm 123
Main Text: Psa. 123:2 As the eyes of slaves look to the hand of their master,
As the eyes of a maid look to the hand of her mistress,
So our eyes look to the LORD our God,
Till he shows us his mercy. (NIV)

We usually look to God for help when we find ourselves with needs that cannot be met by anyone else.

We find it difficult admitting we cannot help ourselves. We know we should suffer penalties for our failures – making promises we failed to keep, speaking words of hatred instead of love, or being less than honest in our relationships. Not only do our hearts condemn us for our failures but there are always those around who will highlight our weaknesses and taunt us for our hypocrisy. We are in need of mercy, someone to say, "I know you blew it, but this will not be held against you." Who can provide this level of mercy to someone so full of self-condemnation?

Let us follow the prescription of the Psalmist and look up to the Lord. His throne is in heaven, unaffected by the jealous games people play on the earth. Only He can determine whether there should be judgment or mercy. By looking to Him, we acknowledge our humble position before Him and our dependence on Him, "like a slave to a master, like a maid to her mistress." We look intently, waiting for His verdict and instruction. We keep looking until He reminds us that He took our sins on Himself and died to pay the penalty for them. So rather than condemnation, He now offers us mercy.

There is no relief when we look around at the "righteous people" who accuse us, or look within at our efforts that ended in failure. When we look up, we find relief in the atonement. The chorus of the song written by Robert Kelly and sung by Whitney Houston states:

I look to you I look to you after all my strength is gone in you I can be strong
I look to you I look to you and when melodies are gone in you I hear a song,
I look to you

Father, our efforts to find relief from those around us have failed, and when we look internally, we are filled with shame because of our weaknesses. Therefore, we look to You for mercy, forgiveness and strength. Thank You for the assurance that You will not disappoint us, because of the grace provided by the cross.

December 6

MANNA SERIES: GLEANINGS FROM THE PSALMS II
FEAR WITHOUT THE DREAD

Reading Passage: Psalm 130
Main Text: Psa. 130:3-4. If you, O LORD, kept a record of sins,
O Lord, who could stand?
But with you there is forgiveness;
Therefore, you are feared. (NIV)

The dictionary defines fear as an unpleasant emotion caused by the belief that someone or something is dangerous, likely to cause pain, or a threat. Fear that is intense is described as a state of dread. When we consider the power, knowledge and holiness of God and how deserving we are of His judgment, our response is usually one of dreadful fear. The Bible frequently commands us to "fear the Lord," and we are left to wonder how we can maintain a close relationship with a Father whom we dread. This Psalm helps us to gain a different perspective on the type of fear we should have of God.

As guilty sinners we ought to fear the wrath of God against sin. But

He is not a God of judgment and wrath only; He is also a God of grace and mercy. The Psalmist muses on the fact that if God kept a record of our sins and dealt with them on their merit, no one could stand before His judgment seat. But He does not punish us as we deserve; rather, in mercy He offers us forgiveness instead of judgment. When we consider the forgiveness of God, it causes us to view Him with awe and honor. God does not overlook or ignore our sins; if so, He would be careless, capricious and unjust. Instead, He takes account of all our sins, considers the related penalty, then makes the decision to accept these penalties on His own account, in order to forgive us and set us free,

Why does He do it? He does it because of His love. On what basis can He do it? By providing someone who became our substitute, accepted the wrath of God on our behalf and died for our sins. Jesus Christ accomplished this by the atonement. How do we respond to someone who rescued us, and to whom we owe our lives, yet all He requires in response is our love? We honor and love Him with a reverential fear or awe. Not with dread, as there is no expectation of pain or a threat.

Consequently, the Psalmist describes His relationship with the Lord in passionate terms, "My soul waits for the Lord more than the watchman waits for the morning" (v. 6). Is this our response to our loving Lord who forgives our sins?

Father, when we consider Your mercy and forgiveness, we are humbled at the thought of Your love to us. We join with the hymn writer and wonder, "Who is a pardoning God like Thee, who has grace so rich and free?" We are filled with wonder, love and respect because of Your grace and mercy toward us.

December 7

MANNA SERIES: GLEANINGS FROM THE PSALMS II
LIKE A WEANED CHILD WITH ITS MOTHER

Reading Passage: Psalm 131
Main Text: Psa. 131:2 But I have stilled and quieted my soul;
Like a weaned child with its mother,
Like a weaned child is my soul within me. (NIV)

The Psalmist has painted a beautiful picture in one of my favorite Psalms. He describes a weaned child snuggling up to his mother. A weaned child no longer needs his mother's milk and is at the stage of exploring his independence and developing his individuality. Although the child in this picture can seemingly survive independent of his mother, he chooses this dependence, relying on her for all his needs. With this comfort and dependence, similar to being in the womb, the child is free from the cares and anxieties of life, leaving these concerns to mother.

The more we develop in adulthood, and the more knowledge we gain, the wiser we believe we become and the less we need to be dependent on anyone. We celebrate the fact that we are known for our intellect while we are on a quest to solve the mysteries of life. However, we soon discover that greater knowledge and independence affect our "hearts" and our "eyes." We develop a proud attitude, thinking ourselves wiser and better than others. We begin looking down at people while looking out for ourselves. We may become successful as we climb the ladders built by ambition, but we soon realize that along with the success come anxious fears, stress and restlessness. These symptoms manifest themselves in our physical and mental health.

In the crisis we create, we long for a time when our souls are stilled and quiet - resting without worry and care, like a child carried by his mother. But this comes at a great price for adults. We have to humble ourselves, admit our inability to cope with life independently, appear weak before others by not getting absorbed in complex matters, and be honest about our inabilities. The rewards are the contentment, security and peace that come from knowing that the One who loves us is caring for us. And in such a state of being, we can rest. The hope of our lives is firmly placed in the Lord.

Where you place your hope will determine the state of your contentment.

Father, it is no wonder Jesus instructed us that we need to become as little children in order to enter the kingdom of God. We do find it difficult to give up our ambition and independence to begin to trust You, as a child trusts its mother. Lord, we humbly submit to You because we don't want to miss out on the rewards of contentment and peace.

December 8

MANNA SERIES: GLEANINGS FROM THE PSALMS II
DON'T LET ADVERSE CIRCUMSTANCES AFFECT YOUR SONG

Reading Passage: Psalm 137
Main Text: Psa. 137:4-6 How can we sing the songs of the LORD
While in a foreign land?
If I forget you, O Jerusalem,
May my right hand forget [its skill].
May my tongue cling to the roof of my mouth
If I do not remember you,
If I do not consider Jerusalem
My highest joy. (NIV)

Have you ever lived in a foreign country surrounded by people whom you cannot identify with? At the same time, you may be suffering persecution and abuse without having the comfort of family and friends. In addition, at such times you may be unable to adjust to the culture, you may feel uncomfortable and unhappy, but may have no hope of returning home. Can you sing in the midst of this adversity? It is possible, but it depends on what you are singing about, and your ability to look beyond your existing circumstance and sing with hope.

The Israelites found themselves as captives in Babylon when the Lord allowed their enemy to take them into exile as punishment for their rebellion. In addition to capturing them, the Babylonians ravished their homeland and completely destroyed their temple in Jerusalem. The Israelites felt lost without a homeland, without national and spiritual identity. To add to their misery, they were taunted by their captors who asked them to sing one of their religious songs. Their depressing response was that they could not sing the songs of the Lord while living in a foreign land.

Admittedly, Jerusalem was destroyed, but their Lord was still alive. Why should they hang up their harps? Remembering Jerusalem brought sorrow and pain, but they had the power to convert present pain into future hope and once again make Jerusalem their "highest joy." This was possible once they were able to focus on the Lord and His ability to turn around the situation, free them from their captors, and rebuild Jerusalem.

When we are struggling to sing songs of joy because we feel as if we are living in a "foreign land," let us change our focus from what we have lost and begin to consider what the Lord is able to do. This will enable us to sing songs of hope regardless of our circumstances.

Consider the song of the prophet Habakkuk in his despair when he heard the news that Babylon would conquer the land of Judah:

> Though the fig tree does not bud, and there are no grapes on the vines,
> Though the olive crop fails, and the fields produce no food,
> Though there are no sheep in the pen, and no cattle in the stalls,
> Yet I will rejoice in the LORD, I will be joyful in God my Savior. (Hab 3:17-18 NIV)

Father, we acknowledge that we find it difficult to sing when we are focused on some of our existing problems. We need your help to be able to look beyond them and see Your ability to miraculously change our circumstances. We will begin to sing songs of hope because of You.

December 9

MANNA SERIES: GLEANINGS FROM THE PSALMS II
APPRECIATING A WORK IN PROGRESS

Reading Passage: Psalm 138
Main Text: Psa. 138:8. The LORD will fulfill [his purpose] for me;
Your love, O LORD, endures forever—
Do not abandon the works of your hands. (NIV)

When we observe a construction project, we can easily jump to the wrong conclusion regarding the progress being made or the intended outcome, if we are unaware of the design of the proposed product and what is required to achieve it. This may be one reason that many builders erect barriers to hide a project from the prying eyes of the ignorant public, perhaps to avoid having to answer foolish questions. Unfortunately, the project of building our lives is open to all, although only God, the architect and builder, knows the stages of our development.

Sometimes we are faced with critics who question whether we are part of God's plan, judging us based on their experience with God and their interpretation of what they think is happening in our lives. They don't know the obstacles we face, our relationship with the Lord, or His purpose revealed to us. Our challenge is not only our critics, but also ourselves. We get frustrated when we think that we have conquered some weakness in our lives, such as a gossiping tongue, or worry, and then find ourselves losing the battle when faced with some new situation. We wonder if we have made any progress, or whether God is about to abandon us as hopeless.

This Psalm encourages us to remember that we are God's work in progress, or as Paul described us, God's workmanship (Eph 2:10). Since He is working on us, He is ready to answer us when we call and will reinforce us with strength (v. 3). When we walk in the midst of trouble that would destroy us, He intervenes to revive our lives (v. 7). An abandoned building is more than an eyesore; it reflects an incompetent builder. We are convinced the Lord will fulfill, or bring to completion the purpose He designed for us. His faithful love looks beyond our present flaws and He keeps working toward His goal. He will not abandon the work of His hands.

Are you feeling frustrated with your spiritual progress, and thinking you will never achieve the destiny of your spiritual maturity? Remember that the One who chose you, called you and designed your destiny is the One who is working to achieve the goal. "Faithful is He who called you, who will accomplish the task."

Lord, we thank You that our lives are not in the hands of our critics, nor are we trying to develop our own lives. We are Your workmanship and are in Your hands, We believe that what You began in us, You are able to bring to completion, because of the finished work of Jesus Christ on the cross.

December 10

MANNA SERIES: GLEANINGS FROM THE PSALMS II
FAR SURPASSING MY SELF-KNOWLEDGE

Reading Passage: Psalm 139
Main Text: Psa. 139:5-6. You hem me in—behind and before;
You have laid your hand upon me.
Such knowledge is too wonderful for me, too lofty for me to
attain. (NIV)

There are some areas of our lives that we prefer to keep a secret because of how vulnerable we feel when we are exposed. Certain exposures are only made in a marriage where there is a relationship of trust and commitment based on a public legal agreement. But even in the most trusted marriage relationship, our private thoughts are not always shared.

In this Psalm, David explained that the Lord's knowledge of us is beyond the knowledge of any one else; in fact, it surpasses our knowledge of ourselves. He states that the Lord knew his daily activities, "when I sit and when I rise... my going out and lying down." Furthermore, the Lord knew the motivation behind these activities; "You perceive my thoughts from afar.... familiar with all my ways." Even before he spoke, the Lord knew what he planned to say. David found this complete knowledge so scary he tried to escape from it, but he could not escape because he was hemmed in on all sides. God's omniscience (knowledge of everything) and omnipresence (His presence everywhere) made escape impossible even if he tried to hide in the most remote place. Indeed, God's knowledge of David predated his existence, having observed his conception and development while in his mother's womb.

The reason we hate being exposed is that we believe such knowledge enables others to think less of us and to seek some control over us, and we cannot trust their intentions toward us. This is not the case with God. He proved His love to us in Jesus Christ in order that we can trust His good intentions for us. Even if we didn't trust God, we could not avoid His knowledge and control of us. However, the fact that we trust Him means we find assurance and comfort by His knowledge, instead of fear and anxiety. Like David, we rest in the fact that God's thoughts to us are precious (vv. 17), which means thoughts that are beautiful and valuable. We can be confident that He will act in our best interests.

Nothing in our lives can surprise the Lord who knows us so intimately. Yet He still loves us. Why shouldn't we trust Him who has such a great love for us?

Father, I am amazed that You know me better than I know myself. But I am comforted in knowing that You were thinking about me even before I began to think about myself. I find assurance that whatever I encounter, You are already aware of it and have made plans for my best interest in the outcome. Thank You Lord.

December 11

MANNA SERIES: GLEANINGS FROM THE PSALMS II
YEARNING FOR LEVEL GROUND

Reading Passage: Psalm 143
Main Text: Psa. 143:10 Teach me to do your will,
For you are my God;
May your good Spirit
Lead me on level ground. (NIV)

One of the challenges we face when spending time on a boat is coping with the instability of the surface beneath us. The floor of the boat shifts at various angles according to the swells of the tide, and if the shift is sudden, we run the risk of falling and may have to grab hold of something in order to secure ourselves. Because of the danger posed by instability, we yearn for firm, predictable, level ground.

Sometimes life, with its uncertainties and sudden changes, causes us to feel as if we are being tossed about and in risk of danger, just as with life at sea. The economy goes into recession and the previously secure jobs have become redundant. We are faced with a sudden illness that ruins our health, reduces our finances, and changes our lifestyle. Volatile political situations in many countries and terrorist activities around the world cause great uncertainty in our lives and increase our lack of confidence concerning the future.

When our circumstances are no longer predictable and we are uncertain about what we should do, like the Psalmist, we cry out to God for help. Our plea is that He would teach us His will. When we walk in His will, we know we experience His protection and our lives are ultimately blessed. Despite the changes in our circumstances and the darkness of our path, with His presence we will feel the stability of level ground and the certainty of His pleasure.

This was the assurance Paul experienced while on the sea in a horrible storm that eventually wrecked the boat in which he was traveling. He reported that the Angel of the Lord came to him in a vision and told him not to fear as no lives would be lost although the ship would be destroyed (Acts 27). When we learn God's will and are guided by His Spirit, we can live without fear or uncertainty, as if walking on level ground. In His will we may not avoid the storms and sudden changes of life, but we will have an inner stability that enables us to go through every storm with a sense of peace.

What storms are you currently encountering? Are you willing to discover, learn and submit to God's will so that He can lead you to level ground?

Father, it may have taken us a long time and many painful experiences, but we have come to the place of acknowledging our need of You. Teach us Your will and grant us Your Spirit to guide us to level ground and stability, by the mercies of Jesus Christ.

December 12

MANNA SERIES: GLEANINGS FROM THE PSALMS II
IT IS CRITICAL WHO WE CHOOSE TO TRUST

Reading Passage: Psalm 146
Main Text: Psa. 146:3-5. Do not put your trust in princes,
    In mortal men, who cannot save.
    When their spirit departs, they return to the ground;
    On that very day their plans come to nothing.
    Blessed is he whose help is the God of Jacob,
    Whose hope is in the LORD his God, (NIV)

We usually deny any accusation that we place our trust in people. But if you listen to our statements of expectations, or expressions of disappointment in people, they reveal a different story. Politicians are expected to convince us that we can achieve prosperity and peace; governments are expected to meet all the needs of society. We are greatly disappointed when our spouses fail to fulfill our expectations, or our pastors fail to achieve divine perfection. It is normal and natural to have expectations of people when we vote to select our leaders or make a vow committing ourselves to partners. However, there is a danger when our trust disregards the fact that these people are humans with all the associated faults, failures and sins, like ourselves. These false expectations will always lead to disappointment. Even if and when their performances are commendable, their lives end in death, and "their plans come to nothing."

Man is always limited in his ability to provide true deliverance. He may succeed in altering the economic or social environment, but he remains powerless to change the nature of humans, which would cause them to have love instead of hate, or to be industrious instead of being lazy. Man is also limited in the duration of his influence because he is mortal and will die.

This leads the Psalmist to observe: "How blessed is he whose help is the God of Jacob." God does more than change our environment; He also changes us, which results in true salvation. Our trust rests in the conviction that our God has control of everything that affects us, and if He doesn't change our circumstances, He will enable us to deal with them. When we trust God, we are not devastated at the failure of anyone, because our hope is not in that one. Indeed, the failure of men helps us to reassess where we placed our trust. Although our favorite politician did not win the election or our preferred manager did not get the top job, and we may be disappointed for a moment, yet we can reaffirm that our God rules over politics, governments and businesses. We will thrive regardless.

To avoid our disappointment in men, which could lead us to despair, remember the words of the hymn, "This is my Father's world, O let me ne'er forget, that though the wrong seems oft so strong. God is the ruler yet."

Father, help us to realize how blessed we are that the God in whom we trust rules over everything and reigns forever. We know we will not be disappointed when we trust in You.

December 13

MANNA SERIES: GLEANINGS FROM THE PSALMS II
AM I DELIGHTFUL TO GOD?

Reading Passage: Psalm 147
Main Text: Psa. 147:10-11 His pleasure is not in the strength of the horse,
Nor his delight in the legs of a man;
The LORD delights in those who fear him,
Who put their hope in his unfailing love. (NIV)

When we consider the greatness of our God as creator and owner of the universe, it is hard to think that He could be impressed by anything or anyone He has created. This does not prevent us from seeking ways to impress Him.

Man is impressed by horsepower; whether in a beautiful swift animal or in powerful engines he designs. He also tries to display his power in other ways. He conquers countries in order to establish large empires, builds elaborate structures including cathedrals, develops large business organizations or large congregations; but none of these things impress God. Manpower means nothing to God, as he does not "delight in the legs (muscles) of man."

What delights the Lord are people who are humble in heart, who recognize the greatness of God and reverence Him. Such people do not glory in their own creations; instead they express their need for God and praise Him. It is difficult to praise the Lord when we are busy admiring our accomplishments. Furthermore, people who are humble are not looking for commendation from God based on their goodness or noble character. Instead they are dependent on His mercy and love. These are the people in whom God takes delight and who impress Him.

This challenges us to constantly examine our lives, by asking the question: "Am I delightful to God?" The question is especially appropriate after any great achievement, or whenever others are acclaiming us. We should also ask the question when we consider the basis of our hope of eternal life. The only basis of our hope is Jesus' atonement for us on the cross, by which He took our sin on Himself and gave us His righteousness.

If, as a result of our self-examination, we are moved to offer praise to God, then we know He will be delighted with us.

Lord, we declare that all we possess come from You, and by ourselves we are nothing. So may all our accomplishments, our good deeds, and also our salvation be a celebration of Your greatness in us, and may You be glorified.

December 14

MANNA SERIES: GLEANINGS FROM THE PSALMS II
SALVATION, EVIDENCE OF GOD'S DELIGHT

Reading Passage: Psalm 149
Main Text: Psa. 149:4-5 For the LORD takes pleasure in His people;
He will beautify the humble with salvation.
Let the saints be joyful in glory;
Let them sing aloud on their beds. (NKJV)

Bondage conveys an ugly picture of those who have been condemned by abusers of power. On the other hand, there are few scenes more beautiful than the picture of someone who was previously bound, but is now experiencing the joy of freedom.

The Psalmist describes the scene of people expressing praise to the Lord by singing and dancing with the accompaniment of various musical instruments. Why are these people so expressive in their praise? Because they recognize that they are the center of God's delight, the source of pleasure to their Creator. Praise becomes the love expression of people who know how much God delights in the praise of His special people. But how do we know we are His special chosen people? Because He provided salvation as evidence of choice, just as a man places a ring on the finger of the bride he has chosen.

Salvation, unlike a ring, may seem an intangible gift. But to the one receiving it, it is substantial and transformative. We remember our previous state when we were under condemnation because of sin. We were oppressed by Satan's accusations, and lived in expectation of God's wrath. Then God in Jesus Christ offered us salvation, by which He took our condemnation and sin, setting us free. We were transformed from a state of dishonor and shame to a state of being adorned with the beauty of salvation. This made us know that we were special. The value of this salvation lies in the fact that it cost God His most precious possession; His only Son. The value of the salvation is that, whereas we lose all our material possessions when we die, it remains effective now and throughout eternity.

When we truly appreciate that we are special to God, that we have received a precious salvation, and God takes pleasure in our praise, we cannot help but be expressively joyful, and sing aloud even on our beds where we have no audience except the Lord.

Father, we thank You for this great salvation which we received when we placed our trust in Jesus Christ. Forgive us for restricting and suppressing our praise, thus depriving You of pleasure. We want to delight in You as You did in us.

December 15

MANNA SERIES: HOPE, ESSENTIAL INGREDIENT FOR SUCCESSFUL LIVING
HOPE MAKES A DAY END IN A DAWN

Reading Passage: Gen. 1:3-23
Main Text: Prov. 4:18. The path of the righteous is like the first gleam of dawn, shining ever brighter till the full light of day. (NIV)

Life without hope is mere existence. There is no looking to the future with expectancy, no motivation to accomplish anything, no dreams of a better life. Life just consists of eating and drinking for survival, like plants and animals.

The Book of Genesis records that the creation of man was different from that of all other created things. Man was formed from the dust of the ground, making him limited to time and space, but God breathed His Spirit into him, giving him "God-likeness" (Gen 1:26). A desire for eternity was placed in our hearts, which causes us to look with expectancy beyond the borders of physical limitation. It is this part of our lives that allows us to communicate with the transcendent God, who is not limited to time and space.

Furthermore, Genesis informs us that God made the day to commence with evening and end in the morning, "there was evening and there was morning, the first day," (Gen 1:5 NIV). (This is how the Hebrew day was determined.) This format of the day places in man, who is limited by his physical nature, a disposition of hope. Regardless of how awful the circumstances of a day may be as the evening turns to night, the day will end with a dawn of hope.

Unfortunately, many people who began life with great enthusiasm and a sense of purpose have allowed the trials and difficulties to drive them to despair and they become hopeless. For them, it becomes very difficult to get out of bed to face a new day. They make no effort to change their circumstances or seek help from God to empower them with new zeal for life. But we were never created to languish in the state of mere existence. God designed our day to end with a dawn. He is described by the apostle Paul as the God of hope, and He is able to change our circumstances and restore our lives so we may "abound in hope" (Rom 15:13 NKJV).

To procure the power of hope from the God of hope, we must place our trust in Him. The act of trusting Him causes us to become righteous and restores God's designed order in our lives. In such a state, rather than deteriorating and becoming more dark and despondent as we grow older, our lives will follow a path that shines brighter, more and more until it ends with the glory of the full light of an eternal day.

Don't let circumstance snuff out your hope, believe in God and let Him restore your day.

Father, we thank You for the hope You provide that allows us to overcome the darkness of our circumstances. We trust You to cause our dark nights to end in dawn, in the name of our Lord Jesus Christ.

December 16

MANNA SERIES: HOPE, ESSENTIAL INGREDIENT FOR SUCCESSFUL LIVING
A PEOPLE OF HOPE

Reading Passage: Gen. 12:1-3
Main Text: Eph. 2:12-13 Remember that at that time you were separate from Christ, excluded from citizenship in Israel and foreigners to the covenants of the promise, without hope and without God in the world. But now in Christ Jesus you who once were far away have been brought near through the blood of Christ. (NIV)

A promise is a spark that lights the fire of hope in a person's life. Until a promise is fulfilled, the beneficiary has to keep a relationship with, and faith in the promisor, in order to maintain hope.

The Lord began His relationship with Abraham and the nation of Israel that he produced, on the basis of a promise. This resulted in their being identified as the "people of hope." They were promised a homeland, that up to the present time they have never fully occupied. They were promised a king (messiah) who would rule over all nations of the world, placing them at the forefront of all nations. This has not yet been realized for them. The fact that these promises to the nation have not been fulfilled, despite the lapse of thousands of years, does not mean the promises were a hoax or that the Promisor was unfaithful.

The Lord desires that His people would deepen their faith and develop their relationship with Him, so they would be known as the people who live with hope of divine intervention because of their faith in God. This hope would sustain them during times when their earthly kings were deposed, their temple destroyed, they were exiled from their homeland, they suffered persecution, and the nation was decimated through a holocaust. Despite all that they suffered, hope allowed the Jews to maintain their identity; to progress and prosper because they looked forward to the time of fulfillment of the promise.

As non-Jews (Gentiles) we did not have their privilege of a relationship with God or the covenants of promise. Paul described Gentiles as being "without hope and without God in the world." However, when Gentiles put their faith in Christ, who is the Jewish messiah and who was sent in fulfillment of the promise given to Abraham, they are incorporated into the "people of hope" with a relationship with God and the promise of a glorious future.

Because of Christ we who were previously hopeless are now full of hope, and have lives of hope that cannot be defeated by any misfortune we encounter. We can endure any attack and recover from any set back because we know our future is secure in our Lord.

Lord, we are so grateful that You provided the means by which we, the outsiders, were given the opportunity to gain a new identity and the basis of hope, because of Jesus. Grant us the desire to maintain this hope so we may live victorious lives.

MANNA SERIES: HOPE, ESSENTIAL
INGREDIENT FOR SUCCESSFUL LIVING
PRISONERS OF HOPE

Reading Passage: Zech. 9:9-17
Main Text: Zech. 9:11-12 As for you, because of the blood of my covenant with you,

> I will free your prisoners from the waterless pit.
> Return to your fortress, O prisoners of hope;
> Even now I announce that I will restore twice as much to you.
> (NIV)

The world can sometimes seem like an imprisoning environment. It appears we are unable to escape the effects of the latest virus or economic disruption, or we are powerless to stem the tide of injustice in our world. When the situation becomes overwhelming, we feel like the Psalmist as he declares, "Oh that I had wings like a dove, I would fly away and be at rest" (Psa. 55:6 NIV). Knowing it is unlikely that we will be able to fulfill the desire to escape, how can we live successfully in an imprisoning environment? We can become prisoners of hope instead of being prisoners of despair.

In the above text, the prophet Zechariah used this phrase to describe the Jews who were exiled in Babylon. They had no king and their own country was under the control of a foreign power. They seemed out of control of their own destiny with no hope of escaping. In that condition, they received a word of prophecy telling them to rejoice because their king was coming to them bringing salvation (Zech. 9:9). The promise was that their prisoners would be delivered from their desolation (waterless pits) and would be returned to a place of security and provision (their fortress). With this promise they were no longer in despair. Instead, they were so inspired by the future that they became prisoners of hope.

The prophecy to the Jews was fulfilled when Jesus rode into Jerusalem (Matt 21:5). His arrival there began the week that culminated in His crucifixion. His death was not for the deliverance of Jews under Roman dominion, but for the deliverance of all mankind who are imprisoned by sin. We no longer have to be imprisoned by the gloom of our circumstances as we have the hope of a future solution. Whether it is personal financial adversity, a crippling health condition or the battle against evil in the society, we can be optimistic knowing that our King has conquered sin, the source of all problems on the earth. Furthermore, He is coming again to reign in righteousness, remedy all our problems and restore peace in the world. Just as the walls of a cell reminds a prisoner of his confinement; the promises of our Lord and the presence of the Holy Spirit continually remind us of our hope of a brighter tomorrow.

What has you imprisoned today, despair or hope? Keep looking for the King.

Father, we thank You that You sent Your King to deliver us from the kingdom of darkness and hopelessness and transfer us to the kingdom of light and hope. Through Jesus we can now reign in life and be victorious over the negatives of life.

December 18

MANNA SERIES: HOPE, ESSENTIAL INGREDIENT FOR SUCCESSFUL LIVING
THE SALVATION ACCOMPLISHED BY HOPE

Reading Passage: Rom. 8:15-25
Main Text: Rom. 8:24-25. For in this hope we were saved. But hope that is seen is no hope at all. Who hopes for what he already has? But if we hope for what we do not yet have, we wait for it patiently. (NIV)

We desired salvation because of our dissatisfaction with the state of our lives as we suffered the consequences of sin. Life was filled with uncertainties, fears, miseries, sicknesses, unhappiness, and it ended with death. The salvation we received through faith in Christ provided the Spirit of God and the new birth making us children of God. However, that immediate internal transformation was not accompanied by a dramatic change in our physical conditions. We still suffer from sicknesses and pain. But what we received at the time of our conversion was hope of a complete salvation: spirit, soul and body.

In today's passage, Paul explained that because we are sons of God and co-heirs with Christ, we have the hope of future glory (vv 16-17). But before that glory is realized, we continue to endure suffering at the present time. Indeed, we groan, awaiting the time when our bodies will be transformed. We are saved, but the glory of the salvation is not yet manifested in our bodies. We are living in the state of hope, which is the state of possession without full realization, and this can sometimes be frustrating. Paul indicated that the earth is in a similar state, but God intended that creation be placed in this state of hope (v 20). Why? Because each painful incident of disruption in creation, and each painful discomfort in our bodies is a powerful reminder of the hope of our future salvation. Each reminder becomes a means of intensifying our desire for salvation. Paul stated "in this hope we were saved" (v. 24).

Any case of hardship and difficulty that reminds us of the imperfections in our physical lives, helps us to focus on our hope. And when we focus on our hope, our appreciation of salvation is enhanced. The Message Bible paraphrases 8:23-25:

These sterile and barren bodies of ours are yearning for full deliverance. That is why waiting does not diminish us, any more than waiting diminishes a pregnant mother. We are enlarged in the waiting. We, of course, don't see what is enlarging us. But the longer we wait, the larger we become, and the more joyful our expectancy.

As Christians we can celebrate even death because it reminds of the hope of resurrection.

We thank You, O Father, for providing us with this wonderful plan by which we can live above all heartache and difficulty in the world. As people of hope, grant us the patience to wait for the glory that will be manifested in our bodies, as we give praise to our Lord.

December 19

MANNA SERIES: HOPE, ESSENTIAL INGREDIENT FOR SUCCESSFUL LIVING
HOPE AS AN ANCHOR OF THE SOUL

Reading Passage: Heb. 6:13-20
Main Text: Heb. 6:19-20. We have this hope as an anchor for the soul, firm and secure. It enters the inner sanctuary behind the curtain, where

Jesus, who went before us, has entered on our behalf. He has become a high priest forever, in the order of Melchizedek. (NIV)

A hurricane warning was issued and the small island was preparing for the onslaught. All planes departed ahead of the storm and most small boats were taken out of the ocean. The captain of the huge cruise ship that was in port knew it was dangerous to keep the ship at the pier, as this would risk damage both to the ship and the dock. He decided to take the ship to open sea and drop anchor in order to weather the storm. When the power of the winds tried to push that floating target further out to sea or cause it to capsize, the strong ropes that were anchored to the rocks on the sea bed held the ship secure.

We can never avoid the stormy seasons in our lives. Sometimes problems occur simultaneously or in quick succession that compound the trauma we suffer. In those times of distress and grief, we are only kept sane and given the strength to keep going, by the hope of a change in our circumstances and a brighter future. Like the anchor of the ship, hope keeps us secure during the storm. However, hope is only as valid as the place to which the anchor is attached. Hope that is placed on grounds that have proven to be unreliable in the past, such as the promise of an unfaithful spouse, is useless and cannot provide any sense of security. Similarly, some people place their hope on vague spiritualism, such as horoscopes and demonic practitioners, but such hope may be mere wishful thinking.

In contrast, hope that is placed in God's word is supported by the fact that God cannot lie, and He gives His oath as additional security (vv. 17-18). This hope becomes an anchor for our souls as it is secured to Jesus, who takes the rope of our hope into the very presence of God. With this type of hope, we are secure against stormy circumstances, demonic attack, and even internal doubts.

Do you have a secure anchor for your life? Consider the words of the ancient hymn by Priscilla J Owens:

> Will your anchor hold in the storms of life,
> When the clouds unfold their wings of strife?
> When the strong tides lift and the cables strain,
> Will your anchor drift, or firm remain?

We have an anchor that keeps the soul
Steadfast and sure while the billows roll,
Fastened to the Rock which cannot move,
Grounded firm and deep in the Savior's love

Father we thank You for the security You have provided us through the hope we have in Jesus Christ. We rest securely in Your promise and His love.

December 20

MANNA SERIES: HOPE, ESSENTIAL INGREDIENT FOR SUCCESSFUL LIVING
HOPE, THE TONIC FOR A MOOD CHANGE

Reading Passage: Lam. 3:19-26
Main Text: Lam. 3:21. Yet this I call to mind
And therefore I have hope:
Because of the LORD'S great love, we are not consumed,
For his compassions never fail.
They are new every morning;
Great is your faithfulness. (NIV)

We sometimes have selective memory when reviewing our past experiences. Because of existing difficulties, we tend to recall only past events that confirm our pessimism regarding the future. The darkness of our lives can become so overwhelming that we are filled with bitterness and gloom. We begin to believe we will never get out of the rut - we can never love or be loved again; nothing will cause us to be happy again; we will be living with meager financial resources for the rest of our lives. Some people try to alleviate these negative emotions by using mind- altering drugs, only to discover later that these never resulted in a change in their situation.

The Prophet Jeremiah found himself in a greatly depressed state when he considered the destruction of his homeland Jerusalem, and the suffering in Judah caused by the Babylonian conquest. The judgment was the result of rebellion by the Jews against the Lord. But Jeremiah felt God had forsaken the nation and disregarded his plea for relief. He cried, "He has driven me away and made me walk in darkness rather than light; indeed, He has turned His hand against me again and again, all day long" (vv. 2-3). He continued, "My splendor is gone and all that I had hoped from the LORD. I remember my affliction and my wandering, the bitterness and the gall" (vv. 18-19). Yet it was at this point that there was an abrupt change in his mood, when he had another recollection. He was still alive when he should have been destroyed by the judgment. While he was moping about his misfortune, he forgot God's mercy to him. Because of the Lord's great love, he could have hope that God would be merciful in the future. Being alive was an indication that the Lord had not abandoned him, and would provide an opportunity for a new day with new possibilities.

This hope is like a tonic for a mood change, providing a glimmer of light in the gloom of overwhelming difficulty. The "bitterness and gall" of yesterday can be transformed to a time of rejoicing tomorrow, as our faithful God removes the dark of our past and provides us with a new dawn. Whenever you are tempted to fall into despair, follow the prescription in Psalm 42:11 NIV, and say with the Psalmist,

> Why are you downcast, O my soul?
> Why so disturbed within me? Put your hope in God,
> For I will yet praise Him, my Savior and my God.

Father, we are thankful that we can find hope in Your mercy. Because of Jesus we are assured of your goodness to us. Great is Your faithfulness.

December 21

MANNA SERIES: HOPE, ESSENTIAL INGREDIENT FOR SUCCESSFUL LIVING
PEOPLE WHO ABOUND IN HOPE

Reading Passage: Rom. 15:7-13
Main Text: Rom. 15:13. May the God of hope fill you with all joy and peace as you trust in him, so that you may overflow with hope by the power of the Holy Spirit. (NIV)

You could see from their body language that the team was feeling dejected. It was just about half-time in the soccer game and they were already down by three goals to nil. In his half-time address, the coach sought to inspire hope in the players. He told them they had another forty-five minutes to produce a win, and they had the skill and strength to exploit the opposition's weaknesses; moreover, he believed in them so they must believe in themselves.

There are several times in life when we begin to despair. We no longer feel we can be successful in the exam, win the coveted job position, meet our sales target, recover from the rejection from our spouse or be restored to health. The game is not over, but in our minds we have lost because we have lost hope. Jesus has called us to an abundant life, not because we are more talented or more deserving than others. In fact, it is not about us; it is about Him and what He is able to do in us. He is able to fill us with hope so that we will abound with hope.

In his epistles, Paul used many descriptions of God in order to help us understand the many ways in which He can meet our various needs. He spoke of the God of endurance and encouragement (v. 5); the God of peace (15:33, 16:20); the God of all comfort (2Cor. 1:3); and the God of love and peace (2Cor. 13:11). To those who put their trust in Him, He can be the God of hope (15:13) who by the power of the Holy Spirit will fill us with hope. Consequently, it does not matter how dark our situation has become, His abounding hope in us will cause us to know that there is nothing impossible with our God. He can turn any seeming defeat into a victory; He can change the heart of the king; He can cause rivers to appear in the deserts; He can send manna from the heavens; He can turn our darkness to dawn.

When we overflow in hope, we will never remain burdened by the situations in life. Hope will always cause us to see the silver lining behind every dark cloud, light at the end of every tunnel, and a resurrection following every death. This is why Jesus came, and this is what Christmas is about. Because of Him, a people in darkness can see a great light, and even the Gentiles can find hope.

The game is not over, so arise and shine for your Light has come!

Jesus, we rejoice in the hope You brought by Your coming to earth. We can look beyond our present darkness with hope because the "Dayspring" from on high will visit us. Thank You Lord.

December 22

MANNA SERIES: ANGELIC ACTIVITY
IN THE ADVENT NARRATIVE
GOOD NEWS IN SURPRISING PLACES

Reading Passage: Luke 1:5-23
Main Text: Luke 1:19-20. The angel answered, "I am Gabriel. I stand in the presence of God, and I have been sent to speak to you and to tell you this good news. And now you will be silent and not able to speak until the day this happens, because you did not believe my words, which will come true at their proper time." (NIV)

The Gospels, which are presented at the beginning of the New Testament canon, begin with great angelic activity. This is significant because after the end of the Old Testament with its many prophetic writings, there was no record of communication from God for a period of approximately 400 years. God resumed His communication to humanity through angels. The meaning of the term angel is "messenger," which describes their basic function, although they perform many other tasks.

The first angelic message was to a man named Zechariah, a priest who was married to Elizabeth. They were both described as righteous and advanced in age. He was performing the duty of burning incense in the temple, a task he would likely perform once in his life. Alone in the temple, amidst his excitement and nervousness at this experience, he was surprised and frightened to see an angel beside the altar. The angel gave him good news. His prayers for a child, that were likely long forgotten and overtaken by age and other priorities, were going to be answered. The promised son, John, was an answer to prayer but had an impact that went beyond Zechariah and Elizabeth. He would prepare the way for God to send His Savior into the world.

Zechariah was so overwhelmed by the events, and puzzled by the message, he responded with doubt. Yet his doubt never changed God's plan or the fulfillment; rather, it provided the "sign of silence" that gave evidence of an incredible experience.

The advent season provides us with a reminder that God has not abandoned His world or forgotten us. He visits at times we least expect

Him, and in ways that will surprise us, to remind us that He is faithful to remember our prayers. But whereas we see only our narrow personal interests, His plans go beyond us to include His purpose for the whole world.

We may not experience an angelic visitor, but our hearts should be prepared to be surprised by good news in surprising places, as we listen to the Christmas messages in Word and song. Let us receive these messages in faith, so we might be reassured that the darkness and gloom of this world and our circumstances cannot disrupt God's plans of hope and goodness through Jesus Christ.

How silently, how silently the wondrous gift is given,
So God imparts to human hearts the blessings of His heaven
No ear may hear His coming, but in this world of sin,
Where meek souls will receive Him still, the dear Christ enters in.

December 23

MANNA SERIES: ANGELIC ACTIVITY IN THE ADVENT NARRATIVE
SURPRISING NEWS TO THE HIGHLY FAVORED

Reading Passage: Luke 1:26-35
Main Text: Luke 1:28-29. The angel went to her and said, "Greetings, you who are highly favored! The Lord is with you." Mary was greatly troubled at his words and wondered what kind of greeting this might be. (NIV)

Imagine being greeted by an angel and being described in terms beyond your wildest imagination. The surprise is not only that you have come face to face with an unusual messenger, but also because you heard that God has selected you for special favor.

The passage records that Mary was greatly troubled at this greeting, and began wondering at its meaning. As far as she was concerned, she was just an ordinary, simple, rural, young lady, who was engaged to Joseph, and was looking forward to her wedding day. She received a special grace from God that provided her with an opportunity for Him to do great things through her. She was not supernatural in any way, but she was "super" available to God and "super" open to whatever He wanted to do through her. When the angel explained that she was going to be the first and only person to have a virgin birth, and that her son would be the expected Messiah, her only question was about how God would accomplish making her pregnant. There was no question about being placed in an embarrassing position, or being unqualified for the role. Because she accepted the grace bestowed on her, and God's ability to perform what He declared, she later stated, "…all generations will call me blessed" (v. 48b).

Christmas reminds us that God has highly favored us. On whomever His favor rests, His presence is assured: "The Lord is with you." As evidence of His favor, He left His place and privilege in glory to come and dwell among us. He calls us "blessed" before He challenges us with His purpose for our lives. We are "blessed with every spiritual blessing in heavenly places in Christ Jesus" (Eph. 1:3). Unlike Mary, we fail to value our special status, so we are reluctant to make ourselves available for whatever He wants to do through us. God wants us to produce what only Holy Spirit can conceive in us. Are we willing to say like Mary, "I am the Lord's servant ... may it be to me as you have said" (v. 38)?

Thou didst leave thy throne and thy kingly crown,
When thou camest to earth for me,
But in Bethlehem's home there was found no room
For thy holy nativity,
O come to my heart Lord Jesus,
There's room in my heart for thee

December 24

MANNA SERIES: ANGELIC ACTIVITY IN THE ADVENT NARRATIVE
DISTURBING NEWS FOR A RIGHTEOUS MAN

Reading Passage: Matt. 1:18-25
Main Text: Matt. 1:19-20 Because Joseph, her husband to be, was a righteous man, and because he did not want to disgrace her, he intended to divorce her privately. When he had contemplated this, an angel of the

Lord appeared to him in a dream and said, "Joseph, son of David, do not be afraid to take Mary as your wife, because the child conceived in her is from the Holy Spirit." (NIV)

Joseph was engaged to Mary, and in accordance with the custom of that society, he was expected to wait for approximately one year before taking her as his wife. The covenant of engagement was binding and required a "bill of divorcement" to terminate it. During the waiting period of the year, there could be no sexual relations between the parties. Meanwhile, the expected husband would prepare accommodation for his bride, and she would demonstrate her faithfulness to her pledge of purity. If she was discovered to be pregnant, she would be disgraced and risked being stoned as an adulteress.

When Joseph discovered Mary was pregnant, he was justified in seeking to divorce her because he considered himself the aggrieved party based on his knowledge of the facts. The angel appeared to him in a dream to inform him that the fact of Mary's pregnancy did not represent the full story because God was doing something supernatural. Righteousness required his acting beyond what the society demanded based on what God revealed to him.

Joseph would have to disrupt his plans and marry Mary immediately. He would protect her against public accusations of unfaithfulness. He would act as Jesus' father, although he knew otherwise, and he would accept the ridicule for any misunderstanding of this mysterious occurrence. This righteousness required Joseph's selflessness so that the divine plan of the Son of God becoming the Son of Man might be accomplished.

Christmas reminds us of the time when God emptied Himself of divinity and took on the form of a servant, to be born in the likeness of men (Phil. 2:7). If God did that for us, are we willing to be selfless for His sake, even if it means ridicule and misunderstanding? Like Joseph, it may involve loving someone whom we would be justified in rejecting, or serving someone society expects us to disregard because of past abuse. We must be willing to ignore the facts as others see it because of the message we have received from God.

May we have the humble mind exhibited by Christ, so we may emulate His righteousness. The following verse from the carol, **Once in Royal David's City** describes the mind of Christ:

He came down to earth from heaven, Who is God and Lord of all,
And His shelter was a stable, And His cradle was a stall;
With the poor, and mean, and lowly, Lived on earth our Savior
holy.

December 25

MANNA SERIES: ANGELIC ACTIVITY IN THE ADVENT NARRATIVE
BREAKING NEWS FOR UNUSUAL MESSENGERS

Reading Passage: Luke 2:8-20
Main Text: Luke 2:10-11 But the angel said to them, "Do not be afraid. I bring you good news of great joy that will be for all the people. Today, in the town of David, a Savior has been born to you; he is Christ the Lord." (NIV)

The greatest event in human history has just occurred. How should this be publicized in a world where there were limited means of communication, no newspapers, and no broadcast facilities? In our day of media specialists, communication experts, and satellite facilities supporting highly resourced broadcast houses, we find it difficult to imagine the challenges of news communication in the first century A.D.

An angel came to shepherds watching over their flocks in the open fields. The shepherds thought they were facing another routine night of drudgery watching for possible robbers, when suddenly, a heavenly messenger interrupted the night. The angel announced he had breaking news that would bring joy to the whole world. The details of the message were sufficiently specific to seem authentic, regarding location and the unexpected sign of a baby in a manger. But what was the significance of a Savior being born? And why were the lowly shepherds the first to know?

The Jews were looking for a political king to deliver the nation from Roman oppression, and this hopefully would eventually result in individual personal benefits. But the shepherds learned that the deliverance was coming first individually, in personal salvation because "a Savior has been born to you." This should be good news to everyone, but the shepherds were especially excited at the privilege of hearing it first. Because of their lowly status in the society, their excitement would be palpable and contagious. The scribes and priests might have questioned the intellectual basis of the announcement. The rich merchants might have stopped to think of the impact the announcement would have on business. The shepherds responded by immediately investigating the news. Then they were filled with praise and glory to God and began to spread the word to everyone. This was an effective method of spreading the Christmas news.

Do we qualify as good evangelists to spread the news of the Savior with the excitement of personal experience, and passion of news carriers? Or do we view the message of Christmas with the routine drudgery of another night of guarding sheep? Let us value the privilege of being chosen to hear and bear the good news that will bring joy to the world.

> *While shepherds kept their watching*
> *Over silent flocks by night,*
> *Behold throughout the heavens,*
> *There shone a holy light:*
> *Go, Tell It On the Mountain,*
> *Over the hills and everywhere;*
> *Go, Tell It On the Mountain*
> *That Jesus Christ is born.*

December 26

MANNA SERIES: ANGELIC ACTIVITY IN THE ADVENT NARRATIVE
MISSING, HIDING FROM A TYRANT

Reading Passage: Matt. 2:1-21
Main Text: Matt. 2:13-14 When they had gone, an angel of the Lord appeared to Joseph in a dream. "Get up," he said, "take the child and his mother and escape to Egypt. Stay there until I tell you, for Herod is going to search for the child to kill him." So he got up, took the child and his mother during the night and left for Egypt, (NIV)

King Herod felt threatened by the news that a new king was born in Bethlehem. Herod, thinking the newborn Jesus posed a threat to his throne, began a search intending to eliminate him. God instructed Joseph to escape to Egypt with Mary and the baby. Jesus was missing from Judea as He was hiding from Herod in Egypt.

The choice of Egypt as the country to hide Jesus is ironic as this was the country from which God delivered the young nation of Israel. One lesson we learn from this incident is that God sometimes moves us away from our usual place of activity for our own protection. Once we sense the voice of God, we should obey, even if he is sending us to an unlikely location. As Christians, we often feel as if we are in enemy territory in our work places or in our neighborhoods because our beliefs and lifestyles are contrary to those around us. The pressures of the society cause us to fear whether we can survive in this alien environment. The account of Jesus' flight to Egypt, and Israel's preservation in Egypt without losing their national identity, convince us that God is able to protect us in enemy territory.

Another lesson from this episode is Matthew's comment that all this happened in order to fulfill the prophecy, "out of Egypt I have called my son" (v. 15). This means God orchestrated Jesus' sojourn in Egypt, so He could be identified with God's pattern of redemption. This pattern involves God's children being in enemy territory, then being redeemed and called out to a new inheritance. God redeemed the children of Israel from Egyptian slavery and called them out to live in the promised land of Canaan. Anyone who is identified as a son of God will have the experience of being called out of the "Egypt" of their past life of slavery to sin, to the new inheritance of life in Christ. Although Jesus was never under the slavery of sin spiritually, God allowed Him to live in Egypt physically, so he could be identified with all sons of God and be called out of Egypt. Have we had the experience of being called out of a sinful lifestyle into a new relationship with God? This experience should provide us with the assurance we are sons of God.

Father, we thank You for paying the price for our redemption so we might experience Your call out from Egypt, and be identified as Your son. We pray that someone reading this devotional will hear Your call for the first time, and experience Your redemption from sin.

MANNA SERIES: ANGELIC ACTIVITY IN THE ADVENT NARRATIVE
WELCOME NEWS FOR EXILES WHO ARE SONS

Reading Passage: Matt. 2:13-23
Main Text: Matt. 2:19-20 After Herod died, an angel of the Lord appeared in a dream to Joseph in Egypt and said, "Get up, take the child and his mother and go to the land of Israel, for those who were trying to take the child's life are dead." (NIV)

One of the unfortunate side effects of conflicts between nations is the creation of exiles trying to escape the effects of war. Currently, there are large groups of people living in temporary shelters in foreign countries, suffering unsanitary and hostile living conditions, because they had to abandon their homes to escape imprisonment or death in their own countries.

Because Herod, the insecure and wicked king of Judea, was intent on eliminating all possible threats to his throne, an angel instructed Joseph to take his family, including Jesus and escape to Egypt. While Herod was on his cruel rampage of killing all boys under the age of two in Bethlehem, Jesus and his family were in exile. After Herod died, an angel again appeared to Joseph with good news. The news was that the enemy who was seeking to destroy them had died and it was now safe for them to return to their inheritance in Israel. The people of Israel experienced similar occurrences in their history. They were placed in exile for an uncertain period and had to wait for the development of events over which they had no control, before they were able to return to their homeland. This experience in Jesus' life demonstrated His identity with the nation of Israel, and with everyone who has a relationship with Him by faith.

The news is that the enemy who was seeking to destroy us has been dealt with; we are now safe to return to our inheritance. In a spiritual sense this enemy is sin, death and the devil, and our exile was in the ungodly world apart from God. But Christmas reminds us that Jesus entered the world to deal with our enemy on the cross. After He sacrificed His life and purchased our redemption, the welcome news can be proclaimed to sons, "leave the place of exile and return home."

If we are sons, we will hear and heed the message. We will bid farewell to the life where we are apart from God and come home. Have you heard the news? Did you sense the call? Have you responded?

> *Good Christian men, rejoice*
> *With heart and soul and voice*
> *Now ye need not fear the grave:*
> *Peace! Peace!*
> *Jesus Christ was born to save*
> *Calls you one and calls you all*
> *To gain His everlasting hall*
> *Christ was born to save*
> *Christ was born to save*

December 28

MANNA SERIES: YEAR-END MUSINGS
WHEN GOD MOVED INTO THE NEIGHBORHOOD

Reading Passage: John 1:1-14
Main Text: John 1:14 The Word became flesh and made his dwelling among us. We have seen his glory, the glory of the One and Only, who came from the Father, full of grace and truth. (NIV)

George graduated from university with a major in sociology. He was fascinated with the poor people in a certain area of his city, who existed on what they foraged from the city dump. Many of the dump dwellers represented several generations of families who lived in that environment without any opportunity for upward mobility in the society. George wanted to know what could be done for these people to provide proper physical and social structures for their development. Because he was from a wealthy family in the upper class of the country, he knew the people would not readily accept his efforts to help them. They would assume that he could not understand their situation and culture, nor could he relate to them. He decided that the only solution was for him to move into their neighborhood and become a part of their lives in order to provide them with opportunity.

The apostle John began his gospel narrative by describing the transcendent nature of God. He existed in eternity past, He created everything, and He was the source of life and light. He wanted a relationship with the world He created, but the world could not recognize Him. God's solution to this problem was for Him to move into the neighborhood of the defiled world by becoming flesh. So the eternal Word became flesh and made His dwelling among us, which allowed us to behold His glory that was full of grace and truth.

By becoming flesh and dwelling among us, God was able to help humanity in ways that could not be accomplished if He remained only a transcendent Spirit. In flesh, God identified with us, becoming familiar with our weaknesses, challenges and temptations with His archenemy, the devil. As a Man, we can accept Him as our perfect representative before the Father in heaven. He also identified with us so He could communicate in terms that we can understand. In eternity He was described as the Word, which means He desires to communicate God-thoughts to humanity. We could not understand what God was saying to us until the Word was incarnated and performed acts, which we could understand.

God became flesh and made His dwelling among us so that by identification and communication, He could provide us with redemption and achieve our transformation. Unlike George, who was hoping that the life of the dump dwellers could be improved by physical and social structures, God knows that there will be no permanent improvement in the lives of humanity until they experience a spiritual transformation. This was God's amazing plan when He sent Jesus to earth to become one with us. He was "born to raise the sons of earth ... and to give them a second birth."

Father, we thank You for the sacrifice You made by providing Your only begotten Son to redeem us from sin and provide us with a new identity. Thank God for Jesus.

MANNA SERIES: YEAR-END MUSINGS
DON'T ASSUME JESUS IS
IN YOUR COMPANY

Reading Passage: Luke 2:41-51

Main Text: Luke 2:43-45 After the Feast was over, while his parents were returning home, the boy Jesus stayed behind in Jerusalem, but they were unaware of it. Thinking he was in their company, they traveled on for a day. Then they began looking for him among their relatives and friends. When they did not find him, they went back to Jerusalem to look for him. (NIV)

We may be familiar with stories of parents arriving home, independent of each other, and realizing that their child is missing because each parent thought the other had collected him from school. An outside observer finds it difficult to understand how the parents could be so negligent, although the facts may prove the situation was simply the result of miscommunication.

When Jesus' parents were returning from the feast in Jerusalem, it was likely they were traveling with a large group including many children. The fact that they went one day's journey before realizing Jesus was missing indicates that their focus was not on Jesus, who had deliberately stayed behind in Jerusalem. Their negligence cost the parents four extra days: one to return and three days searching for Jesus.

We learn from this event how easily we can become distracted and not realize Jesus is not in our company. We may be busy preparing for the Christmas program, or preparing for a worship service, but neglect the Person who should be the focus of our attention. In our celebrations, we can be absorbed with our enjoyment and emotional satisfaction and ignore what should be our primary goal. The goal must always be that Jesus is glorified, and His mission of making new followers is accomplished.

When His parents found Him, Jesus explained that He was busy doing His Father's mission, which required His being in the Father's house. It is frightening to think that while we may be satisfied with our efforts in "serving the Lord," we may not be doing the Father's mission. In fact, Jesus may be missing from our activities and we are not even aware of it.

We will always find the negligence of ignoring Jesus to be costly, because of the effort we will have to make to regain the presence of Jesus.

Do you prioritize having the presence of the Lord in everything you do? Do you try to ensure you are accomplishing the Father's will above fulfilling the traditional program of your church?

Lord, this word challenges us to consider our ways as it is so easy for us to overlook the goal of our celebrations. We don't want to be negligent because we are distracted by our own interests, while You are missing from our company. Help us to keep You and Your mission as the focus of our attention at all times.

December 30

MANNA SERIES: YEAR-END MUSINGS
A FOOT-WASHING OPPORTUNITY

Reading Passage: John 13:2-17
Main Text: John 13:4-5 So he got up from the meal, took off his outer clothing, and wrapped a towel around his waist. After that, he poured water into a basin and began to wash his disciples' feet, drying them with the towel that was wrapped around him. (NIV)

Recently I was reading of some strange New Year's Eve traditions in some countries. In Peru, there is the practice of having boxing matches with neighbors to settle long-standing disputes. One of the strangest is in South Africa where people throw out old furniture and kitchen appliances from their apartment windows into the street. The common idea in these practices is that by clearing out baggage accumulated during the year they ensure these items are not carried into the New Year.

When Jesus met with His disciples for their last meal together before His death on the cross, in addition to instituting the Christian communion, He engaged in a unique exercise as described in John's gospel. Because they had the Passover meal in a room without the attendance of a servant, the disciples sat down to eat without washing their feet. Jesus, noticing their dirty feet, took on the role of the servant and began to wash the disciples' feet. When Peter questioned Jesus' actions and then requested a full bath, Jesus replied that they were basically clean, and required only the washing of their feet.

The reality was that the disciples would have dirty feet because they walked in sandals that left their feet partially uncovered as they trudged the dusty, unpaved streets. Jesus was implying the deeper spiritual meaning that though they were cleansed from their sins because they believed in Him, they would still become contaminated in their spiritual journey by their association with the "dusty" world, and by the manifestations of their "untransformed" sinful nature. They needed continuous washings to maintain their relationship with Him.

Coming to the close of another year, as we reflect on our sins and failings of the year, we are reminded of our need for a washing so we may enter a new year ready for fellowship with our Lord. Because of our faith in Him, our sins do not affect our status as His sons, but they cause a disruption in our fellowship. Although we need to live in a state of continuous repentance, the ending of the old year provides a good opportunity for focusing on the state of our relationship with the Lord, and ensuring there is nothing preventing His favor. Jesus also stated we should follow His example and wash one another's feet. At the end of a year we should get rid of any baggage that disrupts our relationship with God and each other.

Lord, we thank You for Your willingness to wash away the impurities of our lives, even when we dare to come before You with dirty feet. As we end the year, help us to ensure that all impediments to our relationship with You and one another are removed.

December 31

MANNA SERIES: YEAR-END MUSINGS
RECOVERY FROM THIS YEAR'S DISAPPOINTMENTS

Reading Passage: Luke 24:13-27
Main Text: Luke 24:20-21 The chief priests and our rulers handed him over to be sentenced to death, and they crucified him; but we had hoped that he was the one who was going to redeem Israel. And what is more, it is the third day since all this took place. (NIV)

We have come to the end of another calendar year. As is customary, many people will end the year and welcome the next with reflection and celebration. Some celebrate with small parties or grand galas, others at churches or other places of worship. There are various reasons people decide to celebrate the close of a year. Perhaps they are celebrating great achievements, or they may be celebrating the fact that they were able to survive to the end of the year despite difficulties and disappointments.

The celebration of survival is understandable for those who suffered serious sickness, lost a loved one, faced the rejection of spouse or children, or lost their main source of income. We are also aware that there are many who started the year, encountered similar challenges, but did not survive.

For followers of Christ who believe our lives are ordered and directed by God, the disappointments can lead to questions as to why we were allowed to suffer or experience failure. Having gone through those times without getting an explanation from God, we are apprehensive in our celebrations, wondering if we should brace ourselves for a new year with even greater challenges than before.

The two disciples in our passage felt they were ending a chapter of their lives in disappointment. Jesus, whom they were following and on whom they placed their hopes, was crucified and buried. In their disappointment they stated, "We had hoped that He was the One who was going to redeem Israel." They were unaware that the One they were disappointed with, was in fact walking with them. As soon as their "eyes were opened" the disappointment was changed into celebration. What they thought was a dark end became a glorious new beginning.

Rather than commiserate over the disappointments of the year, take time to ensure that you are ending the year walking with the Lord. Appreciate the fact that in His company what seems like a dark end can become an exciting new beginning, what seems hopeless is full of wonderful potential because He is our sovereign, resurrected Lord. If you have Him in your company, you have good reason to celebrate the present and the future, despite the past.

Lord, we are grateful that You keep Your promise never to leave us or forsake us. Even during the dark times when we cannot trace You, we know that You are able to place a rainbow of hope in the darkest cloud. We celebrate Your presence.

CPSIA information can be obtained
at www.ICGtesting.com
Printed in the USA
BVHW041943110521
607065BV00017B/503